THE THEORY OF THE NOVEL

PHILIP STEVICK

THE THEORY
OF
THE NOVEL

THE FREE PRESS
A Division of Macmillan Publishing Co., Inc.
NEW YORK

Collier Macmillan Publishers
LONDON

The Free Press
A Division of Macmillan Publishing Co., Inc.
866 Third Avenue, New York, N.Y. 10022

Collier Macmillan Canada, Ltd.

Library of Congress Catalog Card Number: 67-25335

Printed in the United States of America

printing number
10

CONTENTS

Introduction   1

1. Generic Identity   11

    Maurice Z. Shroder, The Novel as a Genre   13
    Joseph Conrad, Novel as World   29
    Northrop Frye, The Four Forms of Fiction   31

2. Narrative Technique   45

    Phyllis Bentley, Use of Summary   47
             Use of Scene   52
             Art of Narrative   54
    Henry James, The House of Fiction   58
             Emergence of Character   63
             Bewilderment   63
             The Art of Interesting Us In Things   63
             The Ficelle   63
             Adventure   64
             Essence and Form   64
             Scene   64
    Mark Schorer, Technique as Discovery   65

3. Point of View   85

    Wayne C. Booth, Distance and Point-of-View: An
             Essay in Classification   87
    Norman Friedman, Point of View in Fiction: The De-
             velopment of a Critical Concept   108

4. Plot, Structure, and Proportion   139

    R. S. Crane, The Concept of Plot   141
    Norman Friedman, Forms of the Plot   145

Henry James, Foreshortening   166
        Improvisation   167
        Initial Intentions and Final Forms   168
        Time, Development, and Composition   168
        Delicate Adjustments and An Exquisite
                Chemistry   171
Philip Stevick, The Theory of Fictional Chapters   171

5. Style   185

Robert Louis Stevenson, Web, Texture, and the
                        Juggling of Oranges   187
Richard M. Ohmann, Prolegomena to the Analysis of
                        Prose Style   190
Leonard Lutwack, Mixed and Uniform Prose Styles
                        in the Novel   208

6. Character   221

E. M. Forster, Flat and Round Characters   223
W. J. Harvey, The Human Context   231

7. Time and Place   253

A. A. Mendilow, The Position of the Present in Fiction   255
William T. Noon, Modern Literature and the Sense of
                        Time   280
D. S. Bland, Endangering the Reader's Neck: Back-
                        ground Description in the Novel   313

8. Symbol   333

William York Tindall, Excellent Dumb Discourse   335
Ursula Brumm, Symbolism and the Novel   354

9. Life and Art   369

Robert Scholes and
        Robert Kellogg, The Problem of Reality: Illustra-
                        tion and Representation   371
Miguel de Cervantes, Sancho Tells a Tale   384
Henry Fielding, Not an Individual But a Species   387
Laurence Sterne, Tristram Wrestles With the Records   388
Stendhal, The Novel as a Mirror   389

W. M. Thackeray, Box and Puppets 389
Gustave Flaubert, Art and Personality 390
              Everything One Invents is True 390
George Eliot, A Faithful Account of Men and Things
              as They Have Mirrored Themselves
              in My Mind 391
Anthony Trollope, Getting the Facts Right 393
George Meredith, No Dust of the Struggling Outer
              World 394
Emile Zola, Experience and the Naturalistic Novel 394
Henry James, On Writing From Experience 396
Guy. de Maupassant, A Presentment More Striking
              Than Reality Itself 397
Joseph Conrad, The Highest Kind of Justice to the
              Visible Universe 399
André Gide, Edouard on the Tyranny of Resemblance 403
D. H. Lawrence, The One Bright Book of Life 405
James Joyce, A Dividual Chaos, Perilous, Potent,
              Common to Allflesh 406

Selected Bibliography 407

Index 429

INTRODUCTION

AMONG those weary pronouncements that the novel, more than any other genre, evokes—that the novel is dead, for example, and that its dying gasp was breathed by Flaubert, or James, or Joyce—one often encounters the conviction that the novel has no poetics, that it can never and should never have one. It is difficult to think of another area in which the same assumptions have any currency, assumptions which imply that to describe, to define, and to generalize are somehow to sap the vitality of the subject. It is also difficult to think of another area in which they are less appropriate, for the novel is rich enough and intricate enough to demand the greatest of intelligence in responding to it. It is coherent enough as a genre to demand the combined insights of formalist criticism and cultural history in understanding its tradition, and it is vital enough to survive any amount of theory, even if that theory is badly done.

The fact remains, however, that the novel has had no poetics. It is not only, as René Wellek and Austin Warren put it, that "Literary theory and criticism concerned with the novel are much inferior in both quantity and quality to theory and criticism of poetry." It is further true that criticism in the past has given to the novel little sense of its generic uniqueness, no very clear sense of its formal conventions, comparatively little sense of its aesthetic possibilities, and little sense of its origins. The most obvious reason for the lack of a basic body of criticism on the novel is that the novel has had the systematic attention of no great critic, no powerfully synthesizing mind of the order of Aristotle, Johnson, or Coleridge. But beyond this fact lie several conditions which have made the novel an entity without a definition, an art without its own aesthetic, and a tradition without a theory for perceiving its continuity.

The novel, first of all, is a comparatively new genre. In France, the question of whether *La Princesse de Clèves* (1678)

1

is a remarkably mature and penetrating romance or an early novel is a difficult and debatable one. In Spain, there is every reason to call *Don Quixote* (1605–15) a novel, though one can hardly speak of Cervantes' establishment of a Spanish genre. These problems of generic assignment occur in English literature too. Nashe's *The Unfortunate Traveller* (1594) is or is not a novel, depending upon the history one happens to read. Nevertheless, it is clear, of English fiction, that the romances of Congreve and Mrs. Behn in the late seventeenth century belong to an earlier tradition, that the novels of Defoe are genuinely new without Defoe's apparent awareness of their novelty, but that both Fielding and Richardson, by the 1740's, clearly felt themselves to be making a new genre, a feeling that was understood by their readers and their critics. Thus, however one dates the beginnings of the novel, a sense of its generic uniqueness is little more than two hundred years old, a brief time, as artistic forms go, for the establishment of a substantial body of theory.

The novel, moreover, is a mixed genre. Its origins lie in a dozen different forms: essay, romance, history, the "character," biography, comic and sentimental drama, and so on. Traditionally, it is flexible and indeterminate in its form. From time to time critics have offered to define "pure poetry," not a very fruitful enterprise, but one understands its motive. No one, with the possible exception of the practitioners of the "new" French novel, has ever attempted to define a "pure" novel. With a genre so eclectic and various as to include *Emma, Moby Dick,* and *Malone Dies,* the concept of purity is irrelevant, and with a genre so "impure," the demands that theoretical criticism be appropriately flexible are so considerable as almost to inhibit theory altogether.

Furthermore, the novel has suffered from the conviction that it is an inferior form. Like the drama, the novel has been subjected to continuous extra-artistic pressures—from publishers, from serializing editors, from readers with tastes running from the vulgar to the hyper-refined, from the salacious to the over-delicate—all of which tends to limit the taking of its artistic integrity with the same seriousness with which one takes, say, the lyric. A good many of its chief practitioners, too, have willingly conspired to produce the impression that they, and their art, are anti-intellectual, even anti-artistic. No lyric poet of any quality has ever set about undercutting before the public his own claims to artistic seriousness. But in the history of the novel one finds Defoe, the purveyor of true memoirs, Richardson, the earnest moralist, Trollope, the self-confessed hack, Dickens, the public entertainer. One finds the red-skin stances of Mark Twain and Hemingway, beautifully summed up in the notice that precedes *Huckleberry Finn:* "Persons attempting to find a motive in this narrative will be prosecuted; persons attempting to find a moral in it will be banished; persons attempting to find a plot in it will be shot." Even Faulkner enjoyed immensely the sport of pretending not to be a great writer. Thus, the critic who would theorize about the novel is in the position of having to be deeply serious about an art which has often refused to take itself seriously as art.

Finally, the very nature of the novel has supported criticism which is antithetical to general theory. The novel, more than any other genre, is capable of containing large, developed, consistent images of people, and this is one of the reasons that anyone reads novels. Yet the kind of criticism which such a motive is apt to lead to is the "appreciation," the warm, genial essay on Fielding's Parson Adams or Dickens' Micawber, a kind of writing about novels which, for many years, largely took the place of more rigorous forms of criticism. The novel, also, more than any other genre, can give form to a set of attitudes regarding society, history, and the general culture of which the novel is a part, and this too is a reason for reading novels; but the criticism which results from this motive runs the danger of treating fiction as a document, evaluating it less as art than as cultural exhibit and ideological force.

Still, despite the lack of basic definitions, terminologies, and classic descriptions, there are some standard ways of differentiating a novel from narrative prose which is not a novel. Each way of differentiating the novel carries with it implications upon which further criticism has grown. Some of the criteria by which the province of the novel has been established are these.

PERCEPTUAL

NOVELISTS, such an argument asserts, *see* and *hear* what writers of pre-novelist prose do not, or at least they have found a vehicle by means of which their perceptions can be presented.

It is a theory which can be tested by comparing the rather thin and general sensory texture of nearly any work of narrative prose of the seventeenth century with the Hogarthian visual particularity and the ear for speech rhythms of the eighteenth-century novelists. No one would press such an argument toward a precise definition of the novel, remembering the extraordinary range of sensory detail in Chaucer, for example. But as a means for distinguishing the customary density of the novel from the customary absence of a compulsion to render the look and the sound of experience in the immediate antecedents of the novel, such a criterion is useful and suggestive.

STRUCTURAL

ANOTHER way of distinguishing the novel is to propose that novels succeed, as pre-novelistic narratives do not, in constructing actions, with beginning, middle, and end, with the materials of novels deployed in such a way as to give the image of coherence, continuity, and wholeness, and with certain tensions and anticipations regarding the central characters carried through the entire length of the works, to be resolved only at their ends. This, too, leads to no definition of the novel. One expects plays of any period, for example, to cohere as actions. But it is true that Lucian's *True History* is not an action, nor is Rabelais' *Gargantua;* the sixteenth-century fictions of Deloney and Nashe are not actions; and even *Moll Flanders* and *Robinson Crusoe* are not actions in any very strict application of the term. *Pamela* and *Clarissa,* however, *Joseph Andrews* and *Tom Jones* are actions whose structures support, at every point, the wish to make a prose narrative as unified as a good play. And the history of the genre ever since has tended to confirm the idea that a novel is a novel insofar as it is an action and as it ceases to be an action it becomes not a novel but something else.

SOCIOLOGICAL

IT has been obvious to the most disparate of observers—from Samuel Johnson to Karl Marx to Lionel Trilling—that the novel is a middle-class genre. Such an observation has implications both extrinsic and intrinsic. It implies, extrinsically, that the novel emerged as a specific genre at least partly as a response to a new kind of audience, literate, self-conscious in regard to manners and morals, leisured but commercial, aware of itself as a class distinct from the apparent crudities below and the apparent effeteness above. Intrinsically, such an observation implies that the novel, almost by definition, must come to terms with the middle class, either by objectifying middle-class wishes and fears, as in Richardson, or in analyzing a middle-class life style, as in Jane Austen, or in assaulting the middle class, as in Flaubert, or in working out alternatives to middle-class life against a background which is middle class, as in Emily Brontë or in Conrad. At one point in *Pamela*, the heroine is dressed in "fine linen, silk shoes, and fine white cotton stockings, a fine quilted coat, a delicate green Mantea silk gown and coat, a French necklace, and a laced cambric handkerchief and clean gloves." In that catalog, ended with the off-hand "clean gloves," one recognizes the top of the iceberg, the slight details that suggest a whole complex configuration of middle-class attitudes that lie beneath their surface. One hundred sixty years later, Conrad's *Heart of Darkness* undertakes the portrayal of a journey out of manners and morals, out of constraint and convention, but it ends with "a lofty drawing room," furniture with "gilt legs and backs," "a grand piano," polite conversation, and a beautiful, entirely proper middle-class woman.

MYTHIC

NORTHROP FRYE has arranged mythic patterns according to the power of the hero, at the top those heroes who are not men at all but gods, further down the scale those heroes who are men but stronger, wiser, and more resourceful than any of us, still further down the scale those heroes who are like us in their capabilities, and finally the heroes (though the name hero has ceased to be appropriate, of course) who are less capable than we are, the fools and clowns. No one would be satisfied with a romance in which the hero were identifiable with oneself in his capabilities, and conversely no novel can satisfactorily contain a hero of romance or epic proportions. Thackeray called *Vanity*

Fair a novel without a hero. But so, in a sense, is every other novel, for Tom Jones or Pip, Julien Sorel or Emma Bovary exist at a mythic level which every reader occupies in experience. And when a character, Heathcliff in *Wuthering Heights* let us say, becomes "larger than life," we legitimately cease calling the work which contains such a character a novel, calling it a romance instead. Once again, however, to make such an observation is not to define but to point toward a definition, for there are problems in determining the mythic level of certain characters in indisputably novelistic works (Father Zossima in *The Brothers Karamazov* for example) and works of other genres (such as the narrative poems of Crabbe or the plays of Ibsen) often deal with characters of the same mythic level as those of novels.

TYPOGRAPHIC

WHILE novels cannot be differentiated from other printed modern works on such grounds, it has become increasingly fruitful to point out that novels tend to differ from pre-novelistic narrative in the extent to which the novel is a printed, rather than an oral, form. The prose of Bunyan, to be sure, is printed too, but Bunyan's prose has affinities with the sermon, with a spoken tradition, in a way that few novels do. Those endless types and sub-types of English fiction of the seventeenth century, the merry tales, the jest-biographies, the sentimental romances, the beast fables, are oral forms which happen to have been composed and printed. Novels, on the other hand, if they have lost the stylized charm of the formulaic phrase and the ringing diction of purpit orotundity, have made it possible to exploit the apparent authenticity of print and to bring to the private, silent reader, alone with his book, all of the power of those forms which are experienced aurally and publicly.

PHILOSOPHICAL

SINCE Ian Watt's *The Rise of the Novel,* it has become customary to speak of the novel as the product of an intellectual milieu shaped by Descartes and Locke. It is a milieu which

contains an insistence upon the importance of individual experience, a distrust of universals, and an elevation of the data
of the senses as the necessary means by which ideas are formed.
Ideas as such tend to be difficult to contain in novels. Ordinarily
one is not prepared to accept a full-scale character who is
spokesman for a doctrine. In view of this comparative incom-
patibility of the fictional and the explicitly philosophical, it is
especially ironic that the novel, as a genre, should have become
so clearly a vehicle for a philosophical view of experience. One
reflects on how long narrative literature was able to get along
without representing the minute passage of time, precisely located space, and carefully observed appearances and one concludes that novels represent these aspects of experience not
because novelists developed a superior degree of skill but because a particular philosophical climate had made it legitimate
to think of sensory data and individual experience as the very
substance of reality itself.

SUBJECTIVE

AT first thought, the possibility that one might begin to
define novels by considering what novels are about is preposterous. One novel is about a provincial parson whose living is
threatened by a crude but well-meaning reformer. Another novel
is about a country girl, seduced by a wealthy neighbor, married,
abandoned, driven to murder, and executed. A third is about a
fat little soldier in the Austrian army who does everything
wrong. Yet that by now ubiquitous formula "appearance and
reality" is, in fact, an approach to the essence of the novel by
means of naming its subject. Dorothy Van Ghent begins *The
English Novel: Form and Function* by writing, "The subject
matter of novels is human relationships in which are shown the
directions of men's souls." This too, she continues, is the subject
of drama and history; and so she goes on to qualify and elaborate. But initially she has begun to consider particular novels
by stating what novels are about. To Albert S. Cook, for another
example, the subject of the novel is the experience of reality
as process rather than as a fixed, prior, "given" set of beliefs.
Thus, while there is a sense in which the search for the novel's

subject is an impossible task, approached at the appropriate level, the novel as a genre can be said to have its own subject. This way of looking at the novel is nowhere better argued than in the first essay in this collection.

CULTURAL

ALMOST anything that one can say about Western culture from the beginning of the eighteenth century to the present can serve to characterize the novel since it is almost inevitable that the novel will express, criticize, or minister to that aspect of culture. Of society, one may speak of the decline of the organic community and the growth of individualism, the steadily increasing possibilities of class mobility, and the growth of urbanization—and all of these the novel as a genre concerns itself with. Of the transformations of consciousness, one may speak of the decline of belief, the growth of a secular ethic, and the increasing fragmentation of personality into professional and social segments—and the novel reflects, shapes, and enlarges upon these also. Of the great events of intellectual history, one may speak of the growth of psychology, sociology, and scientific method, the thought of Hume and Burke, Marx and Freud— and inevitably the emphases of intellectual history are the emphases of the novel. There is something slightly circular in defining the novel by defining the dominant traits of the culture in which the novel occurs; yet it is a way of looking at the identity of the novel which can hardly be ignored, since the novel tends to insist upon its own cultural relevance. In the long run if not in the short, it is an act of willful perversity to consider *Bleak House* and *Middlemarch, Madame Bovary* and *Germinal* as self-contained forms since they insist upon their force as both products and critiques of their culture on every page. Implicitly, moreover, they insist upon the relevance to the general culture of the genre of which they are a part.

The ideal theorist of the novel, perhaps, would assimilate all of these classic approaches to the genre into a broad, eclectic synthesis. But in fact, aside from the intellectual and temperamental difficulties of being so inclusive as that, not all ways of differentiating the genre are equally capable of being extended into a substantial body of theory. The mythic approach, for example, has enriched our understanding of any number of particular novels; yet as a theoretic instrument for understanding the novel in general, the mythic approach is rather limited. Some approaches, such as the typographic, are too new and too elusive to have established themselves as bases for substantial theory. And potentially the richest of all the ways of thinking about the novel, the cultural, has lent itself so easily to dark predictions at once of the sickness of one's culture and the death of the novel that its successful application to the genre as a whole remains to be demonstrated. Books like Raymond Williams' *Culture and Society* or Richard Chase's *The American Novel and Its Tradition* succeed so well within their chronological and national limitations in their integration of cultural history and literary theory that they promise what can be done by some future critic who seeks to construct a cultural theory of the novel.

Nearly every piece of modern fictional theory, those collected here and those elsewhere, proceeds from the structural orientation sketched above. That is, persuaded that the novel is a formal unit such criticism seeks to establish the ways by which its formal principles can be understood and the ways by which its formal possibilities can be distinguished from those of the other genres. When other general categories, such as style and symbol, are applied to the novel, it is generally understood that these categories must be applied with the special demands of the novel, as its own kind of form, firmly in mind. Other arts have bodies of theory that are more or less atomistic—a good example is the enormous body of writing on metrics and prosody—theory which provisionally ignores the fact that certain elements of a work exist within a total form that is finally indivisible, isolating these elements for purpose of classification and analysis. The novel has provoked no comparable body of theory devoted to "elements" as such. Even E. M. Forster's division of characters into "flat" and "round," which might seem to be a classification of an "element" of fiction, begins by making clear the inextricable relation between any given character and the fictional structure in which it appears. Writing about fiction has not always been so, but for better or worse, the theory of the novel at the present time pursues to varying degrees each of those classic approaches outlined above, all of it growing out of the common assumption, expressed or implied, that theory which does not seek ultimately to explain the form of novels, as organic wholes, is pointless.

By and large, theorists of the novel have not felt compelled to dissociate their analytical rigor from their general human and humanistic concerns. Thus, whatever its deficiencies, one does not need to apologize for the theory of the novel, as if it were a strained and frigid exercise, to be gotten over as quickly as possible so that one can get on with the novels themselves. Now and then one encounters a person who confesses, in a candid moment, that he enjoys reading theory. It is a response which is not inappropriate to the essays that follow since they carry with them the belief that there is nothing incompatible between bringing to bear, on the one hand, all of the precision one can apply to questions of theory and conveying, on the other hand, one's belief in the novel, one's pleasure in its human density, and one's receptivity to its infinite variety.

In the essays that follow, nothing is included for its historical interest. A handful of novelists are represented not because what they say is historically significant, although it is, but because they illuminate questions of the art of fiction in a general and striking way. I have also excluded essays directed toward particular works, even though some such essays contain, incidentally, quite useful theoretical insights. Collections of representative modern criticism directed toward particular novels are by now fairly commonplace. Perhaps the best known is William Van O'Connor's *The Forms of Modern Fiction*. There is always room for another good collection of practical criticism. But the collection which follows grows out of the contrary assumption, not a wish to apply but a wish to examine the premises by which application is made, and out of the further conviction that there is by now so much good general theory that a substantial anthology of the best of it is necessary, both as an act of presentation and as an act of synthesis.

1

GENERIC IDENTITY

Most definitions of the novel tend to be tactical. When Fielding writes that his "new species of writing" is not burlesque or caricature, not true epic and least of all romance, but is rather a comic epic poem in prose, what we have is not really a definition of the novel (though the description does help to locate the novel, as Maurice Shroder points out), not even a very helpful definition of Fielding's novel (though it does aid in understanding certain features of Fielding's tone and construction). Primarily Fielding's description is a tactic, designed to justify Fielding's fiction and to put down the opposition. When Smollett defines the novel as "a large diffused picture of life," it is, again, not a definition but a tactic, urged upon the reader by way of asserting that "diffuseness" can be as great a virtue as the formal control of Fielding. There is nothing wrong, of course, with a tactical definition, if we understand it for what it is, and it may tell us a great deal about how an author regards his own work. One of the brightest, wittiest, most provocative essays on fiction,

Virginia Woolf's "Mr. Bennett and Mrs. Brown," is tactical, and it would be folly to wish it were less strategic and more nearly a proper definition. Even Lionel Trilling's magisterial and highly influential "Manners, Morals, and the Novel" is, in its own way, tactical. It is the nature of the tactical definition, however, to inhibit our response to certain kinds of fiction and thus it is impossible that it function as a necessary first step in the theory of the novel.

Maurice Z. Shroder's "The Novel as a Genre" seeks to define the novel by isolating its essential subject, to do this flexibly enough so that the discussion can embrace the entire genre but precisely enough so that it can serve as an operative definition. The difficulty and the audacity of Shroder's approach can be seen by speculating on how rarely an essentialist definition of the novel has been attempted in the past. The obvious problem with an essentialist approach to the novel is that it lays itself open to exceptions. "What of X work?" the reader may object; "It seems to display the essential characteristics of the novel badly." If such objections are less likely to occur to the reader of Shroder's essay than with similar attempts, it is because of the breadth of Shroder's reference, his combination of mythic and historical methods, and the absence of the tactical impulse.

The idea that the novel contains its own world is encountered so frequently in such phrases as "the world of Dickens" or "the world of Evelyn Waugh" that it is useful to find the idea stated forthrightly and passionately. To speak of the novel in this way is not really to define it, of course, but it is to make a metaphor which invites interpretation. The passage from Conrad which follows states explicitly the difficulty and responsibility involved in setting out to make a fictional world. Implicitly, the idea of the novel as a world carries with it suggestions of unity of tone, consistency of viewpoint, and coherence of vision.

Northrop Frye's discussion of prose fiction seeks to place the novel in a continuum which includes all forms of extended imaginative prose. Frye's definition gains in clarity from his capacity to separate the novel proper from those works, like Scott's romances and Sterne's "anatomies," which are generally treated in histories of the novel but which belong to different traditions. His discussion also destroys the rarely expressed but widely held notion of the novel as a norm, a view which implies

*that narrative works succeed as they are plausible and probable.
On the contrary, the novel, in Frye's discussion, is one of a
series of narrative possibilities, each of which contains its own
potential integrity.*

MAURICE Z. SHRODER

THE NOVEL AS A GENRE

When we speak of "the novel" in general terms, we are—
willingly or unwillingly—accepting the assumption that genre
has more than a theoretical reality. Presumably, then, we should
be able to offer a description of that genre, to say what a novel
is and what distinguishes it from other forms of prose fiction.
Yet students of literature—and even so eminent a witness as
E. M. Forster—seem to be uneasy with any definition of the
novel more elaborate than the formulae familiar to authors of
literary manuals. The novel, according to such handbooks, is
merely "a fictional narrative in prose, of substantial length";
but so, one may add, are the prose *Lancelot, Pilgrim's Progress,*
Ballanche's *Orphée,* and *Finnegans Wake,* none of which could
qualify as novels were we to compare them with *Don Quixote*
or *Madame Bovary, The Egoist* or *The Ambassadors,* "fictional
narratives, etc." that are unquestionably novels and nothing else.

The reluctance to provide more explicit and more substantial
descriptions of the novel may reflect the admirable desire to
avoid the pitfalls of prescriptive theories of genre. But Aristotle's reflections on tragedy have outlasted those "rules" that
later critics dredged from the *Poetics;* and Aristotle's attempt
at description should remain our example. We must really face
the facts of critical responsibility, and we must either drop such
general categories as "the novel," "the romance," and so on,

Reprinted from The Massachusetts Review © *1963, The Massachusetts
Review, Inc.*

or be prepared to offer justifications for such terms, in the form of more extensive descriptions and discussions. This is not a matter of mere academic quibbling; the question is, as Humpty Dumpty neatly puts it to Alice, "which is to be master"—the words we use or we who use them. Especially in the criticism of literature, when we do not define our terms as precisely as possible, we invite exactly that form of bamboozling in which Humpty Dumpty himself indulges.

An adequate definition of the novel would, of course, have to be totally comprehensive, exhaustive, and infallible. It would have to borrow at once from the history of literature, the study of external form, and the study of the fictional matter of novels in general. I cannot pretend that the pages which follow are any more than a suggestion of the direction such a study might take; I am, indeed, more interested in the matter of the novel and in the testimony provided by literary history than I am in questions of external form, specific novelistic techniques and the stylistic peculiarities of individual novelists. My reason is a simple one. The realities of genre underlie individual and external variations—an eclogue is an eclogue in unrhymed iambic pentameter or in alexandrine couplets; and just as we look, in an eclogue, for characteristic imagery and a vision of the world peculiar to the genre, so in examining the novel we should look first at the matter which is susceptible to a variety of shapes. Like any narrative form, the novel has a typical action, with thematic value, which is peculiarly its own.

The matter of the novel—the theme that has informed the genre from *Don Quixote* onward—is relatively uncomplicated. The novel records the passage from a state of innocence to a state of experience, from that ignorance which is bliss to a mature recognition of the actual way of the world. In the less loaded terms of Lionel Trilling, the novel deals with a distinction between appearance and reality. It is not necessarily a question of ontological subtleties: the reality to which the novel appeals is that to which it is historically connected, the reality of bourgeois life, of business, and of the modern city. The first Falstaff, as he stands on the field of Shrewsbury, the thought of money metaphorically coloring his speech—as he questions the value of such aristocratic absolutes as chivalric honor and resolves to be a live coward—Falstaff embodies the sensibility that will make the novel possible. The great expectations of the young Hotspur find ironic responses in the lost illusions of the old Sir John. The protagonist of the novel follows the same pattern of disillusionment—which Harry Levin sees as a major part of what we call realism—from potential fulfillment to actual accomplishment, from a hopeful naïveté to a resigned wisdom.

Thematically, then, the novel distinguishes itself from the romance, in which the protagonist proves himself a hero, actually fulfills his heroic potentiality. *Vanity Fair*—"A Novel Without a Hero"—is rather an exemplary case than an exception. The protagonist of a novel is likely to be an "anti-hero," an "unheroic hero," as Raymond Giraud calls him—a Miniver Cheevy or a Walter Mitty who is able to elaborate his dreams of glory only by ignoring the material realities of his station and his times.

The action of the novel (which receives various episodic developments, as it informs the particular intrigue or plot of any given novel) is essentially a reworking of the basic action of romance—that familiar story which Joseph Campbell discusses, in *The Hero With a Thousand Faces*, as the "monomyth," and to which Northrop Frye, in his *Anatomy of Criticism*, gives the more descriptive name of "the quest." A young man goes forth to discover his own nature and the nature of the world; he is often in search of his name, his father, in search of a mysterious treasure. The completion of the quest proves the young man, if he is the protagonist of a romance, to be what he, and the author, and we the readers knew from the start that he was—a hero. In the novel, the "going forth" may be metaphorical rather than actual; but the voyage often provides the novelistic framework, and the protagonist's movement is always from a narrow environment to a broader one. He may move in space, like Dickens' Pip, from the English countryside to London, and like Balzac's Lucien de Rubempré, from the provinces to Paris; he may move rather in time, with Austen's Emma or Proust's Marcel, from the restricted awareness of childhood to the wider experience of maturity. The goal of the quest—the name and the treasure—may or may not be achieved; but the protagonist of the novel is likely to discover, with Falstaff, that there is no future for heroism, that he himself is a perfectly ordinary man, with the experience and the knowledge that suit his station. The magic name itself proves to be merely an inaccurate pseudonym: Don Quixote, the Knight of the Sad Countenance, is really Alonso Quixano; Lucien de Rubempré—the young "aristocrat"—was born Lucien Chardon.

Although Don Quixote dies with his boots off and Lucien hangs himself in prison, this is not to say that all romances end happily, while all novels end unhappily, that romances incline toward comedy and novels toward tragedy. The hero of a romance may realize his heroic potential only in death—the triumph of the *Liebestod* at the close of the Tristan legend is perhaps our most familiar example. The protagonist of a novel, on the other hand, may—like Elizabeth Bennet and Tom Jones, Eugène de Rastignac and Pierre Bezukhov—live happily ever after; yet all these protagonists succeed only because they have let fall their illusions and their pride. Such a fall, in a novel, is a happy one, since it represents the completion of that educational process with which the novel deals, an education into the realities of the material world and of human life in society.

In other words, the *Bildungsroman* is not merely a special category: the theme of the novel is essentially that of formation, of education. The terms of the education are themselves important, since the process described in the novel is analogous to that described in two other fictional forms, which serve perhaps as the boundaries between which the novelistic sensibility functions. At one extreme stands the romance, with its tale of triumphant adventure and its heroic protagonist. At the other extreme stand such *contes philosophiques* as *Candide* and *Gulliver's Travels,* tales which depend on protagonists who are incredibly naïve and largely unheroic, which deal in the disillusionments one suffers in trying to apply systems to the unsystematic realities of life. The novel, as the French critic Gustave Kahn suggested, is perhaps more like the *conte philosophique* than like the romance, in that it records a similar process of disillusionment; but while philosophical tales cast such disillusionment in ideological terms, novels treat it experientially, in the terms of quotidian reality. Both the novel and the philosophical tale, however, reject that "spirit of romance" which sees the world through a haze of imaginative and subjective interpretation, colored at the least by sentimentality and transformed at the most by the poetry of legend and of myth.

Ortega y Gasset put the matter succinctly in his first book, the recently translated *Meditations on Quixote*. "The myth," Ortega wrote, "is always the starting point of all poetry, including the realistic, except that in the latter we accompany the myth in its descent, in its fall. This collapse of the poetic is the theme of realistic poetry" (p. 144). "Myth" in this context means primarily the thorough transformation—and perhaps elevation—of reality through imaginative projection; the process of the novel (as all critics would, I think, agree) is one of "demythification," the formal or generic equivalent to the experiential disillusionment of the novel's protagonist. Were we to define "myth" in the more limited sense in which it applies to the epic, it would be possible to consider the novel the epic of the modern world, or (in Fielding's phrase) "a comic epic in prose." The mock-heroic passages in *Tom Jones* strengthen the argument, as do such isolated cases as Thackeray's theories of the epic novel and Rémy de Gourmont's reference to *L'Education sentimentale* as the French *Odyssey*—and *Ulysses* would of course fall in line to continue the process into the twentieth century. Nevertheless, the general testimony of literary history suggests that the novel more surely derived from its immediate predecessor, the romance of the Middle Ages and of the Renaissance, than from the epic. The mock-epic—written more often in verse than in prose—all but disappeared with neoclassicism; the mock-romance—a *Roman comique* or a *Roman bourgeois*—is a crucial step in the development of the novel, an imitation of Cervantes' example. Formally or generically, then, the novel is an "anti-romance"—the term, after all, originally designated Sorel's *Berger extravagant*, which literally began where *Don Quixote* left off, with a reduction to the absurd of pastoral romance. Useful as the concept of "demythification" is, however, it is somewhat misleading: it is a critical category, while the terms of the novel are experiential. In such terms, what is revealed as illusory—as mere imaginative projection, "myth" in the pejorative sense of the word—is not quite another genre, the romance, and another literary mode than the realistic (what we are forced to call both the romantic and the romanesque). It is rather the state of mind that evokes and informs that genre and that mode, what we might call (and in so doing avoid the double adjective) the "romance sensibility."

At the root of the romance sensibility lies an active—or, in terms of the novel's process of demythification and disillusionment, an *over*active—imagination. Jane Austen's Emma Woodhouse, for whom romance takes on the popular associations of love and marriage, calls herself an "imaginist"; and her education involves the recognition that the reality of her world is not identical with her wishes and fancies. Flaubert's Emma Bovary suffers from a more critical form of the same disorder, which Jules de Gaultier labeled *le Bovarysme,* a divorce from reality so great that it renders Madame Bovary incapable of accepting her limitations and resigning herself to the dreary provincial towns in which she lives. At its most extreme, the romance sensibility simply turns into madness, imaginative monomania— the spirit of a Don Quixote, which peoples the world with giants and maidens, transforms the world into a theatre for adventure. Don Quixote sees an army with banners in every flock of sheep; it is thus not surprising to find Stendhal's Fabrice del Dongo, after the disillusionment of Waterloo, his own devastating initiation into reality, seeing only a flock of sheep in the retreating and bedraggled French army. But Stendhal is far from finished with his young protagonist: Fabrice's reaction is one of adolescent cynicism, an overstatement as illusory and potentially as dangerous as Don Quixote's romanesque hyperbole. The sensibility that produces novels—I think of Falstaff catechizing himself on the plains of Shrewsbury—asks questions instead of making contrary statements. In what is perhaps the most thoroughly emblematic scene in Cervantes' novel, Don Quixote loudly proclaims that a group of windmills are giants. The adequate response to such a statement is not the contrary assertion, that giants are merely windmills. It is the question asked by the unwilling squire, Sancho Panza: "What giants?" In that crucial question, the innocent Sancho makes explicit the distinction between the novel and the romance.

In the opposition of Don Quixote and Sancho Panza, Cervantes translated into human terms the literary and technical distinctions between his book and the romances he parodied. Don Quixote is the incarnation of the romance sensibility which (while it may be madness) "mythifies," renders the world more poetic and more adventurous. His manner is one of naïveté, a curious combination of innocence and ignorance. Sancho, on the other hand (while just as naïve, and while he may represent so many attitudes that in the second part of *Don Quixote* his nature and his role become increasingly problematic), generally speaks with the voice of the belly and calls his errant master back to reality. He, too, should remind us of a familiar character from the canon of romance, the *vilain*, the comic rustic whose unlovely person and gross personality represent all that is otherwise excluded from the idealized romanesque world. The function of this figure, C. S. Lewis suggests in *The Allegory of Love*, was to serve as "a sop to Silenus"— to give the readers of a romance something to laugh at, to preserve them from the temptation to question and perhaps to mock the romanesque vision itself. But while the *vilain* of romance was more often than not an episodic or a minor character, Sancho Panza accompanies his master to the center of the stage, and his voice is as insistent as is that of the old knight. His call is often a coarse one; his presence often reduces Don Quixote's misadventures to the level of the most crude burlesque; and Byron's reaction—"Cervantes smiled Spain's chivalry away"—is justifiable, if not historically accurate.

But Sancho's quiet question, "What giants?" is not an instance of burlesque: it is the interrogative understatement that complements and confounds Don Quixote's hyperbolic assertion. Sancho, in the episode of the windmills, does not initially reveal the truth of the situation directly and crudely—Byron himself is far less subtle in *Don Juan*, his reductions of romance far more emphatic. The peasant squire simply questions the romanesque premise, the highly-colored overstatement of his master. Without knowing it, Sancho is playing the *eiron* (self-depreciator) to Don Quixote's *alazon* (self-deceiver): Cervantes has recreated the basic comic opposition indicated by Francis Cornford and exhaustively analyzed by Northrop Frye, the opposition of the overly-modest quester after truth and the cocksure pretender.

The *eiron*, however, deliberately understates his side of the case, and while Sancho may qualify as a true *eiron* when he sits in judgment during his term as governor of the Isle Barataria, his irony in the windmill episode is totally unconscious.

Cervantes, on the other hand, is consciously ironic: it is he, after all, who puts the revealing question in Sancho's mouth. The irony of Cervantes, which colors the entire atmosphere of *Don Quixote,* is the most authentic and the most powerful of ironies, that which Aristotle discusses in the *Nicomachean Ethics.* Like Aristotle's *eiron,* Cervantes simulates ignorance: he reaches truth rather by indirection than by dramatic revelation. His·novel—and the paradigm he established surely is, as Harry Levin has indicated, the route to realism—does indeed begin in burlesque and parody, in the confounding of illusion through a confrontation with reality in its most ludicrous and most solid forms. But to pass from the first book of *Don Quixote* to the second, from the absurd imitation of knightly romance to the ambiguous adventures in the Cave of Montesinos and on the magic horse Clavileño, is to move from burlesque to irony. We may note the same progression in the fiction of seventeenth-century France, as we turn from Sorel and Scarron to Madame de La Fayette's ironic treatment of a romanesque situation in *La Princesse de Clèves;* and the sequence of Jane Austen's works —from *Love and Friendship* [*sic*] through *Northanger Abbey* to *Mansfield Park* and *Emma*—illustrates the same development. The progression may be an automatic one if, as David Worcester asserts in *The Art of Satire,* the two modes are relatively lower and higher points on the same scale, irony involving a more subtle contrast of appearance and reality, a more ambiguous form of incongruity, than does burlesque. And irony would thus be singularly appropriate to the purposes of the novel as a genre: the novel treats of disillusionment, of disenchantment, and irony, as Vladimir Jankélévitch writes in *L'Ironie,* "enables us never to be disenchanted, for the simple reason that it resists enchantment" (p. 25). The pleasure we take in seeing an *alazon* shocked out of his illusions—the enchantment of his own imagination— is the pleasure of irony: even the simplest verbal irony depends on the contrast of appearance and reality.

The novel would then seem to be an essentially ironic fictional form, occupying a middle position between the non-ironic romance and the philosophical tale, which is ironic, but in ways often different from those of the novel. The novel shares with the romance an emphasis on human situations rather than on ideas: both deal in experiential reality rather than theoretical questions. The novel shares with the *conte philosophique* a distrust of the romance sensibility, the sentimental and mytho-poeic attitudes that make romances the enchanting and illusory works they are. Like the philosophical tale, too, the novel has a certain didactic purpose: irony has always been one of the major devices of the rhetor, a device by which the speaker separates his audience into the shrewd and the gullible. Within the total audience is an intelligent elite that responds to the rhetor's irony, that understands from the first that Brutus is anything but honorable, that divines the real set of moral values behind the apparent one. In other words, the novel may be a far less "popular" form than we usually assume—far less popular, surely, than the romance, courtly, bourgeois, or historical. Romance persisted (and persists) even after the birth and eventual triumph of the novel, simply by adapting its methods and matter to the fancies of a different social order. It had, after all, survived the late medieval questioning of the secular ethos of courtly romance that resulted in the various Grail cycles. Romance reflects an eternal tendency of the human mind that goes all but un-affected by historical change. In a society of *vilains*—Falstaffs and Sancho Panzas—the heroine of romance is a servant-girl and the hero an orphaned newsboy; but Pamela and Horatio Alger, and the responses they awaken in us, hark back to the codes of Laudine and Yvain. The function of romance has not changed, its action has not changed, although the externals of romanesque setting and intrigue have undergone a great altera-tion. Romance is essentially escapist literature; it appeals to the emotions and imagination of the reader, invites him to marvel at an enchanted world of triumphant adventure—and the tri-umph may be the slaying of a dragon or the unmasking of a corrupt sheriff. The novel, however, leads the reader back to reality by questioning the basis of romance; and the more sophisticated, the more subtle, or the more devastating the process becomes (as it becomes, in various ways, in Stendhal, and James, and Flaubert), the less "popular" the novel is likely to be, the more limited the audience that savors the novelist's irony.

This may well be the result of the nature of novelistic irony, which is more a matter of attitude and of moral orientation than of style. The irony of the philosophical tale—that of Voltaire, let us say, in *Candide*—is largely verbal, and it is the rare reader who does not respond to the oxymoron, hyperbole, and litotes characteristic of such a style. This irony falls under the heading of *tropes*, figures of speech; but the irony of the novel is rather a figure of thought, in the broadest sense. The distinction is at least as old as the *Institutio Oratoria*, and Quintilian's example of the ultimate in irony is the life and manner of Socrates. The Socratic method of apparently innocent questioning—which Sancho Panza adopts as he confronts the windmills—is the method which underlies the irony and the realism of the novel.

However, a further distinction must be made, and the figure of Falstaff is once again useful. Falstaff at Shrewsbury plays the role of the *eiron* as he questions such enchanting abstractions as honor; but Falstaff is an *alazon* as well, a boaster, heir to the long tradition of the *miles gloriosus*, the braggart soldier. Similarly, in relation to romances, all novels are ironic, in that they repeat Sancho Panza's questioning of the romanesque premise, but some novels are clearly more intrinsically ironic than others. Gustave Kahn wrestled with this problem in a brief essay he wrote on the irony of Stendhal and on irony in the French novel in general. There is clearly a contrast, wrote Kahn, between the ironic description of the battle of Waterloo in *La Chartreuse de Parme* and the overblown presentation of the battlefield in *La Débâcle:* Zola's hyperbolic evocation is more reminiscent of Hugo's apocalyptic Romanticism than of Stendhal's detached understatement. Kahn's solution was to distinguish the Stendhalian *roman ironique* from the Romantic or Naturalistic *roman lyrique*. The first term is just enough, but the second unfortunately introduces a new unknown quality; and a better set of terms may be those Harry Levin has used to qualify the ironic manner of Stendhal and the more Romantic method of Balzac, "deflationary" and "inflationary." Romance, perhaps, depends on the art of inflation: the romanesque world is one in which every youth is a hero, every antagonist an ogre, every maiden a masterpiece of nature. Novels are relatively more or less "deflationary": Balzac "deflates" more than does George Sand, Flaubert "deflates" more than does Balzac. An equivalent trio of English novelists might be composed of Walter Scott, Dickens, and James. The question is not merely one of chronology, although these two lists might seem to suggest that the history of modern fiction is the record of a progression from an inflationary to a deflationary manner. On the other hand, the movement from burlesque to irony that appeared as early as *Don Quixote* may be another aspect of the same development.

In the early chapters of *Don Quixote,* Sancho Panza calls his master back to reality; but as they travel through Spain, the knight's imagination fertilizes his squire's mind—and by the time they mount the wooden Clavileño, Sancho is as capable of producing hyperbolic fabrications as is Don Quixote. Cervantes, on the other hand, has become progressively more reticent, less willing to tell us the facts, more prone to force his readers to arrive at the truth by their own efforts of understanding. Cervantes' manner in the second book of *Don Quixote* suggests the manner which triumphs in the nineteenth century, when the novel definitively becomes the vehicle for literary realisms. The irony of his novel, and of later novels, arises less from the presence of an *alazon-eiron* pair like Don Quixote and Sancho Panza, than from the novelist's attitude toward the characters and the fictional world he creates. While (as Ian Watt has indicated) the rise of the novel reflects the rise of the middle class and the spread of the bourgeois ethic, the bourgeois himself receives ironic treatment in the nineteenth-century novel, and M. Homais recalls Don Quixote as much as he does Sancho Panza. It is Flaubert's attitude that counts, and not the social status and intellectual baggage of M. Homais.

The literary *alazon* writes advertisements for himself; he is, in Gustave Kahn's sense, a "lyric" author, no matter what genre he produces. His characters and his world are likely to be the projections of his own wish-dreams, his own imaginative transformations of the humdrum world about him. The "inflationary" novelist—a Balzac or a Zola—deals in a reality familiar to us all, but rendered almost hallucinatory. The real Vidocq becomes the diabolical Vautrin; all of Balzac's characters, Baudelaire remarks, have the genius of their calling and their station. While the romancer transports us to a never-never land of fancy, where all our dreams of glory may be realized, Balzac overloads his reality and loudly proclaims that "all is true." But he protests too much. The "deflationary"—that is, the more ironic—novelist is more likely to disclaim responsibility, to apologize for the story he tells us and the way he tells it. I think of the elaborate fiction Cervantes invents, by which he shifts responsibility for his story to the Arabian chronicler, Cide Hamete Benengeli; of Stendhal's false modesty, as he feigns shock at the morals and motives of his passionate Italians; of Gide's review of the characters in *Les Faux-monnayeurs*, his pretense that he has followed Bernard and Olivier wherever they chose to lead him. As the novelist continues this process, he arrives at what one usually thinks of as the extremity of the realistic method: like Flaubert, like Verga, he disappears completely from his novel, suppresses all explicit moral judgment, and lets his characters fend for themselves. Yet while understating his responsibility and his personality, the ironic novelist remains in complete control. The hero of a romance may run away with his story; the protagonist of a novel is always held more tightly in check. Accepting as we do the theory that the novel tends to approximate a slice of life itself, to represent "real" men and women in "real" situations, it may seem paradoxical to suggest that the closing words of *Vanity Fair*—"Come, children, let us shut up the box and the puppets, for our play is played out"—only make explicit what is implicit in every novel. The novelist is a puppeteer, the novel is a puppet show—and the patented collapsible ending of *La Chartreuse de Parme*, the comic resolution of the intrigue in *Tom Jones*, are merely more obvious examples of a common situation.

What I am suggesting—and what it may not be necessary to state so boldly—is that the heir to Socrates is not Sancho Panza but Cervantes, that the novelist is the *eiron,* while his protagonist (the "imaginist," the romance sensibility in a real world) is an *alazon* who learns, through disillusionment, that he is not a hero after all. Unlike the inflationary novelist, who advertises his characters (if not himself), the deflationary novelist, the ironic author, *appears* to allow his characters to magnify themselves, but is in reality subtly and silently reducing them to their actual stature.

To look at the matter in another light, the novelist is the god of his fictional universe, observing and controlling his characters from above. Hardy, when he invented a "President of the Immortals" in *Tess of the d'Urbervilles,* in no way altered the narrative manner, the general authorial attitude that we find in *The Return of the Native*—but he did, consciously or unconsciously, reveal to us the sense of that attitude, the fact that the malicious deity rebuked by Eustacia Vye was in truth Thomas Hardy himself. Zola, too, in doting the Rougons and the Macquarts with their dreadful heredity, was more like a vengeful god cursing a human house than like the indifferent and objective experimental scientist he somewhat belatedly claimed to be. Flaubert and Joyce, in comparing the novelist to a god absent from his own creation, provide two more examples; but we must not be taken in by that emphasis on absence, any more than we should by Zola's pretense at objectivity, by the similar claims associated with realism as a whole. A novelist's hand may ultimately be less apparent than that of the author who openly dispenses poetic justice to his various characters. Novelists are rather like the god of Tolstoy's parable: they see the truth, but wait. The *alazon* confounds himself by his own pretensions; the *eiron* has only to lead him on. And we have no less an authority than Pascal—relying, indeed, on the Fathers of the Church—to tell us that irony is appropriate for God. In the eleventh of his *Lettres provinciales,* Pascal wrote that the Lord's first words to Adam, after the expulsion of Adam and Eve from Eden, constituted an ironic discourse: "Behold, the man is become as one of us." Adam might take God's words to refer solely to his ill-gained knowledge of good and evil; but the price of that knowledge has been the fall into mortality. Once again we return to that basic theme of the novel, the ironic distinction between the state of innocence (a special variety of ignorance and of moral blindness) and the state of experience. The protagonist of the novel is another Adam, driven out of the paradise of childhood and his own imagination, that paradise which is the country of romance. The novelist plays the role of a god who (like Hardy's Will) may be neither malevolent nor benevolent, but who is constantly ironic.

That the situation of Adam may provoke at once the laughter of the gods and the lamentations of men may help to explain why the novel, with its roots in comedy and comic devices, often approximates tragedy. Irony, after all, modulates between comedy and tragedy—it is, according to J. A. K. Thompson's *Irony,* "the trembling equipoise between jest and earnest" (p. 166). The reason, as Francis Cornford pointed out, is that the comic fault of *alazoneia* is equivalent to the tragic *hybris*. The braggart Falstaff and the over-confident Othello are comic and tragic versions of the same figure, the man blinded to reality by his own pretensions. Thus Don Quixote may be both a grotesque caricature and—for the Romantics—the martyred saint of the imagination. Meredith's Sir Austin Feverel reminds us in his naïve reliance on the virtues of "the System," of Molière's mono-maniacs; but the figure of Sir Austin, at the end of *The Ordeal of Richard Feverel*, is that of a man whose pride has been the cause of madness and death and desolation. Meredith's theory of comedy is perhaps rather a theory of irony, with the Tragic Spirit as one of its Muses. Similarly, the ambiguity of our reactions to Emma Bovary and to Clym Yeobright, to Frédéric Moreau and to Olive Chancellor—are they prentious fools? or is their plight a reflection of the human condition, with all the potentiality for tragic revelation that phrase suggests?—is dictated by the ambiguous nature of the ironic method and manner. If the novel seems to us so successful a vehicle for a realistic picture of the world, it may be that we see in the ambiguous irony of the novel the most accurate reflection of the unsure "realities" of human life. Hardy's title—*Life's Little Ironies*—reflects what may be the general consensus, that life *is* ironic, that only an ironic fiction could reproduce the moral complexities of life. "Now we see through a glass, darkly"—and only the oblique and ironic revelation of the truth is possible for us.

It would follow then that as the novel becomes more thoroughly comic or more thoroughly tragic, it passes beyond irony and beyond realism into a new area of fictive expression, open to more cosmic and more reflective visions of the world. This would seem to be consistent with the development of fiction in the late nineteenth and early twentieth centuries. Irony in the nineteenth century (in prose and in verse) served a specific purpose: it was the mode of reaction to the overstatements of Romanticism, self-advertisement and rampant sentimentality, the "spirit of romance" in one of its most emphatic manifestations.

> We had fed the heart on fantasies,
> The heart's grown brutal from the fare—

these lines from Yeats might serve as a motto for the mid-century reaction of such French authors as Flaubert, Baudelaire, and Leconte de Lisle. While certain statements of Matthew

Arnold are similar to those of his French contemporaries, the reaction in England had come earlier, with Byron and Peacock —even, to a degree, with Jane Austen—and was less embittered, less violent. But once having made its point, the ironic manner that produced the great realistic novels had no place to go. (Were it not for the subsistence of Romanticism itself throughout the nineteenth century, it would even be surprising to find in Flaubert and Twain and Turgenev methods and lessons which we can trace back to Cervantes, Madame de La Fayette, and Fielding.) Once Flaubert moved from the individual case of Emma Bovary to the generation of Frédéric Moreau, he had gone as far as his variety of realism could carry him. Thus the last decades of the nineteenth century are marked by a change in fiction, the tendency either to become more emphatically psychological, to look for ironies deeper within the individual sensibility, or to become more openly "cosmic," to see all men as blind pretenders and truth as the prerogative of an omniscient god. The methods and the concerns of realistic fiction continue to appear in novels of the early—and, one should add, of the middle—twentieth century, just as the romance survived the coming of the novel: François Mauriac and C. P. Snow are only two of the living novelists writing in the nineteenth-century manner. But the concern for point of view in James, the stream of consciousness in Virginia Woolf, the subtle analyses of the conscious and unconscious mind in Gide and Proust reflect changes in our attitude toward the nature of reality that had of necessity to affect modern fiction. We associate these new developments with the work of such men as Bergson and Freud; we might look to Sir J. G. Frazer for an equivalent to other changes in the nature of fiction. With such authors as Zola and Hardy, the novel opens itself to a process that we might call "remythification," the tendency to see human life in terms of myth and legend, to appropriate the processes and effects which earlier novelists had avoided as the province of poetry. The pattern for many early novelists was to begin with a parody of romance and to end as realists. The pattern that becomes increasingly obvious after 1900 is a curious reversal of Cervantes' paradigm: Joyce and Mann, for example, begin in realism and end in mythopoeia. As realism had burlesqued romance, so the authors of the new fiction turned the processes of realistic novels themselves into objects of ridicule. Proust's pastiches of his predecessors, his caricature of the realistic novelist—that detached *poseur* who, when questioned on his cold aloofness, responds, "J'observe!"—are exemplary, as is Joyce's burlesque of catalogue realism in the "Ithaca" chapter of *Ulysses*.

I am not trying to suggest that by the early twentieth century, fiction had completed a perfect circle. This would be far from the truth. The ironic matter of the novel (corresponding as it did to certain changes in the social order, in science, and in philosophy) left ineradicable effects on the nature of fiction: Proust's Marcel grows from the age of names to the age of things, Joyce's *Ulysses* is set in a modern city, and Joyce's use of myth is in itself often ironic. But if we are to deal with the various forms of fiction in terms of their essential qualities, we must recognize that the ironic realism of the novel from Cervantes to the late nineteenth century gives way to other fictional modes in the twentieth. We may be forced to continue to use the term "novel" for the fiction of the twentieth century, as French has been forced to employ the word *roman* for both the romance and the novel; but we must recognize that our expectations may be wrong—as wrong as they often are when we turn from the fiction of England and of France to that of other countries, even in the nineteenth century. The novel was at one moment the dominant form of fiction in England and in France; this seems to have been less surely so in, let us say, America and Russia. "The American novel" is a phrase we use almost indiscriminately; were we to follow Richard Chase and to distinguish the American novel from the American romance (in all likelihood a form both more abundant and more accurately a reflection of the American imagination), we might discover that we had cleared up an unfortunate critical confusion, one that Nathaniel Hawthorne noted in his preface to *The House of the Seven Gables*. And, while there is indeed a tradition of ironic fiction in Russia (a tradition represented by Gogol, Goncharov, Saltykov, Turgenev, and Chekhov), the more impressive works of Dostoevsky and Tolstoy belong rather to the body of literature that E. M. Forster calls "prophetic fiction"—novels, perhaps, but not novels of the stricter sort deriving from *Don Quixote*. As Forster says, one needs a different set of tools to examine such fiction, and so it often is with English and French literature of our own century. Brunetière's theory of the evolution of genres, since it confused evolution and progress, was incorrect; but genres do change, and as the novel grew out of the romance through the ironic attitude and manner that we call realism, so—as our views of reality have changed, and as the ironic fiction that depicted the contrast of appearance and reality had made its point—something new has grown out of the novel.

JOSEPH CONRAD

NOVEL AS WORLD

Of all books, novels, which the Muses should love, make a serious claim on our compassion. The art of the novelist is simple. At the same time it is the most elusive of all creative arts, the most liable to be obscured by the scruples of its servants and votaries, the one pre-eminently destined to bring trouble to the mind and the heart of the artist. After all, the creation of a world is not a small undertaking except perhaps to the divinely gifted. In truth every novelist must begin by creating for himself a world, great or little, in which he can honestly believe. This world cannot be made otherwise than in his own image: it is fated to remain individual and a little mysterious, and yet it must resemble something already familiar to the experience, the thoughts and the sensations of his readers. At the heart of fiction, even the least worthy of the name, some sort of truth can be found—if only the truth of a childish theatrical ardour in the game of life, as in the novels of Dumas the father. But the fair truth of human delicacy can be found in Mr. Henry James's novels; and the comical, appalling truth of human rapacity let loose amongst the spoils of existence lives in the monstrous world

The selection is part of an essay entitled "Books" which appeared in The Speaker _in 1905. It is reprinted here from Conrad's_ Notes on Life and Letters (_London, 1921_).

created by Balzac. The pursuit of happiness by means lawful and unlawful, through resignation or revolt, by the clever manipulation of conventions or by solemn hanging on to the skirts of the latest scientific theory, is the only theme that can be legitimately developed by the novelist who is the chronicler of the adventures of mankind amongst the dangers of the kingdom of the earth. And the kingdom of this earth itself, the ground upon which his individualities stand, stumble, or die, must enter into his scheme of faithful record. To encompass all this in one harmonious conception is a great feat; and even to attempt it deliberately with serious intention, not from the senseless prompting of an ignorant heart, is an honourable ambition. For it requires some courage to step in calmly where fools may be eager to rush. As a distinguished and successful French novelist once observed of fiction, "C'est un art *trop* difficile."

It is natural that the novelist should doubt his ability to cope with his task. He imagines it more gigantic than it is. And yet literary creation being only one of the legitimate forms of human activity has no value but on the condition of not excluding the fullest recognition of all the more distinct forms of action. This condition is sometimes forgotten by the man of letters, who often, especially in his youth, is inclined to lay a claim of exclusive superiority for his own amongst all the other tasks of the human mind. The mass of verse and prose may glimmer here and there with the glow of a divine spark, but in the sum of human effort it has no special importance. There is no justificative formula for its existence any more than for any other artistic achievement. With the rest of them it is destined to be forgotten, without, perhaps, leaving the faintest trace. Where a novelist has an advantage over the workers in other fields of thought is in his privilege of freedom—the freedom of expression and the freedom of confessing his innermost beliefs—which should console him for the hard slavery of the pen.

NORTHROP FRYE

THE FOUR FORMS OF FICTION

In assigning the term fiction to the genre of the written word, in which prose tends to become the predominating rhythm, we collide with the view that the real meaning of fiction is falsehood or unreality. Thus an autobiography coming into a library would be classified as non-fiction if the librarian believed the author, and as fiction if she thought he was lying. It is difficult to see what use such a distinction can be to a literary critic. Surely the word fiction, which, like poetry, means etymologically something made for its own sake, could be applied in criticism to any work of literary art in a radically continuous form, which almost always means a work of art in prose. Or, if that is too much to ask, at least some protest can be entered against the sloppy habit of identifying fiction with the one genuine form of fiction which we know as the novel.

Let us look at a few of the unclassified books lying on the boundary of "non-fiction" and "literature." Is *Tristam Shandy* a novel? Nearly everyone would say yes, in spite of its easygoing disregard of "story values." Is *Gulliver's Travels* a novel? Here most would demur, including the Dewey decimal system, which puts it under "Satire and Humor." But surely everyone would call it fiction, and if it is fiction, a distinction appears between fiction as a genus and the novel as a species of that genus. Shifting the ground to fiction, then, is *Sartor Resartus* fiction? If not, why not? If it is, is *The Anatomy of Melancholy* fiction? Is it a literary form or only a work of "non-fiction" written with "style"? Is Borrow's *Lavengro* fiction? Everyman's Library says yes; the World's Classics puts it under "Travel and Topography."

The literary historian who identifies fiction with the novel is greatly embarrassed by the length of time that the world managed to get along without the novel, and until he reaches his great deliverance in Defoe, his perspective is intolerably cramped. He is compelled to reduce Tudor fiction to a series of tentative essays in the novel form, which works well enough for Deloney but makes nonsense of Sidney. He postulates a great fictional gap in the seventeenth century which exactly covers the golden age of rhetorical prose. He finally discovers that the word novel, which up to about 1900 was still the name of a more or less recognizable form, has since expanded into a catchall term which can be applied to practically any prose book that is not "on" something. Clearly, this novel-centered view of prose fiction is a Ptolemaic perspective which is now too complicated to be any longer workable, and some more relative and Copernican view must take its place.

When we start to think seriously about the novel, not as fiction, but as a form of fiction, we feel that its characteristics, whatever they are, are such as make, say, Defoe, Fielding, Austen, and James central in its tradition, and Borrow, Peacock, Melville, and Emily Brontë somehow peripheral. This is not an estimate of merit: we may think *Moby Dick* "greater" than *The Egoist* and yet feel that Meredith's book is closer to being a typical novel. Fielding's conception of the novel as a comic epic in prose seems fundamental to the tradition he did so much to establish. In novels that we think of as typical, like those of Jane Austen, plot and dialogue are closely linked to the conventions of the comedy of manners. The conventions of *Wuthering Heights* are linked rather with the tale and the ballad. They seem to have more affinity with tragedy, and the tragic emotions of passion and fury, which would shatter the balance of tone in Jane Austen, can be safely accommodated here. So can the supernatural, or the suggestion of it, which is difficult to get into a novel. The shape of the plot is different: instead of manoeuvering around a central situation, as Jane Austen does, Emily Brontë tells her story with linear accents, and she seems to need the help of a narrator, who would be absurdly out of place in Jane Austen. Conventions so different justify us in regarding *Wuthering Heights* as a different form of prose fiction from the novel, a form which we shall here call the romance. Here again we have to use the same word in several different contexts, but romance seems on the whole better than tale, which appears to fit a somewhat shorter form.

The essential difference between novel and romance lies in the conception of characterization. The romancer does not attempt to create "real people" so much as stylized figures which expand into psychological archetypes. It is in the romance that we find Jung's libido, anima, and shadow reflected in the hero, heroine, and villain respectively. That is why the romance so often radiates a glow of subjective intensity that the novel lacks, and why a suggestion of allegory is constantly creeping in around its fringes. Certain elements of character are released in the romance which make it naturally a more revolutionary form than the novel. The novelist deals with personality, with characters wearing their *personae* or social masks. He needs the framework of a stable society, and many of our best novelists have been conventional to the verge of fussiness. The romancer deals with individuality, with characters *in vacuo* idealized by revery, and, however conservative he may be, something nihilistic and untamable is likely to keep breaking out of his pages.

The prose romance, then, is an independent form of fiction to be distinguished from the novel and extracted from the miscellaneous heap of prose works now covered by that term. Even in the other heap known as short stories one can isolate the tale form used by Poe, which bears the same relation to the full romance that the stories of Chekhov or Katherine Mansfield do to the novel. "Pure" examples of either form are never found; there is hardly any modern romance that could not be made out to be a novel, and vice versa. The forms of prose fiction are mixed, like racial strains in human beings, not separable like the sexes. In fact the popular demand in fiction is always for a mixed form, a romantic novel just romantic enough for the reader to project his libido on the hero and his anima on the heroine, and just novel enough to keep these projections in a familiar world. It may be asked, therefore, what is the use of making the above distinction, especially when, though undeveloped in criticism, it is by no means unrealized. It is no surprise to hear that Trollope wrote novels and William Morris romances.

The reason is that a great romancer should be examined in terms of the conventions he chose. William Morris should not

be left on the side lines of prose fiction merely because the critic
has not learned to take the romance form seriously. Nor, in
view of what has been said about the revolutionary nature of
the romance, should his choice of that form be regarded as an
"escape" from his social attitude. If Scott has any claims to be
a romancer, it is not good criticism to deal only with his defects
as a novelist. The romantic qualities of *The Pilgrim's Progress*,
too, its archetypal characterization and its revolutionary approach to religious experience, make it a well-rounded example
of a literary form: it is not merely a book swallowed by English
literature to get some religious bulk in its diet. Finally, when
Hawthorne, in the preface to *The House of the Seven Gables*,
insists that his story should be read as romance and not as novel,
it is possible that he meant what he said, even though he indicates that the prestige of the rival form has induced the
romancer to apologize for not using it.

Romance is older than the novel, a fact which has developed
the historical illusion that it is something to be outgrown, a
juvenile and undeveloped form. The social affinities of the romance, with its grave idealizing of heroism and purity, are with
the aristocracy (for the apparent inconsistency of this with the
revolutionary nature of the form just mentioned, see the introductory comment on the *mythos* of romance in the previous
essay). It revived in the period we call Romantic as part of the
Romantic tendency to archaic feudalism and a cult of the hero,
or idealized libido. In England the romances of Scott and, in
less degree, the Brontës, are part of a mysterious Northumbrian
renaissance, a Romantic reaction against the new industrialism
in the Midlands, which also produced the poetry of Wordsworth
and Burns and the philosophy of Carlyle. It is not surprising,
therefore, that an important theme in the more bourgeois novel
should be the parody of the romance and its ideals. The tradition established by *Don Quixote* continues in a type of novel
which looks at a romantic situation from its own point of view,
so that the conventions of the two forms make up an ironic
compound instead of a sentimental mixture. Examples range
from *Northanger Abbey* to *Madame Bovary* and *Lord Jim*.

The tendency to allegory in the romance may be conscious,
as in *The Pilgrim's Progress*, or unconscious, as in the very
obvious sexual mythopoeia in William Morris. The romance,

which deals with heroes, is intermediate between the novel, which deals with men, and the myth, which deals with gods. Prose romance first appears as a late development of Classical mythology, and the prose Sagas of Iceland follow close on the mythical Eddas. The novel tends rather to expand into a fictional approach to history. The soundness of Fielding's instinct in calling *Tom Jones* a history is confirmed by the general rule that the larger the scheme of a novel becomes, the more obviously its historical nature appears. As it is creative history, however, the novelist usually prefers his material in a plastic, or roughly contemporary state, and feels cramped by a fixed historical pattern. *Waverley* is dated about sixty years back from the time of writing and *Little Dorrit* about forty years, but the historical pattern is fixed in the romance and plastic in the novel, suggesting the general principle that most "historical novels" are romances. Similarly a novel becomes more romantic in its appeal when the life it reflects has passed away: thus the novels of Trollope were read primarily as romances during the Second World War. It is perhaps the link with history and a sense of temporal context that has confined the novel, in striking contrast to the worldwide romance, to the alliance of time and Western man.

Autobiography is another form which merges with the novel by a series of insensible gradations. Most autobiographies are inspired by a creative, and therefore fictional, impulse to select only those events and experiences in the writer's life that go to build up an integrated pattern. This pattern may be something larger than himself with which he has come to identify himself, or simply the coherence of his character and attitudes. We may call this very important form of prose fiction the confession form, following St. Augustine, who appears to have invented it, and Rousseau, who established a modern type of it. The earlier tradition gave *Religio Medici, Grace Abounding*, and Newman's *Apologia* to English literature, besides the related but subtly different type of confession favored by the mystics.

Here again, as with the romance, there is some value in recognizing a distinct prose form in the confession. It gives several of our best prose works a definable place in fiction instead of keeping them in a vague limbo of books which are not quite literature because they are "thought," and not quite religion or philosophy because they are Examples of Prose Style. The confession, too, like the novel and the romance, has its own short form, the familiar essay, and Montaigne's *livre de bonne foy* is a confession made up of essays in which only the continuous narrative of the longer form is missing. Montaigne's scheme is to the confession what a work of fiction made up of short stories, such as Joyce's *Dubliners* or Boccaccio's *Decameron*, is to the novel or romance.

After Rousseau—in fact in Rousseau—the confession flows into the novel, and the mixture produces the fictional autobiography, the *Künstler-roman,* and kindred types. There is no literary reason why the subject of a confession should always be the author himself, and dramatic confessions have been used in the novel at least since *Moll Flanders*. The "stream of consciousness" technique permits of a much more concentrated fusion of the two forms, but even here the characteristics peculiar to the confession form show up clearly. Nearly always some theoretical and intellectual interest in religion, politics, or art plays a leading role in the confession. It is his success in integrating his mind on such subjects that makes the author of a confession feel that his life is worth writing about. But this interest in ideas and theoretical statements is alien to the genius of the novel proper, where the technical problem is to dissolve all theory into personal relationships. In Jane Austen, to take a familiar instance, church, state, and culture are never examined except as social data, and Henry James has been described as having a mind so fine that no idea could violate it. The novelist who cannot get along without ideas, or has not the patience to digest them in the way that James did, instinctively resorts to what Mill calls a "mental history" of a single character. And when we find that a technical discussion of a theory of aesthetics forms the climax of Joyce's *Portrait,* we realize that what makes this possible is the presence in that novel of another tradition of prose fiction.

The novel tends to be extroverted and personal; its chief interest is in human character as it manifests itself in society. The romance tends to be introverted and personal: it also deals with characters, but in a more subjective way. (Subjective here refers to treatment, not subject-matter. The characters of romance are heroic and therefore inscrutable; the novelist is freer to enter his characters' minds because he is more objective.) The confession is also introverted, but intellectualized in content. Our next step is evidently to discover a fourth form of fiction which is extroverted and intellectual.

We remarked earlier that most people would call *Gulliver's Travels* fiction but not a novel. It must then be another form of fiction, as it certainly has a form, and we feel that we are turning from the novel to this form, whatever it is, when we turn from Rousseau's *Emile* to Voltaire's *Candide,* or from Butler's *The Way of All Flesh* to the Erewhon books, or from Huxley's *Point Counterpoint* to *Brave New World.* The form thus has its own traditions, and, as the examples of Butler and Huxley show, has preserved some integrity even under the ascendancy of the novel. Its existence is easy enough to demonstrate, and no one will challenge the statement that the literary ancestry of *Gulliver's Travels* and *Candide* runs through Rabelais and Erasmus to Lucian. But while much has been said about the style and thought of Rabelais, Swift, and Voltaire, very little has been made of them as craftsmen working in a specific medium, a point no one dealing with a novelist would ignore. Another great writer in this tradition, Huxley's master, Peacock, has fared even worse; for, his form not being understood, a general impression has grown up that his status in the development of prose fiction is that of a slapdash eccentric. Actually, he is as exquisite and precise an artist in his medium as Jane Austen is in hers.

The form used by these authors is the Menippean satire, also more rarely called the Varronian satire, allegedly invented by a Greek cynic named Menippus. His works are lost, but he had two great disciples, the Greek Lucian and the Roman Varro, and the tradition of Varro, who has not survived either except in fragments, was caried on by Petronius and Apuleius. The Menippean satire appears to have developed out of verse satire through the practice of adding prose interludes, but we know it only as a prose form, though one of its recurrent features (seen in Peacock) is the use of incidental verse.

The Menippean satire deals less with people as such than with mental attitudes. Pedants, bigots, cranks, parvenus, virtuosi, enthusiasts, rapacious and incompetent professional men of all kinds, are handled in terms of their occupational approach to life as distinct from their social behavior. The Menippean satire thus resembles the confession in its ability to handle abstract ideas and theories, and differs from the novel in its characterization, which is stylized rather than naturalistic, and presents people as mouthpieces of the ideas they represent. Here again no sharp boundary lines can or should be drawn, but if we compare a character in Jane Austen with a similar character in Peacock we can immediately feel the difference between the two forms. Squire Western belongs to the novel, but Thwackum and Square have Menippean blood in them. A constant theme in the tradition is the ridicule of the *philosophus gloriosus*, already discussed. The novelist sees evil and folly as social diseases, but the Menippean satirist sees them as diseases of the intellect, as a kind of maddened pedantry which the *philosophus gloriosus* at once symbolizes and defines.

Petronius, Apuleius, Rabelais, Swift, and Voltaire all use a loosejointed narrative form often confused with the romance. It differs from the romance, however (though there is a strong admixture of romance in Rabelais), as it is not primarily concerned with the exploits of heroes, but relies on the free play of intellectual fancy and the kind of humorous observation that produces caricature. It differs also from the picaresque form, which has the novel's interest in the actual structure of society. At its most concentrated the Menippean satire presents us with a vision of the world in terms of a single intellectual pattern. The intellectual structure built up from the story makes for violent dislocations in the customary logic of narrative, though the appearance of carelessness that results reflects only the carelessness of the reader or his tendency to judge by a novel-centered conception of fiction.

The word "satire," in Roman and Renaissance times, meant either of two specific literary forms of that name, one (this one) prose and the other verse. Now it means a structural principle or attitude, what we have called a *mythos*. In the Menippean satires we have been discussing, the name of the form also applies to the attitude. As the name of an attitude, satire is, we have seen, a combination of fantasy and morality. But as the name of a form, the term satire, though confined to literature (for as a *mythos* it may appear in any art, a cartoon, for example), is more flexible, and can be either entirely fantastic or entirely moral. The Menippean adventure story may thus be pure fantasy, as it is in the literary fairy tale. The Alice books are perfect Menippean satires, and so is *The Water-Babies*, which has been influenced by Rabelais. The purely moral type is a serious vision of society as a single intellectual pattern, in other words a Utopia.

The short form of the Menippean satire is usually a dialogue or colloquy, in which the dramatic interest is in a conflict of ideas rather than of character. This is the favorite form of Erasmus, and is common in Voltaire. Here again the form is not invariably satiric in attitude, but shades off into more purely fanciful or moral discussions, like the *Imaginary Conversations* of Landor or the "dialogue of the dead." Sometimes this form expands to full length, and more than two speakers are used: the setting then is usually a *cena* or symposium, like the one that looms so large in Petronius. Plato, though much earlier in the field than Menippus, is a strong influence on this type, which stretches in an unbroken tradition down through those urbane and leisurely conversations which define the ideal courtier in Castiglione or the doctrine and discipline of angling in Walton. A modern development produces the country-house weekends in Peacock, Huxley, and their imitators in which the opinions and ideas and cultural interests expressed are as important as the love-making.

The novelist shows his exuberance either by an exhaustive analysis of human relationships, as in Henry James, or of social phenomena, as in Tolstoy. The Menippean satirist, dealing with intellectual themes and attitudes, shows his exuberance in intellectual ways, by piling up an enormous mass of erudition about his theme or in overwhelming his pedantic targets with an avalanche of their own jargon. A species, or rather subspecies, of the form is the kind of encyclopaedic farrago represented by Athenaeus' *Deipnosophists* and Macrobius' *Saturnalia*, where people sit at a banquet and pour out a vast mass of erudition on every subject that might conceivably come up in a conversation. The display of erudition had probably been associated with the Menippean tradition by Varro, who was enough of a polymath to make Quintilian, if not stare and gasp,

at any rate call him *vir Romanorum eruditissimus.* The tendency to expand into an encyclopaedic farrago is clearly marked
in Rabelais, notably in the great catalogues of torcheculs and
epithets of codpieces and methods of divination. The encyclopaedic compilations produced in the line of duty by Erasmus
and Voltaire suggest that a magpie instinct to collect facts is
not unrelated to the type of ability that has made them famous
as artists. Flaubert's encyclopaedic approach to the construction
of *Bouvard et Pecuchet* is quite comprehensible if we explain it
as marking an affinity with the Menippean tradition.

This creative treatment of exhaustive erudition is the organizing principle of the greatest Menippean satire in English
before Swift, Burton's *Anatomy of Melancholy.* Here human
society is studied in terms of the intellectual pattern provided
by the conception of melancholy, a symposium of books replaces
dialogue, and the result is the most comprehensive survey of
human life in one book that English literature had seen since
Chaucer, one of Burton's favorite authors. We may note in
passing the Utopia in his introduction and his "digressions,"
which when examined turn out to be scholarly distillations of
Menippean forms: the digression of air, of the marvellous journey; the digression of spirits, of the ironic use of erudition; the
digression of the miseries of scholars, of the satire on the *philosophus gloriosus.* The word "anatomy" in Burton's title means
a dissection or analysis, and expresses very accurately the intellectualized approach of his form. We may as well adopt it as a
convenient name to replace the cumbersome and in modern
times rather misleading "Menippean satire."

The anatomy, of course, eventually begins to merge with the
novel, producing various hybrids including the *roman à thèse*
and novels in which the characters are symbols of social or other
ideas, like the proletarian novels of the thirties in this century.
It was Sterne, however, the disciple of Burton and Rabelais,
who combined them with greatest success. *Tristram Shandy* may
be, as was said at the beginning, a novel, but the digressing
narrative, the catalogues, the stylizing of character along
"humor" lines, the marvellous journey of the great nose, the
symposium discussions, and the constant ridicule of philosophers and pedantic critics are all features that belong to the
anatomy.

A clearer understanding of the form and traditions of the anatomy would make a good many elements in the history of literature come into focus. Boethius' *Consolation of Philosophy*, with its dialogue form, its verse interludes and its pervading tone of contemplative irony, is a pure anatomy, a fact of considerable importance for the understanding of its vast influence. *The Compleat Angler* is an anatomy because of its mixture of prose and verse, its rural *cena* setting, its dialogue form, its deipnosophistical interest in food, and its gentle Menippean raillery of a society which considers everything more important than fishing and yet has discovered very few better things to do. In nearly every period of literature there are many romances, confessions, and anatomies that are neglected only because the categories to which they belong are unrecognized. In the period between Sterne and Peacock, for example, we have, among romances, *Melmoth the Wanderer;* among confessions, Hogg's *Confessions of a Justified Sinner;* among anatomies, Southey's *Doctor,* Amory's *John Buncle,* and the *Noctes Ambrosianae.*

To sum up then; when we examine fiction from the point of view of form, we can see four chief strands binding it together, novel, confession, anatomy, and romance. The six possible combinations of these forms all exist, and we have shown how the novel has combined with each of the other three. Exclusive concentration on one form is rare: the early novels of George Eliot, for instance, are influenced by the romance, and the later ones by the anatomy. The romance-confession hybrid is found, naturally, in the autobiography of a romantic temperament, and is represented in English by the extroverted George Borrow and the introverted De Quincey. The romance-anatomy one we have noticed in Rabelais; a later example is *Moby Dick,* where the romantic theme of the wild hunt expands into an encyclopaedic anatomy of the whale. Confession and anatomy are united in *Sartor Resartus* and in some of Kierkegaard's strikingly original experiments in prose fiction form, including *Either/Or.* More comprehensive fictional schemes usually employ at least three forms: we can see strains of novel, romance, and confession in *Pamela,* of novel, romance, and anatomy in *Don Quixote,* of novel, confession, and anatomy in Proust, and of romance, confession, and anatomy in Apuleius.

I deliberately make this sound schematic in order to suggest the advantage of having a simple and logical explanation for the form of, say, *Moby Dick* or *Tristram Shandy*. The usual critical approach to the form of such works resembles that of the doctors in Brobdingnag, who after great wrangling finally pronounced Gulliver a *lusus naturae*. It is the anatomy in particular that has baffled critics, and there is hardly any fiction writer deeply influenced by it who has not been accused of disorderly conduct. The reader may be reminded here of Joyce, for describing Joyce's books as monstrous has become a nervous tic. I find "demogorgon," "behemoth," and "white elephant" in good critics; the bad ones could probably do much better. The care that Joyce took to organize *Ulysses* and *Finnegans Wake* amounted nearly to obsession, but as they are not organized on familiar principles of prose fiction, the impression of shapelessness remains. Let us try our formulas on him.

If a reader were asked to set down a list of the things that had most impressed him about *Ulysses*, it might reasonably be somewhat as follows. First, the clarity with which the sights and sounds and smells of Dublin come to life, the rotundity of the character-drawing, and the naturalness of the dialogue. Second, the elaborate way that the story and characters are parodied by being set against archetypal heroic patterns, notably the one provided by the *Odyssey*. Third, the revelation of character and incident through the searching use of the stream-of-consciousness technique. Fourth, the constant tendency to be encyclopaedic and exhaustive both in technique and in subject matter, and to see both in highly intellectualized terms. It should not be too hard for us by now to see that these four points describe elements in the book which relate to the novel, romance, confession, and anatomy respectively. *Ulysses*, then, is a complete prose epic with all four forms employed in it, all of practically equal importance, and all essential to one another, so that the book is a unity and not an aggregate.

This unity is built up from an intricate scheme of parallel contrasts. The romantic archetypes of Hamlet and Ulysses are like remote stars in a literary heaven looking down quizzically on the shabby creatures of Dublin obediently intertwining themselves in the patterns set by their influences. In the "Cyclops" and "Circe" episodes particularly there is a continuous parody of realistic patterns by romantic ones which reminds us, though the irony leans in the opposite direction, of *Madame Bovary*. The relation of novel and confession techniques is similar; the author jumps into his characters' minds to follow their stream of consciousness, and out again to describe them externally. In the novel-anatomy combination, too, found in the "Ithaca" chapter, the sense of lurking antagonism between the personal and intellectual aspects of the scene accounts for much of its pathos. The same principle of parallel contrast holds good for the other three combinations: of romance and confession in "Nausicaa" and "Penelope," of confession and anatomy in "Proteus" and "The Lotos-Eaters," of romance and anatomy (a rare and fitful combination) in "Sirens" and parts of "Circe."

In *Finnegans Wake* the unity of design goes far beyond this. The dingy story of the sodden HCE and his pinched wife is not contrasted with the archetypes of Tristram and the divine king: HCE is himself Tristram and the divine king. As the setting is a dream, no contrast is possible between confession and novel, between a stream of consciousness inside the mind and the appearances of other people outside it. Nor is the experiential world of the novel to be separated from the intelligible world of the anatomy. The forms we have been isolating in fiction, and which depend for their existence on the commonsense dichotomies of the daylight consciousness, vanish in *Finnegans Wake* into a fifth and quintessential form. This form is the one traditionally associated with scriptures and sacred books, and treats life in terms of the fall and awakening of the human soul and the creation and apocalypse of nature. The Bible is the definitive example of it; the Egyptian Book of the Dead and the Icelandic Prose Edda, both of which have left deep imprints on *Finnegans Wake,* also belong to it.

2

NARRATIVE TECHNIQUE

No one is in a position to recognize the difficulty of even the simplest choices among fictional techniques better than one (and there must be very many) who has imagined himself a potential novelist, has tried writing fiction, and has given it up for an easier trade. What does one develop and what does one summarize? In which directions should one develop? Does the appearance of the characters matter? Must one imagine and report their exact words? How much of the physical surroundings is it essential to show? Of two more-or-less equally developed passages, why does one seem thin while the other seems cluttered? How does one make time pass? Where do motives begin and how far back is one obliged to analyze them? How does one get the characters from one place to another? What is the relation between the complexity of the situation one starts with and the texture of the finished fiction?

No theory exactly answers these questions, of course, but theoretical discussions can illuminate the problems which the questions raise all the same. What such theory requires is first a fairly non-partisan analytical curiosity. Some of the greatest of novelists have never wondered publicly, and perhaps not even privately, how they were doing what they were doing. How consciously Dickens may have thought through the principles of his art as he sketched out the work sheets for the serial installments of his novels is, of course, impossible to say. But one can safely conclude that Trollope, with his 250 words every quarter hour, wrote out of a spontaneous feeling for the demands of his material which he could not have translated into conceptual form. Secondly, a theory of narrative technique needs a terminology, for without a rich enough vocabulary the necessary discriminations and comparisons can scarcely be made.

In addition, a theory of narrative technique requires that the critic make, at least implicitly, two assumptions. The first of these is that techniques have no existence apart from their employment in particular novels, that one cannot begin to judge the effectiveness of one way of telling a story over another without judging the relation between that technique and the whole structure of the novel in which it appears. A theory of technique also requires that the critic assume that the subject matter of a novel—its ideas, its themes, its system of values—cannot be separated from its technique, since it is only by means of technique that these themes and values have any existence at all.

The selection from Phyllis Bentley that follows demonstrates a fine balance between the wish to generalize and the capacity to see every technique in its particular employment in unique novels. It demonstrates as well how much intelligence can be brought to so basic a question as the rhythm of summary and scene. The selections from James, taken from the Prefaces to the New York Edition were written near the end of his career while he was at the height of his powers. They have provided an example for novelists and critics ever since because of the penetration of his critical insights into the technique of his own work; and they have added much to the terminology in which such matters are still discussed. The essay by Mark Schorer has proved to be a watershed in the criticism of fiction. For, of those two assumptions a critic must make, the latter, that the content and the technique of fiction are indivisible, has gained currency only very slowly. The brilliance of Schorer's essay has established, with an irrefutable authority, that "technique is the only means [the novelist] has of discovering, exploring, developing his subject, of conveying its meaning, and, finally, of evaluating it."

PHYLLIS BENTLEY

USE OF SUMMARY

The scene and the summary have quite distinct uses, distinct parts to play, in fiction. The place of the summary is very well explained by Fielding in *Tom Jones:*

> We intend in it [the novel] rather to pursue the method of those writers who profess to disclose the revolutions of countries, than to imitate the painful and voluminous historian, who, to preserve the regularity of his series, thinks himself obliged to fill up as much paper with the details of months and years in which nothing remarkable happened, as he employs upon those notable eras when the greatest scenes have been transacted on the human stage. Such histories as these do in reality very much resemble a newspaper, which consists of just the same number of words, whether there be any news in it or not . . .
>
> Now it is our purpose in the ensuing pages to pursue a contrary method: when any extraordinary scene presents itself, as we trust will often be the case, we shall spare no pains nor paper to open it at large to our reader; but if whole years should pass without producing any thing worthy of his notice, we shall not be afraid of a chasm in our history, but shall hasten on to matters of consequence. . . . .
>
> (Book II, chapter i.)
>
> Good writers will, indeed, do well to imitate the ingenious traveller . . . who always proportions his stay at any place to the beauties, elegances, and curiosities which it affords.
>
> (Book XI, chapter ix.)

That is to say, when the novelist requires to traverse rapidly large tracts of the world of the novel which are necessary to the story, but not worth dwelling long upon—not worth narrating

From Some Observations on the Art of Narrative, *1947. Reprinted by permission of A. D. Peters & Co.*

in the specific detail of a scene—the summary is what he uses. For example:

> We lived in an uninterrupted course of ease and content for five years . . . .
>> (Daniel Defoe: *Moll Flanders.*)

> They travelled as expeditiously as possible; and, sleeping one night on the road, reached Longbourn by dinner-time the next day.
>> (Jane Austen: *Pride and Prejudice*, Ch. 47.)

> Elizabeth passed the chief of the night in her sister's room.
>> (Jane Austen: *Pride and Prejudice*, Ch. 9.)

> In the course of the day I was enrolled a member of the fourth class, and regular tasks and occupations were assigned me.
>> (Charlotte Brontë: *Jane Eyre*, Ch. vi.)

> Mr. Dick and I soon became the best of friends.
> In less than a fortnight I was quite at home, and happy, amongst my new companions.
>> (Charles Dickens: *David Copperfield*, Ch. xv.)

> She had been led through the best galleries, had been taken to the chief points of view, had been shown the grandest ruins and the most glorious churches . . . .
>> (George Eliot: *Middlemarch*, Ch. 20.)

> Some months of homely courtship ensued.
>> (George Meredith: *The Egoist*, Ch. iii.)

> The news became known in trading circles throughout the town.
>> (Arnold Bennett: *The Old Wives' Tale*, Ch. iv.)

> Sir Francis's career had not come up to his expectations.
>> (Virginia Woolf: *Night and Day.*)

> Mary spent her first week in London very quietly. She visited a few shops, but for the most part she stayed in [her] rooms, and read, or thought of John. . . . At the end of a week she wanted action. She ordered herself a plum-coloured habit and hired a horse and a groom to ride with her in the Park.
>> (Storm Jameson: *The Lovely Ship.*)

Note how in that last passage the summary goes down the sliding scale of specificity towards the scene. The first two sentences are highly condensed summary, the third sentence less so. In the fourth sentence we receive such specific details as the colour of the habit and the ordering of a groom, though we are not told the incidents in which Mary orders and buys them. The following sentence begins: "The morning of her first ride was cold"—a specific time is established, and we glide off into a scene, where Mary rides in the Park, has her horse disturbed by a hat scudding between his feet, receives the apologies of the young man who owns the hat, and so on.

The summary is particularly useful, too, when a whole way of life is to be indicated as a background to the main characters' specific activities. There are some fine passages of summary of this kind in Thackeray's chapter "How to Live Well on Nothing a Year" in *Vanity Fair*. To have told all the activities summarised there in specific action would have occupied infinitely more space and labour than they were worth to the story. A neat example of a social summary occurs in Galsworthy's *The Man of Property:*

> They had all done so well for themselves, these Forsytes, that they were all what is called "of a certain position." They had shares in all sorts of things, not as yet in consols, for they had no dread in life like that of 3 per cent. for their money. They collected pictures, too, and were supporters of such charitable institutions as might be beneficial to their sick domestics . . . .
>
> (Galsworthy: *The Man of Property*, Ch. i.)

One of the most important and frequent uses of the summary is to convey rapidly a stretch of *past* life. The novelist, having excited our interest in his characters by telling a scene to us, suddenly whizzes his pageant back, then forward, giving us a rapid summary of their past history, a retrospect. Percy Lubbock has discussed the theory and practice of the retrospect with such penetration and such erudition that it would be idle to enter deeply into the subject here, but one or two examples of fine retrospects may be interesting. In *Clayhanger* Edwin sees a tear on the cheek of an old Sunday-school teacher. The tear is explained (Chapter iv) by a retrospective summary, some twelve pages long, which sums up the whole of the life of Edwin's father—and the whole of the life of pottery operatives in the early 19th century as well. Trollope's retrospective summary of the tragic history of Mary's birth in *Dr. Thorne* is famous for its vitality and interest, though somewhat overlong. An amusingly laconic summary, of which the brevity forms the bite, is Aldous Huxley's account of the course of the intrigue between Walter Bidlake and Marjorie Carling, which occupies eight lines of the first page of *Point Counterpoint*.

The summary if unskilfully handled can become exceedingly tedious. "What is the use of a book without pictures or conversations?" thought Alice just before the White Rabbit ran by, in condemnation of the book her sister was reading, and this childish comment is supported by novel-readers of all degrees of intelligence. Long close paragraphs of print are in themselves apt to dismay the less serious readers and their instinct here is a sound one, for an excess of summary and an insufficiency of scene in a novel makes the story seem remote, without bite, second-hand; for in a summary the novelist is selecting, so to speak, from his own selection; we feel we might have summarised differently if we had seen more fully. Besides, the summary tends to throw the events summarised into the past; we feel that they must have happened long ago or time would have lacked for the process of summarising.

Possibly the worst example in good English fiction of the misuse of summary occurs at the beginning of *Waverley*. Omitting chapter one, which discusses the kind of story Scott intends to write, as not really part of the novel, we begin chapter two by a somewhat indirect but specific statement that sixty years ago Edward Waverley took leave of his family to join a regiment of dragoons in which he had lately obtained a commission, and that it was a melancholy day at Waverley-Honour when the young officer parted with Sir Everard, his uncle. This is a hopeful start; for the sake of the battles and adventures it seems to promise, most readers would be perfectly willing to tackle a few paragraphs, or even a few pages, of retrospective summary explaining who the two Waverleys are, with their respective situations. But Scott gives us four chapters of summary without a single scene. Not until the opening of chapter six do we leave retrospect and come to: "It was upon the evening of this memorable Sunday that Sir Everard entered the library. . . ." It is a specific action; at last we are being given a scene, where the kind of action we call speech is soon vouchsafed to us. The naïve monotony, the stale secondhand air, of an unbroken summary, four chapters long, would be intolerable to the sophisticated modern reader.

The placing and introduction of the summary is a matter

requiring great skill. Perhaps I may be forgiven if I cite a personal instance of bad placing. In a novel of mine called *The Spinner of the Years*, a family, the Armitages, are sitting at dinner when the bell rings; the son of the house goes out to see who has arrived, and returns, bringing with him a young lad, Johnnie Talland. At this point I broke off, and gave eight pages of retrospective summary, covering Johnnie's career since the Armitages last saw him. When the novel was published a critic complained of this. The criticism vexed me, for it was clear that the critic knew nothing about the art of narrative, he had no idea that all summary occurred between two scenes. But in fact the critic, though less well informed in the technique of fiction, had a sounder story-telling instinct than I, for the summary was undoubtedly ill-placed. I had not sufficiently excited the readers' curiosity about Johnnie to make them want a summary about him; all they were eager about at the moment was what the young Imogen Armitage, upon whom interest had been concentrated, felt at the meeting. A few more sentences, an uncertainty in Johnnie's manner which hinted an inconvenience in his life, would have reconciled the reader to a summary which satisfied his curiosity.

The transition from one kind of narrative to another is also a ticklish job. It can be done in the baldest, crudest way, as when Defoe (*Moll Flanders*) in the middle of a scene breaks into summary by remarking: "Here he gave me a long history of his life, which indeed would make a very strange history, and be infinitely diverting. He told me . . ." or George Eliot begins a chapter of retrospective summary on Tertius Lydgate's career by announcing with equal frankness: "At present I have to make the new settler Lydgate better known to anyone interested in him. . . ." (*Middlemarch*). But other novelists, whether of the 18th, 19th or 20th century, show such an infinite subtlety in making their transitions that a very pointed tool is necessary to disentangle the interweavings. A great part of the vigour, the vivacity and the readability of Dickens derives from his innumerable interweavings of scene and summary; his general method is to keep summary to the barest essential minimum, a mere sentence or two here and there between the incredibly fertile burgeoning of his scenes. Thus the fabric of his narrative remains always very closely woven.

The later novelists, too, employ endless devices to make summary appear as scene and thus rob it of its tedium, casting it in the guise of one character's reflections upon another, dialogue between two characters, and so on. But of the contemporary disrepute of summary I shall speak later.

USE OF SCENE

It will not be necessary to furnish many examples of scenes from fiction, since the whole weight of fiction criticism hitherto seems directed upon nothing else. Here are a few short examples, extracts from narrative scenes in well-known novels. To avoid confusing the issue, I have chosen several passages which are not "scenes" in the violent sense of the word.

> Upon opening the clothes, to his great surprise he beheld an infant wrapped up in some coarse linen, in a sweet and profound slumber, between his sheets.
>> (Fielding: *Tom Jones.*)

> Mr. Darcy smiled; but Elizabeth thought she could perceive that he was rather offended, and therefore checked her laugh.
>> (Jane Austen: *Pride and Prejudice.*)

> All at once, without speaking, he struck suddenly and strongly. I tottered, and on regaining my equilibrium retired back a step or two from his chair.
>> (Charlotte Brontë: *Jane Eyre.*)

> "When will you see her?" said the signora with a start.
> "See whom?" said the bishop.
> "My child," said the mother.
> "What is the young lady's age?" asked the bishop.
> "She is just seven," said the signora.
> "Oh," said the bishop, shaking his head: "She is much too young—very much too young."
>> (Trollope: *Barchester Towers.*)

> The card of Lieutenant Patterne was handed to Sir Willoughby, who laid it on the salver, saying to the footman: "Not at home."
>> (Meredith: *The Egoist.*)

> Mrs. Durrant sat in the drawing-room by a lamp winding a ball of wool. Mr. Clutterbuck read *The Times*. In the distance stood a second lamp, and round it sat the young ladies, flashing scissors. . . . Mr. Wortley read a book.

"Yes; he is perfectly right," said Mrs. Durrant, drawing herself up and ceasing to wind her wool.

(Virginia Woolf: *Jacob's Room.*)

In all the above passages, specific actions are narrated: the characters see, speak, strike, smile, think, kneel, read, push, wind wool; a card is handed, scissors flash.

The scene gives the reader a feeling of participating in the action very intensely, for he is hearing about it contemporaneously, exactly as it occurs and the moment it has occurred; the only interval between its occurring and the reader hearing about it is that occupied by the novelist's voice telling it. The scene is therefore used for intense moments. The crisis, the climax, of a sequence of actions is always (by novelists who know their craft) narrated in scene. When Darcy proposes to Elizabeth, when Rochester's wedding to Jane is interrupted; when Micawber reveals Uriah Heep's wickedness, when Paul Dombey dies; when Rawdon discovers Becky's unfaithfulness with Lord Steyne, when Constance Baines hurls Mr. Povey's tooth from the window; when Ferrand talks about English hypocrisy to Dick Shelton, when Aziz undergoes his trial for assault, when Jess Oakroyd tears up his insurance card—whenever an important action occurs, whenever an important decision is taken—it is presented in scene. The Victorian novelists, however, did not waste full-dress scenes on minor incidents. Dickens with his light touch, his agile grace, is in and out of a minor scene in a couple of sentences; the heavier-handed write fewer and longer scenes, fewer and longer summaries.

It is not possible to convey the same *amount*, the same *volume* of information in a scene as in a summary of the same length, but by a highly significant or symbolic scene an equally valid impression of the portion of life being presented may be created. (Some would say a more valid, a more truthful, as well as a more vivid, impression.) The difference in method is between loading a single incident with significance or taking the essence of many incidents, between offering some terms to represent the mathematical series, or offering the summation of the whole; between selection and integration.

The scene method alone cannot give an extensive background, cannot give a long stretch of past history, cannot give explanations—at least, it can do so only by employing a great number of scenes, thus wasting the reader's time and attention, and throwing the story out of proportion. Percy Lubbock makes the interesting point that in *Anna Karenina* Tolstoy destroys one of his finest effects by not using summary (which Lubbock calls retrospect) sufficiently. Anna renounces her world for love—but Tolstoy never gives us a panorama of her glittering social world through summary, he employs scenes alone. These scenes, concludes Lubbock, are not numerous enough or significant enough to give an impression of St. Petersburg society against which Anna's later loneliness would stand out strongly. Few would cavil at any method employed in a novel so essentially satisfying as *Anna Karenina*, but there are many instances (I believe) in modern novels where a greater use of summary would have improved the work. In Virginia Woolf's *The Years*, for example, where the fortunes of the Pargiter family from 1880 to 1937 are presented in scenes only, we are conscious of great gaps in our knowledge of the family, for lack of linking and explanatory summary. We are conscious too, I think, of tedium in the constant re-establishing of time and place. North Pargiter complains that he is always finding himself on another strange doorstep, and the great difficulty of the "maximum scene" method is that somehow or other the location, type and ownership of the fresh doorstep has every time to be indicated. The modern novelist enjoys making these locations in subtle and indirect fashion, but in his efforts to avoid the crudity and monotony of repeated direct statements his subtlety sometimes becomes obscurity and the reader is involved in a guessing competition.

The scene is undoubtedly the most important, the most significant and the most entertaining of the novelist's available types of narrative. But it is not the only type.

ART OF NARRATIVE

The proper use, the right mingling, of scene, description and summary is the art of fictitious narrative.

It is difficult to give many examples without overweighting this text with slabs of quotation involving whole pages of fiction, so perhaps I may be allowed to give the text of one brief passage only, to illustrate the method of analysis, and then analyse the opening pages of *Vanity Fair*, as an example to serve as typical of many.

Description:	The moon was set, and it was very dark;
Scene:	Bessie carried a lantern, whose light glanced on wet steps and gravel road . . .
Description:	Raw and chill was the winter morning;
Scene:	My teeth chattered as I hastened down the drive. . . . The distant roll of the wheels announced the coming coach; I went to the door and watched its lamps approach rapidly through the gloom. . . . The coach drew up . . . my trunk was hoisted up; I was taken from Bessie's neck, to which I clung with kisses. "Be sure and take good care of her!" cried she to the guard. "Ay, ay!" was the answer; the door was slapped to, and on we drove.
Summary:	We appeared to travel over hundreds of miles. . . . We passed through several towns,
Scene:	and in one, a very large one, the coach stopped; the horses were taken out, and the passengers alighted to dine. I was carried into an inn. . . .

(Charlotte Brontë: *Jane Eyre.*)

The close interweaving of the types of narrative in that short passage may be noted as typical. Let us now analyse a more extended piece, from a master hand.

Vanity Fair opens thus:

> While the present century was in its teens, and on one sunshiny morning in June, there drove up to the great iron gate of Miss Pinkerton's Academy for young ladies, on Chiswick Mall, a large family coach. . . .

"There drove up a coach"—we are being told of a specific action at a specific time in a specific place; that is a scene. The scene continues for three or four pages; Miss Jemima Pinkerton sees the coach, comments on it to her sister; they talk; in their talk it transpires that Amelia Sedley is leaving the Academy that day and that another pupil, Becky Sharp, is accompanying her. Miss Pinkerton inscribes a farewell copy of Johnson's Dictionary for Amelia, declines Jemima's request to inscribe one for Becky Sharp. Then Thackeray glides off into a mingled summary and description, telling us what Amelia was like and certain passages of her past history. This takes a couple of pages. Then (page 6) we hear: "The hour of parting came."

Miss Pinkerton and Amelia part (summary gliding into the specific); Miss Pinkerton and Becky part (definitely scene— Becky makes her farewells in French which her schoolmistress does not understand); there is a rapid account of the parting with the pupils; the two girls enter Amelia's coach (scene); Jemima hands in some sandwiches and a copy of the Dictionary for Becky, though uninscribed (scene); Becky throws the Dictionary out of the window (scene); the carriage rolls away and the gates are closed (scene), and chapter one is over.

Chapter two begins with a scene between Amelia and Becky in the coach; then Thackeray goes into a four-page retrospect, chiefly summary mingled with a little short scene here and there, telling us Becky's past.

> Many a dun had she talked to, and turned away from her father's door; many a tradesman had she coaxed and wheedled into good-humour . . . The rigid formality of the place suffocated her . . . She had not been much of a dissembler, until now her loneliness taught her to feign . . . .

When Thackeray has finished summarising Becky's past, he glides into scene:

> When at length home was reached, Miss Amelia Sedley skipped out on Sambo's arm. . . . She showed Rebecca over every room in the house. . . . She insisted upon Rebecca accepting the white cornelian . . . she determined in her heart to ask her mother's permission to present her white Cashmere shawl to her friend.

The white Cashmere shawl had been brought home from India by Amelia's brother Joseph, and the scene continues and becomes even more specific as Amelia and Sedley talk about Joseph. The dinner-bell rings and the two girls go down to dinner (scene) and the chapter ends.

Chapter three begins with a scene between the girls and Joseph, then goes off into a retrospective summary about Joseph Sedley.

> His bulk caused Joseph much anxious thought and alarm. Now and again he would make a desperate attempt to get rid of his super-abundant fat; but his indolence and love of good living speedily got the better of these endeavours at reform. . . . He took the hugest pains to adorn his big person and passed many hours daily in that occupation. . . .

If we were given an account of one specific occasion when Joseph at a specific time and place stood before his mirror dressing for hours, that would be a scene; but Thackeray rightly judged that the Collector of Boggley Wallah at his dressing-table was not worth so long pausing over, and summarises him in a page and a half. But Joseph taking Becky into dinner, and Becky's attempts to capture his interest, are worth a scene and get one which lasts till the end of the chapter.

> Downstairs, then, they went, Joseph very red and blushing, Rebecca very modest, and holding her green eyes downwards. . . . I must be quiet, thought Rebecca, and very much interested about India.

Chapter four begins with a brief summary:

> Poor Joe's panic lasted for two or three days. . . . As for Mr. Sedley's jokes, Rebecca laughed at them with a cordiality and perseverance. . . .

And so on for two paragraphs. Then:

> Once, in looking over some drawings which Amelia had sent from school, Rebecca came upon one which caused her to burst into tears and leave the room.

This is scene again.

And so it goes on through this and every other English novel written between 1719 and 1919: scene, summary, description, scene, summary. The blend of scene, summary and description is—or was between 1719 and 1919 (Defoe and Woolf)—the novelist's medium, his fictitious prose narrative; through and by this he must present his material; through and by this he must portray characters and actions representative of reality in a plot of more or less complexity; through and by this he must give us that patterned impression of dynamic life which is the purpose of all art.

HENRY JAMES

THE HOUSE OF FICTION

The house of fiction has in short not one window, but a million—a number of possible windows not to be reckoned, rather; every one of which has been pierced, or is still pierceable, in its vast front, by the need of the individual vision and by the pressure of the individual will. These apertures, of dissimilar shape and size, hang so, all together, over the human scene that we might have expected of them a greater sameness of report than we find. They are but windows at the best, mere holes in a dead wall, disconnected, perched aloft; they are not hinged doors opening straight upon life. But they have this mark of their own that at each of them stands a figure with a pair of eyes, or at least with a field-glass, which forms, again and again, for observation, a unique instrument, insuring to the person making use of it an impression distinct from every other. He and his neighbours are watching the same show, but one seeing more where the other sees less, one seeing black where the other sees white, one seeing big where the other sees small, one seeing coarse where the other sees fine. And so on, and so on; there is fortunately no saying on what, for the particular pair of eyes, the window may *not* open; "fortunately" by reason, precisely, of this incalculability of range. The spreading field, the human scene, is the "choice of subject"; the pierced aperture, either broad or balconied or slit-like and low-browed, is the "literary form"; but they are, singly or together, as nothing without the posted presence of the watcher—without, in other words, the consciousness of the artist. Tell me what the artist is, and I will tell you of what he has *been* conscious. Thereby I

From the Preface to The Portrait of a Lady. *This and the following selections from the Prefaces are reprinted from* The Art of the Novel *(New York, 1934).*

shall express to you at once his boundless freedom and his "moral" reference.

All this is a long way round, however, for my word about my dim first move toward "The Portrait," which was exactly my grasp of a single character—an acquisition I had made, moreover, after a fashion not here to be retraced. Enough that I was, as seemed to me, in complete possession of it, that I had been so for a long time, that this had made it familiar and yet had not blurred its charm, and that, all urgently, all tormentingly, I saw it in motion and so to speak, in transit. This amounts to saying that I saw it as bent upon its fate—some fate or other; *which*, among the possibilities, being precisely the question. Thus I had my vivid individual—vivid, so strangely, in spite of being still at large, not confined by the conditions, not engaged in the tangle, to which we look for much of the impress that constitutes an identity. . . .

This single small corner-stone, the conception of a certain young woman affronting her destiny, had begun with being all my outfit for the large building of "The Portrait of a Lady." It came to be a square and spacious house—or has at least seemed so to me in this going over it again; but, such as it is, it had to be put up round my young woman while she stood there in perfect isolation. That is to me, artistically speaking, the circumstance of interest; for I have lost myself once more, I confess, in the curiosity of analysing the structure. By what process of logical accretion was this slight "personality," the mere slim shade of an intelligent but presumptuous girl, to find itself endowed with the high attributes of a Subject?—and indeed by what thinness, at the best, would such a subject not be vitiated? Millions of presumptuous girls, intelligent or not intelligent, daily affront their destiny, and what is it open to their destiny to *be*, at the most, that we should make an ado about it? The novel is of its very nature an "ado," an ado about something, and the larger the form it takes the greater of course the ado. Therefore, consciously, that was what one was in for—for positively organizing an ado about Isabel Archer.

One looked it well in the face, I seem to remember, this extravagance; and with the effect precisely of recognising the charm of the problem. Challenge any such problem with any

intelligence, and you immediately see how full it is of substance; the wonder being, all the while, as we look at the
world, how absolutely, how inordinately, the Isabel Archers,
and even much smaller female fry, insist on mattering. George
Eliot has admirably noted it—"In these frail vessels is borne
onward through the ages the treasure of human affection." In
"Romeo and Juliet" Juliet has to be important, just as, in
"Adam Bede" and "The Mill on the Floss" and "Middlemarch"
and "Daniel Deronda," Hetty Sorel and Maggie Tulliver and
Rosamond Vincy and Gwendolen Harleth have to be; with that
much of firm ground, that much of bracing air, at the disposal
all the while of their feet and their lungs. They are typical,
none the less, of a class difficult, in the individual case, to make
a centre of interest; so difficult in fact that many an expert
painter, as for instance Dickens and Walter Scott, as for instance even, in the main, so subtle a hand as that of R. L.
Stevenson, has preferred to leave the task unattempted. There
are in fact writers as to whom we make out that their refuge
from this is to assume it to be not worth their attempting; by
which pusillanimity in truth their honour is scantly saved. It
is never an attestation of a value, or even of our imperfect sense
of one, it is never a tribute to any truth at all, that we shall
represent that value badly. It never makes up, artistically, for
an artist's dim feeling about a thing that he shall "do" the
thing as ill as possible. There are beter ways than that, the best
of all of which is to begin with less stupidity.

It may be answered meanwhile, in regard to Shakespeare's
and to George Eliot's testimony, that their concession to the
"importance" of their Juliets and Cleopatras and Portias (even
with Portia as the very type and model of the young person intelligent and presumptuous) and to that of their Hettys and
Maggies and Rosamonds and Gwendolens, suffers the abatement
that these slimnesses are, when figuring as the main props of
the theme, never suffered to be sole ministers of its appeal, but
have their inadequacy eked out with comic relief and under-
plots, as the playwrights say, when not with murders and
battles and the great mutations of the world. If they are shown
as "mattering" as much as they could possibly pretend to,
the proof of it is in a hundred other persons, made of much
stouter stuff, and each involved moreover in a hundred rela-

tions which matter to *them* concomitantly with that one. Cleopatra matters, beyond bounds, to Antony, but his colleagues, his antagonists, the state of Rome and the impending battle also prodigiously matter; Portia matters to Antonio, and to Shylock, and to the Prince of Morocco, to the fifty aspiring princes, but for these gentry there are other lively concerns; for Antonio, notably, there are Shylock and Bassanio and his lost ventures and the extremity of his predicament. This extremity indeed, by the same token, matters to Portia—though its doing so becomes of interest all by the fact that Portia matters to *us*. That she does so, at any rate, and that almost everything comes round to it again, supports my contention as to this fine example of the value recognized in the mere young thing. . . .

Now to see deep difficulty braved is at any time, for the really addicted artist, to feel almost even as a pang the beautiful incentive, and to feel it verily in such sort as to wish the danger intensified. The difficulty most worth tackling can only be for him, in these conditions, the greatest the case permits of. So I remember feeling here (in presence, always, that is, of the particular uncertainty of my ground), that there would be one way better than another—oh, ever so much better than any other!—of making it fight out its battle. The frail vessel, that charged with George Eliot's "treasure," and thereby of such importance to those who curiously approach it, has likewise possibilities of importance to itself, possibilities which permit of treatment and in fact peculiarly require it from the moment they are considered at all. There is always the escape from any close account of the weak agent of such spells by using as a bridge for evasion, for retreat and flight, the view of her relation to those surrounding her. Make it predominantly a view of *their* relation and the trick is played: you give the general sense of her effect, and you give it, so far as the raising on it of a superstructure goes, with the maximum of ease. Well, I recall perfectly how little, in my now quite established connexion, the maximum of ease appealed to me, and how I seemed to get rid of it by an honest transposition of the weights in the two scales. "Place the centre of the subject in the young woman's own consciousness," I said to myself, "and you get as interesting and as beautiful a difficulty as you could wish. Stick to *that*—for the centre; put the heaviest weight into *that* scale, which will be so largely the scale of her relation to herself. Make her only interested enough, at the same time, in the things that are not herself, and this relation need n't fear to be too limited. Place meanwhile in the other scale the lighter weight (which is usually the one that tips the balance of interest) : press least hard, in short, on the consciousness of your heroine's satellites, especially the male; make it an interest contributive only to the greater one. See, at all events, what can be done in this way. What better field could there be for a due ingenuity? The girl hovers, inextinguishable, as a charming creature, and the job will be to translate her into the highest terms of that formula, and as nearly as possible moreover into *all* of them. To depend upon her and her little concerns wholly to see you through will necessitate, remember, your really 'doing' her."

So far I reasoned, and it took nothing less than that technical rigour, I now easily see, to inspire me with the right confidence for erecting on such a plot of ground the neat and careful and proportioned pile of bricks that arches over it and that was thus to form, constructionally speaking, a literary monument. Such is the aspect that to-day "The Portrait" wears for me: a structure reared with an "architectural" competence, as Turgenieff would have said, that makes it, to the author's own sense, the most proportioned of his productions after "The Ambassadors" —which was to follow it so many years later and which has, no doubt, a superior roundness. On one thing I was determined; that, though I should clearly have to pile brick upon brick for the creation of an interest, I would leave no pretext for saying that anything is out of line, scale or perspective. I would build large—in fine embossed vaults and painted arches, as who should say, and yet never let it appear that the chequered pavement, the ground under the reader's feet, fails to stretch at every point to the base of the walls. That precautionary spirit, on re-perusal of the book, is the old note that most touches me: it testifies so, for my own ear, to the anxiety of my provision for the reader's amusement. I felt, in view of the possible limitations of my subject, that no such provision could be excessive, and the development of the latter was simply the general form of that earnest quest. And I find indeed that this is the only account I can give myself of the evolution of the fable: it is all under the head thus named that I conceive the needful accretion as having taken place, the right complications as having started.

EMERGENCE OF CHARACTER

A character is interesting as it comes out, and by the process and duration of that emergence; just as a procession is effective by the way it unrolls, turning to a mere mob if all of it passes at once.

From the Preface to The Princess Casamassima.

BEWILDERMENT

It seems probable that if we were never bewildered there would never be a story to tell about us; we should partake of the superior nature of the all-knowing immortals whose annals are dreadfully dull so long as flurried humans are not, for the positive relief of bored Olympians, mixed up with them. Therefore it is that the wary reader for the most part warns the novelist against making his characters too *interpretative* of the muddle of fate, or in other words too divinely, too priggishly clever.

From the Preface to Roderick Hudson.

THE ART OF INTERESTING US IN THINGS

[The novelist] embarks, rash adventurer, under the star of "representation," and is pledged thereby to remember that the art of interesting us in things—once these things are the right ones for his case—can *only* be the art of representing them. This relation to them, for invoked interest, involves his accordingly "doing"; and it is for him to settle with his intelligence what that variable process shall commit him to.

From the Preface to The Spoils of Poynton.

THE FICELLE

[Maria Gostrey] is the reader's friend . . . in consequence of dispositions that make him so eminently require one; and she acts in that capacity, and *really* in that capacity alone, with

From the Preface to The Ambassadors.

exemplary devotion, from beginning to end of the book. She is an enrolled, a direct, aid to lucidity; she is in fine, to tear off her mask, the most unmitigated and abandoned of *ficelles*.

ADVENTURE

It is, not surprisingly, one of the rudiments of criticism that a human, a personal "adventure" is no *a priori*, no positive and absolute and inelastic thing, but just a matter of relation and appreciation—a name we conveniently give, after the fact, to any passage, to any situation, that has added the sharp taste of uncertainty to a quickened sense of life. Therefore the thing is, all beautifully, a matter of interpretation and of the particular conditions; without a view of which latter some of the most prodigious adventures, as one has often had occasion to say, may vulgarly show for nothing.

From the Preface to Daisy Miller.

ESSENCE AND FORM

It is a familiar truth to the novelist, at the strenuous hour, that, as certain elements in any work are of the essence, so others are only of the form; that as this or that character, this or that disposition of the material, belongs to the subject directly, so to speak, so this or that other belongs to it but indirectly—belongs intimately to the treatment. This is a truth, however, of which he rarely gets the benefit—since it could be assured to him, really, but by criticism based upon perception, criticism which is too little of this world.

From the Preface to The Portrait of a Lady.

SCENE

If I speak, as just above, of the *action* embodied, each time, in these so "quiet" recitals, it is under renewed recognition of the inveterate instinct with which they keep conforming to the

From the Preface to What Maisie Knew.

"scenic" law. They demean themselves for all the world—they quite insist on it, that is, whenever they have a chance—as little constituted dramas, little exhibitions founded on the logic of the "scene," the unit of the scene, the general scenic consistency, and knowing little more than that. To read them over has been to find them on this ground never at fault. The process repeats and renews itself, moving in the light it has once for all adopted. . . . Going over the pages here placed together has been for me, at all events, quite to watch the scenic system at play. The treatment by "scene" regularly, quite rhythmically recurs; the intervals between, the massing of the elements to a different effect and by a quite other law, remain, in this fashion, all preparative, just as the scenic occasions in themselves become, at a given moment, illustrative, each of the agents, true to its function, taking up the theme from the other very much as the fiddles, in an orchestra, may take it up from the cornets and flutes, or the wind-instruments take it up from the violins. The point, however, is that the scenic passages are *wholly* and logically scenic, having for their rule of beauty the principle of the "conduct," the organic development, of a scene—the entire succession of values that flower and bear fruit on ground solidly laid for them. The great advantage for the total effect is that we feel, with the definite alternation, how the theme *is* being treated.

MARK SCHORER

TECHNIQUE AS DISCOVERY

Modern criticism, through its exacting scrutiny of literary texts, has demonstrated with finality that in art beauty and truth are indivisible and one. The Keatsian overtones of these terms are

Reprinted from the Hudson Review, *I (1948), by permission of the author. Copyright by Mark Schorer.*

mitigated and an old dilemma solved if for beauty we substitute form, and for truth, content. We may, without risk of loss, narrow them even more, and speak of technique and subject matter. Modern criticism has shown us that to speak of content as such is not to speak of art at all, but of experience; and that it is only when we speak of the *achieved* content, the form, the work of art as a work of art, that we speak as critics. The difference between content, or experience, and achieved content, or art, is technique.

When we speak of technique, then, we speak of nearly everything. For technique is the means by which the writer's experience, which is his subject matter, compels him to attend to it; technique is the only means he has of discovering, exploring, developing his subject, of conveying its meaning, and, finally, of evaluating it. And surely it follows that certain techniques are sharper tools than others, and will discover more; that the writer capable of the most exacting technical scrutiny of his subject matter will produce works with the most satisfying content, works with thickness and resonance, works which reverberate, works with maximum meaning.

We are no longer able to regard as seriously intended criticism of poetry which does not assume these generalizations; but the case for fiction has not yet been established. The novel is still read as though its content has some value in itself, as though the subject matter of fiction has greater or lesser value in itself, and as though technique were not a primary but a supplementary element, capable perhaps of not unattractive embellishments upon the surface of the subject, but hardly of its essence. Or technique is thought of in blunter terms than those which one associates with poetry, as such relatively obvious matters as the arrangement of events to create plot; or, within plot, of suspense and climax; or as the means of revealing character motivation, relationship, and development; or as the use of point of view, but point of view as some nearly arbitrary device for the heightening of dramatic interest through the narrowing or broadening of perspective upon the material, rather than as a means toward the positive definition of theme. As for the resources of language, these, somehow, we almost never think of as a part of the technique of fiction—language as used to create a certain texture and tone which in themselves state and define themes and meanings; or language, the counters of our ordinary speech, as forced, through conscious manipulation, into all those larger meanings which our ordinary speech almost never intends. Technique in fiction, all this is a way of saying, we somehow continue to regard as merely a means to organizing material which is "given" rather than as the means of exploring and defining the values in an area of experience which, for the first time *then*, are being given.

Is fiction still regarded in this odd, divided way because it is really less tractable before the critical suppositions which now seem inevitable to poetry? Let us look at some examples: two well-known novels of the past, both by writers who may be described as "primitive," although their relative innocence of technique is of a different sort—Defoe's *Moll Flanders* and Emily Brontë's *Wuthering Heights;* and three well-known novels of this century—*Tono Bungay,* by a writer who claimed to eschew technique; *Sons and Lovers,* by a novelist who, because his ideal of subject matter ("the poetry of the immediate present") led him at last into the fallacy of spontaneous and unchangeable composition, in effect eschewed technique; and *A Portrait of the Artist as a Young Man,* by a novelist whose practice made claims for the supremacy of technique beyond those made by anyone in the past or by anyone else in this century.

Technique in fiction is, of course, all those obvious forms of it which are usually taken to be the whole of it, and many others; but for present purposes, let it be thought of in two respects particularly: the uses to which language, as language, is put to express the quality of the experience in question; and the uses of point of view not only as a mode of dramatic delimitation, but more particularly, of thematic definition. Technique is really what T. S. Eliot means by "convention": any selection, structure, or distortion, any form or rhythm imposed upon the world of action; by means of which, it should be added, our apprehension of the world of action is enriched or renewed. In this sense, everything is technique which is not the lump of experience itself, and one cannot properly say that a writer has no technique, or that he eschews technique, for, being a writer, he cannot do so. We can speak of good and bad technique, of adequate and inadequate, of technique which serves the novel's purpose, or disserves.

II

IN THE prefatory remarks to *Moll Flanders*, Defoe tells us that he is not writing fiction at all, but editing the journals of a woman of notorious character, and rather to instruct us in the necessities and the joys of virtue than to please us. We do not, of course, take these professions seriously, since nothing in the conduct of the narrative indicates that virtue is either more necessary or more enjoyable than vice. On the contrary, we discover that Moll turns virtuous only after a life of vice has enabled her to do so with security; yet it is precisely for this reason that Defoe's profession of didactic purpose has interest. For the actual morality which the novel enforces is the morality of any commercial culture, the belief that virtue pays—in worldly goods. It is a morality somewhat less than skin deep, having no relation to motives arising from a sense of good and evil, least of all, of evil-*in*-good, but exclusively from the presence or absence of food, drink, linen, damask, silver, and timepieces. It is the morality of measurement, and without in the least intending it, *Moll Flanders* is our classic revelation of the mercantile mind: the morality of measurement, which Defoe has completely neglected to measure. He fails not only to evaluate this material in his announced way, but to evaluate it at all. His announced purpose is, we admit, a pious humbug, and he meant us to read the book as a series of scandalous events; and thanks to his inexhaustible pleasure in excess and exaggeration, this element in the book continues to amuse us. Long before the book has been finished, however, this element has also become an absurdity; but not half the absurdity as that which Defoe did not intend at all—the notion that Moll could live a rich and full life of crime, and yet, repenting, emerge spotless in the end. The point is, of course, that she has no moral being, nor has the book any moral life. Everything is external. Everything can be weighed, measured, handled, paid for in gold, or expiated by a prison term. To this, the whole texture of the novel testifies—the bolts of goods, the inventories, the itemized accounts, the landlady's bills, the lists, the ledgers—all this, which taken together comprises what we call Defoe's method of circumstantial realism.

He did not come upon that method by any deliberation; it represents precisely his own world of value, the importance of external circumstance to Defoe. The point of view of Moll is indistinguishable from the point of view of her creator. We discover the meaning of the novel (at unnecessary length, without economy, without emphasis, with almost none of the distortions or the advantages of art) in spite of Defoe, not because of him. Thus the book is not the true chronicle of a disreputable female, but the true allegory of an impoverished soul, the author's; not an anatomy of the criminal class, but of the middle class. And we read it as an unintended comic revelation of self and of a social mode. Because he had no adequate resources of technique to separate himself from his material, thereby to discover and to define the meanings of his material, his contribution is not to fiction but to the history of fiction, and to social history.

The situation in *Wuthering Heights* is at once somewhat the same and yet very different. Here, too, the whole novel turns upon itself, but this time to its estimable advantage; here, too, is a revelation of what is perhaps the author's secret world of value, but this time, through what may be an accident of technique, the revelation is meaningfully accomplished. Emily Brontë may merely have stumbled upon the perspectives which define the form and the theme of her book. Whether she knew from the outset, or even at the end, what she was doing, we may doubt; but what she did and did superbly we can see.

We can assume, without at all becoming involved in the author's life but merely from the tone of somnambulistic excess which is generated by the writing itself, that this world of monstrous passion, of dark and gigantic emotional and nervous energy, is for the author, or was in the first place, a world of ideal value; and that the book sets out to persuade us of the moral magnificence of such unmoral passion. We are, I think, expected, in the first place, to take at their own valuation these demonic beings, Heathcliff and Cathy: as special creatures, set apart from the cloddish world about them by their heightened capacity for feeling, set apart, even, from the ordinary objects of human passion as, in their transcendent, sexless relationship, they identify themselves with an uncompromising landscape and cosmic force. Yet this is absurd, as much of the detail that surrounds it ("Other dogs lurked in other recesses") is absurd. The novelist Emily

Brontë had to discover these absurdities to the girl Emily; her technique had to evaluate them for what they were, so that we are persuaded that it is not Emily who is mistaken in her estimate of her characters, but they who are mistaken in their estimate of themselves. The theme of the moral magnificence of unmoral passion is an impossible theme to sustain, and what interests us is that it was device—and this time, mere, mechanical device—which taught Emily Brontë—the needs of her temperament to the contrary, all personal longing and reverie to the contrary, perhaps—that this was indeed not at all what her material must mean as art. Technique objectifies.

To lay before us the full character of this passion, to show us how it first comes into being and then comes to dominate the world about it and the life that follows upon it, Emily Brontë gives her material a broad scope in time, lets it, in fact, cut across three generations. And to manage material which is so extensive, she must find a means of narration, points of view, which can encompass that material, and, in her somewhat crude concept of motive, justify its telling. So she chooses a foppish traveler who stumbles into this world of passionate violence, a traveler representing the thin and conventional emotional life of the far world of fashion, who wishes to hear the tale; and for her teller she chooses, almost inevitably, the old family retainer who knows everything, a character as conventional as the other, but this one representing not the conventions of fashion, but the conventions of the humblest moralism.

What has happened is, first, that she has chosen as her narrative perspective those very elements, conventional emotion and conventional morality, which her hero and heroine are meant to transcend with such spectacular magnificence; and second, that she has permitted this perspective to operate throughout a long period of time. And these two elements compel the novelist to see what her unmoral passions come to. Moral magnificence? Not at all; rather, a devastating spectacle of human waste; ashes. For the time of the novel is carried on long enough to show Heathcliff at last an emptied man, burned out by his fever ragings, exhausted and will-less, his passion meaningless at last. And it goes even a little further, to Lockwood, the fop, in the graveyard, sententiously contemplating headstones. Thus in the end the triumph is all on the side of the cloddish world, which survives.

Perhaps not all on that side. For, like Densher at the end of *The Wings of the Dove*, we say, and surely Hareton and the second Cathy say, "We shall never be again as we were!" But there is more point in observing that a certain body of materials, a girl's romantic daydreams, have, through the most conventional devices of fiction, been pushed beyond their inception in fancy to their meanings, their conception as a written book—that they, that is, are not at all as they were.

III

TECHNIQUE alone objectifies the materials of art; hence technique alone evaluates those materials. This is the axiom which demonstrates itself so devastatingly whenever a writer declares under the urgent sense of the importance of his materials—whether these are autobiography, or social ideas, or personal passions—whenever such a writer declares that he cannot linger with technical refinements. That art will not tolerate such a writer H. G. Wells handsomely proves. His enormous literary energy included no respect for the techniques of his medium, and his medium takes its revenge upon his bumptiousness. "I have never taken any very great pains about writing. I am outside the hierarchy of conscious and deliberate writers altogether. I am the absolute antithesis of Mr. James Joyce. . . . Long ago, living in close conversational proximity to Henry James, Joseph Conrad, and Mr. Ford Madox Hueffer, I escaped from under their immense artistic preoccupations by calling myself a journalist." Precisely. And he escaped—he disappeared—from literature into the annals of an era.

Yet what confidence! "Literature," Wells said, "is not jewelry, it has quite other aims than perfection, and the more one thinks of 'how it is done' the less one gets it done. These critical indulgences lead along a fatal path, away from every natural interest towards a preposterous emptiness of technical effort, a monstrous egotism of artistry, of which the later work of Henry James is the monumental warning. 'It,' the subject, the thing or the thought, has long since disappeared in these amazing works; nothing remains but the way it has been manipulated." Seldom has a literary theorist been so totally wrong; for what we learn as James grows for us and Wells disappears is that without what he calls "manipulation," there *is* no "it," no "subject" in art. There is again only social history.

The virtue of the modern novelist—from James and Conrad down—is not only that he pays so much attention to his medium, but that, when he pays most, he discovers through it a new subject matter, and a greater one. Under the "immense artistic preoccupations" of James and Conrad and Joyce, the form of the novel changed, and with the technical change, analogous changes took place in substance, in point of view, in the whole conception of fiction. And the final lesson of the modern novel is that technique is not the secondary thing that it seemed to Wells, some external machination, a mechanical affair, but a deep and primary operation; not only that technique *contains* intellectual and moral implications, but that it *discovers* them. For a writer like Wells, who wished to give us the intellectual and the moral history of our times, the lesson is a hard one; it tells us that the order of intellect and the order of morality do not exist at all, in art, except as they are organized in the order of art.

Wells' ambitions were very large. "Before we have done, we will have all life within the scope of the novel." But that is where life already is, within the scope of the novel; where it needs to be brought is into novels. In Wells we have all the important topics in life, but no good novels. He was not asking too much of art, or asking that it include more than it happily can; he was not asking anything of it—as art, which is all that it can give, and that is everything.

A novel like *Tono Bungay*, generally thought to be Wells' best, is therefore instructive. "I want to tell—*myself*," says George, the hero, "and my impressions of the thing as a whole"—the thing as a whole being the collapse of traditional British institutions in the twentieth century. George "tells himself" in terms of three stages in his life which have rough equivalents in modern British social history, and this is, to be sure, a plan, a framework; but it is the framework of Wells' abstract thinking, not of his craftsmanship, and the primary demand which one makes of such a book as this—that means be discovered whereby the dimensions of the hero contain the experiences he recounts—is never met. The novelist flounders through a series of literary imitations

—from an early Dickensian episode, through a kind of Shavian interlude, through a Conradian episode, to a Jules Verne vision at the end. The significant failure is in that end, and in the way that it defeats not only the entire social analysis of the bulk of the novel, but Wells' own ends as a thinker. For at last George finds a purpose in science. "I decided that in power and knowledge lay the salvation of my life; the secret that would fill my need; that to these things I would give myself."

But science, power, and knowledge are summed up at last in a destroyer. As far as one can tell Wells intends no irony, although he may here have come upon the essence of the major irony in modern history. The novel ends in a kind of meditative rhapsody which denies every value that the book had been aiming toward. For of all the kinds of social waste which Wells has been describing, this is the most inclusive, the final waste. Thus he gives us in the end not a novel, but a hypothesis; not an individual destiny, but a theory of the future; and not his theory of the future, but a nihilistic vision quite opposite from everything that he meant to represent. With a minimum of attention to the virtues of technique, Wells might still not have written a good novel; but he would at any rate have established a point of view and a tone which would have told us what he meant.

To say what one means in art is never easy, and the more intimately one is implicated in one's material, the more difficult it is. If, besides, one commits fiction to a therapeutic function which is to be operative not on the audience but on the author, declaring, as D. H. Lawrence did, that "One sheds one's sicknesses in books, repeats and presents again one's emotions to be master of them," the difficulty is vast. It is an acceptable theory only with the qualification that technique, which objectifies, is under no other circumstances so imperative. For merely to repeat one's emotions, merely to look into one's heart and write, is also merely to repeat the round of emotional bondage. If our books are to be exercises in self-analysis, then technique must—and alone can—take the place of the absent analyst.

Lawrence, in the relatively late Introduction to his *Collected Poems*, made that distinction of the amateur between his "real" poems and his "composed" poems, between the poems which expressed his demon directly and created their own form "willy-nilly," and the poems which, through the hocus-pocus of technique, he spuriously put together and could, if necessary, revise. His belief in a "poetry of the immediate present," poetry in which nothing is fixed, static, or final, where all is shimmeriness and impermanence and vitalistic essence, arose from this mistaken notion of technique. And from this notion, an unsympathetic critic like D. S. Savage can construct a case which shows Lawrence driven "concurrently to the dissolution of personality and the dissolution of art." The argument suggests that Lawrence's early, crucial novel, *Sons and Lovers*, is another example of meanings confused by an impatience with technical resources.

The novel has two themes: the crippling effects of a mother's love on the emotional development of her son; and the "split" between kinds of love, physical and spiritual, which the son develops, the kinds represented by two young women, Clara and Miriam. The two themes should, of course, work together, the second being, actually, the result of the first: this "split" is the "crippling." So one would expect to see the novel developed, and so Lawrence, in his famous letter to Edward Garnett, where he says that Paul is left at the end with the "drift towards death," apparently thought he had developed it. Yet in the last few sentences of the novel, Paul rejects his desire for extinction and turns toward "the faintly humming, glowing town," to life—as nothing in his previous history persuades us that he could unfalteringly do.

The discrepancy suggests that the book may reveal certain confusions between intention and performance.

One of these is the contradiction between Lawrence's explicit characterizations of the mother and father and his tonal evaluations of them. It is a problem not only of style (of the contradiction between expressed moral epithets and the more general texture of the prose which applies to them) but of point of view. Morel and Lawrence are never separated, which is a way of saying that Lawrence maintains for himself in this book the confused attitude of his character. The mother is a "proud, *honorable* soul," but the father has a "small, *mean* head." This is the sustained contrast; the epithets are characteristic of the whole, and they represent half of Lawrence's feelings. But what is the other half? Which of these characters is given his real sympathy—the hard, self-righteous, aggressive, demanding mother who comes through to us, or the simple, direct, gentle, downright, fumbling, ruined father? There are two attitudes here. Lawrence (and Morel) loves his mother, but he also hates her for compelling his love; and he hates his father with the true Freudian jealousy, but he also loves him for what he is in himself, and he sympathizes more deeply with him because his wholeness has been destroyed by the mother's domination, just as his, Lawrence-Morel's has been.

This is a psychological tension which disrupts the form of the novel and obscures its meaning, because neither the contradiction in style nor the confusion in point of view is made to right itself. Lawrence is merely repeating his emotions, and he avoids an austerer technical scrutiny of his material because it would compel him to master them. He would not let the artist be stronger than the man.

The result is that, at the same time that the book condemns the mother, it justifies her; at the same time that it shows Paul's failure, it offers rationalizations which place the failure elsewhere. The handling of the girl, Miriam, if viewed closely, is pathetic in what it signifies for Lawrence, both as man and artist. For Miriam is made the mother's scapegoat, and in a different way from the way that she was in life. The central section of the novel is shot through with alternate statements as to the source of the difficulty: Paul is unable to love Miriam wholly, and Miriam can love only his spirit. These contradictions appear sometimes within single paragraphs, and the point of view is never adequately objectified and sustained to tell us which is true. The material is never seen as material; the writer is caught in it exactly as firmly as he was caught in his experience of it. "That's how women are with me," said Paul. "They want me like mad, but they don't want to belong to me." So he might have said, and believed it; but at the end of the novel, Lawrence is still saying that, and himself believing it.

For the full history of this technical failure, one must read *Sons and Lovers* carefully and then learn the history of the manuscript from the book called *D. H. Lawrence: A Personal Record*, by one E. T., who was Miriam in life. The basic situation is clear enough. The first theme—the crippling effects of the mother's love—is developed right through to the end; and then suddenly, in the last few sentences, turns on itself, and Paul gives himself to life, not death. But all the way through, the insidious rationalizations of the second theme have crept in to destroy the artistic coherence of the work. A "split" would occur in Paul; but as the split is treated, it is superimposed upon rather than developed in support of the first theme. It is a rationalization made from it. If Miriam is made to insist on spiritual love, the meaning and the power of theme one are reduced; yet Paul's weakness is disguised. Lawrence could not separate the investigating analyst, who must be objective, from Lawrence, the subject of the book; and the sickness was not healed, the emotion not mastered, the novel not perfected. All this, and the character of a whole career, would have been altered if Lawrence had allowed his technique to discover the full meaning of his subject.

A Portrait of the Artist as a Young Man, like *Tono Bungay* and *Sons and Lovers*, is autobiographical, but unlike these it analyzes its material rigorously, and it defines the value and the quality of its experience not by appended comment or moral epithet, but by the texture of the style. The theme of *A Portrait*, a young artist's alienation from his environment, is explored and evaluated through three different styles and methods as Stephen Dedalus moves from childhood through boyhood into maturity. The opening pages are written in something like the Ulyssesean stream of consciousness, as the environment impinges directly on the consciousness of the infant and the child, a strange, opening world which the mind does not yet subject to questioning, selection, or judgment. But this style changes very soon, as the boy begins to explore his surroundings; and as his sensuous experience of the world is enlarged, it takes on heavier and heavier rhythms and a fuller and fuller body of sensuous detail, until it reaches a crescendo of romantic opulence in the emotional climaxes which mark Stephen's rejection of domestic and religious values. Then gradually the style subsides into the austere intellectuality of the final sections, as he defines to himself the outlines of the artistic task which is to usurp his maturity.

A highly self-conscious use of style and method defines the quality of experience in each of these sections, and, it is worth pointing out in connection with the third and concluding section, the style and method evaluate the experience. What has happened to Stephen is, of course, a progressive alienation from the life around him as he progressed in his initiation into it, and by the end of the novel, the alienation is complete. The final portion of the novel, fascinating as it may be for the developing esthetic creed of Stephen-Joyce, is peculiarly bare. The life experience was not bare, as we know from *Stephen Hero;* but Joyce is forcing technique to comment. In essence, Stephen's alienation is a denial of the human environment; it is a loss; and the austere discourse of the final section, abstract and almost wholly without sensuous detail or strong rhythm, tells us of that loss. It is a loss so great that the texture of the notation-like prose here suggests that the end is really all an illusion, that when Stephen tells us and himself that he is going forth to forge in the smithy of his soul the uncreated conscience of his race, we are to infer from the very quality of the icy, abstract void he now inhabits, the implausibility of his aim. For *Ulysses* does not create the conscience of the race; it creates our consciousness.

In the very last two or three paragraphs of the novel, the style changes once more, reverts from the bare, notative kind to the romantic prose of Stephen's adolescence. "Away! Away! The spell of arms and voices: the white arms of roads, their promise of close embraces and the black arms of tall ships that stand against the moon, their tale of distant nations. They are held out to say: We are alone—come." Might one not say that the austere ambition is founded on adolescent longing? That the excessive intellectual severity of one style is the counterpart of the excessive lyric relaxation of the other? And that the final passage of *A Portrait* punctuates the illusory nature of the whole ambition?

For *Ulysses* does not create a conscience. Stephen, in *Ulysses,* is a little older, and gripped now by guilt, but he is still the cold young man divorced from the human no less than the institutional environment. The environment of urban life finds a separate embodiment in the character of Bloom, and Bloom is as lost as Stephen, though touchingly groping for moorings. Each of the two is weakened by his inability to reach out, or to do more than reach out to the other. Here, then, is the theme again, more fully stated, as it were in counterpoint.

But if Stephen is not much older, Joyce is. He is older as an artist not only because he can create and lavish his godlike pity on a Leopold Bloom, but also because he knows now what both Stephen and Bloom mean, and *how much,* through the most brilliant technical operation ever made in fiction, they can be made to mean. Thus *Ulysses,* through the imaginative force which its techniques direct, is like a pattern of concentric circles, with the immediate human situation at its center, this passing on and out to the whole dilemma of modern life, this passing on and out beyond that to a vision of the cosmos, and this to the mythical limits of our experience. If we read *Ulysses* with more satisfaction than any other novel of this century, it is because its author held an attitude toward technique and the technical scrutiny of subject matter which enabled him to order, within a single work and with superb coherence, the greatest amount of our experience.

IV

IN THE United States during the last twenty-five years, we have had many big novels but few good ones. A writer like James T. Farrell apparently assumes that by endless redundancy in the description of the surface of American life, he will somehow write a book with the scope of *Ulysses*. Thomas Wolfe apparently assumed that by the mere disgorging of the raw material of his experience he would give us at last our epic. But except in a physical sense, these men have hardly written novels at all.

The books of Thomas Wolfe were, of course, journals, and the primary role of his publisher in transforming these journals into the semblance of novels is notorious. For the crucial act of the artist, the unique act which is composition, a sympathetic editorial blue pencil and scissors were substituted. The result has excited many people, especially the young, and the ostensibly critical have observed the prodigal talent with the wish that it might have been controlled. Talent there was, if one means by talent inexhaustible verbal energy, excessive response to personal experience, and a great capacity for auditory imitativeness, yet all of this has nothing to do with the novelistic quality of the written result; for until the talent is controlled, the material organized, the content achieved, there is simply the man and his life. It remains to be demonstrated that Wolfe's conversations were any less interesting as novels than his books, which is to say that his books are without interest as novels. As with Lawrence, our response to the books is determined, not by their qualities as novels, but by our response to him and his qualities as a temperament.

This is another way of saying that Thomas Wolfe never really knew what he was writing *about*. *Of Time and the River* is merely a euphemism for "Of a Man and his Ego." It is possible that had his conception of himself and of art included an adequate respect for technique and the capacity to pursue it, Wolfe would have written a great novel on his true subject—the dilemma of romantic genius; it was his true subject, but it remains his undiscovered subject, it is the subject which *we* must dig out for him, because he himself had neither the lamp nor the pick to find it in and mine it out of the labryinths of his experience. Like Emily Brontë, Wolfe needed a point of view beyond his own which would separate his material and its effect.

With Farrell, the situation is opposite. He knows quite well what his subject is and what he wishes to tell us about it, but he hardly needs the novel to do so. It is significant that in sheer clumsiness of style no living writer exceeds him, for his prose is asked to perform no service beyond communication of the most rudimentary kind of fact. For his ambitions the style of the newspaper and the lens of the documentary camera would be quite adequate, yet consider the diminution which Leopold Bloom, for example, would suffer, if he were to be viewed from these, the technical perspectives of James Farrell. Under the eye of this technique, the material does not yield up enough; indeed, it shrinks.

More and more writers in this century have felt that naturalism as a method imposes on them strictures which prevent them from exploring through all the resources of technique the full amplifications of their subjects, and that thus it seriously limits the possible breadth of esthetic meaning and response. James Farrell is almost unique in the complacency with which he submits to the blunt techniques of naturalism; and his fiction is correspondingly repetitive and flat.

That naturalism had a sociological and disciplinary value in the nineteenth century is obvious; it enabled the novel to grasp materials and make analyses which had eluded it in the past, and to grasp them boldly; but even then it did not tell us enough of what, in Virginia Woolf's phrase, is "really real," nor did it provide the means to the maximum of reality coherently contained.

Even the Flaubertian ideal of objectivity seems, today, an un-necessarily limited view of objectivity, for as almost every good writer of this century shows us, it is quite as possible to be ob-jective about subjective states as it is to be objective about the circumstantial surfaces of life. Dublin, in *Ulysses*, is a moral set-ting: not only a city portrayed in the naturalistic fashion of Dickens' London, but also a map of the modern psyche with its oblique and baffled purposes. The second level of reality in no way invalidates the first, and a writer like Joyce shows us that, if the artist truly respects his medium, he can be objective about both at once. What we need in fiction is a devoted fidelity to every technique which will help us to discover and to evaluate our subject matter, and more than that, to discover the amplifica-tions of meaning of which our subject matter is capable.

Most modern novelists have felt this demand upon them. André Gide allowed one of his artist-heroes to make an observa-tion which considerably resembles an observation we have quoted from Wells. "My novel hasn't got a subject . . . Let's say, if you prefer it, it hasn't got *one* subject . . . 'A slice of life,' the natu-ralist school said. The great defect of that school is that it always cuts its slice in the same direction; in time, lengthwise. Why not in breadth? Or in depth? As for me I should like not to cut at all. Please understand; I should like to put everything into my novel." Wells, with his equally large blob of potential material, did not know how to cut it to the novel's taste; Gide cut, of course— in every possible direction. Gide and others. And those "cuts" are all the new techniques which modern fiction has given us. None, perhaps, is more important than that inheritance from French symbolism which Huxley, in the glittering wake of Gide, called "the musicalization of fiction." Conrad anticipated both when he wrote that the novel "must strenuously aspire to the plasticity of sculpture, to the colour of painting, and to the magic suggestiveness of music—which is the art of arts," and when he said of that early but wonderful piece of symbolist fiction, *The Heart of Darkness*, "It was like another art altogether. That sombre theme had to be given a sinister resonance, a tonality of its own, a continued vibration that, I hoped, would hang in the air and dwell on the ear after the last note had been struck."

The analogy with music, except as a metaphor, is inexact, and except as it points to techniques which fiction can employ as fiction, not very useful to our sense of craftsmanship. It has had an approximate exactness in only one work, Joyce's final effort, an effort unique in literary history, *Finnegans Wake*, and here, of course, those readers willing to make the effort Joyce demands, discovering an inexhaustible wealth and scope, are most forcibly reminded of the primary importance of technique to subject, and of their indivisibility.

The techniques of naturalism inevitably curtail subject and often leave it in its original area, that of undefined social experience. Those of our writers who, stemming from this tradition, yet, at their best, achieve a novelistic definition of social experience— writers like the occasional Sherwood Anderson, William Carlos Williams, the occasional Erskine Caldwell, Nathanael West, and Ira Wolfert in *Tucker's People*—have done so by pressing naturalism far beyond itself, into positively Gothic distortions. The structural machinations of Dos Passos and the lyrical interruptions of Steinbeck are the desperate maneuvers of men committed to a method of whose limitations they despair. They are our symbolists *manqué*, who end as allegorists.

Our most accomplished novels leave no such impressions of desperate and intentional struggle, yet their precise technique and their determination to make their prose work in the service of their subjects have been the measure of their accomplishment. Hemingway's *The Sun Also Rises* and Wescott's *The Pilgrim Hawk* are consummate works of art not because they may be measured by some external, neoclassic notion of form, but because their forms are so exactly equivalent with their subjects, and because the evaluation of their subjects exists in their styles.

Hemingway has recently said that his contribution to younger writers lay in a certain necessary purification of the language; but the claim has doubtful value. The contribution of his prose was to his subject, and the terseness of style for which his early work is justly celebrated is no more valuable, as an end in itself, than the baroque involutedness of Faulkner's prose, or the cold elegance of Wescott's. Hemingway's early subject, the exhaustion of value, was perfectly investigated and invested by his bare style, and in story after story, no meaning at all is to be inferred from the fiction except as the style itself suggests that there is no meaning in life. This style, more than that, was the perfect technical substitute for the conventional commentator; it expresses and it measures that peculiar morality of the stiff lip which Hemingway borrowed from athletes. It is an instructive lesson, furthermore, to observe how the style breaks down when Hemingway moves into the less congenial subject matter of social affirmation: how the style breaks down, the effect of verbal economy as mute suffering is lost, the personality of the writer, no longer protected by the objectification of an adequate technique, begins its offensive intrusion, and the entire structural integrity slackens. Inversely, in the stories and the early novels, the technique was the perfect embodiment of the subject and it gave that subject its astonishing largeness of effect and of meaning.

One should correct Buffon and say that style is the subject. In Wescott's *Pilgrim Hawk*—a novel which bewildered its many friendly critics by the apparent absence of subject—the subject, the story, is again in the style itself. This novel, which is a triumph of the sustained point of view, is only bewildering if we try to make a story out of the narrator's observations upon others; but if we read his observations as oblique and unrecognized observations upon himself the story emerges with perfect coherence, and it reverberates with meaning, is as suited to continuing reflection as the greatest lyrics.

The rewards of such respect for the medium as the early Hemingway and the occasional Wescott have shown may be observed in every good writer we have. The involutions of Faulkner's style are the perfect equivalent of his involved structures, and the two together are the perfect representation of the moral labyrinths he explores, and of the ruined world which his novels repeatedly invoke and in which these labyrinths exist. The cultivated sensuousity of Katherine Anne Porter's style—as of Eudora Welty's and Jean Stafford's—has charm in itself, of course, but no more than with these others does it have esthetic value in itself; its values lie in the subtle means by which sensuous details become symbols, and in the way the symbols provide a network which is the story, and which at the same time provides the writer and us with a refined moral insight by means of which to test it. When we put such writers against a writer like William Saroyan, whose respect is reserved for his own temperament, we are appalled by the stylistic irresponsibility we find in him, and by the almost total absence of theme, or defined subject matter, and the abundance of unwarranted feeling. Such a writer inevitably becomes a sentimentalist because he has no means by which to measure his emotion. Technique, at last, is measure.

These writers, from Defoe to Porter, are of unequal and very different talent, and technique and talent are, of course, after a point, two different things. What Joyce gives us in one direction, Lawrence, for all his imperfections as a technician, gives us in another, even though it is not usually the direction of art. Only in some of his stories and in a few of his poems, where the demands of technique are less sustained and the subject matter is not autobiographical, Lawrence, in a different way from Joyce, comes to the same esthetic fulfillment. Emily Brontë, with what was perhaps her intuitive grasp of the need to establish a tension between her subject matter and her perspective upon it, achieves a similar fulfillment; and, curiously, in the same way and certainly by intuition alone, Hemingway's early work makes a moving splendor from nothingness.

And yet, whatever one must allow to talent and forgive in technique, one risks no generalization in saying that modern fiction at its best has been peculiarly conscious of itself and of its tools. The technique of modern fiction, at once greedy and fastidious, achieves as its subject matter not some singleness, some topic or thesis, but the whole of the modern consciousness. It discovers the complexity of the modern spirit, the difficulty of personal morality, and the fact of evil—all the untractable elements under the surface which a technique of the surface alone cannot approach. It shows us—in Conrad's words, from *Victory*—that we all live in an "age in which we are camped like bewildered travellers in a garish, unrestful hotel," and while it puts its hard light on our environment, it penetrates, with its sharp weapons, the depths of our bewilderment. These are not two things, but only an adequate technique can show them as one. In a realist like Farrell, we have the environment only, which we know from the newspapers; in a subjectivist like Wolfe, we have the bewilderment only, which we record in our diaries and letters. But the true novelist gives them to us together, and thereby increases the effect of each, and reveals each in its full significance.

Elizabeth Bowen, writing of Lawrence, said of modern fiction, "We want the naturalistic surface, but with a kind of internal burning. In Lawrence every bush burns." But the bush burns brighter in some places than in others, and it burns brightest when a passionate private vision finds its objectification in exacting technical search. If the vision finds no such objectification, as in Wolfe and Saroyan, there is a burning without a bush. In our committed realists, who deny the resources of art for the sake of life, whose technique forgives both innocence and slovenliness—in Defoe and Wells and Farrell—there is a bush but it does not burn. There, at first glance, the bush is only a bush; and then, when we look again, we see that, really, the thing is dead.

3

POINT OF VIEW

The phrase point of view is perhaps an unfortunate one since it applies equally to the intellectual orientation of a work (a Christian point of view, for example, or a Marxist point of view), to the emotional stance of the writer as it is reflected in the tone of a work (a sardonic point of view, for example), and to the angle from which a fictional work is narrated. But despite its ambiguity, the phrase, in its third sense, has become fixed and attempts to supplant it with more precise phrases such as "focus of narration" have not been successful. No other aspect of fictional technique has been more widely discussed, analyzed, and debated, at least among modern critics of the novel. It has even been a rallying point for movements in fiction. When Ford Madox Ford demotes most classic English novelists to the sub-category of "nuvvelists," it is largely because he disapproves of their management of point of view.

Why the question of point of view has loomed as large as it has in modern discussions of the novel is easy to see. James thought and wrote often about the problems of how his fiction was to be narrated, by whom, and to what effect. And he experimented with different degrees of control and arbitrary narrowness in the views of his narrators, experimented further with narrators whose veracity we can accept and narrators whose vision we understand to be seriously limited. Following the example of James, Percy Lubbock, in his influential The Craft of Fiction, made point of view the single most significant category in his assessment of particular novels. Profitable discussion of almost any modern novelist—Conrad, Faulkner, Virginia Woolf, Mann, Joyce, Camus, Joyce Cary—might well begin with point of view, not only because of modern experiments in narration but because of modern preoccupations with the perceiving mind. It is not only the more modern and psychological of novels, however, that require a clear perception by the reader of their point of view. Of any novel, our understanding of its point of view determines to a large extent our perception of the novel's value system and its complex of attitudes. It is even true that in a slightly uncomfortable way our judgment of the worth of a novel depends upon our perception of its point of view.

In 1938 Edmund Wilson, reviewing Henry Miller's Tropic of Cancer, found Miller's portrayal of his hero to be a penetratingly ironic, comic demolition of the American bum in Paris, with his Pernod and his meretricious dreams. Miller replied to the review, in a rather dismayed and defensive letter, protesting that his book was without irony and distance, that "the narrator, or the hero, as your critic puts it, is also myself." The immediate impasse in this exchange between novelist and critic is point of view. But dependent upon that central matter of technique is every other value in the novel. Presumably, if Edmund Wilson were to accept Henry Miller's own statement of intention, he would be obliged to find Tropic of Cancer not a detached and perceptive work at all but a banal and silly one. A whole history of the novel, in fact, could be written around just such problems in the perception of point of view. Are the facile pieties of Moll Flanders Defoe's own pieties or are they the rather hypocritical effusions of a first-person narrator who is at some distance from Defoe? Does Richardson create a far more attractive villain than he ever intended by giving Lovelace an elegant, ingenious first-person voice? Is Fielding an oafish, overbearing extrovert who insists upon managing both the reader and his characters, or is

"Fielding" an artful contrivance of Fielding, the authorial commentary of whom furnishes a kind of moral world surrounding the characters and whose temperament always exists in a context of ironic play? And where, in the intricacies of Jane Austen's fiction, is the authentic voice of Jane Austen to be found? Questions such as these begin with technique and end with the novelist's entire view of life.

Only a few critics have managed to treat point of view without partisanship and preconception, out of a wish not to legislate but to describe. Two of the best of them are represented here.

WAYNE C. BOOTH

DISTANCE AND POINT-OF-VIEW
AN ESSAY IN CLASSIFICATION

> 'But he [the narrator] little knows what surprises lie in wait for him, if someone were to set about analysing the mass of truths and falsehoods which he has collected here.'
>
> 'Dr. S.', in Confessions of Zeno

Like other notions used in talking about fiction, point-of-view has proved less useful than was expected by the critics who first brought it to our attention. When Percy Lubbock hailed the triumph of Henry James's dramatic use of the 'central intelligence,' and told us that 'the whole intricate question of method, in the craft of fiction,' is governed by 'the relation in which the narrator stands to the story,' he might have predicted that many critics would, like E. M. Forster, disagree with him. But he could hardly have predicted that his converts would produce, in forty years of elaborate investigations of point-of-view, so little help to the author or critic who must decide whether this or that technique in a particular work is appropriate to this or that effect. On the one hand we have been given classifications

From Essays in Criticism, XI (1961). Reprinted by permission of Essays in Criticism.

and descriptions which leave us wondering why we have bothered
to clasify and describe; the author who counted the number of
times the word 'I' appears in each of Jane Austen's novels may
be more obviously absurd than the innumerable scholars who
have traced in endless detail the *'Ich-Erzählung,'* or *'erlebte Rede,'*
or *'monologue intérieur'* from Dickens to Joyce or from James
to Robbe-Grillet. But he is no more irrelevant to literary judgment. To describe particulars may be interesting but it is only
the preliminary to the kind of knowledge that might help us
explain the success or failure of individual works.

On the other hand, our efforts at formulating useful principles
have been of little more use because they have been overtly prescriptive. If to count the number of times 'I' occurs tells us
nothing about how many times 'I' should occur, to formulate
abstract appeals for more 'showing' and less 'telling,' for less
authorial commentary and more drama, for more realistic consistency and fewer arbitrary shifts which remind the reader that
he is reading a book, gives us the illusion of having discovered
criteria when we really have not. While it is certainly true that
some effects are best achieved by avoiding some kinds of telling,
too often our prescriptions have been for 'the novel' entire, ignoring what James himself knew well: there are '5,000,000 ways
to tell a story,' depending on one's overall purposes. Too many
Jamesians have tried to establish in advance the precise degree
of realistic intensity or irony or objectivity or 'aesthetic distance'
his work should display.

It is true that dissenting voices are now heard more and more
frequently, perhaps the most important being Kathleen Tillotson's recent inaugural lecture at The University of London,
The Tale and the Teller. But the clichés about the superiority
of dramatic showing over mere telling are still to be found
everywhere: in scholarly journals, in the literary quarterlies, in
the weekly reviews, in the latest book on how to read a novel,
and in dust-jacket blurbs. 'The author does not tell you directly
but you find out for yourself from their [the characters'] every
word, gesture, and act,' a Modern Library jacket tells us about
Salinger's *Nine Stories*. That this is praise, that Salinger would
be in error if he were found telling us anything directly, is taken
for granted.

Since the novelist's choices are in fact practically unlimited, in judging their effectiveness we can only fall back on the kind of reasoning used by Aristotle in the *Poetics*: *if* such-and-such an effect is desired, *then* such-and-such points-of-view will be good or bad. We all agree that point-of-view is in some sense a technical matter, a means to larger ends; whether we say that technique is the artist's way of discovering his artistic meaning or that it is his way of working his will upon his audience, we still can judge it only in the light of the larger meanings or effects which it is designed to serve. Though we all at times violate our own convictions, most of us are convinced that we have no right to impose on the artist abstract criteria derived from other kinds of work.

But even when we have decided to put our judgments in the hypothetical 'if-then' form, we are still faced with an overwhelming variety of choices. One of the most striking features of our criticism is the casual way in which we allow ourselves to reduce this variety, thoughtlessly, carelessly, to simple categories, the impoverishment of which is evident whenever we look at any existing novel. On the side of effect critics at one time had a fairly large number of terms to play with—terms like tragedy, comedy, tragi-comedy, epic, farce, satire, elegy, and the like. Though the neo-classical kinds were often employed in inflexible form, they did provide a frame of discourse which allowed the critic and artist to communicate with each other: 'if the effect you want is what we have traditionally expected under the concept "tragedy," then your technique here is inadequate.' If what we are working for is a first-rate comedy, Dryden tells us in 'An Essay of Dramatic Poesy,' then here are some rules we can count on; they may be difficult to apply, they may require painstaking discussion, and they will certainly require genius if they are to be made to work, but they can still be of help to artist and critic because they are based on an agreement about a recognised literary effect.

In place of the earlier kinds, we have generally substituted a criticism based on qualities that are supposed to be sought in all works. All novels are said to be aiming for a common degree of realistic intensity; ambiguity and irony are discussed as if they were always beauties, never blemishes. Point-of-view should always be used 'consistently,' because otherwise the realistic illusion will be destroyed.

When technical means are related to such simplified ends, it is hardly surprising that they are themselves simplified. Yet we all know that our experience of particular works is more complex than the simple terminology suggests. The prescriptions against 'telling' cannot satisfy any reader who has experienced *Tom Jones, The Egoist, Light in August*, or *Ulysses* (the claim that the author does not address us directly in the last of these is one of the most astonishingly persistent myths in modern criticism). They explicitly contradict our experience of dozens of good novels of the past fifteen years which, like Joyce Cary's posthumous *The Captive and the Free*, have rediscovered for us how lively 'telling' can be. We all know, of course, that 'too much' of the author's voice is, as Aristotle said, unpoetic. But how much is too much? Is there an abstract rule applicable to 'the novel,' quite aside from the needs of particular works or kinds?

Our experience with the great novels tells us that there is not. Most novels, like most plays, cannot be purely dramatic, entirely shown as taking place in the moment. There are always what Dryden called 'relations,' narrative summaries of action that takes place 'off-stage.' And try as we will to ignore the troublesome fact, 'some parts of the action are more fit to be represented, some to be related.' But related by whom? When? At what length? The dramatist must decide, and his decision will be based in large part on the particular needs of the work in hand. The novelist's case is different mainly in that he has more devices to choose from; he may speak with all of the voices available to the dramatist, and he may also choose—some would say he is also tempted by—some forms of telling not easily adapted to the stage.

Unfortunately our terminology for the author's many voices has been inadequate. If we name over three or four of the great narrators—say Cervantes' Cid Hamete Benengeli, Tristram Shandy, the 'author' of *Middlemarch* and Strether in *The Ambassadors* (with his nearly effaced 'author' using his mind as a reflector of events)—we find again that to describe any of them with conventional terms like 'first-person' and 'omniscient' tells us little about how they differ from each other, and consequently it tells us little about why they succeed while others, described in the same terms, fail. Some critics do, indeed, talk about the problem of 'authority,' showing that first-person tales produce difficulties in stories which do not allow any one person to know all that goes on; having made this point, which seems so obvious, they are often then driven to find fault with stories like *Moby Dick,* in which the author allows his narrator to know of events that happen outside his designated sphere of authority.

We can never be sure that enriching our terms will improve our criticism. But we can be quite sure that the terms with which we have long been forced to work cannot help us in discriminating among effects too subtle—as are all actual literary effects—to be caught in such loose-meshed nets. Even at the risk of pedantry, then, it should be worth our while to attempt a richer tabulation of the forms the author's voice can take.

1

PERHAPS the most overworked distinction is that of 'person.' To say that a story is told in the first or the third person, and to group novels into one or the other kind, will tell us nothing of importance unless we become more precise and describe how the particular qualities of the narrators relate to specific desired effects. It is true that choice of the first person is sometimes unduly limiting; if the 'I' has inadequate access to necessary information, the author may be led into improbabilities. But we can hardly expect to find useful criteria in a distinction that would throw all fiction into two, or at most three, heaps. In *this* pile we see *Henry Esmond,* 'A Cask of Amontillado,' *Gulliver's Travels* and *Tristram Shandy.* In *that* we have *Vanity Fair, Tom Jones, The Ambassadors,* and *Brave New World.* But the commentary in *Vanity Fair* and *Tom Jones* is in the first person, often resembling more the intimate effect of *Tristram Shandy* than that of many third person works. And again, the effect of *The Ambassadors* is much closer to that of the great first-person novels, since Strether in large parts 'narrates' his own story, even though he is always referred to in the third person.

Further evidence that this distinction is ordinarily overemphasised is seen in the fact that all of the following functional distinctions apply to both first and third-person narration alike.

2

THERE are *dramatised* narrators and *undramatised* narrators. The former are always and the latter are usually distinct from the implied author who is responsible for their creation.

a. The Implied Author (the author's 'second self')

Even the novel in which no narrator is dramatised creates an implicit picture of an author who stands behind the scenes, whether as stage-manager, as puppeteer, or as an indifferent God, silently paring his fingernails. This implied author is always distinct from the 'real man'—whatever we may take him to be—who creates a superior version of himself as he creates his work; any successful novel makes us believe in an 'author' who amounts to a kind of 'second self.' This second self is usually a highly refined and selected version, wiser, more sensitive, more perceptive than any real man could be.

In so far as a novel does not refer directly to this author, there will be no distinction between him and the implied, undramatised narrator; for example, in Hemingway's *The Killers* there is no narrator other than the implicit second self that Hemingway creates as he writes.

b. Undramatised Narrators

Stories are usually not as rigorously scenic as *The Killers;* most tales are presented as passing through the consciousness of a teller, whether an 'I' or a 'he.' Even in drama much of what we are given is narrated by someone, and we are often as much interested in the effect on the narrator's own mind and heart as we are in learning what *else* the author has to tell us. When Horatio tells of his first encounter with the ghost in *Hamlet,* his own character, though never mentioned explicitly as part of the narrative event, is important to us as we listen. In fiction, as soon as we encounter an 'I' we are conscious of an experiencing mind whose views of the experience will come between us and the event. When there is no such 'I,' as in *The Killers*, the inexperienced reader may make the mistake of thinking that the story comes to him unmediated. But even the most naïve reader must recognise that something mediating and transforming has come into a story from the moment that the author explicitly places a narrator into the tale, even if he is given no personal characteristics whatever.

One of the most frequent reading faults comes from a naïve identification of such narrators with the authors who create them. But in fact there is always a distinction, even though the author himself may not have been aware of it as he wrote. The created author, the 'second self,' is built up in our minds from our experience with all of the elements of the presented story. When one of those elements is an explicit reference to an experiencing narrator, our view of the author is derived in part from our notion of how the presented 'I' relates to what he claims to present. Even when the 'I' or 'he' thus created is ostensibly the author himself—Fielding, Jane Austen, Dickens, Meredith—we can always distinguish between the narrator and the created author who presents him. But though the distinction is always present, it is usually important to criticism only when the narrator is explicitly dramatised.

c. *Dramatised Narrators*

In a sense even the most reticent narrator has been 'dramatised' as soon as he refers to himself as 'I,' or, like Flaubert, tells us that 'we' were in the classroom when Charles Bovary entered. But many novels dramatise their narrators with great fullness. In some works the narrator becomes a major person of great physical, mental and moral vividness (*Tristram Shandy*, *Remembrance of Things Past*, and *Dr. Faustus*); in such works the narrator is often radically different from the implied author who creates him, and whose own character is built up in our minds partly by the way in which the narrator is made to differ from him. The range of human types that have been dramatised as narrators is almost as great as the range of other fictional characters—one must say 'almost' because there are some characters who are unqualified to narrate or reflect a story.

We should remind ourselves that many dramatised narrators are never explicitly labelled as narrators at all. In a sense, every speech, every gesture, narrates; most works contain disguised narrators who, like Molière's *raisonneurs,* are used to tell the audience what it needs to know, while seeming merely to act out their roles. The most important unacknowledged narrators are, however, the third-person 'centres of consciousness' through whom authors filter their narrative. Whether such 'reflectors,' as James sometimes called them, are highly-polished, lucid mirrors reflecting complex mental experience, or the rather turbid, sense-bound 'camera eyes' of much fiction since James, they fill precisely the function of avowed narrators.

> Gabriel had not gone to the door with the others. He was in a dark part of the hall gazing up the staircase. A woman was standing near the top of the first flight, in the shadow also. He could not see her face but he could see the terracotta and salmon-pink panels of her skirt which the shadow made appear black and white. It was his wife. She was leaning on the banisters, listening to something. Gabriel was surprised at her stillness and strained his ear to listen also. But he could hear little save the noise of laughter and dispute on the front steps, a few chords struck on the piano and a few notes of a man's voice singing . . . He asked himself what is a woman standing on the stairs in the shadow, listening to distant music, a symbol of.

The very real advantages of this method, for some purposes, have been a dominant note in modern criticism. Indeed, so long as our attention is on such qualities as naturalness and vividness, the advantages seem overwhelming. It is only as we break out of the fashionable assumption that all good fiction seeks these qualities in the same degree that we are forced to recognise disadvantages. The third-person reflector is only one mode among many, suitable for some effects but cumbersome and even harmful when other effects are desired.

3

AMONG dramatised narrators, whether first-person or third-person reflectors, there are mere *observers* (the 'I' of *Tom Jones, The Egoist, Troilus and Criseyde*), and there are *narrator-agents* who produce some measurable effect on the course of events (ranging from the minor involvement of Nick in *The Great Gatsby* to the central role of Tristram Shandy, Moll Flanders, Huckleberry Finn, and—in the third-person—Paul Morel in *Sons and Lovers*). Clearly any rules we might discover about observers may or may not apply to narrator-agents, yet the distinction is seldom made in talk about point-of-view.

4

ALL narrators and observers, whether first or third-person, can relay their tales to us primarily as *scene* ('The Killers,' *The Awkward Age*), primarily as *summary* or what Lubbock called 'picture' (Addison's almost completely non-scenic tales in *The Spectator*) or, most commonly, as a combination of the two.

Like Aristotle's distinction between dramatic and narrative manners, the somewhat different modern distinction between telling and showing does cover the ground. But the trouble is that it pays for broad coverage with gross imprecision. Narrators of all shapes and shades must either report dialogue alone or support it with 'stage directions' and description of setting. But when we think of the radically different effect of a scene reported by Huck Finn and a scene reported by Poe's Montresor, we see that the quality of being 'scenic' suggests very little about literary effect. And compare the delightful summary of twelve years given in two pages of *Tom Jones* (III, i), with the tedious showing of even ten minutes of uncurtailed conversation in the hands of a Sartre when he allows his passion for 'durational realism' to dictate a scene when summary is called for. We can only conclude that the contrast between scene and summary, between showing and telling—indeed, between any two dialectical terms that try to cover so much ground—is not prescriptive or normative but loosely descriptive only. And as description, it is likely to tell us very little until we specify the kind of narrator who is providing the scene or the summary.

5

NARRATORS who allow themselves to tell as well as show vary greatly depending on the amount and kind of *commentary* allowed in addition to a direct relating of events in scene and summary. Such commentary can, of course, range over any aspect of human experience, and it can be related to the main business in innumerable ways and degrees. To treat of it as if it were somehow a single device is to ignore important differences between commentary that is merely ornamental, commentary that serves a rhetorical purpose but is not part of the dramatic structure, and commentary that is integral to the dramatic structure, as in *Tristram Shandy*.

6

CUTTING across the distinction between observers and narrator-agents of all these kinds is the distinction between *self-conscious narrators,* aware of themselves as writers (*Tom Jones, Tristram Shandy, Barchester Towers, The Catcher in the Rye, Remembrance of Things Past, Dr. Faustus*), and narrators or observers who rarely if ever discuss their writing chores (*Huckleberry Finn*) or who seem unaware that they are writing, thinking, speaking, or 'reflecting' a literary work (Camus' *The Stranger,* Lardner's *Haircut,* Bellow's *The Victim*).

7

WHETHER or not they are involved in the action as agents, narrators and third-person reflectors differ markedly according to the degree and kind of *distance* that separates them from the author, the reader, and the other characters of the story they relate or reflect. Such distance is often discussed under terms like 'irony,' or 'tone,' but our experience is in fact much more diverse than such terms are likely to suggest. 'Aesthetic distance' has been especially popular in recent years as a catch-all term for any lack of identification between the reader and the various norms in the work. But surely this useful term should be reserved to describe the degree to which the reader or spectator is asked to forget the artificiality of the work and 'lose himself' in it; whatever makes him aware that he is dealing with an aesthetic object and not real life increases 'aesthetic distance,' in this sense. What I am dealing with is more complex and more difficult to describe, and it includes 'aesthetic distance' as one of its elements.

In any reading experience there is an implied dialogue among author, narrator, the other characters, and the reader. Each of the four can range, in relation to each of the others, from identification to complete opposition, on any axis of value or judgment; moral, intellectual, aesthetic, and even physical (does the reader who stammers react to the stammering of H. C. Earwicker as I do? Surely not). The elements usually discussed under 'aesthetic distance' enter in of course; distance in time and space, differences of social class or conventions of speech or dress—these and many others serve to control our sense that we are dealing with an aesthetic object, just as the paper moons and other unrealistic stage effects of some modern drama have had an 'alienation' effect. But we must not confuse these effects with the equally important effects of personal beliefs and qualities, in author, narrator, reader, and all others in the cast of characters. Though we cannot hope to deal with all of the varieties of control over distance that narrative technique can achieve, we can at least remind ourselves that we deal here with something more than the question of whether the author attempts to maintain or destroy the illusion of reality.

a.

The *narrator* may be more or less distant from the *implied author*. The distance may be moral (Jason vs. Faulkner; the barber vs. Lardner; the narrator vs. Fielding in *Jonathan Wild*). It may be intellectual (Twain and Huck Finn, Sterne and

Tristram Shandy in the matter of bigotry about the influence of noses, Richardson and Clarissa). It may be physical or temporal: most authors are distant from even the most knowing narrator in that they presumably know how 'everything turns out in the end'; and so on.

b.

The *narrator* also may be more or less distant from the *characters* in the story he tells. He may differ, for example, morally, intellectually and temporally (the mature narrator and his younger self in *Great Expectations* or *Redburn*), morally and intellectually (Fowler the narrator and Pyle the American in Greene's *The Quiet American*, both departing radically from the author's norms but in different directions), morally and emotionally (Maupassant's 'The Necklace,' and Huxley's 'Nuns at Luncheon,' in which the narrators affect less emotional involvement than Maupassant and Huxley clearly expect from the reader).

c.

The *narrator* may be more or less distant from the *reader's* own norms, e.g., physically and emotionally (Kafka's *The Metamorphosis*); morally and emotionally (Pinkie in *Brighton Rock*, the miser in Mauriac's *Knot of Vipers*; the many moral degenerates that modern fiction has managed to make into convincing human beings).

One of the standard sources of plot in modern fiction—often advanced in the name of repudiating plot—is the portrayal of narrators whose characteristics change in the course of the works they narrate. Ever since Shakespeare taught the modern world what the Greeks had overlooked in neglecting character change (compare *Macbeth* and *Lear* with *Oedipus*), stories of character development or degeneration have become more and more popular. But it was not until we had discovered the full uses of the third-person reflector that we found how to show a narrator changing *as he narrates*. The mature Pip, in *Great*

Expectations, is presented as a generous man whose heart is where the reader's is supposed to be; he watches his young self move away from the reader, as it were, and then back again. But the third-person reflector can be shown, technically in the past tense but in effect present before our eyes, moving toward or away from values that the reader holds dear. The twentieth-century has proceeded almost as if determined to work out all of the permutations and combinations on this effect: start far and end near; start near and end far; start far, move close, but lose the prize and end far; start near, like Pip, move away but see the light and return close; start far and move farther (many modern 'tragedies' are so little tragic because the hero is too distant from us at the beginning for us to care that he is, like Macbeth, even further at the end); start near and end nearer . . . I can think of no theoretical possibilities that haven't been tried; anyone who has read widely in modern fiction can fill in examples.

d.

The *implied author* may be more or less distant from the *reader.* The distance may be intellectual (the implied author of *Tristram Shandy,* not of course to be identified with Tristram, is more interested in and knows more about recondite classical lore than any of his readers), moral (the works of Sade), and so on. From the author's viewpoint, a successful reading of his book will reduce to zero the distance between the essential norms of his implied author and the norms of the postulated reader. Often enough there is very little distance to begin with; Jane Austen does not have to convince us that pride and pre-judice are undesirable. A bad book, on the other hand, is often a book whose implied author clearly asks that we judge according to norms we cannot accept.

e.

The *implied author* (and reader) may be more or less distant from *other characters,* ranging from Jane Austen's complete approval of Jane Fairfax in *Emma* to her contempt for Wickham in *Pride and Prejudice*. The complexity that marks our pleasure in all significant literature can be seen by contrasting the kinds of distance in these two situations. In *Emma*, the *narrator* is non-committal toward Jane Fairfax, though there is no sign of disapproval. The *author* can be inferred as approving of her almost completely. But the chief *reflector*, *Emma*, who has the largest share of the job of narration, is definitely disapproving of Jane Fairfax for most of the way. In *Pride and Prejudice*, on the other hand, the narrator is non-committal toward Wickham for as long as possible, hoping to mystify us; the author is secretly disapproving; and the chief reflector, Elizabeth, is definitely approving for the first half of the book.

It is obvious that on each of these scales my examples do not begin to cover the possibilities. What we call 'involvement' or 'sympathy' or 'identification,' is usually made up of many reactions to authors, narrators, observers, and other characters. And narrators may differ from their authors or readers in various kinds of involvement or detachment, ranging from deep personal concern (Nick in *The Great Gatsby*, MacKellar in *The Master of Ballantrae*, Zeitblom in *Dr. Faustus*) to a bland or mildly amused or merely curious detachment (Waugh's *Decline and Fall*).

In talk about point-of-view in fiction, the most seriously neglected of these kinds of distance is that between the fallible or unreliable narrator and the implied author who carries the reader with him as against the narrator. If the reason for discussing point-of-view is to find how it relates to literary effects, then surely the moral and intellectual qualities of the narrator are more important to our judgment than whether he is referred to as 'I' or 'he,' or whether he is privileged or limited, and so on. If he is discovered to be untrustworthy, then the total effect of the work he relays to us is transformed.

Our terminology for this kind of distance in narrators is almost hopelessly inadequate. For lack of better terms, I shall call a narrator *reliable* when he speaks for or acts in accordance with the norms of the work (which is to say, the implied author's norms), *unreliable* when he does not. It is true that most of the great reliable narrators indulge in large amounts of incidental irony, and they are thus 'unreliable' in the sense of being potentially deceptive. But difficult irony is not sufficient to make a narrator unreliable. We should reserve the term unreliable for those narrators who are presented as if they spoke *throughout* for the norms of the book and who do not in fact do so. Unreliability is not ordinarily a matter of lying, although deliberately deceptive narrators have been a major resource of some modern novelists (Camus' *The Fall*, Calder Willingham's *Natural Child*, etc.). It is most often a matter of what James calls *inconscience;* the narrator is mistaken, or he pretends to qualities which the author denies him. Or, as in *Huckleberry Finn*, the narrator claims to be naturally wicked while the author silently praises his virtues, as it were, behind his back.

Unreliable narrators thus differ markedly depending on how far and in what direction they depart from their author's norms; the older term 'tone,' like the currently fashionable 'distance,' covers many effects that we should distinguish. Some narrators, like Barry Lyndon, are placed as far 'away' from author and reader as possible, in respect to every virtue except a kind of interesting vitality. Some, like Fleda Vetch, the reflector in James's *The Spoils of Poynton*, come close to representing the author's ideal of taste, judgment, and moral sense. All of them make stronger demands on the reader's powers of inference than does reliable narration.

8

BOTH reliable and unreliable narrators can be *isolated*, unsupported or uncorrected by other narrators (Gully Jimson in *The Horse's Mouth*, Henderson in Bellow's *Henderson the Rain King*) or supported or corrected (*The Sound and the Fury*). Sometimes it is almost impossible to infer whether or to what degree a narrator is fallible; sometimes explicit corroborating or conflicting testimony makes the inference easy. Support or correction differs radically, it should be noted, depending on whether it is provided from within the action, so that the narrator-agent might benefit (Faulkner's *Intruder in the Dust*) or is simply provided externally, to help the reader correct or reinforce his own views *as against the narrator's* (Graham

Greene's *The Power and the Glory*). Obviously the effects of isolation will be radically different in the two cases.

9

OBSERVERS and narrator-agents, whether self-conscious or not, reliable or not, commenting or silent, isolated or supported, can be either *privileged* to know what could not be learned by strictly natural means or *limited* to realistic vision and inference. Complete privilege is what we usually call omniscience. But there are many kinds of privilege and very few 'omniscient' narrators are allowed to know or show as much as their authors know.

We need a good study of the varieties of limitation and their function. Some limitations are only temporary, or even playful, like the ignorance Fielding sometimes imposes on his 'I' (as when he doubts his own powers of narration and invokes the Muses for aid, e.g., *Tom Jones* XIII, i). Some are more nearly permanent but subject to momentary relaxation, like the generally limited, humanly realistic Ishmael in *Moby Dick*, who can yet break through his human limitations when the story requires (' "He waxes brave, but nevertheless obeys; most careful bravery that!" murmured Ahab'—with no one present to report to the narrator). And some are confined to what their literal condition would allow them to know (first person, Huck Finn; third person, Miranda and Laura in Katherine Anne Porter's stories).

The most important single privilege is that of obtaining an inside view, because of the rhetorical power that such a privilege conveys upon a narrator. A curious ambiguity in our notions of 'omniscience' is ordinarily hidden by our terminology. Many modern works that we usually classify as narrated dramatically, with everything relayed to us through the limited views of the characters, postulate fully as much omniscience in the silent author as Fielding claims for himself. Our roving visitation into the minds of sixteen characters in Faulkner's *As I Lay Dying*, seeing nothing but what those minds contain, may seem in one sense not to depend on an omniscient narrator. But this method is omniscience with teeth in it: the implied author demands our absolute faith in his powers of divination. We must never for a moment doubt that he knows everything about each of these sixteen minds, or that he has chosen correctly how much to show of each. In short the choice of the most rigorously limited point-of-view is really no escape from omniscience—the true narrator is as 'unnaturally' all-knowing as he ever was. If evident artificiality were a fault—which it is not —modern narration would be as faulty as Trollope's.

Another way of suggesting the same ambiguity is to look closely at the concept of 'dramatic' story-telling. The author can present his characters in a dramatic situation without in the least presenting them in what we normally think of as a dramatic manner. When Joseph Andrews, who has been stripped and beaten by thieves, is overtaken by a stage-coach, Fielding presents the scene in what by some modern standards must seem an inconsistent and undramatic mode. 'The poor wretch, who lay motionless a long time, just began to recover his senses as a stage-coach came by. The postilion hearing a man's groans, stopped his horses, and told the coachman, he was certain there was a dead man lying in the ditch . . . A lady, who heard what the postilion said, and likewise heard the groan, called eagerly to the coachman to stop and see what was the matter. Upon which he bid the postilion alight, and look into the ditch. He did so, and returned, "That there was a man sitting upright, as naked as ever he was born." ' There follows a splendid description, hardly meriting the name of *scene*, in which the selfish reactions of each passenger are recorded. A young lawyer points out that they might be legally liable if they refuse to take Joseph up. 'These words had a sensible effect on the coachman, who was well acquainted with the person who spoke them; and the old gentleman above mentioned, thinking the naked man would afford him frequent opportunities of showing his wit to the lady, offered to join with the company in giving a mug of beer for his fare; till partly alarmed by the threats of the one, and partly by the promises of the other, and being perhaps a little moved with compassion at the poor creature's condition, who stood bleeding and shivering with the cold, he at length agreed.' Once Joseph is in the coach, the same kind of indirect reporting of the 'scene' continues, with frequent excursions, however superficial, into the minds and hearts of the assembly of fools and knaves, and occasional guesses when complete knowledge seems inadvisable. If to be dramatic is to show characters dramatically engaged with each other, motive clashing with motive, the outcome depending upon the resolution of motives, then this scene is dramatic. But if it is to give the impression that the story is taking place by itself, with the characters existing in a dramatic relationship vis-a-vis the spectator, unmediated by a narrator and decipherable only through inferential matching of word to word and word to deed, then this is a relatively undramatic scene.

On the other hand, an author can present a character in this latter kind of dramatic relationship with the reader without involving that character in any internal drama at all. Many lyric poems are dramatic in this sense and totally undramatic in any other. 'That is no country for old men—' Who says? Yeats, or his 'mask,' says. To whom? To us. How do we know that it is Yeats and not some character as remote from him as Caliban is remote from Browning in 'Caliban upon Setebos'? We infer it as the dramatised statement unfolds; the need for the inference is what makes the lyric *dramatic* in this sense. Caliban, in short, is dramatic in two senses; he is in a dramatic situation with other characters and he is in a dramatic situation over-against us. Yeats, or if we prefer 'Yeats' mask,' is dramatic in only one sense.

The ambiguities of the word dramatic are even more complicated in fiction than attempts to dramatise states of consciousness directly. Is *A Portrait of the Artist as a Young Man* dramatic? In some respects, yes. We are not told about Stephen. He is placed on the stage before us, acting out his destiny with only disguised helps or comments from his author. But it is not his actions that are dramatised directly, not his speech that we hear unmediated. What is dramatised is his mental record of everything that happens. We see his consciousness at work on the world. Sometimes what it records is itself dramatic, as when Stephen observes himself in a scene with other characters. But the report itself, the internal record, is dramatic in the second sense only. The report we are given of what goes on in Stephen's mind is a monologue uninvolved in any modifying dramatic context. And it is an *infallible* report, even less subject to critical doubts than the typical Elizabethan soliloquy. We accept, by convention, the claim that what is reported as going on in Stephen's mind really goes on there, or in other words, that Joyce knows how Stephen's mind works. 'The equation of the page of his scribbler began to spread out a widening tail, eyed and starred like a peacock's; and, when the eyes and stars of its indices had been eliminated, began slowly to fold itself together again. The indices appearing and disappearing were eyes opening and closing; the eyes opening and closing were stars . . .' Who says so? Not Stephen, but the omniscient, infallible author. The report is direct, and it is clearly unmodified by any 'dramatic' context—that is, unlike a speech in a dramatic scene, we do not suspect that the report has here been in any way aimed at an effect on anyone but the reader. We are thus in a dramatic relation with Stephen only in a limited sense— the sense in which a lyrical poem is dramatic.

Indeed if we compare the act of reporting in *Tom Jones* with the act of reporting in *Portrait*, the former is in one sense considerably more dramatic; Fielding dramatises himself and his telling, and even though he is essentially reliable we must be constantly on our toes in comparing word to word and word to deed. 'It is an observation sometimes made, that to indicate our idea of a simple fellow, we say, he is easily to be seen through: nor do I believe it a more improper denotation of simple book. Instead of applying this to any particular performance, we choose rather to remark the contrary in this history, where the scene opens itself by small degrees; and he is a sagacious reader who can see two chapters before him.' Our running battle to keep up with these incidental ironies in Fielding's narration is matched, in *Portrait*, with an act of absolute, unquestioning credulity.

We should note finally that the author who eschews both forms of artificiality, both the traditional omniscience and the modern manipulation of inside views, confining himself to 'objective' surfaces only, is not necessarily identical with the 'undramatised author' under (2) above. In *The Awkward Age*, for example, James allows himself to comment frequently, but only to conjecture about the meaning of surfaces; the author is dramatised, but dramatised as partially ignorant of what is happening.

10

FINALLY, narrators who provide inside views differ in the depth and the axis of their plunge. Boccaccio can give inside views, but they are extremely shallow. Jane Austen goes relatively deep morally, but scarcely skims the surface psychologically. All authors of stream-of-consciousness narration attempt to go deep psychologically, but some of them deliberately remain shallow in the moral dimension. We should remind ourselves that any sustained inside view, of whatever depth, temporarily turns the character whose mind is shown into a narrator; inside views are thus subject to variations in all of the qualities we have described above, and most importantly in the degree of unreliability. Generally speaking, the deeper our plunge, the more unreliability we will accept without loss of sympathy. The whole question of how inside views and moral sympathy interrelate has been seriously neglected.

Narration is an art, not a science, but this does not mean that we are necessarily doomed to fail when we attempt to formulate principles about it. There are systematic elements in every art, and criticism of fiction can never avoid the responsibility of trying to explain technical successes and failures by reference to general principles. But the question is that of where the general principles are to be found. Fiction, the novel, point-of-view— these terms are not in fact subject to the kind of definition that alone makes critical generalisations and rules meaningful. A given technique cannot be judged according to its service to 'the novel,' or 'fiction,' but only according to its success in particular works or kinds of work.

It is not surprising to hear practising novelists report that they have never had help from critics about point-of-view. In dealing with point-of-view the novelist must always deal with the individual work: which particular character shall tell this particular story, or part of a story, with what precise degree of reliability, privilege, freedom to comment, and so on. Shall he be given dramatic vividness? Even if the novelist has decided on a narrator who will fit one of the critic's classifications—'omniscient,' 'first-person,' 'limited omniscient,' 'objective,' 'roving,' 'effaced,' and so on—his troubles have just begun. He simply cannot find answers to his immediate, precise, practical problems by referring to statements that the 'omniscient is the most flexible method,' or 'the objective the most rapid or vivid,' or whatever. Even the soundest of generalisations at this level will be of little use to him in his page-by-page progress through his novel. As Henry James's detailed records show, the novelist discovers his narrative technique as he tries to achieve for his readers the potentialities of his developing idea. The majority of his choices are consequently choices of degree, not kind. To decide that your narrator shall not be omniscient decides practically nothing. The hard question is, just how *inconscient* shall he be? To decide that you will use first-person narration decides again almost nothing. What kind of first-person? How fully characterised? How much aware of himself as a narrator? How reliable? How much confined to realistic inference, how far privileged to go beyond realism? At what points shall he speak truth and at what points utter no judgment or even utter falsehood? [1]

There are no doubt *kinds* of effect to which the author can refer—e.g., if he wants to make a scene more amusing, poignant, vivid, or ambiguous, or if he wants to make a character more sympathetic or more convincing, such-and-such practices may be indicated. But it is not surprising that in his search for help in his decisions, he should find the practice of his peers more helpful than the abstract rules of the textbooks: the sensitive author who reads the great novels finds in them a storehouse of precise examples, examples of how *this* effect, as distinct from all other possible effects, was heightened by the proper narrative choice. In dealing with the types of narration, the critic must always limp behind, referring constantly to the varied practice which alone can correct his temptations to over-generalise.

---

[1] I try to deal with some of these questions in *The Rhetoric of Fiction*, published in 1961 by the University of Chicago Press. This article is an expanded version of Chapter VI from that book.

NORMAN FRIEDMAN

POINT OF VIEW IN FICTION
THE DEVELOPMENT OF A CRITICAL CONCEPT

> *"Let me only add that in this Art, as in the others,*
> *there is, and will be always, whatever has been done*
> *already, something new to discover, something new*
> *to express, something new to describe."*
> —*Walter Besant, The Art of Fiction* (1885).

Aldous Huxley, speaking through Philip Quarles's "Note-book," questioned some twenty-five years ago the contemporary distaste for the omniscient author in fiction: "But need the author be so retiring? I think we're a bit too squeamish about these personal appearances nowadays." Yet four years later Joseph Warren Beach could write: "In a bird's eye view of the English novel from Fielding to Ford, the one thing that will impress you more than any other is the disappearance of the author." Accordingly, Bradford A. Booth wrote in 1950: "It has been said that the most significant change in the fiction of our time is the disappearance of the author. Conversely, the trade mark of the Victorian novel is the presence of the author, ever poised to intrude a comment, to interpret the characters, or to write an essay on cabbages and kings." For better or for worse, then, it seems that our "squeamishness" has won the day.[1]

The importance of this fastidiousness is conceived by many today, however, as of the highest. "This is the great outstanding feature of technique since the time of Henry James," claims Beach, "that the story shall tell itself, being conducted through the impressions of the characters. It is this which finally differ-

[1] Huxley, *Point Counter Point* (1928), Ch. xxii; Beach, *The Twentieth Century Novel: Studies in Technique* (New York and London, 1932), p. 14; Booth, "Form and Technique in the Novel," *The Reinterpretation of Victorian Literature*, ed. Joseph E. Baker (Princeton, 1950), p. 79.

Reprinted by permission of the Modern Language Association of America from PMLA, LXX (1955).

entiates fiction from history and philosophy and science." Mark Schorer's concern is even more rigorous; it is time, he announces, that we read fiction as if technique were something more crucial than mere embellishment, for "technique is the only means [the writer] has of discovering, exploring, developing his subject, of conveying its meaning, and finally, of evaluating it." And he speaks chiefly of the aesthetic relationship between the author and his work. "We are no longer able to regard as seriously intended," he continues, "criticism of poetry which does not assume these generalizations; but the case for fiction has not yet been established." If fiction's case has not yet been established, there are strong forces at work in the process of establishing it. "Point of View" is becoming one of the most useful critical distinctions available to the student of fiction today.[2]

It is the purpose of this paper to sketch in the aestheic background of this concept and its emergence as a critical tool, to outline and exemplify its basic principles, and finally to discuss its significance in relation to the problem of artistic technique generally.

I

THE art of literature, as opposed to the other arts, is by virtue of its verbal medium both cursed and blessed with a fatal capacity for talk. Its vices are the defects of its virtues: on the one hand, its range and depth of significance far exceed the scope of painting, music, or sculpture; on the other, its ability to project the sensory qualities of person, place, and event is correspondingly less. While it can express more ideas and attitudes, it presents qualitatively weaker images. It is enough for the painter to attend to his palette, to get the proper shade in the proper place; but the writer is torn continually between the difficulty of showing what a thing is and the ease of telling how he feels about it. The sculptor can only show; the musician, program music notwithstanding, can never tell. But literature

---

[2] Beach, ibid., pp. 15–16; Schorer, "Technique as Discovery," *Essays in Modern Literary Criticism*, ed. Ray B. West, Jr. (New York and Toronto, 1952), pp. 190–191 (reprinted from the *Hudson Review*, 1948).

derives its very life from this conflict—which is basic to all its forms—and the history of its aesthetic could in part be written in terms of this fundamental tension, to which the particular problem of point of view in fiction is related as part to whole. For the general distinction was being made, from Plato and Aristotle to Joyce and Eliot, in order that the specific one could take shape. From the ancient rhetorician's directions regarding "vividness" (*enargia*) to the modern aesthetician's study of "projection" (empathy), the relationship between the author's values and attitudes, their embodiment in his work, and their effect upon the reader, have been and continue to be of crucial concern.

For our purpose it will suffice to fix the two opposite points in time between which the history of this concept may be plotted. Plato, to begin with, made a distinction, when discussing the "style" of epic poetry,[3] between "simple narration" on the one hand an "imitation" on the other. When the poet speaks in the person of another we may say that he assimilates his style to that person's manner of talking; this assimilation of himself to another, either by the use of voice or gesture, is an *imitation* of the person whose character he assumes. But, if the poet everywhere appears and never conceals himself, then the imitation

[3] *The Republic* (Plato died 347 B.C.), III, 392–394. For some representative high spots in the history of aesthetics and criticism regarding this distinction, see the following: Aristotle, *Rhetoric* (ca. 330 B.C.), III, xi, 2–4; Quintilian, *Institutes* (fr. ca. A.D. 88), IV, ii, 63; VI, ii, 28–34; VIII, iii, 61–62; Sidney, *An Apology for Poetry* (ca. 1583, printed 1595), in *Elizabethan Critical Essays,* ed. G. Gregory Smith (London, 1904), I, 201; John Hoskins, *Directions for Speech and Style* (ca. 1600), ed. Hoyt H. Hudson (Princeton, 1935), p. 42; Bacon, *De Augmentis* (1623), v, v; Dryden, "A letter to the Honorable Sir Robert Howard," prefacing *Annus Mirabilis* (1666); Alexander Gerard, *Essay on Taste* (London, 1759), Part III, Sec. vi, pp. 197–198, and *Essay on Genius* (London, 1774), Part II, Sec. iii, pp. 169–174; Henry Home, Lord Kames, *Elements of Criticism* (Edinburgh, 1762), Ch. xvii, pp. 483–484 (cf. Mihail M. Morozov, "The Individualization of Shakespeare's Characters through Imagery," *Shakespeare Survey* 2, Cambridge, Eng., 1949, pp. 83–106); Coleridge, "Shakespeare as a Poet Generally," first published 1836, but probably delivered as a lecture in 1818, or even 1808; Keats, Letter to Bailey, Sat., 22 Nov. 1817, Letter to George and Thomas Keats, Sun., 21 Dec. 1817; Hazlitt, "On Shakespeare and Milton," Lecture II, *Lectures on the English Poets* (1818); Arnold, preface to *Poems,* 1853 ed.; Meredith, Letter to Miss J- H-, 22 Nov. 1864, *Letters of George Meredith,* coll. and ed. by his son (New York, 1912), I, 163.

I am indebted to my colleague, Mr. Charles A. McLaughlin, for calling my attention to the first 7 of these references.

is dropped and his poetry becomes *simple narration*. Plato then illustrates this difference by "translating" a passage from the beginning of *The Iliad* out of the direct form of discourse into the indirect—chiefly by substituting "he said *that*" or "he bade him *to*" for quoted dialogue—thus changing an imitative passage to simple narrative. He goes on to note that the opposite extreme—dialogue only—approaches the style of the drama, which is wholly imitative (with the exception, we might add, of choral comment and messenger-narration). Homer, of course, mixes the two—as do most of his successors. We have, on the other hand, that form which uses the poet's voice only: for example, the dithyramb (lyric). As we shall see below, however, dialogue is not the only factor which distinguishes imitation from narration.

Coming now to the opposite end of the curve of history, we recall a similar distinction developed by Joyce in the person of Stephen, between the lyric and the dramatic forms, with the epic as intermediary, which in no way differs in its essential outlines from that of Plato. He is speaking here of the evolution of literature from the lyric cry to the impersonalized dramatic projection: "The narrative is no longer purely personal. The personality of the artist passes into the narration itself, flowing round and round the persons and the actions like a vital sea. . . . The dramatic form is reached when the vitality which has flowed and eddied round each person fills every person with such vital force that he or she assumes a proper and intangible esthetic life." There follows the by now famous passage about the disappearance of the author: "The personality of the artist, at first a cry or a cadence or a mood [lyric] and then a fluid and lambent narrative [epic], finally refines itself out of existence [drama], impersonalizes itself, so to speak." [4]

Let us now consider briefly the emergence of the specific application of this basic distinction to the analysis of point of view in fiction, for point of view provides a *modus operandi*

---

[4] *A Portrait of the Artist as a Young Man* (dated Dublin 1904, Trieste 1914, published 1916), middle of Ch. v. Cf. Eliot, "Tradition and the Individual Talent" (1917), "Hamlet and His Problems" (1919). For technical discussion of "aesthetic distance" see Melvin Rader, *A Modern Book of Aesthetics,* rev. ed. (New York, 1952), pp. 381–465, where the work of Munsterberg, Bullough, Ortega y Gasset, Worringer, and Vernon Lee is presented and discussed.

for distinguishing the possible degrees of authorial extinction in the narrative art.

Regarding the particular problem of the relation between the author, the narrator, and the story subject, Edith Wharton complained in 1925, "It seems as though such a question must precede any study of the subject chosen, since the subject is conditioned by the answer; but no critic appears to have propounded it, and it was left to Henry James to do so in one of those entangled prefaces to the Definitive Edition from which the technical axioms ought some day to be piously detached." [5] As it turns out, she was more nearly correct than she knew, for not only have James's prefaces become the source and fount of critical theory in this matter but also no fewer than two full-length interpretations of them had already appeared before she wrote these words—that of Beach in 1918 and that of Lubbock in 1921. But first let us examine some of the pronouncements of the master himself.

James in his prefaces (1907–09) tells us he was obsessed by the problem of finding a "centre," a "focus," for his stories, and that it was in large measure solved by considering how the narrative vehicle could be limited by framing the action inside the consciousness of one of the characters within the plot itself. "A beautiful infatuation this," he comments, "always, I think, the intensity of the creative effort to get into the skin of the creature . . ." Thus, since the irresponsible illusion-breaking of the garrulous omniscient author, who tells the story as *he* perceives it rather than as one of his characters perceives it, is eliminated by this device, the story gains in intensity, vividness, and coherence. "There is no economy of treatment without an adopted, a related point of view, and though I understand, under certain degrees of pressure, a represented community of vision between several parties to the action when it makes for concentration, I understand no breaking-up of the register, no sacrifice of the recording consistency, that doesn't rather scatter and weaken." [6]

Professor Beach undertook to organize the theory of this "method" and to apply it to James's own fiction. He distinguishes among several kinds of points of view and discriminates between James's calculated shifts in focus and "that arbitrary and unconsidered shift of point of view within the chapter, within the paragraph, that visible manipulation of the puppets from without, which is so great a menace to illusion and intimacy." The problem as a whole, however, "is a most complex and difficult one, and the practice of story-tellers is manifold. It would be impossible to give a brief summary of the common usage, even if one had made a sufficiently careful survey of the field to feel certain of all the facts." [7] The time was ripe, apparently, for the next step.

It remained to Percy Lubbock to apply the general distinction between direct and indirect presentation—a distinction common, as we have suggested, throughout the history of aesthetics and criticism—to a discussion of James's particular concern with point of view in fiction. "The art of fiction," he claims, "does not begin until the novelist thinks of his story as a matter to be *shown,* to be so exhibited that it will tell itself [rather than being *told* by the author]. . . . the thing has to *look* true, and that is all. It is not made to look true by simple statement." If artistic "truth" is a matter of compelling rendition, of creating the illusion of reality, then an author speaking in his own person about the lives and fortunes of others is placing an extra obstacle between his illusion and the reader by virtue of his very presence. In order to remove this obstacle the author may choose to limit the functions of his own personal voice in one way or another: "The only law that binds him throughout, whatever course he is pursuing, is the need to be consistent on *some* plan, to follow the principle he has adopted; and of course it is one of the first of his precepts, as with every artist in any kind, to allow himself no more latitude than he requires." One of the chief means to this end, the one James himself not only announced in theory but followed in practice, is to have the story told as if by a character in the story, but told in the third person. In this way the reader perceives the action as it filters through the consciousness of one of the characters involved, yet perceives it *directly* as it impinges upon that consciousness, thus avoiding that removal to a distance necessitated by retrospective first-person narration: "the difference is that instead of receiving

[7] *The Method of Henry James* (New Haven, 1918), pp. 56–71.

his report we now see him in the act of judging and reflecting; his consciousness, no longer a matter of hearsay, a matter for which we must take his word, is now before us in its original agitation." [8] Mental awareness is thus dramatized directly instead of being reported and explained indirectly by the narrator's voice, much in the same way that words and gestures may be dramatized directly (*scene*) rather than being summarized by the narrator (*panorama*).

Although one may find many shrewd observations on this point scattered throughout the writings of novelists and critics before the prefaces of James served to crystallize the main issue —for his notions did not spring full-blown from the head of Jove [9]—we must perforce limit ourselves to a brief consideration of what happened to them after they were expounded by Beach and Lubbock. An exception may be made, however, for the work of Selden L. Whitcomb, entitled *The Study of a Novel* (1905), the first to my knowledge which devotes a formal section to the rubric, "The Narrator. His Point of View." Here it is claimed that "the unity of a passage or a plot depends largely on the clearness and stability of [the narrator's] position." [10] This notion, coming as it does a year or two before James's prefaces, seems remarkably prophetic of things to come, since

[8] *The Craft of Fiction* (New York, 1921), pp. 62, 66–67, 71–72, 139–143.
[9] See, e.g., the remarks of MacKenzie, Defoe, Richardson, Fielding, and Scott, in *Novelists on Novels*, ed. R. Brimley Johnson (London, 1928), pp. 13, 25, 41–45, 58–59, 94, 173, 180–184, 199–200; of Thackeray and de Maupassant in *The Writer's Art*, ed. Rollo Walter Brown (Cambridge, Mass., 1921), pp. 202–204, 271; Nassau William Senior, *Essays on Fiction* (London, 1864—written 1821–57), pp. 189 ff., 349–351, 391–392; Sidney Lanier, *The English Novel*, Centennial Ed., Vol. iv, eds. Clarence Gohdes and Kemp Malone (Baltimore, 1945), pp. 22, 172–173, 190, 220–222; Walter Besant, *The Art of Fiction* (Boston, 1885—a lecture delivered at the Royal Institution in 1884), p. 3; Henry James, *The Art of Fiction and Other Essays*, ed. Morris Roberts (New York, 1948), pp. 4–6; cf. "A Humble Remonstrance" (1884), by R. L. Stevenson; Daniel Greenleaf Thompson, *The Philosophy of Fiction in Literature* (London and New York, 1890), pp. 211–212; William Dean Howells, *Criticism in Fiction* (New York, 1891), pp. 19–21, 75–76; Brander Matthews, *Aspects of Fiction* (New York, 1896), pp. 185–186, 198–199, 223, 234; Bliss Perry, *A Study of Prose Fiction* (Boston, 1902), pp. 48–72; Frank Norris, *The Responsibilities of the Novelist* (New York, 1903), pp. 27–28, 206, 246.
[10] Boston, 1905, pp. 15–21, 31–38, 49 ff., 66–72, 101; cf. Evelyn May Albright, *The Short-Story* (New York, 1907), pp. 54–55, 66–70.

from this point on almost every manual published on the art of fiction contains a similar section. During the next ten years or so we find a spate of such manuals which soon grows into an avalanche, and the specific analysis of point of view becomes common property.[11]

The most significant work in the field after Beach and Lubbock, although as we have seen she seems curiously unaware of them, is that of Mrs. Wharton herself in 1925: "It should be the story-teller's first care to choose his reflecting mind deliberately, as one would choose a building-site . . . and when this is done, to live inside the mind chosen, trying to feel, see and react exactly as the latter would, no more, no less, and, above all, no otherwise. Only thus can the writer avoid attributing incongruities of thought and metaphor to his chosen interpreter." And from now on the manuals are always with us.[12]

The remainder of the second decade is distinguished by the demurral of E. M. Forster in 1927, who glances briefly at our problem only to pass it up as a trivial technicality. Allowing Lubbock full credit for his "formulae," he prefers to regard the novel otherwise: the novelist's chief specialty is unhampered omniscience whereby "he commands all the secret life, and he must not be robbed of this privilege. 'How did the writer know that?' it is sometimes said. 'What's his standpoint? He is not being consistent, he's shifting his point of view from the limited to the omniscient, and now he's edging back again'. Questions like these have too much the atmosphere of the law courts about

[11] Clayton Hamilton, *Materials and Methods of Fiction* (New York, 1908—reprinted as *A Manual of the Art of Fiction* in 1918), pp. 120–138; Charles F. Horne, *The Technique of the Novel* (New York and London, 1908), pp. v, 243–263; J. Berg Esenwein, *Writing the Short-Story* (Springfield, Mass., 1909), pp. 109–124; Walter B. Pitkin, *The Art and Business of Story Writing* (New York, 1912), pp. 174–187; Carl H. Grabo, *The Art of the Short Story* (New York, 1913), pp. 21–36, 159; Ethan Allen Cross, *The Short Story* (Chicago, 1914), pp. 80–86; Harry T. Baker, *The Contemporary Short Story* (New York, 1916), pp. 52, 111–112; Blanche Colton Williams, *A Handbook on Story Writing* (New York, 1917 [2nd ed. rev. 1930]), pp. 129–166; Henry Burrowes Lathrop, *The Art of the Novelist* (London, 1921), pp. 252–282.

[12] Wharton, pp. 11–16, 43–46, 70–75, 86–95; Glenn Clark, *A Manual of the Short Story Art* (New York, 1922), pp. 89–95; Elizabeth A. Drew, *The Modern Novel* (New York, 1926), pp. 246–262; Michael Joseph, *How to Write a Short Story* (New York, 1926), pp. 47–56.

them. All that matters to the reader is whether the shifting of attitude and the secret life are convincing." [13]

The third decade is graced chiefly by Beach's monumental study, in 1932, of the technique of the twentieth-century novel, which is characterized, he says, mainly by virtue of the fact that "the story tells itself; the story speaks for itself. The author does not apologize for his characters; he does not even tell us what they do but has them tell us, themselves. Above all, he has them tell us what they think, what they feel, what impressions beat in on their minds from the situations in which they find themselves." Apparently encouraged by the work of Lubbock, which followed shortly after his own early study of James, Beach now makes a concerted and massive onslaught upon the telling-showing problem as it appears in hundreds of modern novels.[14]

In an essay dated 1941 we find Allen Tate taking up the gauntlet cast down by Forster: "The limited and thus credible authority for the action, which is gained by putting the knower of the action inside its frame, is perhaps the distinctive feature of the modern novel; and it is, in all the infinite shifts of focus of which it is capable, the specific feature which more than any other has made it possible for the novelist to achieve an objective structure." Accordingly, Phyllis Bentley, in 1947, is constrained to remark: "The gradual decline in the use of direct

[13] *Aspects of the Novel* (New York, 1927), pp. 118–128. Cf. Grant Overton, *The Philosophy of Fiction* (New York, 1928), pp. 59, 131–135; Carl H. Grabo, *The Technique of the Novel* (New York, 1928), pp. 65, 81; Van Meter Ames, *Aesthetics of the Novel* (Chicago, 1928), pp. 177–193; Stewart Beach, *Short-Story Technique* (Boston, 1929), pp. 4–13, 103–120, 136–158; Mary Burchard Orvis, *Short Story Writing* (New York, 1928), pp. 111–121; Edith Mirrielees, *Writing the Short Story* (New York, 1929), pp. 81–121; John Gallishaw, *Twenty Problems of the Fiction Writer* (New York and London, 1929), pp. vii–x, 88–167.

[14] *The Twentieth Century Novel* (New York and London, 1932), p. 15, et passim. Cf. Ford Madox Ford, "Techniques," *Southern Review*, i (1935), 20–35; Gordon Hall Gerould, *How to Read Fiction* (Princeton, 1937), pp. 54–55, 66–67, 71–73; Douglas Bement, *Weaving the Short Story* (New York, 1931), pp. 169–173; John T. Frederick, *A Handbook of Short Story Writing*, rev. ed. (New York, 1932), pp. 34–35; Thomas H. Uzzell, *Narrative Technique*, 3rd ed. (New York, 1934), pp. 410–437, and "New Techniques in the Novel," *English Journal* xxiv (1935), 355–363; Arthur Sullivant Hoffman, *The Writing of Fiction* (Boston, 1934), pp. 69, 317–367; James Weber Linn and Houghton Wells Taylor, *Foreword to Fiction* (New York and London, 1935), pp. 27–45, 57–60; Edward J. O'Brien, *The Short Story Case Book* (New York, 1935), pp. 13–32.

comment, till at last heaved overboard with a splash by the twentieth century, is a fascinating study which should be attempted by a contemporary critic in the interest of . . . [that rather neglected aesthetics of fiction] I mentioned in my introduction." [15]

The really significant advance in the theory of point of view which occurred in the forties is the work of Mark Schorer in 1948. If Lubbock was concerned with the point of view as a means to a coherent and vivid presentation, Schorer takes it one step further by examining "the uses of point of view not only as a mode of dramatic delimitation, but, more particularly, of thematic definition." A novel, he says, normally reveals a created world of values and attitudes, and an author is assisted in his search for an artistic definition of these values and attitudes by the controlling medium offered by the devices of point of view; through these devices he is able to disentangle his own prejudices and predispositions from those of his characters and thereby to evaluate those of his characters dramatically in relation to one another within their own frame. He has here the concurrence of Ellen Glasgow, who wrote in 1943: "To be too near, it appears, is more fatal in literature than to be too far away; for it is better that the creative writer should resort to imagination than that he should be overwhelmed by emotion." The novelist must "separate the subject from the object in the act of creation"; he does this by "total immersion" or "projection" into the materials of his story. Finally, that the telling-showing distinction is established as a commonplace of the criticism of fiction is evidenced by its latest reiteration in the work of Bernard De Voto in 1950, as well as in the current handbooks—not only of fiction writing and reading but also of freshman composition.[16]

---

[15] Tate, "The Post of Observation in Fiction," *Maryland Quart.,* II (1944), 61–64; Bentley, *Some Observations on the Art of Narrative* (New York, 1947), pp. 35–39.

[16] Glasgow, *A Certain Measure* (New York, 1943), pp. 18–19, 41–43, 70, 99, 114, 150, 168, 180–183, 189–192; Schorer, "Technique as Discovery," loc. cit. Cf. W. H. Rogers, "Form in the Art-Novel," *Helicon,* II (1939), 1–17; De Voto, "The Invisible Novelist," *The World of Fiction* (Boston, 1950), pp. 205–228; Arthur E. Dubois, "The Art of Fiction," *South Atlantic Quart.,* XL (1941), 112–122; Cleanth Brooks and R. P. Warren, *Understanding Fiction* (New York and London, 1943), pp. 588–596; William Foster-Harris, *The Basic Formulas of Fiction* (Norman, Okla., 1944), pp. 22–53; A. L. Bader, "The Structure of the Modern Short Story," *College English,* VII (1945),

II

HAVING traced the development of this key concept, we may now attempt a concrete and coherent definition of its parts and their relationships. Such a definition will, I think, be produced if we can manage to codify the questions of which these distinctions are answers, and if we can arrange these answers into some semblance of logical sequence.

Since the problem of the narrator is adequate transmission of his story to the reader, the questions must be something like the following: 1) Who talks to the reader? (author in third or first person, character in first, or ostensibly no one); 2) From what position (angle) regarding the story does he tell it? (above, periphery, center, front, or shifting); 3) What channels of information does the narrator use to convey the story to the reader? (author's words, thoughts, perceptions, feelings; or character's words and actions; or character's thoughts, perceptions, and feelings: through which of these or combination of these three possible media does information regarding mental states, setting, situation, and character come?); and 4) At what distance does he place the reader from the story? (near, far, or shifting). And since, further, our major distinction is between "telling" and "showing," the sequence of our answers should proceed by de-

86–92; Elizabeth Bowen, "Notes on Writing a Novel" (1945), *Collected Impressions* (New York, 1950), pp. 249–263; Kenneth Payson Kempton, *The Short Story* (Cambridge, Mass., 1947), pp. 82–145; Dorothy McCleary, *Creative Fiction Writing* (Boston, 1947), pp. 61–69, 70–85, 99–104; Mary Burchard Orvis, *The Art of Writing Fiction* (New York, 1948), pp. 70–91, 113–133, 135–151; Alex Comfort, *The Novel and Our Time* (Denver, 1948), pp. 33–43; Richard Summers, *Craft of the Short Story* (New York and Toronto, 1948), pp. 47–48; René Wellek and Austin Warren, *Theory of Literature* (New York, 1949), pp. 223–234; Brooks and Warren, *Fundamentals of Good Writing* (New York, 1949), pp. 267–288; Manuel Komroff, *How to Write a Novel* (New York and Boston, 1950), pp. 62–95; Mark Schorer, *The Story: A Critical Anthology* (New York, 1950), pp. 16–17, 65; Fred B. Millet, *Reading Fiction* (New York, 1950), pp. 14–25; Vincent McHugh, *Primer of the Novel* (New York, 1950), pp. 4, 16, 113–124; Caroline Gordon and Allen Tate, *The House of Fiction* (New York, 1950), pp. 621–634; A. A. Mendilow, *Time and the Novel* (London, 1952), pp. 96–115; Francis Connolly, *A Rhetoric Case Book* (New York, 1953), pp. 588–589.

grees from the one extreme to the other: from statement to inference, from exposition to presentation, from narrative to drama,
from explicit to implicit, from idea to image.

Editorial Omniscience

Regarding the modes of transmission of story material, we have
first therefore to define concretely our major distinction: summary narrative (telling) vs. immediate scene (showing). Ben
Franklin, on his way as a lad to Philadelphia, came across a copy
of *Pilgrim's Progress* in Dutch, and commented somewhat un-
historically. "Honest John was the first that I know of who mix'd
Narration and Dialogue, a Method of Writing very engaging to
the Reader, who in the most interesting Parts finds himself, as it
were, brought into the Company, and present at the Discourse.
De foe [sic] in his Cruso [sic], his Moll Flanders, Religious
Courtship, Family Instructor, and other Pieces, has imitated it
with Success. And Richardson has done the same in his Pamela,
etc.—" While this is our distinction, I am not so sure that, for
our purposes, dialogue is the crucial factor. Edward Overton,
the narrator in Butler's *The Way of All Flesh,* informs us in the
opening chapter that "My father's face would always brighten
when old Pontifex's name was mentioned. 'I tell you, Edward',
he would say to me, 'old Pontifex was not only an able man, but
he was one of the very ablest men that I ever knew'. This was
more than I as a young man was prepared to stand. 'My dear
father', I answered, 'what did he do?' " [17] It can hardly be said
that the dialogue here constitutes a scene—other factors would
seem to be required. Notice that the verb form is past imperfect,
and that as a result the time and place are indefinite.

In order, then, that the event be placed immediately before the
reader, there is required at least a definite point in space and
time. The chief difference between narrative and scene is accordingly of the general-particular type: summary narrative is
a generalized account or report of a series of events covering
some extended period and a variety of locales, and seems to be

[17] Franklin, *Autobiography* (fr. 1793 on, Franklin died in 1790); Butler,
first published posthumously in 1903 (Butler died in 1902, but ceased work
on this novel in 1884).

the normal untutored mode of storytelling; immediate scene emerges as soon as the specific, continuous, and successive details of time, place, action, character, and dialogue begin to appear. Not dialogue alone but concrete detail within a specific time-place frame is the *sine qua non* of scene.

Butler again will supply us with an example of pure summary narrative: "Old Mr. Pontifex had married in the year 1750, but for fifteen years his wife bore no children. At the end of that time Mrs. Pontifex astonished the whole village by showing unmistakable signs of a disposition to present her husband with an heir or heiress. Hers had long ago been considered a hopeless case, and when on consulting the doctor concerning the meaning of certain symptoms she was informed of their significance, she became very angry and abused the doctor roundly for talking nonsense" (opening of Ch. II). Notice here that, in spite of the specific date (1765), it is the narrator's tone rather than the event itself which dominates—"unmistakable signs," "certain symptoms," and so on, reveal Overton's delight in the irony of the situation rather than the situation itself. We are not shown Mrs. Pontifex's appearance directly (although we can of course infer its general outlines), nor her visit to the doctor, nor her words of anger and abuse, and so on.

For an example of immediate scene we might as well select the obvious—Hemingway is its master: "The rain stopped as Nick turned into the road that went up through the orchard. The fruit had been picked and the fall wind blew through the bare trees. Nick stopped and picked up a Wagner apple from beside the road, shiny in the brown grass from the rain. He put the apple in the pocket of his Mackinaw coat." [18] Here, although no one has yet spoken, we have Hemingway's typically patient presentation of sensory detail: setting (weather: rain, wind; background: road, trees, apple, grass), action (Nick turned, stopped, picked up, put), and character (Nick and his Mackinaw coat). The event itself rather than the overt attitude of the narrator dominates.

These modes of rendering, the one second-hand and indirect, the other immediate and direct, rarely occur in their pure form. Indeed, the chief virtue of the narrative medium is its infinite flexibility, now expanding into vivid detail, now contracting into

[18] "The Three-Day Blow," from *In our Time* (1925).

economical summary; yet one might hazard the loose generalization that modern fiction is characterized by its emphasis on the scene (in the mind or in speech and action), while conventional fiction is characterized by its emphasis on narration. But even the most abstract of narrations will have embedded somewhere within it hints and suggestions of scenes, and even the most concrete of scenes will require the exposition of some summary material. The *tendency*, however, in Editorial Omniscience is away from scene, for it is the author's voice which dominates the material, speaking frequently as "I" or "we."

Here "omniscience" signifies literally a completely unlimited —and hence difficult to control—point of view. The story may be seen from any or all angles at will: from a godlike vantage point beyond time and place, from the center, the periphery, or front. There is nothing to keep the author from choosing any of them, or from shifting from one to the other as often or rarely as he pleases.

The reader accordingly has access to the complete range of possible kinds of information, the distinguishing feature of this category being the thoughts, feelings, and perceptions of the author himself; he is free not only to inform us of the ideas and emotions within the minds of his characters but also of his own. The characteristic mark, then, of Editorial Omniscience is the presence of authorial intrusions and generalizations about life, manners, and morals, which may or may not be explicitly related to the story at hand. Thus, for example, Fielding in *Tom Jones* and Tolstoy in *War and Peace* have interpolated their essays as separate chapters within the body of the work, and hence they are easily detachable. Hardy, on the other hand, makes no such formal distinction commenting here and there in the midst of the action as he sees fit.

One may indeed investigate this sometimes ambiguous relationship between the author's commentary and the story itself. The results are almost always interesting, if not enlightening. Hardy is a case in point: in *Tess of the D'Urbervilles* he indulges in one of his characteristic editorializing passages: "In the ill-judged execution of the well-judged plan of things, the call seldom produces the comer, the man to love rarely coincides with the hour for loving." He continues on about the general unlikelihood of this uneven situation ever improving, and then attempts explicitly to relate this observation to the story at hand: "Enough that in the present case, as in millions, the two halves of an approximately perfect whole did not confront each other at the perfect moment. . . . Out of which maladroit delay sprang anxieties, disappointments, shocks, catastrophes—and what was called a strange destiny" (1891: end of Ch. v).

We may therefore expect the story to illustrate this cause and effect relationship: if Tess's misery has its source in plain bad luck, then it should properly have no cause in her temperament; either the fault is in ourselves or in our stars. Yet Hardy, in his analysis of the motivation of his people, seems at times to be implying something quite different. Tess has screwed up her courage, for example, to tell Angel the horrible truth, but ends (as usual) by ducking the issue: "At the last moment her courage failed her, she feared his blame for not telling him sooner; her instinct of self-preservation was stronger than her candor" (middle of Ch. xxx). There is an internal conflict, then; one which she cannot resolve. Apparently there is more here than mere clumsy mischance. Again, she decides to visit his parents in an effort to settle things, but again quails at the critical moment: "She went her way without knowing that the greatest misfortune of her life was this feminine loss of courage at the last critical moment" (middle of Ch. xliv).

Things need not have been so bad for her, on the other hand, if Angel's character had been different: "Within the remote depths of his constitution, so gentle and affectionate as he was in general, there lay hidden a hard logical deposit, like a vein of metal in a soft loam, which turned the edge of everything that attempted to traverse it. It had blocked his way with the Church; it blocked his way with Tess" (middle of Ch. xxxvi). It is obviously an open question whether a novelist can create characters wholly devoid of significant motivation, even in the service of a naturalistic fatalism.

At any rate, it is a natural consequence of the editorial attitude that the author will not only *report* what goes on in the minds of his characters, but he will also *criticize* it. Thus Hardy depicts poor Tess wandering disconsolately about the countryside after her disastrous encounter with Alex, imagining natural sights and sounds as proclaiming her guilt. He then overtly informs the reader that the unfortunate girl was wrong in feeling this way:

"But this encompassment of her own characterization, based upon shreds of convention, peopled by phantoms and voices antipathetic to her, was a sorry and mistaken creation of Tess's fancy—a cloud of moral hobgoblins by which she was terrified without reason" (end of Ch. XIII). Because she never discovers this, all we can say is that it is just too bad she has less perception than her creator.

Neutral Omniscience

Since the next step toward objectification differs from Editorial Omniscience only in the absence of direct authoral intrusions (the author speaks impersonally in the third person), we may continue our discussion of the various media available for the transmission of story material here. The absence of intrusions does not imply, however, that the author necessarily denies himself a voice when using the Neutral Omniscient frame; such people as Mark Rampion and Philip Quarles in *Point Counter Point* are obviously projections of one or another of Huxley's own attitudes (at that time), as we know from the external evidence, even though Huxley never editorializes in his own voice.

Regarding characterization, although an omniscient author may have a predilection for scene and consequently may allow his people to speak and act for themselves, his predominant tendency is to describe and explain them to the reader in his own voice. Thus Tess meets Alex for the first time, hesitating uncertainly before him: ". . . a figure came forth from the dark triangular door of the tent. It was that of a tall young man, smoking." Now, although Tess is standing there and observing, Alex is described as seen by Hardy and not by his heroine: "He had an almost swarthy complexion, with full lips, badly moulded, though red and smooth, above which was a well-groomed black mustache with curled points though his age could not be more than three- or four-and-twenty. Yet despite the touches of barbarism in his contours, there was a singular force in the gentleman's face, and in his bold rolling eyes" (middle of Ch. v).

By way of illustrating this characteristic indirection concretely, I have re-written the passage by placing this description more directly within Tess's sensory frame: "*She saw* a figure come forth from the dark triangular door of the tent. It was that of a tall young man, smoking. *She noticed* his swarthy complexion, his full lips, badly moulded though red and smooth, and above them a well-groomed mustache with curled points. Though he cannot be more than three- or four-and-twenty, *she thought.* Yet despite the apparent touches of barbarism in his features, *she sensed* a singular force in the gentleman's face and in his bold rolling eyes."

Similarly, the mental states and the settings which evoke them are *narrated* indirectly as if they have already occurred—discussed, analyzed, and explained—rather than presented *scenically* if they were occurring now. If we return to the passage where Tess is wandering guiltily about the countryside, we read: "On the lonely hills and dales her quiescent glide was of a piece with the element she moved in. . . . At times her whimsical fancy would intensify natural processes around her till they seemed a part of her own story. . . . The midnight airs and gusts, moaning among the tightly wrapped buds and bark of the winter twigs, were formulae of bitter reproach." In contrast, I have again tried revising the scene by showing it occurring directly within Tess's mind: "At times *she felt* the scenery as part of her own story. *She heard* the midnight airs and gusts, moaning among the tightly wrapped buds and bark of the winter twigs, *reproaching her* bitterly."

Finally, since summary narrative and immediate scene are equally available (the latter largely for external speech and action), the distance between the story and the reader may be near or far, and it may shift at will—often whimsically and without apparent design. The prevailing characteristic of omniscience, however, is that the author is always ready to intervene himself between the reader and the story, and that even when he does set a scene, he will render it as he sees it rather than as his people see it.

"I" as Witness

Our progress toward direct presentation charts the course of surrender; one by one, as the concentric rings of an onion are peeled, the author's channels of information and his possible vantage points are given up. As he denied himself personal commentary in moving from Editorial to Neutral Omniscience, so here, in moving to the "I" as Witness category, he hands his job completely over to another. Albeit the narrator is a creation of the author, the latter is from now on denied any direct voice in the proceedings at all. The witness-narrator is a character on his own right *within* the story itself, more or less involved in the action, more or less acquainted with its chief personages, who speaks to the reader in the first person.

The natural consequence of this narrative frame is that the witness has no more than ordinary access to the mental states of others; its distinguishing characteristic, then, is that the author has surrendered his omniscience altogether regarding all the other characters involved, and has chosen to allow his witness to tell the reader only what he as observer may legitimately discover. The reader has available to him only the thoughts, feelings, and perceptions of the witness-narrator; he therefore views the story from what may be called the wandering periphery.

What the witness may legitimately transmit to the reader is not as restricted as may at first appear: he can talk to the various people within the story and can get their views on matters of concern (notice how carefully Conrad and Fitzgerald have troubled to characterize Marlow and Carraway as men in whom others feel compelled to confide); particularly he can have interviews with the protagonist himself; and finally he can secure letters, diaries, and other writings which may offer glimpses of the mental states of others. At the utmost limit of his tether, he can draw *inferences* as to how others are feeling and what they are thinking. Thus Nick Carraway speculates, after Gatsby's solitary death, about what went on in his mind before he was shot: "No telephone message arrived. . . . *I have an idea* that Gatsby himself didn't believe it would come, and *perhaps* he no longer cared. If that was true *he must have felt* that he had lost the old warm world, paid a high price for living too long with a single dream. *He must have looked up* at an unfamiliar sky through frightening leaves and shivered as he found what a grotesque thing a rose is and how raw the sunlight was upon the scarcely created grass." [19]

But Butler wanders uncertainly beyond his limits in *The Way*

[19] End of Ch. VIII (1925). Italics mine.

of All Flesh more often than one could wish. His witness-narrator does, in fact, explicitly inform us of his boundaries: "But what were the feelings of Theobald and Christina when the village was passed and.they were rolling [in their honeymoon carriage] quietly by the fir plantation? . . . For some time the pair said nothing: what they must have felt during their first half-hour, the reader must guess, for it is beyond my power to tell him." What, then, are we to make of this passage immediately preceding? "Christina and he [Theobald] had got on, *he thought to himself,* very nicely for a great number of years; why—why— why should they not continue to go on as they were doing now for the rest of their lives?" (beginning of Ch. XIII). Or again, " 'I hope,' said Theobald *to himself,* 'I hope he'll [Ernest] work —or else that Skinner will make him' " (beginning of Ch. XXIV).

It is true that Overton is a contemporary and close friend of Theobald, as well as the godfather and guardian of Ernest, and that Theobald in these instances might have told him later about what went on in his mind, but Overton too frequently gives us no clue whatever as to his authority for such information.

Since the witness-narrator can summarize his narrative at any given point as well as present a scene, the distance between the reader and story may be either near or far, or both. We may note here that the scenes are usually presented directly as the witness sees them.[20]

"I" as Protagonist

With the shift of the narrative burden from a witness to one of the chief personages, who tells his own story in the first person, a few more channels of information are given up and a few more vantage points are lost.[21] Because of his subordinate role in the story itself, the witness-narrator has much greater mobility and

[20] One may speculate, if he wishes, as to the relation between the "I" as Witness frame in fiction and the convention of the messenger in Greek drama. E.g., the re-telling of the catastrophe at the end of *Oedipus Rex* or *Oedipus at Colonus* by an eye-witness.

[21] There is an intermediary category, albeit a minor one, to be mentioned here. It is characterized by the fact that, although the protagonist tells his own story, he tells it not to the reader but rather to someone of his acquaintance who thereupon relays it to the reader in his own person. Something of a combination "I" as Witness and "I" as Protagonist frame.

consequently a greater range and variety of sources of information than the protagonist proper, who is centrally involved in the action. The protagonist-narrator, therefore, is limited almost entirely to his own thoughts, feelings, and perceptions. Similarly, the angle of view is that of the fixed center.

And, since the protagonist-narrator can summarize or present directly in much the same way as the witness, the distance may be near or far, or both. One of the best examples of this mode is to be found in *Great Expectations*.

Multiple Selective Omniscience

In spite of the fact that both the "I" as Witness and the "I" as Protagonist modes are limited to the narrator's mind, there is still *someone* doing the talking, *someone* is still narrating. The next step toward the objectification of the story material is the elimination of not only the author who disappeared with the "I" as Witness frame, but also of any narrator whatsoever. Here the reader ostensibly listens to no one; the story comes directly through the minds of the characters as it leaves its mark there. As a result, the tendency is almost wholly in the direction of scene, both inside the mind and externally with speech and action; and narrative summary, if it appears at all, is either supplied unobtrusively by the author by way of "stage direction" or emerges through the thoughts and words of the characters themselves.

The appearance of the characters, what they do and say, the setting—all the story materials, therefore—can be transmitted to the reader only through the mind of someone present. Thus Mrs. Ramsay's age and appearance are rendered in Virginia Woolf's *To the Lighthouse:* "They must find a way out of it all. There might be some simpler way, some less laborious way, *she sighed.* When *she looked* in the glass and *saw* her hair grey, her cheek sunk, at fifty, *she thought,* possibly, she might have managed things better—her husband; money; his book." [22]

It might be questioned as to exactly how this mode of presentation, where the author *shows* us internal states, differs from normal omniscience, where the author peers into the minds of his

[22] Harbrace Modern Classics ed. (1927), pp. 13–14. Italics mine.

characters and *tells* us what is going on there. It is chiefly that the one renders thoughts, perceptions, and feelings as they occur consecutively and in detail passing through the mind (scene), while the other summarizes and explains them after they have occurred (narrative). A "translation" of another passage from Mrs. Woolf will illustrate the precise point of difference: "Such was the complexity of things [thinks Lily Briscoe]. For what happened to her, especially staying with the Ramsays, was to be made to feel violently two opposite things at the same time; that's what you feel, was one; that's what I feel, was the other, and then they fought together in her mind, as now. It is so beautiful, so exciting, this love, that I tremble on the verge of it." [23] The shift to normal omniscience is effected by changing to indirect discourse, standardizing the personal pronouns to the third person (one often thinks of oneself in the first, second, or third person), and normalizing the syntax: "It seemed to Lily *that* things were quite complex. Staying with the Ramsays, especially, made her feel *that* she was being pulled in two opposite directions at the same time. On the one hand, *there were* the feelings of others; and, on the other, *there were one's own* feelings. Sometimes love appeared so beautiful and exciting *that she* trembled on the verge of it." A less patient omniscient author might simply remark: "Lily felt ambivalent about love, especially with the Ramsays."

Selective Omniscience

Here the reader is limited to the mind of only one of the characters. Instead, therefore, of being allowed a composite of viewing angles, he is at the fixed center. The other questions are answered as they were for the previous category.

It remains merely to illustrate. A vivid example of exactly how the story materials are transmitted directly to the reader through a character's mind is found in Joyce's *A Portrait:* "Consciousness of place *came ebbing back to him* [Stephen] slowly over a vast tract of time unlit, unfelt, unlived. The squalid scene

[23] Ibid., p. 154. Ramon Fernandez, in *Messages* (1926), trans. from the French by Montgomery Belgion (New York, 1927), makes a very keen distinction, apparently independently, between the "novel" (showing) and the "recital" (telling), pp. 61–69.

composed itself around him; the common accents, the burning gasjets in the shops, odours of fish and spirits and wet sawdust, moving men and women. An old woman was about to cross the street, an oilcan in her hand. He bent down and asked was there a chapel near?" [24]

The abrupt beginnings and much of the distortion characteristic of modern stories and novels are due to the use of Multiple and Selective Omniscience, for, if the aim is to dramatize mental states, and depending upon how far "down" into the mind you go, the logic and syntax of normal daytime public discourse begin to disappear. Of course, there is no necessary connection: Henry James, staying on the "upper" levels of his characters' minds, which are usually of the highly articulate type anyway, cannot be called a "stream-of-consciousness" writer. Woolf, who might be said to dwell on the "middle" level of her characters' minds (which are characteristically chaste), and Joyce, who knows no bottom, are correspondingly more difficult.[25]

The Dramatic Mode

Having eliminated the author, and then the narrator, we are now ready to dispose of mental states altogether. The information available to the reader in the Dramatic Mode is limited largely to what the characters do and say; their appearance and the setting may be supplied by the author as in stage directions;

---

[24] End of Ch. III (1916). I am in fundamental agreement with Ellsworth Mason, who maintains that the Joyce canon is "dramatic" from beginning to end, displaying no progression from "lyric" to "epic" to "drama," as has commonly been supposed. See "Joyce's Categories," *Sewanee Review,* LXI (1953), 427–432.

[25] Cf. Louis Hasley, "The Stream-of-Consciousness Method," *Catholic World,* CXLVI (1937), 210–213; Lawrence Bowling, "What is the Stream of Consciousness Technique?" *PMLA,* LXV (1950), 333–345; Robert Humphrey, " 'Stream of Consciousness': Technique or Genre?" *PQ,* XXX (1951), 434–437. Bowling makes a very useful distinction between mental analysis, interior monologue, and stream of consciousness; the latter two represent the more and the less articulate manner of directly rendering internal states, the first the indirect omniscient manner. See also Gleb Struve, "Monologue Interieur: The Origins of the Formula and the First Statement of its Possibilities," *PMLA,* LXIX (1954), 1101–11; and Robert Humphrey, *Stream of Consciousness in the Modern Novel,* Perspectives in Criticism: 3 (Berkeley and Los Angeles, 1954)—both of which appeared after this article was completed.

there is never, however, any direct indication of what they perceive (a character may *look* out of the window—an objective act—but what he *sees* is his own business), what they think, or how they feel. This is not to say of course, that mental states may not be *inferred* from action and dialogue.

We have here, in effect, a stage play cast into the typographical mold of fiction. But there is some difference: fiction is meant to be read, drama to be seen and heard, and there will be a corresponding difference in scope, range, fluidity, and subtlety. The analogy, however, does largely hold, in that the reader apparently listens to no one but the characters themselves, who move as it were upon a stage; his angle of view is that of the fixed front (third row center), and the distance must always be near (since the presentation is wholly scenic). Hemingway comes into his own here (mainly in short stories such as *Hills Like White Elephants*), and mention might be made of James's *The Awkward Age* (1899), which is something of a tour de force—the gains in immediacy hardly compensating for the difficulties of sustaining a full-length novel within this mode.[26]

The Camera

Largely for the sake of symmetry, our account of the kinds of points of view may be concluded with what seems the ultimate in authorial exclusion. Here the aim is to transmit, without apparent selection or arrangement, a "slice of life" as it passes before the recording medium: "I am a camera," begins Isherwood's narrator at the opening of *Goodbye to Berlin* (1945), "with its shutter open, quite passive recording, not thinking. Recording the man shaving at the window opposite and the woman in the kimono washing her hair. Someday, all this will have to be developed, carefully printed, fixed." [27]

[26] For a discussion of the reverse of this problem, see Herman M. Weisman, "An Investigation of Methods and Techniques in the Dramatization of Fiction," *Speech Monographs*, XIX (1952), 48–59.

[27] Tolstoy is reported to have recorded camera-style, as his first attempt at authorship in March 1851, everything that he saw and felt for one day. Cf. Prince D. S. Mirsky, *A History of Russian Literature* (New York, 1934 [1927]), pp. 329–330; and Janko Lavrin, *Tolstoy: An Approach* (London, 1944), p. 21. It is called *The History* [or *An Account*] *of Yesterday*, but I have not been able to obtain a copy.

Perhaps, however, with the final extinction of the author, fiction as an art will become extinct as well, for this art, while requiring some degree at least of objective vividness, requires as well, it seems to me, a structure, the product of a guiding intelligence which is implicit in the narrative and which shapes the material so as to arouse the reader's expectations with regard to the probable course of events, to cross those expectations with an equally probable contrary course, and then to allay these expectations so that the resultant outcome seems after all the necessary one. Nor need this statement be taken as a plea for a return to novels in which "something happens," in the sense of melodramatic action; "events" refers equally, as we have argued above, to mental states as to overt action, and a writer—such as Mrs. Woolf, for example—can become infinitely subtle in these matters without entirely abandoning structure. To argue that the function of literature is to transmit unaltered a slice of life is to misconceive the fundamental nature of language itself: the very act of writing is a process of abstraction, selection, omission, and arrangement. But why, finally, need we go to a novel for a slice of life when we can go to the nearest street corner for a much more vivid one which we can experience at first hand?

III

WHAT, it may be asked, is the result of all this "squeamishness"? Does not all this fuss over technique by an author end in a cold detachment, a clinical, passionless objectivity? Thus Bradford Booth objects that "if the Victorian intrusive author failed, he failed on a grand scale, for he attempted much. In the eyes of many of us, however, he did not fail. It is charged that he does not maintain a consistent point of view. What matter, if his characters live? It is charged that he sees human nature only from the outside. What matter, if his view be not distorted?" Are not Scott and Dickens, after all, more delightful than James, with his obsessive scrupulosity? For Beach, the answer is relative, a matter of taste: "We cannot be the worse for the wisdom of these big men, these large souls [i.e., the Victorian novelists]. But, for better or worse, the fashion has changed; we like fiction unadulterated; we like the sense of taking part in an actual, a present experience, without the interference of an authorial guide." [28]

But is it really so largely a matter of "fashion"? And does not Booth beg some crucial questions? We have indicated above that it has been all along a commonplace of aesthetic theory that effective presentation and "impersonality" go hand in hand; [29] and the difference between Dickens and James regarding liveliness is also a function of their characteristic choice of materials, not merely of technique. But perhaps the whole question can be rephrased in terms of ends and means: has the novelist utilized the available techniques in such a way as to produce the effect intended? or has he allowed opportunities to pass and obstacles to arise between the reader and the desired illusion?

The basic assumption, then, of those who are seriously concerned over technique, as James himself so long ago pointed out, is that the prime end of fiction is to produce as complete a story-illusion as possible. Given material potentially interesting, concentration and intensity, and hence vividness, are the results of working within limits, albeit self-imposed, and any lapse thereof is in all probability the result either of not establishing a limiting frame to begin with or of breaking the one already established. Surely this is one of the basic principles of artistic technique in general.

Thus the choice of a point of view in the writing of fiction is at least as crucial as the choice of a verse form in the composing of a poem; just as there are certain things which cannot get said in a sonnet, so each of the categories we have detailed has a probable range of functions it can perform within its limits. The question of effectiveness, therefore, is one of the suitability of a given technique for the achievement of certain kinds of effects, for each kind of story requires the establishment of a

[28] Booth, pp. 94–96; Beach, *Twentieth Century Novel*, pp. 15–16. Booth informs me that his stand in this matter has since undergone some modification.

[29] See, e.g., Aristotle's *Poetics*, 1460^a 5: "Homer, admirable as he is in every other respect, is especially so in this, that he alone among epic poets is not unaware of the part to be played by the poet himself in the poem. The poet should say very little *in propria persona,* as he is no imitator when doing that. Whereas the other poets are perpetually coming forward in person, and say but little, and that only here and there, as imitators, Homer after a brief preface brings in forthwith a man, or woman, or some other Character—no one of them characterless, but each with distinctive characteristics" (Bywater trans.).

particular kind of an illusion to sustain it. Editorial Omni-science, for example, may be called the "free verse" of fiction: its limits are so wholly internal that an unwary novelist has more opportunities for illusion-breaking here than with the others. How much of Whitman, Sandburg, or Masters is flat and dull? And how much of *War and Peace*—to take the highest —could easily be dispensed with? On the other hand, when the personality of the author-narrator has a definite function to ful-fill in relation to his story—say of irony, compassion, philosophi-cal range and depth, and so on—he need not retire behind his work, so long as his point of view is adequately established and coherently maintained. It is more a matter of consistency than of this or that degree of "impersonality." But the author-narrator has a more complicated problem on his hands here, and had best look to his devices. Free verse is not "free" after all, as Eliot has somewhere remarked; but to establish a pattern within it is more difficult and hence more liable to disruption. In this respect, Fielding's *Tom Jones* is more successful than *War and Peace:* the intellectual tone and pedantic material of Tolstoy's interchapters are often at variance with the tenor and impact of the story itself, which has as its theme the glorification (in Pierre, Kutuzov, Karataev, Nikolay, Natasha) of the instinctive and intuitive forces in life. There is thus revealed, for all its majesty, a fatally unresolved ambiguity at the core of this novel: it is commonly agreed that Andrey and Pierre are symbolic projections of Tolstoy's own ambivalence, and it is as if, after having killed off Andrey, the author-narrator could not allow Andrey's attitude to disappear altogether from the story and so kept it alive, as it were, in the interchapters. However we may view them, they are basically undramatic.

Thus, if it is essential to an author's purpose that the minds of many be revealed freely and at will—to achieve, for example, the effect of a social milieu in the manner of Huxley—and if the author's superior and explanatory tone is to dominate the perception and awareness of his characters—to achieve that typi-cal Huxleyan effect of smallness and futility and indignity— then Neutral Omniscience is the logical choice. If the element of suspense is to be foremost—as, say, in mystery stories and detective fiction—if a situation is to be gradually built up and revealed piecemeal—as, for example, in *Lord Jim*—then the witness-narrator seems more likely than any other. If the problem is one of tracing the growth of a personality as it reacts to experience, the protagonist-narrator will prove most useful—as in *Great Expectations*—assuming that he has sufficient sensitivity and intelligence to develop and to perceive the significance of that development (a naïve protagonist may, of course, be used for an ironic effect). If the author is concerned with the way in which personality and experience emerge as a mosaic from their impingement upon the sensibilities of several individuals, then Multiple Selective Omniscience provides a way—as in *To the Lighthouse*. If the intent is to catch a mind in a moment of discovery—as in *A Portrait of the Artist*—Selective Omniscience is the means. And finally, if the author's purpose is to produce in the reader's mind a moment of revelation—as in Hemingway's *Hills Like White Elephants*—then the Dramatic Mode, with its tendency to imply more than it states, provides the logical approach. The analysis of technique, then, is crucial, as Schorer maintains, when it is seen as revealing the author's purpose and, even more fundamentally, the basic structure of values which he has embodied by means of that technique.

Consistency and not cold-bloodedness is all, for consistency —within however large and diverse and complex a frame— signifies that the parts have been adjusted to the whole, the means to the end, and hence that the maximum effect has been rendered. It is, however, a necessary rather than a sufficient cause; the over-all consistency of a great but clumsy novelist may emerge *in spite of* his technical inadequacies, while the consistency of a lesser talent will not in itself produce masterpieces, succeeding within a smaller frame than that which genius may attempt. Sometimes a noble failure is more exciting than a petty victory. But how many of our most ambitious and brilliant novels would have been even more successful if closer attention had been directed toward these matters? [30] There is surely no necessary contradiction between genius and technical mastery.

[30] I have in mind here, for example, the obvious inconsistencies in the narrative of *Don Quixote* as well as the often burdensome references to Cid Hamet, the author of the "original" MS. (cf. Wayne C. Booth, "The Self-Conscious Narrator in Comic Fiction before *Tristram Shandy*," *PMLA*, LXVII [1952], 163–185); or Melville's continual bursting of his original witness-narrator frame in *Moby Dick;* or the frequent absurdities engendered in the course of the narrative by Richardson's epistolary technique in *Pamela;* or the curiously split structure of *Moll Flanders;* or the excesses and lapses in emphasis in Wolfe's bulky novels (cf. n. 32 below).

D. H. Lawrence is a case in point, and Schorer has outlined the basic cause of the curious restlessness with which the reader is left after reading, say, *Sons and Lovers*. In spite of its "modern" concern with sex and the unconscious, this story is still narrated within the frameless frame of old-fashioned Editorial Omniscience, and the danger of authorial identification with the protagonist—and hence of partisanship and dice-loading—has not been obviated. The author-narrator thus analyzes Miriam's thoughts: "So in May she asked him [Paul] to come to Willey Farm and meet Mrs. Dawes. There was something he hankered after. She saw him, whenever they spoke of Clara Dawes, rouse and get slightly angry. He said he did not like her. Yet he was keen to know about her. Well, he should put himself to the test. She believed that there were in him desires for higher things, and desires for lower, and that the desires for the higher would conquer. At any rate, he should try." And then Lawrence adds, "She forgot that her 'higher' and 'lower' were arbitrary." [31]

Both Schorer and Diana Trilling point out that there is consequently a contradiction in the book's theme: Paul Morel cannot achieve a satisfactory sexual relationship either because of his enervating mother-fixation or because Miriam can encompass only the "spiritual" aspects of such a relationship. And these two themes are mutually exclusive—the fault is the mother's or Miriam's—and the trouble is that Lawrence has been unable sufficiently to dissociate himself from Paul to tell one from the other, with the result that he tries to have it both ways. But the reader remains frustrated; lack of consistency means loss of effect. Yet the irony is that Lawrence himself believed in the efficacy of dramatic projection as a way of clarifying and understanding his own emotional problems: "One sheds one's sicknesses in books—repeats and presents again one's emotions, to be master of them." E. T., however, the original of Miriam, knew that in this case he had failed: ". . . he burked the real issue. It was his old inability to face his problem squarely. His mother had to be supreme. . . . So instead of a release and a deliverance from bondage, the bondage was glorified and made absolute. . . . The best I could think of him

---

[31] Schorer, "Technique as Discovery," *op. cit.*, pp. 197–198; Lawrence (1913), Modern Library Edition, p. 269.

was that he had run with the hare and hunted with the hounds." [32]

By way of contrast, we may note Joyce's presentation of Stephen in *A Portrait*, where, in spite of the common tendency to treat it as autobiographical, the story of the hero's coming-of-age is completely objectified. Because Joyce has strictly limited the flow of information only to those scenes, perceptions, thoughts, and feelings which Stephen's mind records, he has eliminated the possibility of authorial partisanship which so vitiates the structure of *Sons and Lovers*. As a result, we get such a clear picture of the protagonist that one of his friends can say to him: "It is a curious thing, do you know—Cranly said dispassionately—how your mind is supersaturated with the religion in which you say you disbelieve." One cannot conceive of Lawrence, given his lack of control, as allowing Miriam to say to Paul: "It is a curious thing, do you know, how your rather excessive love for your mother causes you unwittingly to seek a sexual outlet with younger women which will be devoid of spiritual content. Passion and devotion are split in your mind by guilt, and therefore you react violently when a woman asks you for both together, accusing her of wanting to draw the soul out of you. Your soul has already been given to your mother. So you misconceive me completely when you say I want only your spiritual love." (Due allowance will, I hope, be made for the fact that I am not a novelist; but I believe, from the evidence in E. T.'s book, that Miriam was fully capable of such penetration. Lawrence, however, renders her as agonizingly inarticulate.)

Such is the success of Joyce's projection that, in spite of the fact that both he and his hero deliberately rejected Catholicism, literary Catholics can nevertheless relish his portrayal of religious life in the book. Thus Thomas Merton comments regarding the famous Hell passages: "What impressed me was not the

[32] Trilling, Introd. to *The Portable D. H. Lawrence* (New York, 1947), pp. 19–20; Lawrence, quoted in the same place; E. T., *D. H. Lawrence: A Personal Record* (London, 1935), pp. 201–204. For another interesting firsthand acount of the problem of objectivity in fiction, see Thomas Wolfe's *The Story of a Novel* (1936): "The nature of my method, the desire fully to explore my material had led me into another error. The whole effect of those five years of incessant writing had been to make me feel not only that everything had to be used, but that everything had to be told, that nothing could be implied." Penguin ed. of Wolfe's short stories (New York, 1947 [variously entitled *Short Stories* and *Only the Dead Know Brooklyn*]), pp. 117–118, 146.

fear of hell, but the expertness of the sermon. . . . So then I continued to read Joyce, more and more fascinated by the pictures of priests and Catholic life that came up here and there in his books." Similarly, Caroline Gordon can say, "I suspect that this book has been misread by a whole generation. It is not primarily a picture of the artist rebelling against constituted authority. It is, rather, the picture of a soul that is being damned for time and eternity caught in the act of foreseeing and foreknowing its damnation." [33] While I think that this is perverse sophistry, I think also that it is a tribute to Joyce's dramatic genius that a Catholic can sympathize with the portrayal of Catholic values in the novel which the hero rejects.

All this is merely to say, in effect, that when an author surrenders in fiction, he does so in order to conquer; he gives up certain privileges and imposes certain limits in order the more effectively to render his story-illusion, which constitutes artistic truth in fiction. And it is in the service of this truth that he spends his creative life.

[33] Merton, *The Seven Storey Mountain*, Signet ed. (New York, 1952 [1948]), pp. 255–256; Gordon, "Some Readings and Misreadings," *Sewanee Rev.* LXI (1953), 384–407.

PLOT, STRUCTURE, AND PROPORTION

Jacques Barzun once compiled a list of meanings and connotations that have attached themselves to the word romantic. And since the word has been used as a hopefully precise designation, a vaguely suggestive epithet, and a polemical weapon, his list is diverse, amusing, and totally lacking in any consensus. Romantic means irrational, mysterious, formless, bombastic, and so on, for several pages. The same kind of glossary could be compiled for plot since that word, too, occurs in contexts which make it neutrally descriptive, honorific, and pejorative. Plot means essence, story, overt action, formula, skeleton, mechanism, contrivance—the very reason for which a narrative work exists, the means by which a narrative work conveys what it really wishes to say, or the cheapest kind of trickery, of the sort that promises chocolate ice cream if we eat our meat and potatoes. As long as the word occurs in contexts such as Plot Outlines of the World's

Great Novels, it will be capable of meaning the action of a work in its skeletal, paraphrasable form. Yet one reflects on how useless to criticism is the naming of an element of a work, of Madame Bovary say, which can be represented in this way: a provincial young woman whose view of life is derived from romance marries a coarse but earnest country doctor, quickly tires of him—and so on. Plot can be a useful category only when the word enters the critical vocabulary neutral of values and defined in a larger, more inclusive sense than that summary sense above, so that the word designates something of the total work, in all of its uniqueness, complexity, and power.

It is out of a wish to recover the Aristotelian validity of the word plot and to define it so as to make it genuinely useful to criticism that R. S. Crane's influential essay originates. The passage that follows is part of a long essay which brilliantly elucidates the unity of Tom Jones and protests against the facile equation of its plot with its bare structure of action. Norman Friedman's essay proceeds from Crane's position to build a systematic account of the way in which fictional plots operate, playing anticipation against realization, arousing expectation and providing fulfillment, presenting possibilities and offering resolutions.

Novelists of different periods have concerned themselves with structure and proportion in different ways: the architectonic concerns of Fielding with their roots in the drama, the epic, and history; the balance, the poise, and the economy of Jane Austen; the frames, the contrasts, and the alterations of Emily Brontë; the claims of serialization upon most of the major Victorian novelists; the rhythms of symbol and motif in Conrad; the stylized symmetry of James; the intricate symbolic and analogical structure of Joyce. The assumptions that underlie these different solutions to problems of structure are recoverable in various ways, by observing the process of revision, as one can do for example with Jane Austen's Persuasion, by access to work sheets or note books, by inference from the novel itself, and in a few occasions from the remarks of the novelists. James is one of the few to have explained something of what it means, in his own work, to have overtreated or undertreated, to have concentrated or dissipated, to have arranged badly or well, and to have found the structural equivalents of his own imaginative vision.

The last essay in the section takes what is either ignored or regarded as one of the least interesting aspects of fictional structure, division into chapters, and attempts a defense of its importance, a psychological explanation, and the beginnings of a historical account.

R. S. CRANE

THE CONCEPT OF PLOT

Any novel or drama not constructed on didactic principles is a composite of three elements, which unite to determine its quality and effect—the things that are imitated (or "rendered") in it, the linguistic medium in which they are imitated, and the manner or technique of imitation; and I shall assume further that the things imitated necessarily involve human beings interacting with one another in ways determined by, and in turn affecting, their moral characters and their states of mind (i.e., their reasonings, emotions, and attitudes). If this is granted, we may say that the plot of any novel or drama is the particular temporal synthesis effected by the writer of the elements of action, character, and thought that constitute the matter of his invention. It is impossible, therefore, to state adequately what any plot is unless we include in our formula all three of the elements or causes of which the plot is the synthesis; and it follows also that plots will differ in structure according as one or another of the three causal ingredients is employed as the synthesizing principle. There are, thus, plots of action, plots of character, and plots of thought. In the first, the synthesizing principle is a completed change, gradual or sudden, in the situation of the protagonist, determined and effected by character and thought (as in *Oedipus* and *The Brothers Karamazov*);

From "The Concept of Plot and the Plot of 'Tom Jones.' " *Reprinted from* Critics and Criticism: Ancient and Modern, *ed. R. S. Crane by permission of The University of Chicago Press.* © 1952 *by The University of Chicago.*

in the second, the principle is a completed process of change in the moral character of the protagonist, precipitated or molded by action, and made manifest both in it and in thought and feeling (as in James's *The Portrait of a Lady*); in the third, the principle is a completed process of change in the thought of the protagonist and consequently in his feelings, conditioned and directed by character and action (as in Pater's *Marius the Epicurean*). All these types of construction, and not merely the first, are plots in the meaning of our definition; and it is mainly, perhaps, because most of the familiar classic plots, including that of *Tom Jones*, have been of the first kind that so many critics have tended to reduce plot to action alone.[1]

If this is granted, we may go farther. For a plot, in the enlarged sense here given to the term, is not merely a particular synthesis of particular materials of character, thought, and action, but such a synthesis endowed necessarily, because it imitates in words a sequence of human activities, with a power to affect our opinions and emotions in a certain way. We are bound, as we read or listen, to form expectations about what is coming and to feel more or less determinate desires relatively to our expectations. At the very least, if we are interested at all, we desire to know what is going to happen or how the problems faced by the characters are going to be solved. This is a necessary condition of our pleasure in all plots, and there are many good ones—in the classics of pure detective fiction, for example, or in some modern psychiatric novels—the power of which depends almost exclusively on the pleasure we take in inferring progessively, from complex or ambiguous signs, the true state of affairs. For some readers and even some critics this would seem to be the chief source of delight in many plots that have obviously been constructed on more specific principles: not only *Tom Jones*, as we have seen, but *Oedipus* has been praised as a mystery story, and it is likely that much of Henry James's popularity is due to his remarkable capacity for provoking a superior kind of inferential activity. What distinguishes all the more developed forms of imaginative literature,

---

[1] This accounts in large part, I think, for the depreciation of "plot" in E. M. Forster's *Aspects of the Novel*, and for his notion of a rivalry between "plot" and "character," in which one or the other may "triumph." For a view much closer to that argued in this essay see Elizabeth Bowen, "Notes on Writing a Novel," *Orion*, II (1945), 18 ff.

however, is that, though they presuppose this instinctive pleasure in learning, they go beyond it and give us plots of which the effects derive in a much more immediate way from the particular ethical qualities manifested in their agents' actions and thoughts vis-à-vis the human situations in which they are engaged. When this is the case, we cannot help becoming, in a greater or less degree, emotionally involved; for some of the characters we wish good, for others ill, and, depending on our inferences as to the events, we feel hope or fear, pity or satisfaction, or some modification of these or similar emotions. The peculiar power of any plot of this kind, as it unfolds, is a result of our state of knowledge at any point in complex interaction with our desires for the characters as morally differentiated beings; and we may be said to have grasped the plot in the full artistic sense only when we have analyzed this interplay of desires and expectations sequentially in relation to the incidents by which it is produced.

It is, of course, an essential condition of such an effect that the writer should so have combined his elements of action, character, and thought as to have achieved a complete and ordered whole, with all the parts needed to carry the protagonist, by probable or necessary stages, from the beginning to the end of his change: we should not have, otherwise, any connected series of expectations wherewith to guide our desires. In itself, however, this structure is only the matter or content of the plot and not its form; the form of the plot—in the sense of that which makes its matter into a definite artistic thing—is rather its distinctive "working or power," as the form of the plot in tragedy, for example, is the capacity of its unified sequence of actions to effect through pity and fear a catharsis of such emotions.

But if this is granted, then certain consequences follow for the criticism of dramas and novels. It is evident, in the first place, that no plot of this order can be judged excellent *merely* in terms of the unity of its action, the number and variety of its incidents, or the extent to which it produces suspense and surprise. These are but properties of its matter, and their achievement, even to a high degree, in any particular plot does not inevitably mean that the emotional effect of the whole will not still be diffused or weak. They are, therefore, necessary, but not sufficient, conditions of a good plot, the positive excellence of which depends upon the power of its peculiar synthesis of character, action, and thought, as inferable from the sequence of words, to move our feelings powerfully and pleasurably in a certain definite way.

But this power, which constitutes the form of the plot, is obviously, from an artistic point of view, the most important virtue any drama or novel can have; it is that, indeed, which most sharply distinguishes works of imitation from all other kinds of literary productions. It follows, consequently, that the plot, considered formally, of any imitative work is, in relation to the work as a whole, not simply a means—a "framework" or "mere mechanism"—but rather the final end which everything in the work, if that is to be felt as a whole, must be made, directly or indirectly, to serve. For the critic, therefore, the form of the plot is a first principle, which he must grasp as clearly as possible for any work he proposes to examine before he can deal adequately with the questions raised by its parts. This does not mean that we cannot derive other relevant principles of judgment from the general causes of pleasure operative in all artistic imitations, irrespective of the particular effect, serious or comic, that is aimed at in a given work. One of these is the imitative principle itself, the principle that we are in general more convinced and moved when things are "rendered" for us through probable signs than when they are given merely in "statement," without illusion, after the fashion of a scenario.[2] Critical judgments, valid enough if they are not taken absolutely, may also be drawn from considerations of the general powers of language as a literary medium, of the known potentialities or requirements of a given manner of representation (e.g., dramatic or narrative), and of the various conditions of suspense and surprise. We are not likely to feel strongly the emotional effect of a work in which the worse rather than the better alternatives among these different expedients are consistently chosen or chosen in crucial scenes. The same thing, too, can be said of works in which the thought, however clearly serving an artistic

---

[2] The meaning and force of this will be clear to anyone who has compared in detail the text of *The Ambassadors* with James's preliminary synopsis of the novel (*The Notebooks of Henry James* [New York, 1947], pp. 372–415). See also the excellent remarks of Allen Tate, apropos of *Madame Bovary*, in his "Techniques of Fiction" (*Forms of Modern Fiction*, ed. William Van O'Connor [Minneapolis, 1948], esp. pp. 37–45).

use, is generally uninteresting or stale, or in which the characters of the agents, though right enough in conception for the intended effect, are less than adequately "done" or fail to impress themselves upon our memory and imagination, or in which we perceive that the most has not been made of the possibilities implicit in the incidents. And there is also a kind of judgment, distinct from any of these, the object of which is not so much the traits of a work that follow from its general character as an imitative drama or novel as the qualities of intelligence and moral sensibility in its author which are reflected in his conception and handling of its subject and which warrant us in ascribing "greatness," "seriousness," or "maturity" to some products of art and in denying these values to others no matter how excellent, in a formal sense, the latter may be.

Such criticism of parts in the light of general principles is indispensable, but it is no substitute for—and its conclusions, affirmative as well as negative, have constantly to be checked by —the more specific kind of criticism of a work that takes the form of the plot as its starting point and then inquires how far and in what way its peculiar power is maximized by the writer's invention and development of episodes, his step-by-step rendering of the characters of his people, his use and elaboration of thought, his handling of diction and imagery, and his decisions as to the order, method, scale, and point of view of his representation.

NORMAN FRIEDMAN

FORMS OF THE PLOT

Surely the plot summary of novels and plays will take its place beside the prose paraphrase of poems in the history of classroom roadblocks. While it is heartening to see such con-

From Journal of General Education, *VIII (1955). Reprinted by permission of* Journal of General Education.

crete demonstrations of students having actually read and retained the material, we teachers are always saying that the important thing about a literary work is not the story it tells, roughly speaking, but rather what its author makes of it. By this we mean, of course, that the essential problem in reading a poem, play, or novel is a determination of its artistic form.

Just as the student's translation of a poem into his own words leaves out exactly those elements which are essential to the poem as an artistic whole—the dramatic situation in which its speaker is located, the listener he addresses, and the rhetorical aim which he is trying to achieve—so too does the student's bare recital of the events in a play or novel leave out those elements which are necessary to a grasp of the shaping principle binding them together: the character and motives of the protagonist, his state of mind, the change he undergoes, and the crucial chain of cause and effect leading him from one condition to another.

By way of illustration, we may ask our students to imagine a given "story"—say, protagonist meets loved one, wins loved one, loses loved one—as it might be treated by several different writers—say, Hardy, D. H. Lawrence, F. Scott Fitzgerald, Hemingway, and George Orwell. Clearly the same story turns out to be five altogether different things in *Tess of the d'Urbervilles, Sons and Lovers, The Great Gatsby, A Farewell to Arms,* and *1984,* and it is exactly this difference which we are after—the *art* involved. What is the whole, we ask; what holds it all together; what is the principle of unity which governs the selection and arrangement of parts and their embodiment in language?

I

THERE is available, of course, a generally current theory of form with which we are all familiar. A narrative is organized, we have been told often enough, so that its diverse elements of action, character, background, and theme have been reconciled into an organic whole. And certain general formulas have been evolved in order to account for this reconciliation, such as purpose, passion, perception, or tension, conflict, resolution.

"Irony" is the key term here, and, while the message may never be simple and overt, the important formal principle is found in the sensibility of the author, in his ability to recognize and represent the complexities of the human situation, to see both sides, to put opposites into some kind of working and harmonious relationship. Within this framework, then, the student is taught to discern the elaborate systems of similarity and contrast which obtain among the various elements of the plot.

Such a theory is helpful as far as it goes and is clearly a step in the right direction. But it does not go far enough, and, what is more damaging, it blurs some of the very distinctions it purports to make. In the first place, it is a framework into which we can fit *all* literary works, whether they be poems, short stories, novelettes, plays, or novels. It is monolithic and therefore does not serve to establish those crucial differences mentioned above. Second, it is a circular or static theory of form in which the whole is seen as emerging, somehow, out of co-ordinate relationships established, somehow, among equal parts. Everything is related to everything else, the story goes, and everything works together. As a result, with the narrative art especially, the essential flow of cause and effect in time—the concept of levels of subordination among the parts, one serving as means or material to the next—gets lost in the shuffle. And, finally, since theme contradictorily gets top billing, even though it is modified by qualifications about "total meaning," this theory commits us out of hand to a didactic interpretation of all of literature. While it is true that most of the works which we value as serious and important deal with moral and philosophical ideas, it does not necessarily follow that those works are organized formally by those ideas.[1]

If all plots, nay, if all literary works, are seen as being shaped according to the same general principles, then we have not gone far toward solving the problem of how to see and define the many differences which common sense tells us exist among the various poems, plays, and novels we have read. What we still need, then, is a theory of wholes which will make available to us as many different alternative hypotheses as are needed

---

[1] Cf. Bruce Harkness, "Imitation and Theme," *JAAC*, XII (1954), 499–508, and Charles A. McLaughlin, "A Note on 'Imitation and Theme' in Literary Criticism," *JAAC*, XIII (1954), 267–70.

in order to do this job—a theory which will not commit us in advance to finding a set pattern in everything we read, and a pattern of irony at that. For, if we make our theory general enough, it is clear that it will "work" for anything, and who is to gainsay a student who claims that he has "found" a reconciled opposition in a given work "empirically" when that is what we have taught him to look for?

II

HOW may we construct a theory of the whole from which we will be able to derive a set of distinctions allowing us to define as closely as possible the unique form of a particular plot? We need, to begin with, a concept which will free us from the limitations of the current static, or closed-circle, notion of the whole outlined above. It is not enough to say that all the parts relate to all the other parts and that the whole equals this relationship. If we think, however, of the whole as an "end" and the parts and devices as "means," we will bring a sense of developmental progression back into our thinking. Parts and devices are there in the work not just to "relate" but to do a job, to forward a purpose, and that purpose is its end or form. Any piece of writing is intended by its author, whether deliberately or instinctively or both, to effect some sort of end, and it is this end which serves as the principle by which he guides himself when facing such crucial artistic questions as where to begin, how much to include and in what order, where to emphasize and where de-emphasize, where and how to end, and so on.

Nor is this the same sort of "intention" which has recently been ruled out of the classroom as "fallacious," [2] for what we are really after here is not what the writer says he intended or hopes he achieved—although I can see no reason why this should not be allowed as evidence—but rather what we can infer from reading the work itself, even if it has not been com-

---

[2] W. K. Wimsatt, Jr., and M. C. Beardsley, "The Intentional Fallacy," reprinted in *Essays in Modern Literary Criticism*, ed. Ray B. West, Jr. (New York, 1952), pp. 174–89.

pletely realized. And do we not do this all the time ourselves when correcting student themes? It is clearly not enough to tell a student that a certain paragraph is out of place or extraneous, that his ending is weak and ineffective, or that his choice of words is inappropriate. How is he to see *why* and then correct it? Do we not say to him: "You are trying to convince such-and-such an audience that a certain idea or course of action is either right or wrong with regard to a given problem; therefore, since this paragraph doesn't logically follow from the way you have set up your problem, or since its topic isn't pertinent to the problem you are trying to resolve, or since this ending leaves your audience undecided about what you would have them think or do, or since your diction is too formal or too informal properly to move this audience—*therefore* it is out of place, or extraneous, or weak, or ineffective, or inappropriate."

Thus the reader interested in perceiving and defining the form of any piece of writing, so that he may use this sense of the whole to guide him in discussing the relevance and efficacy of its parts and their manner of presentation, must begin by trying to recover by inference the end effect aimed at. The purpose of this essay, therefore, is to determine how far and in what ways we can go toward defining the different kinds of ends we are likely to meet in that species of imaginative literature the magnitude of whose represented actions is that of the whole plot, in the hope that we will emerge with a set of preliminary lines of differentiation, derived from actual examples in stories, plays, and novels, which will make available to us a range of alternative hypotheses to apply to any given plot when trying to analyze its organization.

I say "imaginative literature" in order to distinguish the kinds of work which I wish to deal with here, whose general end is to arouse and allay a sequence of emotions in the reader with regard to the career of some particular imagined character for the sake of that imaginative response itself, such as *Great Expectations* or *Washington Square*, from that kind whose general end is to inform us about, or persuade us to adopt, a given idea or course of action with regard to some "real-life" problem, such as Orwell's *1984* or Koestler's *Darkness at Noon*.[3]

[3] Cf. R. S. Crane, "Literature, Philosophy, and the History of Ideas," *MP*, LII (1954), 73–83.

And I say "magnitude of the whole plot" in order to distinguish the nature of the action represented in a plot from other literary forms whose actions are smaller: the *speech,* in which one person acts verbally without being answered (the action represented in most short poems); the *scene,* in which two or more persons speak and act in a single closed situation, the number of persons remaining constant throughout (the action represented in some short poems and many short stories); the *episode,* a system of such scenes grouped around a central incident (the action represented in most short stories and novelettes); and the *plot,* a group of two or more episodes effecting a completed process of change in the main character (the action represented in most plays and novels).[4]

III

THE end of a plot, then, is to represent some completed process of change in the protagonist for the sake of the sequence of emotions which that process evokes in the reader. On the basis of this theory we commit ourselves and our students to a dynamic conception of form—a conception which puts its whole emphasis upon what everyone feels to be the essential quality of plots, that is to say, the sequential flow of events in time and its means and causes, effects and ends. Now, in order to differentiate one plot from another, we must define the kinds of changes we are likely to meet in plays and novels and the corresponding sequences of imaginative response they arouse in the reader.

To understand and respond to this process of change, we need to know its related causes and conditions. The causes of a man's actions—the immediate ones, at least[5]—are to be found

[4] I have taken these terms and distinctions, as well as much else of value, from Elder Olson's "Outline of Poetic Theory," in *Critics and Criticism,* ed. R. S. Crane (Chicago, 1952), pp. 546–66.

[5] There are remoter causes, of course, such as heredity, for example, and the psychological impact upon personality of childhood environment; and these may be used dramatically by an author, as in Butler's *The Way of All Flesh* or the various psychological novels which have become recently quite frequent, as in Jo Sinclair's *Wasteland* (New York, 1946). I suspect, however, that such factors find their way eventually into the terms discussed in the present paragraph.

in the way he conceives of things, in the nature of his goals and purposes, and in the environmental circumstances in which he finds himself. These, then, are the three variables we must consider in defining and understanding the central change around which plots are built: the protagonist's state of mind, his character and behavior, and his situation with regard to the external environment. For example, it is clear that, in *Tom Jones*, much of Tom's failure to maintain his honor and reputation is due to misconceptions of various sorts on his part as well as on the part of others; that we are meant to respond in a certain way to his liaison with Jennie Jones because he does not realize who she is; that we wish him well, in spite of his somewhat careless nature, because he is a sympathetic person who has been put upon by others less admirable than he; and so on.

Professor R. S. Crane has already laid the groundwork for such an approach in "The Plot of *Tom Jones*," [6] where he argues that a "plot" may be conceived of as something more than "merely the material continuity of the story" in relation to the degree of ingenuity revealed by "the variety of incidents it contains, [and] the amount of suspense and surprise it evokes." We may more profitably consider "plot," he says, as a composite of action, character, and thought rather than merely equating it with "action" apart from "the moral qualities of the characters and the operations of their thought." Since there are these three variables involved in any process of change, it follows that a change in any one of them may serve as the unifying principle of a plot, with the remaining two factors—either changing or remaining constant—related as means to that end. "There are, thus, plots of action, plots of character, and plots of thought."

Crane argues further that, in order to determine the form of a given plot, we must continue on and examine the imaginative responses which its unified sequence of events is calculated to evoke in us, for therein lies the ultimate effect or end of this kind of literary work. For it is the desire to arouse our sympathy or aversion, for example, which dictates to an author the kinds of people he portrays and the things he has them do; the desire

[6] This essay first appeared in the *Journal of General Education*. IV (1950), 112–30, and was subsequently included, slightly altered, in *Critics and Criticism*, pp. 616–48, under the title "The Concept of Plot and the Plot of *Tom Jones*."

to provoke our pity or indignation, for example, which determines the sort of fate he designs for a certain character. In this case, the form of a plot is a matter of the relationship between two things: the unified sequence of events involved in the completed process of change, which depends upon whether the synthesizing change is one of action, character, or thought; and the particular sequence of emotions aroused as we read, which depends upon the moving power invested in these events. Thus "we may be said to have grasped the plot in the full artistic sense only when we have analyzed the interplay of desires and expectations sequentially in relation to the incidents by which it is produced." The form of the whole plot, then, is a question of "the capacity of its peculiar synthesis of character, action, and thought to move our feelings powerfully and pleasurably in a certain definite way."

So, in discouraging our students from making plot summaries, we may teach them the alternative procedure of constructing "arguments," that is to say, a synopsis of the unique combination of action, character, and thought which will include in one succinct statement the parts necessary to an understanding of the synthesizing principle binding the whole plot together: the kind of man the protagonist is, what his change is, the degree of his responsibility for what he does and undergoes, and the essential stages of cause and effect bringing about his change. Such a procedure defines for us the form of the action in terms of which the play or novel is constructed but is not a full account of that play or novel itself, since it omits those elements therein which exist for the sake of making the form probable, intelligible, vivid, and moving—elements without which there would be no play or novel in the first place. For the work itself embodies the form in language; this embodiment, what is actually set before us, Crane calls the "scenario." And it is precisely this distinction between the necessary and the probable which a plot summary fails to make, an error of serious consequences in many cases, and especially in such a novel as *Lord Jim*, whose devices of representation include such complexities as frequent chronological shifts and a multiplicity of character narrators.

The argument of the plot of *Great Expectations*, for example, might run somewhat as follows: a young and sensitive boy, born in humble circumstances, conceives and puts into effect, with the help of an anonymous benefactor, an ambitious plan to become a moneyed gentleman in order to prove himself worthy, as he thinks, of a handsome and wealthy girl whom he has come to love; in the process, however, he becomes an idle and worthless snob, feeling ashamed of, and doing all he can to avoid, his old and humble friends and haunts, until the convict who, in secret, has given him the money to establish himself thus reappears and reveals himself; the shock of this discovery produces in our by now young man a change in attitude, so that he finally sees what he has become; he then proceeds to make amends by returning in humility to his old home and friends.

So much for the argument, the parts necessary to the form of the plot. All else in the novel may be accounted for as giving this form body, probability, and moving power. And further critical inquiry would, beginning with such a definition of its form, bring us into a consideration of the devices of representation. The role of Mrs. Joe, for example, Pip's older sister who acts as his stepmother, is a representational one: her ill-natured badgering does not cause Pip to want to leave home—it is Estella's scorn which does that—but it does help preserve partial sympathy for Pip in his rejection of this life—that sympathy which would have been lost altogether if Mrs. Joe had been as noble and admirable as Joe himself. It is necessary, however, as we have seen from the argument above, only that the boy conceive of his ambition to leave home and receive the means to do so. The scenario, therefore, includes many such devices functioning to insure the proper response in the reader, in addition to those scenes where Pip brings food and file to Magwitch, where he is insulted by Estella, where he receives his inheritance, where the convict reappears, and so on, which are necessary to bring about the particular change which organizes the plot. Additional examination of the scenario would cover such topics as the role of the protagonist as narrator; the function of such subordinate characters as Biddy, Orlick, Herbert, Clara, and so on; the figures of speech and symbolic devices; and many more.

Thus far does Professor Crane take us; but since he has contented himself so far (in his published writings) with this general preamble to the problem—in enumerating only the three most basic types of plot and in distinguishing between the form and its embodiment—and a detailed analysis of one novel by way of illustration, I should like to carry his suggestions somewhat further, concentrating for present purposes on the general principles by which we can define the forms of plots rather than on that "more specific kind of criticism of a work which takes the form of the plot as its starting point" and then inquires into the construction of the scenario.[7] For it soon becomes evident to anyone investigating Crane's distinctions that a whole host of subdivisions is required in order that they may be applied with profit to different plots.[8]

IV

BEFORE we can suggest to our students a set of alternative hypotheses for defining the form of a given plot, we must establish the procedure for doing so and define its key terms. The first question we ask is: Who is the protagonist? And we must caution against assuming out of hand that it is always the character whose name appears in the title (it is Brutus and not Caesar who is the protagonist of Shakespeare's *Julius Caesar*, for example), or the one for whom we feel most sympathy and admiration (my male students frequently applaud Stan Kowolski, in *A Streetcar Named Desire*, feeling that Blanche is indeed a fake). The protagonist is the one who undergoes the major change, the one whose career serves as the chief focus of interest, the one around whom all else in the plot revolves. In some instances, such as *The Scarlet Letter* or *All the King's Men* or *The Caine Mutiny*, this is not immediately apparent and requires some close reasoning.

Second, what is his or her character, and how do we respond to it? What is his or her fortune, and do we fear it will become worse and hope it will become better? And what is his or her

[7] I have, however, a detailed analysis of the problem of point of view in fiction which appears in *PMLA*, December, 1955. [See section 3 of this anthology—*Ed.*]

[8] The responsibility for what follows is entirely mine, however, and not Professor Crane's.

thought, and do we feel he or she is sufficiently aware of the facts of the situation and the consequences of his or her behavior in order to be held responsible for what he or she does and undergoes?

Third, which of these three factors undergoes a change as the plot unfolds and reaches its conclusion? There must be at least one change for us to have a plot at all, but if there are two or three, as is frequently the case, we must determine which of these changes is the main change, and how the others are related to that change. It is evident, for example, that the protagonist of *Great Expectations* undergoes a change in thought at the end of the second part of the novel when he discovers who his benefactor is, a change in fortune when he subsequently becomes ill, and a change in character when he returns in humility to the places and friends of his childhood. Yet, it should be equally evident that the plot hinges upon his changes in character and that the other changes are material to that end. How do we know this?—because he has partially alienated our sympathies early in the book by becoming a snob, and our expectations and desires are not allayed until he actually makes overt amends for his bad behavior. We are simply not satisfied when he merely sees himself in a new and proper light, or when he falls sick, for there are still people back home whom he has snubbed and for whom we feel great sympathy and respect—Joe and Biddy. No formula, theory, or procedure can substitute for a careful, imaginative, and intelligent reading; what we do hope for, however, is that these things will make our students more careful, imaginative, and intelligent readers than they were before.

And, finally, we ask for a statement of the argument of the plot which will include all the foregoing in a cause-and-effect relationship. If the student, at this point, has available to him a preliminary list of general possibilities, he will be aided greatly in making up his mind as to what kind of a plot it is with which he is dealing and will all the more easily be able to determine crucial similarities and differences between one plot and another. But he must also be taught to realize that placing a plot in a category, however accurately, is the beginning and not the end of his analysis; the goal is to grasp its artistic organization and not merely to label it and then forget about it. The categories derived below are to be taken as suggestive of the varieties of plots rather than as definitive of their limitations and are designed to provoke rather than bypass thought. Nor is there anything sacred or inviolate about them: it is the critic and not the artistic work which must give way when any question arises, making his terms to suit the work and not forcing the work to suit his terms.

It remains, before going on to that list, to define our key terms a bit more fully. "Action" or "fortune" refers to the protagonist's honor, status, and reputation, his goods, loved ones, health, and well-being. Fortune is revealed in what happens to him—happiness or misery—and to his plans—success or failure. "Character" refers to the protagonist's motives, purposes, and goals, his habits, behavior, and will, and may be noble or base, good or bad, sympathetic or unsympathetic, complete or incomplete, mature or immature. Character is revealed when he decides voluntarily to pursue or abandon a course of action and in whether he can indeed put his decision into effect. And "thought" refers to the protagonist's states of mind, attitudes, reasonings, emotions, beliefs, conceptions, and knowledge. Thought is revealed either omnisciently, as in many novels, or in what the character says when stating a general proposition, arguing a particular point, or explaining his view of a situation.

Since, in any well-organized plot, these three factors—either changing or remaining constant—are inextricably interwoven, one serving as material to another, or as its cause, or as its occasion, or as its sign or manifestation, we must take care not to confuse them. Although they are thus related, they are nonetheless distinct. Thus the protagonist's suicide, as the culmination of a plot, may represent a noble character's decision to atone for the evil he has unwittingly done and the misfortunes he has caused to fall on his head, as in *Othello;* or it may represent the last despairing gesture of a protagonist whose character is no longer sufficient to cope with the problems of his life, as in *The Seagull.* And the difference lies in the latitude of choice we think he has in deciding to live or to die. Or a person's goals (character) may indeed be related to his conceptions (thought), and a change in the latter may cause a change in the former, as in *Great Expectations;* but they may also change independently or even in different directions, as when Bernick, in *Pillars of the Community,* admits his hypocrisy in private long before he decides to do anything about it publicly. Or, again, a person may have a certain goal (character) and yet may be prevented from reaching it by circumstances beyond his control (fortune), as when Prewitt, in *From Here to Eternity,* is destroyed by the group within which he has attempted to preserve some measure of personal autonomy. If a person's goal, however, refers to the attainment of some such moral quality, and if his success or failure in this depends upon his own will power, patience, and self-confidence, as in *The Secret Sharer,* rather than upon circumstance, then it is a problem of character and not of fortune.

We will derive, then, our alternative possibilities in the following manner: we ask first whether the major change is in fortune, character, or thought and derive therefrom our three main categories; we ask further, within each category, whether the particular change is from a satisfactory state to a less satisfactory state or from a less satisfactory to a more satisfactory one; and we ask, finally, how the remaining two factors are related as material to this end. We will then attempt to define the distinctive power of each type "to move our feelings powerfully and pleasurably in a certain definite way," as Crane says. This is not easy to do without going into the details of each plot; but, since this would enlarge an already sizable essay beyond reasonable bounds, we must content ourselves with the barest of hints and suggestions regarding the general range of possibilities. It is sufficiently clear, however, that a good man achieving good fortune, a good man suffering bad fortune, a bad man achieving good fortune, and a bad man suffering bad fortune, for example, produce different effects and therefore comprise different kinds of plots.

In the light of the foregoing distinctions, then, and in relation to these variables, let us see what kinds of plots will emerge.

V

Plots of Fortune

THE ACTION PLOT   The first and most primitive type of plot under this heading is also, I daresay, the most common in terms of the reading public as a whole. The primary, and often the sole, interest lies in "what happens next," and the characters and their thought are portrayed minimally in terms of the bare necessities required to forward the action. That is to say, we rarely, if ever, become involved here in any serious moral or intellectual issue; nor does the outcome have any far-reaching consequences for the fortune, character, or thought of the protagonist, leaving him free to start all over again, it may be, in a sequel; and the pleasures we experience are almost wholly those of suspense, expectation, and surprise, the plot being organized around a basic puzzle and solution cycle. There is a gangster to track down, a murderer to discover and apprehend, a treasure to be gotten, or a planet to be reached. Examples of this type are most frequently found in those classes of fiction called adventure, detective, western, and science-fiction stories. This is not to say, however, that the action plot need always be a subliterary form, since there are many respectable examples which have deservedly become classics of their kind—the novels of R. L. Stevenson, for example, the stories of Sir Arthur Conan Doyle, the mysteries of Wilkie Collins, and so on.

THE PATHETIC PLOT   Here we have a sympathetic protagonist who undergoes misfortune through no particular fault of his own, and hence this type is primarily a plot of suffering. It is frequently the case that his will is in some way weak and his thought naïve and deficient. I call it "pathetic," since our long-range fears for him actually materialize, being scarcely alleviated by sporadic and intermittent short-range hopes, resulting ultimately in sheer pity for his suffering. Notice, for example, how Hardy dwells, in *Tess of the D'Urbervilles*, upon the shameful inadequacy of his heroine's home and school background as a cause of her unfortunate career; this, coupled with the rather supine quality of her determination, the irresistible workings of Nature's fecund processes, and the fact that she had, after all, murdered her unwelcome lover, is sufficient to produce the desired emotional effect at the end when she is arrested and executed.

This type seems indeed a favorite of the "naturalists," as, for example, in such works as *Tess, The Three Sisters, Death of a Salesman, A Streetcar Named Desire, From Here to Eternity,* or *Maggie: A Girl of the Streets,* where a brooding sense of human frailty and futility pervades the whole, leaving one with only a frustrated feeling of pity, sorrow, and loss in the face of the inscrutably deterministic steamroller of circumstance crushing the mewling kitten of human hopes.

THE TRAGIC PLOT If, however, a sympathetic protagonist has also strength of will in addition to a certain degree of sophistication or ability to change his thought, his responsibility for what he does or causes to happen may be correspondingly greater. When such a man suffers misfortune, part or all of which he is responsible for through some serious mistake or error in judgment on his part, and subsequently discovers his error only too late, then we have the tragic plot strictly speaking. There is here the same long-range fear provoked by threatened misfortune and pity for its materialization as in the pathetic plot, but there is also here a more complicated relationship among fortune, character, and thought, resulting in that much-vexed "catharsis" which Aristotle innocently let loose upon the critical world. We may take it to mean for the present purpose, simply that our fear and then our pity are followed by a sense of justice and emotional satisfaction, since the tragic hero not only has had a hand in his own downfall but has also come to recognize that involvement. His ensuing agony of spirit, therefore, although frequently resulting in the death of a good man, is somehow deserved; is, indeed, the best possible end for him, given what he has done or suffered, or is even a necessary atonement for his somewhat imperfect or arrogant nature. Surely this is a complex form, one of the most noble of artistic achievements; but instances may almost be numbered—alas!—on the fingers of one hand: *Oedipus Rex, Antigone, Othello, Hamlet, Lear, Julius Caesar*—and how many others?

THE PUNITIVE PLOT [9] Here we have a protagonist whose character is essentially unsympathetic, in that his goals and purposes are repugnant, yet who may perhaps be admirable for his strength of will and intellectual sophistication, suffering well-deserved misfortune. It is in this type that we most frequently encounter the "satanic" or "Machiavellian" hero-villain close to the hearts of the Elizabethan and Jacobean writers, as in *Doctor Faustus* and *The Duchess of Malfi*, for example, or in Milton's

[9] The term is Olson's (*op. cit.*).

Satan, and which was revived by such nineteenth-century romantics as Byron, Huysmans, Goethe, and so on.

At first our admiration and indignation are curiously compounded as the hero-villain sets in motion his immoral schemes and rises above the ineffectual and moralizing fools by whom he is surrounded. But, when he succeeds in victimizing truly good and admirable people as well, these emotions give way to horror and outrage, and finally we feel a profound sense of satisfied vindication when he reaches his ultimate downfall. Whatever pity we feel is directed toward his victims rather than the protagonist himself, so that the final emotional equilibrium reached here is not to be confused with tragic catharsis. Other instances may be found in *Hedda Gabler, Volpone, Tartuffe,* B. Traven's *The Treasure of Sierra Madre,* Hellman's *The Little Foxes, Richard III,* and *The Changeling.*

THE SENTIMENTAL PLOT Coming now to those plots in which the change in fortune is for the better, we have a very common type involving a sympathetic protagonist who survives the threat of misfortune and comes out all right at the end, although this, too, like the pathetic plot, is a plot of suffering. Our emotional responses here are the obverse of those for the pathetic plot, since the long-range hopes which are aroused ultimately materialize, while the corresponding short-range fears are allayed, the final effect being one of joyous relief at the sight of virtue receiving its just reward. An essential cause of this effect is that, although the protagonist remains steadfast throughout, he is acted upon rather than acting; neither his bad nor his good fortune depends directly upon the quality of his thought or character. *Anna Christie* is a good example of this type, since Anna's final winning of Mat Burke does not depend upon anything she can do or say. *Cymbeline* is another; and, of course, we will find instances aplenty in the nearest motion-picture theater.

THE ADMIRATION PLOT [10] A change in fortune for the better which is caused by a sympathetic protagonist's nobility of character results in a somewhat different effect. Here he gains primarily in honor and reputation and, it may be, even in spite of

[10] I am indebted to Mr. McLaughlin for this term and for much else as well.

a loss of some sort in his material welfare. Our long-range hopes are fulfilled, as in the sentimental plot, but with the difference that our final response is respect and admiration for a man out-doing himself and the expectations of others concerning what a man is normally capable of. *The Conquest of Granada* is the prime example of this type, while the stage version of *Mr. Roberts* and a story by H. L. Davis entitled "Open Winter" provide modern instances.

VI
Plots of Character

THE MATURING PLOT   It may be more instructive, in dealing with plots which turn upon a change in character, to begin with those types in which the change is for the better, of which there seem, happily, to be a greater number. The most common of these involves a sympathetic protagonist whose goals are either mistakenly conceived or undetermined, and whose will is consequently rudderless and vacillating. This insufficiency is frequently the result of inexperience and naïveté, or even of absolute wrongheadedness, in his beliefs and attitudes. If this latter is the cause, some means must be devised for changing his thought; in any case, his character must be given strength and direction, and this may be accomplished through some drastic, or even fatal, misfortune—as when the protagonist in *Lord Jim* gladly accepts death as a way of finally proving his regained strength and purpose. Since this type frequently involves the coming-of-age of young people, we may call it the maturing plot. Our long-range hopes that the protagonist will choose the right course after all are confirmed, and our final response is a sense of righteous satisfaction. And it is this crucial element of choice, of coming finally to a radical decision, which is the distinguishing quality of this type. *Great Expectations* is as pure an example of this type as we are likely to find; other instances are to be found in *The Way of All Flesh, Diana of the Crossways, A Portrait of the Artist as a Young Man, The Secret Sharer, The Portrait of a Lady,* Ferner Nuhn's *Ten,* or Faulkner's *The Bear.*

THE REFORM PLOT Somewhat similar is another form of character change for the better, with the difference that the protagonist's thought is sufficient from the beginning. That is to say, he is doing wrong and he knows it, but his weakness of will causes him to fall away from what he himself knows to be the just and proper path. Faced with the problem either of revealing to others his weakness or of concealing it under a mask of virtue and respectability, he chooses the latter course at the outset. The problem then becomes one of devising the means of forcing his hand, of making him choose the alternative course. Thus, after having been led to admire him at the beginning, we feel impatience and irritation when we begin seeing through his mask, and then indignation and outrage when he continues to deceive others, and, finally, a sense of confirmed and righteous satisfaction when he makes the proper choice at last. In the maturing plot there is some pity for the protagonist, because he acts and suffers under a mistaken view of things, but it is exactly this element which is missing in the reform plot. The two chief examples of this type which come to mind are *The Scarlet Letter* and *The Pillars of the Community*. And in certain respects it resembles the punitive plot in that the protagonist is a pious hypocrite or charlatan impostor of some sort but is different in that he is reformed at the end rather than merely punished.

THE TESTING PLOT The distinctive quality of this type is that a sympathetic, strong, and purposeful character is pressured, in one way or another, to compromise or surrender his noble ends and habits: he either takes the bribe or he suffers the consequences. He wavers, and the plot turns on the question of whether or not he will remain steadfast. Our sympathies here are curiously compounded, since he places himself in danger of misfortune if he persists, and the temptation he withstands would, if yielded to, better his material welfare. Thus we feel he should give it up and save his neck, and yet if he does, he will pay a price by losing his own self-respect and our respect for him as well. When he makes the only proper choice, we end with a feeling of satisfaction that our faith in him has been justified. The chief exhibit of this type would be *For Whom the Bell Tolls*, and I have noticed a trend in this direction in many television plays of the more serious sort.

THE DEGENERATION PLOT   A character change for the worse occurs when we start with a protagonist who was at one time sympathetic and full of ambition and subject him to some crucial loss which results in his utter disillusionment. He then has to choose between picking up the threads of his life and starting over again; or giving up his goals and ambitions altogether. If he chooses the former course, we have what may be termed "the resignation plot," but, since I know of only one such plot—*Uncle Vanya*—I have not reserved a special section for it. Chekhov, indeed, seems to have been obsessed with the problem of how a person can live after all his ideals, hopes, and goals have been shattered, but he most frequently had his protagonists choose the latter course, as in *Ivanov* and *The Seagull*. There is a sequence of feeble and short-range hopes followed by the materialization of long-range fears, but I am not sure whether the final effect is one of pity or of impatience and contempt for such weakness. It all depends upon how convinced we have become that the protagonist has in fact only one real choice he can make, upon how impossible staying alive and trying again seems to be. My own students, for example, do not respond as sympathetically to Chekhov's gloom as I do, but that may be due to the ever widening gulf between our ages. Other examples are to be found in *The Emperor Jones* and *Tender Is the Night*.

VII
Plots of Thought

THE EDUCATION PLOT   Since those plots which turn upon a change in thought seem to be a comparatively recent development in the history of the art—and here it would take an Erich Auerbach to explain the cultural causes of this phenomenon—there are fewer works to talk about. The most common type, however, involves a change in thought for the better in terms of the protagonist's conceptions, beliefs, and attitudes. It resembles the maturing plot in that his thought at the outset is somehow inadequate and is then improved, but it does not continue on to demonstrate the effects of this beneficial change on his behavior. This inadequacy may be either sophisticated, where the protagonist has been through a series of disillusioning experiences and has therefore become cynical or fatalistic, as in *All the King's Men* and *The Confidential Agent;* or naïve, where he has simply not yet been exposed to alternative possibilities, as in *How Beautiful with Shoes* and *The Death of Ivan Ilyich.* The problem is now to subject him to some sort of threat or trial which will serve to change his conceptions in the direction of a more comprehensive view; or, as the rather verbose Jack Burden expresses it in the closing pages of *All the King's Men,* "It is the story of a man who lived in the world and to him the world looked one way for a long time and then it looked another and very different way."

The curve of our emotional responses here follows a cycle of short-range fears and long-range hopes, in that a sympathetic person undergoes a threat of some sort and emerges into a new and better kind of wholeness at the end, with a final sense of relief, satisfaction, and pleasure. Other examples of this type are to be found in *Huckleberry Finn, Marius the Epicurean, To the Lighthouse, War and Peace,* Irwin Shaw's *An Act of Faith, Winterset,* and Gorki's *One Autumn Night.*

THE REVELATION PLOT This type hinges upon the protagonist's ignorance concerning the essential facts of his situation. It is not, then, a question of his attitudes and beliefs but rather of his knowledge, and he must discover the truth before he can come to a decision. The clearest and neatest example I know of is Roald Dahl's *Beware of the Dog,* in which the protagonist, a wounded R.A.F. pilot, comes to discover that he is in enemy hands and thereby avoids the danger of unwittingly revealing classified combat information. He wakes from his coma in a hospital which, to all appearances, is in England. A faint sense of suspicion gradually grows in his mind, until he manages to confirm it beyond a doubt, and at the end he gives only his name, rank, and serial number when questioned. We begin by feeling that everything is fine; our short-range fears develop and then are superseded by our long-range hopes—he is in enemy hands all right, but he has found it out just in time—followed by a final sense of relief and pleasure.

THE AFFECTIVE PLOT There is a change in attitude and belief here but not of the general and philosophical sort which characterizes the education plot. The problem in this type is to come to see some other person in a different and truer light than before, which involves a change in feeling. This change, depending upon whether the discovery is pleasant or unpleasant, will leave the protagonist happy and hopeful or sad and resigned, and our emotional responses will vary accordingly. Examples of this type are to be found in *Pride and Prejudice,* O'Connor's *My Oedipus Complex, Daisy Miller, The Petrified Man,* Jean Stafford's *A Country Love Story,* Wharton's *The Other Two,* Maugham's *Mackintosh,* Ruth Suckow's *Golden Wedding,* James's *Paste,* Strindberg's *Autumn,* and Shaw's *Arms and the Man.*

THE DISILLUSIONMENT PLOT   In opposition to the education plot, we have that type in which a sympathetic protagonist starts out in the full bloom of faith in a certain set of ideals and, after being subjected to some kind of loss, threat, or trial, loses that faith entirely. Such is the case in *The Great Gatsby,* for example, where Gatsby's "dream" depends upon his winning back Daisy, upon whom that dream has come to depend. When his grandstand play to do so fails, however, and he sees that she is not worthy of his conception of her, he has nothing left to live for, and his subsequent death at the hands of Wilson is an act of mercy. Since this plot leaves its hero at the end somewhat like a puppet without wires or a clock with a broken mainspring, our long-range fears eventually succeed in thwarting our short-range hopes, and we are left with a final sense of loss and pity. We find in O'Neill's *The Hairy Ape,* Joyce's *A Little Cloud,* and O'Connor's *The Storyteller* further examples of this type.

VIII

HAVING named, defined, and illustrated some fourteen types of plot forms, what have we accomplished after all? Another set of pigeonholes into which our students can stuff literary works and forget about them? Surely not, for no one can decide which type the form of a given plot is without, first, reading it very attentively and, second, thinking back over it with extreme care.

This, at least, is a gain not to be despised, even if the student comes out with an erroneous theory after all. And when that happens, which is not infrequently the case, it falls upon the teacher and the class to reason through the whole problem again, in the light of those remaining alternatives which seem most plausible, in an effort to hit upon a more satisfactory theory. There are no a priori or prescriptive answers, then, in this procedure, nor does the right answer rule the classroom by the weight of the teacher's authority alone.

And, finally, if we want our students to go on and discuss the parts and devices and how they are related to the whole, then it follows that we must have a conception of the whole which will enable them to do so. We do not isolate techniques for the sake of analysis only; it is our definition of the whole which makes relevant our interpretation of these techniques. Not categories for their own sake, then, but a variety of possible ways of seeing wholes has been the aim of this essay. For if we would examine the pertinence and efficiency of the parts and devices of a given plot, we must begin with a hypothesis as to *what* those things are relevant *to* and effective *for*. A definition of the whole, in sum, provides the enveloping context, the limit or control, in terms of which whatever else we may say about a plot derives its significance and its point.

HENRY JAMES

FORESHORTENING

There was always the difficulty—I have in the course of these so numerous preliminary observations repeatedly referred to it, but the point is so interesting that it can scarce be made too often—that the simplest truth about a human entity, a situation, a relation, an aspect of life, however small, on behalf of which

From the Preface to Daisy Miller.

the claim to charmed attention is made, strains ever, under one's hand, more intensely, *most* intensely, to justify that claim; strains ever, as it were, toward the uttermost end or aim of one's meaning or of its own numerous connexions; struggles at each step, and in defiance of one's raised admonitory finger, fully and completely to express itself. Any real art of representation is, I make out, a controlled and guarded acceptance, in fact a perfect economic mastery, of that conflict: the general sense of the expansive, the explosive principle in one's material thoroughly noted, adroitly allowed to flush and colour and animate the disputed value, but with its other appetites and treacheries, its characteristic space-hunger and space-cunning, kept down. The fair flower of this artful compromise is to my sense the secret of "foreshortening"—the particular economic device for which one must have a name and which has in its single blessedness and its determined pitch, I think, a higher price than twenty other clustered loosenesses; and just because full-fed statement, just because the picture of as many of the conditions as possible made and kept proportionate, just because the surface iridescent, even in the short piece, by what is beneath it and what throbs and gleams through, are things all conducive to the only compactness that has a charm, to the only spareness that has a force, to the only simplicity that has a grace—those, in each order, that produce the *rich* effect.

IMPROVISATION

Nothing is so easy as improvisation, the running on and on of invention; it is sadly compromised, however, from the moment its stream breaks bounds and gets into flood. Then the waters may spread indeed, gathering houses and herds and crops and cities into their arms and wrenching off, for our amusement, the whole face of the land—only violating by the same stroke our sense of the course and the channel, which is our sense of the uses of a stream and the virtue of a story. . . . To improvise with extreme freedom and yet at the same time without the possibility of ravage, without the hint of a flood; to keep the stream, in a word, on something like ideal terms with itself: that was

From the Preface to The Aspern Papers.

here my definite business. The thing was to aim at absolute single-ness, clearness and roundness, and yet to depend on an imagination working freely, working (call it) with extravagance; by which law it would n't be thinkable except as free and would n't be amusing except as controlled.

INITIAL INTENTIONS AND FINAL FORMS

When I think indeed of those of my many false measurements that have resulted, after much anguish, in decent symmetries, I find the whole case, I profess, a theme for the philosopher. The little ideas one would n't have treated save for the design of keeping them small, the developed situations that one would never with malice prepense have undertaken, the long stories that had thoroughly meant to be short, the short subjects that had underhandedly plotted to be long, the hypocrisy of modest beginnings, the audacity of misplaced middles, the triumph of intentions never entertained—with these patches, as I look about, I see my experience paved: an experience to which nothing is wanting save, I confess, some grasp of its final lesson.

From the Preface to The Awkward Age.

TIME, DEVELOPMENT, AND COMPOSITION

To re-read "Roderick Hudson" was to find one remark so promptly and so urgently prescribed that I could at once only take it as pointing almost too stern a moral. It stared me in the face that the time-scheme of the story is quite inadequate, and positively to that degree that the fault but just fails to wreck it. The thing escapes, I conceive, with its life: the effect sought is fortunately more achieved than missed, since the interest of the subject bears down, auspiciously dissimulates, this particular flaw in the treatment. Everything occurs, none the less, too punctually and moves too fast: Roderick's disintegration, a gradual process, and of which the exhibitional interest is exactly that it *is* gradual and occasional, and thereby traceable and watchable, swallows two years in a mouthful, proceeds quite *not*

From the Preface to Roderick Hudson.

by years, but by weeks and months, and thus renders the whole view the disservice of appearing to present him as a morbidly special case. The very claim of the fable is naturally that he *is* special, that his great gift makes and keeps him highly exceptional; but that is not for a moment supposed to preclude his appearing typical (of the general type) as well; for the fictive hero successfully appeals to us only as an eminent instance, as eminent as we like, of our own conscious kind. My mistake on Roderick's behalf—and not in the least of conception, but of composition and expression—is that, at the rate at which he falls to pieces, he seems to place himself beyond our understanding and our sympathy. These are not our rates, we say; we ourselves certainly, under like pressure,—for what is it after all?—would make more of a fight. We conceive going to pieces—nothing is easier, since we see people do it, one way or another, all round us; but this young man must either have had less of the principle of development to have had so much of the principle of collapse, or less of the principle of collapse to have had so much of the principle of development. "On the basis of so great a weakness," one hears the reader say, "where was your idea of the interest? On the basis of so great an interest, where is the provision for so much weakness?" One feels indeed, in the light of this challenge, on how much too scantly projected and suggested a field poor Roderick and his large capacity for ruin are made to turn round. It has all begun too soon. as I say, and too simply, and the determinant function attributed to Christina Light, the character of well-nigh sole agent of his catastrophe that this unfortunate young woman has forced upon her, fails to commend itself to our sense of truth and proportion.

It was not, however, that I was at ease on this score even in the first fond good faith of composition; I felt too, all the while, how many more ups and downs, how many more adventures and complications my young man would have had to know, how much more experience it would have taken, in short, either to make him go under or to make him triumph. The greater complexity, the superior truth, was all more or less present to me; only the question was, too dreadfully, how make it present to the reader? How boil down so many facts in the alembic, so that the distilled result, the produced appearance, should have intensity, lucidity, brevity, beauty, all the merits required for my effect? How, when it was already so difficult, as I found, to proceed even as I *was* proceeding? It did n't help, alas, it only maddened, to remember that Balzac would have known how, and would have yet asked no additional credit for it. All the difficulty I could dodge still struck me, at any rate, as leaving more than enough; and yet I was already consciously in presence, here, of the most interesting question the artist has to consider. To give the image and the sense of certain things while still keeping them subordinate to his plan, keeping them in relation to matters more immediate and apparent, to give all the sense, in a word, without all the substance or all the surface, and so to summarize and foreshorten, so to make values both rich and sharp, that the mere procession of items and profiles is not only, for the occasion, superseded, but is, for essential quality, almost "compromised"—such a case of delicacy proposes itself at every turn to the painter of life who wishes both to treat his chosen subject and to confine his necessary picture. It is only by doing such things that art becomes exquisite, and it is only by positively becoming exquisite that it keeps clear of becoming vulgar, repudiates the coarse industries that masquerade in its name. This eternal time-question is accordingly, for the novelist, always there and always formidable; always insisting on the *effect* of the great lapse and passage, of the "dark backward and abysm," by the terms of truth, and on the effect of compression, of composition and form, by the terms of literary arrangement. It is really a business to terrify all but stout hearts into abject omission and mutilation, though the terror would indeed be more general were the general consciousness of the difficulty greater. It is not by consciousness of difficulty, in truth, that the story-teller is mostly ridden; so prodigious a number of stories would otherwise scarce get themselves (shall it be called?) "told." None was ever very well told, I think, under the law of mere elimination—inordinately as that device appears in many quarters to be depended on. I remember doing my best not to be reduced to it for "Roderick," at the same time that I did so helplessly and consciously beg a thousand questions. What I clung to as my principle of simplification was the precious truth that I was dealing, after all, essentially with an Action, and that no action, further, was ever made historically vivid without a certain factitious compactness; though this logic indeed opened up

horizons and abysses of its own. But into these we must plunge
on some other occasion.

DELICATE ADUSTMENTS AND AN EXQUISITE CHEMISTRY

To put all that is possible of one's idea into a form and com-
pass that will contain and express it only by delicate adjustments
and an exquisite chemistry, so that there will at the end be
neither a drop of one's liquor left nor a hair's breadth of the rim
of one's glass to spare—every artist will remember how often
that sort of necessity has carried with it its particular inspiration. Therein lies the secret of the appeal, to his mind, of the
successfully *foreshortened* thing, where representation is arrived
at, as I have already elsewhere had occasion to urge, not by the
addition of items (a light that has for its attendant shadow a possible dryness) but by the art of figuring synthetically, a compactness into which the imagination may cut thick, as into the
rich density of wedding-cake.

From the Preface to The Tragic Muse.

PHILIP STEVICK

THE THEORY OF FICTIONAL CHAPTERS

I

"Really, universally, relations stop nowhere," writes Henry
James in the preface to *Roderick Hudson*, "and the exquisite
problem of the artist is eternally but to draw, by a geometry of
his own, the circle within which they shall happily *appear* to do
so. He is in the perpetual predicament that the continuity of
things is the whole matter, for him, of comedy and tragedy;

From The Western Humanities Review, *XX (1966). Reprinted by permission of* The Western Humanities Review.

that this continuity is never, by the space of an instant or an inch, broken, and that, to do anything at all, he has at once intensely to consult and intensely to ignore it." [1] It is not only fiction, of course, that must end. All art ends, music with silence, the painting with its frame or its wall, literature of any genre at least with the covers of the book. But it is the special fate of the artist in extended prose, his "perpetual predicament" in James's phrase, that his art must "end" not only once but again and again. His problem is perhaps not different in kind from that of the dramatist or the writer of extended narrative poetry, but it is different in degree and intensity. For the central tradition of the novel represents a search for artistic equivalents of change and continuity, the artistic equivalents of the amplitude and variety of experience, in a way that narrative poetry and the drama seldom do. As the one genre which most consistently displays an awareness of time in its minutely ordinary passage, it is especially paradoxical that traditionally this very temporal continuity should be so frequently interrupted. Thirty-seven times in *The Wings of the Dove* white space interrupts its richly detailed continuity, in *Vanity Fair* sixty-seven times, and in *Don Quixote* one hundred twenty-six. Although "continuity" must have meant something vastly different to the author of *Lazarillo de Tormes*, to Fielding, to Sterne, to Galsworthy, and to the Joyce of *Finnegans Wake*, yet for all of them, to make a continuous prose fiction was to make it out of partly discrete, partly enclosed units. Of a formal principle so nearly universal, so apparently central to the purposes of fiction, it is worth asking why.

One way of finding an answer is to seek a common ground between experience and art, particularly in the impulse to enclose, to make a pattern. At its simplest this impulse demonstrates itself in that paradigmatic gestalt formation by which an observer sees three dots and perceives the possibility that they may become corners of a triangle. An observer of the sky separates figure from ground and perceives that one group of stars resembles a "W" and another resembles a crab. An observer sees a depression in the earth, contrasts the depression with its surrounding plane, and makes it a gestalt by calling it a "hole." As Köhler points out, built into every language are hundreds of

[1] *The Art of the Novel*, ed. R. P. Blackmur (New York, 1934), p. 5.

words which refer to this pattern-making faculty: brink, edge, beginning, end, close, piece, part, rest, remainder, proceeding, finishing, continuing, deviating, bending, retarding, and so on. Thus the impulse to enclose is a basic property of the mind. And consequently, the impulse to shape narratives into patterns is simply the ineluctable result of the human perceptions that lie at its basis. Moreover the effect of literature, as Susanne Langer maintains, is to create a mode of "virtual memory" in which this pattern-making impulse is more capable of fulfillment than in immediate experience.

If the impulse to make gestalts is universal, both in experience and in art, it is not always equally possible to fulfill. In the rather thin ground which surrounds Cassiopeia, one can easily separate the constellation. Within the Milky Way, separate figures are all but impossible. Beyond a certain point, if the raw data of experience are numerous enough and indistinguishable enough, the gestalt perception fails. To shift from experience to art, an observer, from a single point in space and in a rather short period of time, can respond to most paintings, even one so crowded, say, as an historical panorama by David, as a satisfyingly enclosed gestalt. In the case of extended narrative, this capacity to respond directly to the formal enclosure of a work is frustrated, frustrated by those qualities that make it all but impossible to see figures and grounds in the Milky Way. Extended narrative, that is, is experienced at length; and inevitably it far exceeds most paintings, most sculptures, most lyric poems in the sheer bulk of its detail. The classic description of this inability to experience extended narrative directly is in the eloquent first page of Percy Lubbock's *The Craft of Fiction:*

> To grasp the shadowy and fantasmal form of a book, to hold it fast, to turn it over and survey it at leisure—that is the effort of a critic of books, and it is perpetually defeated. Nothing, no power, will keep a book steady and motionless before us, so that we may have time to examine its shape and design. As quickly as we read, it melts and shifts in the memory; even at the moment when the last page is turned, a great part of the book, its finer detail, is already vague and doubtful. A little later, after a few days or months, how much is really left of it? A cluster of impressions, some clear points emerging from a mist of uncertainty, this is all we can hope to possess, generally speaking, in the name of a book. . . . Nobody would venture to criticize a building, a statue, a picture, with nothing before him but the memory of a single

glimpse caught in passing; yet the critic of literature, on the whole, has to found his opinion upon little more.[2]

The short story can be read in a sitting. Both in its classic theory and in its practice, the short story seeks to achieve an economy and unity of form which enable the reader to experience it as, in fact, a gestalt. James was fond of speaking of the short novel as "the shapely nouvelle," suggesting that even at the length of forty or fifty pages, a narrative is capable of being so managed as to enable the reader to respond directly to its form, in its entirety. But narrative of the length of epic, romance, and novel exceeds the limits of the reader's pattern-making faculty. Perhaps the ideal reader of extended narrative is one who reads the work at a single sitting, without diversion and without interruption. But even if this were frequently done, it is not at all likely that the frustrations which Percy Lubbock describes would be prevented.

If art in general, then, demands in creator and observer a heightening of the gestalt perception which organizes experience itself, then the writer of extended narrative is obliged to make his work out of subordinate, distinguishable parts, each of which can be seen as a form in itself. Thus the writer induces anticipations which can be fulfilled at different levels, days which begin and end, alliances which are made and broken, locations which are visited temporarily, antagonists that are vanquished. Since, as I have argued, the bulk of a narrative work exceeds one's gestalt perception, one sees the pattern of the whole work, the moral education of the hero, say, or the vicissitudes of a love affair, by seeing its subordinate configurations in turn. Or, to put it another way, one responds to the form of an epic by responding to the successive forms of its books; one responds to the form of a novel by responding to its chapters. And without the possibility of responding to the form of its chapters, as more or less discrete units, an understanding of the whole work would be infinitely more difficult than it now is.

Of these subordinate configurations, the writer has several theoretical options open to him. First, he can present the data of his book, or chapter, or episode along with their enclosure. In terms of gestalt psychology, the writer here gives us three dots

[2]   (New York, 1921), pp. 1–2.

and then proceeds to show us, by drawing lines, how his three dots form a triangle. Secondly, the writer can present the materials of an apparent gestalt but enclose these materials in a way different from our expectations. Here the writer gives us three dots, but just as we expect the drawing of a triangle, he surprises us and connects the dots by means of a circle instead. Wertheimer has defined the critical intelligence as "the process of destroying one gestalt in favor of a better one," [3] a definition capable, certainly, of referring to aspects of the narrative imagination. Third, the writer can provide us with materials suggesting the means for their enclosure yet withholding from us the enclosure itself. Here he gives us three dots and ends his presentation, leaving us with the responsibility for recognizing the possibility of a triangle if we wish. Fourth, the writer can present us with materials which suggest an ambiguity of enclosures. Here he gives us an irregular sprinkling of dots; we may experiment, if we wish, with lines and curves and figures, but any enclosure which we make is uncertain, subjective, and arbitrary, like interpretations of Rorschach ink-blots. In each of these four situations, an order and a shape is imposed upon events in time. And it is this order which is the rationale of the chapter.

More than a heightened sense of meaning, however, the division of a long narrative provides a purely esthetic pleasure, one of the few comparatively abstract pleasures which an art so little abstract as narrative art can provide. Kenneth Burke writes of the categorical expectations which one brings to art of all kinds. One begins a sonnet expecting that it will contain fourteen lines, one begins Pope expecting couplets, one begins an epic expecting an invocation. Contrary to those expectations which arise during the reading of a work, categorical expectations exist anterior to the reading. As these expectations are fulfilled, they provide what Burke calls the appeal of "conventional form," the appeal "of form *as form*." Burke cites the example of "the final Beethoven rejoicing of a Beethoven finale." "The audience 'awaits' it," Burke argues, "before the first bar of the music has been played." [4] At least since Homer, audiences of extended narratives

---

[3] Quoted in R. W. Gerard, "The Biological Basis of Imagination," in *The Creative Process,* ed. Brewster Ghiselin (New York, 1955), p. 231.

[4] *Counterstatement* (Chicago, 1957), pp. 126–27.

have expected categorically that the work will be divided, that it will contain within its beginning and end a series of subordinate beginnings and endings. And the fulfillment of this expectation evokes in the reader something not unlike the abstract formal pleasure one finds in a Chinese vase. Jane Austen begins a chapter of *Emma* thus: "The hair was curled, and the maid sent away, and Emma sat down to think and be miserable.—It was a wretched business indeed!" (Ch. 16) If part of the pleasure one finds in those two sentences is in the ironic juxtaposition of the curling of hair and the onset of misery, part of one's pleasure may also derive from the perception that the ancient art of beginning a new episode has been carried off with consummate skill.

Susanne Langer has written of the impulse, the necessity really, to compose the chapters of experience as an act of understanding. She cites a passage of *Sons and Lovers* in which Mrs. Morel must compose events before she can cope with them. "For a while she could not control her consciousness; mechanically she went over the last scene, then over it again, certain moments coming each time like a brand red-hot down on her soul; and each time she enacted again the past hour, each time the brand came down at the same points, till the mark was burnt in, and the pain burnt out, and at last she came to herself." "Life," Mrs. Langer continues, "is incoherent unless we give it form. Usually the process of formulating our own situations and our own biography is not as conscious as Mrs. Morel's struggle to conceive the outrage she suffered; but it follows the same pattern— we 'put it into words,' tell it to ourselves, compose it in terms of 'scenes,' so that in our minds we can enact all its important moments." [5] We have learned how to do this, how to arrange and organize experience so as to cope with it emotionally, from all the literature we have ever read, argues Mrs. Langer, from nursery tales to the most sophisticated fiction. Conversely, as 1 have argued, every writer has learned from experience the necessity for composing his art into intelligible parts when the whole exceeds the limits of the esthetic understanding.

[5] *Feeling and Form* (New York, 1953), p. 400.

II

THE great novelists of the English eighteenth century faced the problem of making chapters in rather different ways. Their different responses shed some significant light, beyond those categorical reasons I have advanced above, on the question of why chapters should exist in any given novel. In *Moll Flanders*, Defoe makes no apparent chapters; the novel is typographically continuous. Nevertheless, it does contain narrative units. One such unit ends thus:

> But this affair had its end too; for after about a year, I found that he did not come so often as usual, and at last he left it off altogether without any dislike or bidding adieu; and so there was an end of that short scene of life, which added no great store to me, only to make more work for repentance.

Clearly such a passage indicates the end of a "chapter," even though such a unit is not numbered and set apart typographically from what follows it. What Defoe, or rather Moll, summarizes suggests the rationale for such narrative division. Moll's life, as the summary indicates, is neither cumulative nor climatic but serial. Despite certain mechanisms of Defoe designed to show her growth in callousness or her progress toward repentance, her life is composed not of stages in her education or her moral development but of episodes which do not have (or seldom have) any necessary causal relation with what follows. A narrative unit in Defoe lasts as long as the particular dramatic situation of Moll lasts; when the episode is finished—an affair, a new career, a journey—the narrative unit is finished and a new one begins. Defoe's lack of structural subtlety is in danger of seeming a bit unrewarding to the reader. But the point is that some lives are climactic, some cumulative and some merely serial, and Moll's happens to be one of the latter. She gains little insight as the novel proceeds except for the acquisition of the cunning that comes with experience; but great numbers of people outside of novels gain little insight into themselves as they live their lives and it would be presumptuous to insist that such a life style cannot be adapted to novelistic purposes. Moll is motivated by no transcendent goal in a dramatically interesting and coherent way; but again, outside of novels, few people consistently pursue an intelligible goal. In other words, an episodic organization is as legitimate as any other because experience, from a particular point of view, is episodic. Birth, marriage, death, accusation, exoneration, renunciation—events such as these are real beginnings and endings. And thus Defoe's technique, with its absence of physical division and its bare minimum of progressive movement, with its barely differentiated series of loves and losses, crimes and punishments, its virtual elimination of the possibility of crisis and decision, is a remarkably persuasive mimetic structure, fashioned as it is because that is the way experience is felt.

In Richardson, the nearly discrete episodes that life contains not only do not provide the organizing principle, as they do in Defoe, but Richardson's multiple narration and amplitude of detail blur these divisions so as to make them seem almost not to exist. That is, if the end of an action is contained within a letter from Clarissa, it will probably recur in a letter from Lovelace, perhaps in another letter from Anna Howe, and perhaps the events will be further reflected upon by Jack Belford. No event is likely to seem very gratifyingly ended in such circumstances. The separate books within Richardson's novels are arbitrary divisions, divisions in which the formal necessity to finish and enclose does not exist, and the individual letter contains within its own stylized rhetoric all the beginnings and endings that an epistolary novelist ever needs.

This is not to say, however, that dividing a narrative by means of letters is only mechanical or expedient, that the division itself has nothing to do with the formal effects of the narrative. Midway through a letter to her mother, Clarissa writes:

> If I do *not* answer him, he will be made desperate, and think himself justified in resenting the treatment he complains of: if I *do*, and if, in compliment to me, he forbears to resent what he thinks himself entitled to resent; be pleased, madam, to consider the obligation he will suppose he lays me under.

The same letter ends thus:

> And so leaving the whole to your own wisdom, and whether you choose to consult my papa and uncles upon this humble application, or not;

or whether I shall be allowed to write an answer to Mr. Lovelace or not (and if allowed so to do, I beg your direction, by whom to send it); I remain, Honoured Madam,

> Your unhappy, but ever dutiful daughter,
> *Cl. Harlowe.*[6]

The rhetoric of eighteen-century correspondence provides the letter with its own resolution. Indeed, probably no other unit of prose ends so conclusively and satisfyingly as the archaic epistolary form, with its syntactic continuity with the signature. Yet the letter itself could not have been more inconclusive. With its qualifications and parentheses, its piled-up conditional clauses, the letter is a masterful representation of uncertainty. Thus, in the tension between formal units which begin and end hundreds of times and a psychological content which never ends, Richardson builds a formal structure of great power. Formally, *Clarissa* expresses the agonies of stopping and starting, of waiting until tomorrow, of waiting for replies, of asking deliverance and expressing resignation. In short, it is in part because the individual letters of *Clarissa* each must end, and because they do so with such power, that the novel achieves the sustained and continuously tragic suspense that it does.

Fielding is the first (and one of the very few) English novelists to theorize on chapter division. But his theory comes in a chapter so arch, so puzzlingly ironic as to leave quite unclear what he meant to assert. The common reader, he begins, may imagine that the division of a narrative is intended only "to swell our works to a much larger bulk than they would otherwise be extended to." On the contrary, divisions are for the convenience of the reader, not the author. A space between chapters may be regarded as "an inn or resting-place," and thus may give occasion for a retrospective reflection on the preceding chapter. A work without such occasions for rest and reflection "resembles the opening of wilds or seas, which tires the eye and fatigues the spirit when entered upon." Secondly, chapter division gives the author an opportunity for inscribing at the beginning of a chapter what is to come. Chapter divisions, moreover, prevent the dog-earing of a book. And besides, they have the sanction of antiquity, since Homer and Virgil divided their epics into books. Fielding's chapter on chapters ends with this metaphor: "it be-

6 Modern Library edition, p. 74.

comes an author generally to divide a book, as it does a butcher to joint his meat, for such assistance is of great help to both the reader and the carver." [7]

Certainly Fielding's final metaphor is ironic, as is his image of Homer bringing out the *Odyssey* book by book, hawking each one separately. Yet it is difficult to assume that the entire chapter is flippant. Fielding's initial point, that chapter division permits rest and reflection while the absence of division results in a kind of spiritual fatigue, makes perfect esthetic sense when esthetic principles are reasoned by psychological values. The idea is not unlike the principle which I have argued for in the preceding section, the need for limiting the size of the fictional unit to the capacity of the reader's gestalt-making faculty. Evidence of Fielding's seriousness, however, lies finally in his practice. For he does seem often to divide his narrative according to the duration of attention which he can legitimately ask of his readers. His chapters, that is, are often more or less arbitrarily ended units which are over when it is time for narrator and reader (and perhaps the characters themselves) to reflect on what has just happened. A chapter from *Tom Jones,* for example, involves the identity of Mrs. Waters, reflection on the Man of the Hill, Partridge's rustic wit, the belligerence of a sergeant, the effects of a considerable quantity of alehouse liquor, the appearance of Sophia, and so on. It is the kind of chapter which could go on for many times its length. But it ends after just about as many pages as any chapter in Fielding with the reflections:

> The beauty of Jones highly charmed her [Mrs. Waters'] eye; but as she could not see his heart, she gave herself no concern about it. She could feast heartily at the table of love, without reflecting that some other already had been, or hereafter might be, feasted with the same repast. A sentiment which, if it deals but little in refinements, deals, however, much in substance; and is less capricious, and perhaps less ill-natured and selfish, than the desire of those females who can be contented enough to abstain from the possession of their lovers, provided they are sufficiently satisfied that no one else possesses them.[8]

That is, after all the mock sententiousness and misapplied learning, the misunderstood intentions and the language gone wrong, the passionate earnestness and the calculated insincerity of the

[7] *Joseph Andrews,* ed. Martin Battestin (Boston, 1961), pp. 73–75.
[8] Modern Library edition, p. 441.

chapter, it is time to get back to Jones, to his temptations, his love, and to the nature of woman. It is not that the chapter is an episode in any conventional sense of the word, with its own beginning, middle, and its own inevitable end; it is not that it ends out of any internal necessity; it has simply gone on long enough. Such a chapter makes, of course, only the most fragile of gestalts, but there is still a certain configural validity in the kind of chapter which might be entitled "Many Things Happened Which Are Here Related."

All of this is not to say that chapter divisions in Fielding are all so arbitrary as the one I have described or that chapters exist only for the accommodation of the reader's interest. In fact, Fielding's technique is so various that it provides a broad range of justifications for the convention. Certainly it is possible to change a scene more conveniently between chapters, as Fielding usually does, than within them. And it is possible to omit irrelevant periods of time between chapters more easily than to offer a perfunctory summary at mid-chapter, again as Fielding usually does. It is possible for Fielding to use a chapter break for an adjustment of his tone; and thus the modulations from the narrator's discussion of his art in Fielding's prolegomenous chapters to his narrative proper, from the broad irony of a chapter on, say, Partridge to the narrative intensity of a chapter on Sophia in distress—these adjustments and modulations are considerably facilitated by the device of the chapter. *Tom Jones*, too, as a good many critics have said and as Fielding himself remarks, is a structure of contrasts. The chapter title "In which Master Blifil and Jones appear in different lights" is a characteristic one. We are expected, as we read Fielding, to see people and events "in different lights," to see what was in contrast to what is, to see reality in contrast with its guises. Such a structure of contrasts is more easily built with the flexibility of frequent chapter divisions. Finally, as Andrew Wright has remarked,[9] Fielding again and again presents the reader with a "tableau," a comparatively static, almost "posed" picture, in the manner of Hogarth. Perhaps the most conspicuous example is the prison scene at the beginning of *Amelia*. It is a narrative technique, again, which can be imagined as existing, perhaps, in a completely continuous narration. But it is difficult to imagine it as

[9] *Henry Fielding: Mask and Feast* (London, 1965), pp. 122–145.

being so successful as it is when, in Fielding, the tableau is roughly coexistent with the limits of the chapter in which it appears.

So far I have suggested that novelists, at least eighteenth-century novelists, may write in chapters because experience itself can be said to consist of chapters, because the alternating frustrations and fulfillments of life can be given a powerfully dramatic form simply by the act of segmenting the narrative, because the attention and the imagination of the reader are adaptable to small narrative units rather than to long, unbroken ones, and because the technical demands of writing a novel, with its scenic shifts, its omissions, and so on, are easier to meet when the narrative is divided. None of the reasons applies to Sterne. Life, for Sterne, is not lived in chapters:

> My mother, you must know,—but I have fifty things more necessary to let you know first,—I have a hundred difficulties which I have promised to clear up, and a thousand distresses and domestic misadventures crowding in upon me thick and three-fold, one upon the neck of another,—a cow broke in (tomorrow morning) to my uncle *Toby's* fortifications, and eat up two ratios and a half of dried grass, tearing up the sods with it, which faced his horn-work and covered way.—*Trim* insists upon being tried by a court-martial,—the cow to be shot,—*Slop* to be *crucifixed*,—myself to be *tristramed*, and at my very baptism made a martyr of;—poor unhappy devils that we all are! [10]

By his chapter divisions, Sterne achieves a large range of comic effects; but his comic effects are made at the deliberate expense of the conventional advantages of narrative division. Rather than intensifying the dramatic progression of his novel by dividing it, Sterne dissipates its drama. Chapters in *Tristram Shandy* are a few lines long, others nearly interminable, all with little of the apparent regard which Fielding expresses for the reader's interest. And although the technical demands Sterne makes upon himself are considerable, they are so unconventional as to constitute a parody of conventional technique. One chapter ends, "Imagine to yourself;—but this had better begin a new chapter." And the next chapter begins: "CHAPTER NINE—Imagine to yourself a little squat, uncourtly figure of a Doctor *Slop*. . . ." At the end of *Middlemarch*, George Eliot suggests that every end is at the same time a beginning. Sterne does her one better.

[10] *Tristram Shandy*, Rinehart edition, p. 206.

What his manipulation of the chapter suggests is a use of chapters to indicate a distrust of chapters, more than a recognition of beginnings in ends, a denial of the reality of the narrative unit. Time after time, what looks like an episode is no episode, what looks like a digression is no digression. What this internal, associationist, apparently capricious organization effects is precisely that radical reorientation of the gestalt-making mechanism which I have suggested above is possible in fiction, in this case by playing the mind of Tristram against the conventions of fiction. Without its chapters, no doubt, *Tristram Shandy* would be less funny and quite likely unreadable. And without its chapters, the appearance, which Sterne carefully induces, of an anxious Tristram wrestling with his intractable material would be lost. But finally, Sterne can write chapters of such comic exuberance precisely because he does not believe in chapters.

The eighteenth-century novelists, then, represent the technique of the chapter come full circle, from an unawareness, almost, of its usefulness, to a full exploitation of its power and its variety, to a parody of it. In one sense there is nothing more to be said about the chapter as an aspect of fictional technique. The beginnings and endings, the technical shifts, the relations between chapters in Jane Austen alone are so subtle and various as to justify a book in themselves. But her chapters do rather little which was not latent in the technical virtuosity of the eighteenth century. In another sense, however, the novelists of the nineteenth century used the chapter in a way which was beyond the concerns of the eighteenth-century novelists. Novelists of the nineteenth century learned how to make their characters grow and change; they learned, in James's word, to make them "emerge"; they learned how to reveal the pressure of environment. And these new causal and developmental concerns are intimately related to the way in which novels are divided.

In *Middlemarch*, for example, the chapters on Dorothea perform rather the function of drops in the Chinese water torture. They gradually alter the personality of Dorothea. And it is difficult to imagine how this alteration might have taken place without the appearance of stages, degrees, interior crises, and small progressions. The early chapters of *The Way of All Flesh* build up, layer by layer, the genetic and environmental enclosure from which Ernest cannot escape. And again, it is difficult to imagine how the sense of heavy impenetrability could have been evoked by Butler without the structural possibilities of chaptered narration. In *The Aspern Papers* one has the sense of growing familiarity with the nameless narrator who reveals himself, by stages, as he becomes more involved in his personal intrigue; at the same time, one follows those small events that mark the breakdown of Miss Tita's reserve as well as those other small events that mark the growth of Miss Bordereau's understanding. Again, it is not that chapter division interrupts the tale; it makes the narration possible.

Critics of fiction have rarely been comfortable with the technical analysis of conventions, excepting, perhaps, the question of point of view, preferring instead the application of large concepts—moral, psychological, and cultural—to the uncircumscribed genre of the novel. It is not, however, to detract from the vitality and the human significance of the novel to insist that part of the responsibility of any novelist is to make his own adjustments to certain broadly esthetic and specifically narrative conventions. Of these, the convention of the chapter, limiting though it may sometimes be, has arisen and has continued through so many kinds of prose fiction precisely because, as I have argued, it is first a way of making the narrative intelligible but more than that because it is a device which enables the narrative to contain all the truth it will bear.

5

STYLE

Linguists have coined the word idiolect for the peculiar use of language by a particular speaker. Every novelist, of course, possesses his own idiolect and that fact alone makes a general theory of style almost impossible. What kinds of generalizations about style could one offer, for example, that would illuminate such strikingly individual uses of words as those in Emily Brontë and Meredith, Mark Twain and Henry James? The varieties of point of view are finite; but the ways in which words can be used for fictional purposes are infinite. All of this is reflected in the fact that most good studies of style are attempts to demonstrate how a single writer puts his idiolect to his own artistic purposes.

Nevertheless, there are some ways in which one can and in fact must talk about style in general. The question of method, first of all, requires a theoretical answer. What does style mean and how does one go about describing a style? The problem of the mode and purpose of artistic language, secondly, can be settled only at a philosophical, general level. Is there an essential difference between the way that language is used in fiction and the way that language is used in ordinary, nonartistic discourse? Thirdly, certain broad rhetorical categories can form the basis for useful generalizations, if they are used with tact and flexibility. Is not part of one's obligation in dealing with Mark Twain, for example, to use the general category American colloquial, not as a device for over-simplifying Twain but as a means for defining a stylistic tradition and for differentiating Twain's place in it from, say, Hemingway's? In still another direction, conventional descriptions of period style tend to be less applicable to the novel than to other forms, but it is possible, nonetheless, to relate certain stylistic traits to the unity of an age. What, for example, is the stylistic source of that impression which dozens of critics have stated of shared traits of perception and judgment in the verbal habits of Fielding, Dr. Johnson, and Jane Austen? Finally, one can seek to justify, in a general way, one's subjective response to stylistic effects. Granting the infinity of fictional contexts and purposes, can one still state principles by means of which one judges one sentence to be graceful and satisfying and another sentence to be clumsy and inept?

The study of style has undergone some serious transformations in the past thirty years. These are too complex to be summarized here, though a sense of the wish to redefine both the nature and the method of stylistic study can be seen in Richard Ohmann's essay. The selection from Stevenson is a thoroughly ingratiating survival from another age. Yet, if it is innocent of methodological rigor, Stevenson's essay expresses quite incomparably the total involvement of the writer with the shape of the words on the page. Leonard Lutwack's essay takes the antithesis of stylistic uniformity and diversity and pursues it in several directions. Some of the sections of this anthology may seem to represent an area of theory that is, for the time being, more or less complete, the section on point of view for example. The three essays on style, on the other hand, should suggest an area of theory in which the ground has scarcely been broken. Starting with the premise that style and substance are organically inseparable, nearly everything about style remains to be said.

ROBERT LOUIS STEVENSON

WEB, TEXTURE, AND THE JUGGLING OF ORANGES

Literature, although it stands apart by reason of the great destiny and general use of its medium in the affairs of men, is yet an art like other arts. Of these we may distinguish two great classes: those arts, like sculpture, painting, acting, which are representative, or, as used to be said very clumsily, imitative; and those, like architecture, music, and the dance, which are self-sufficient, and merely presentative. Each class, in right of this distinction, obeys principles apart; yet both may claim a common ground of existence, and it may be said with sufficient justice that the motive and end of any art whatever is to make a pattern; a pattern, it may be, of colours, of sounds, of changing attitudes, geometrical figures, or imitative lines; but still a pattern. That is the plane on which these sisters meet; it is by this that they are arts; and if it be well they should at times forget their childish origin, addressing their intelligence to virile tasks, and performing unconsciously that necessary function of their life, to make a pattern, it is still imperative that the pattern shall be made.

Music and literature, the two temporal arts, contrive their pattern of sounds in time; or, in other words, of sounds and pauses. Communication may be made in broken words, the business of life be carried on with substantives alone; but that is not what we call literature; and the true business of the literary artist is to plait or weave his meaning, involving it around itself; so that each sentence, by successive phrases, shall first come into a kind of knot, and then, after a moment of suspended meaning, solve and clear itself. In every properly

From "On Some Technical Elements of Style in Literature," first published in The Contemporary Review, *April, 1885. Reprinted from* Works, Volume XXII *(New York, 1898)*.

constructed sentence there should be observed this knot or hitch; so that (however delicately) we are led to foresee, to expect, and then to welcome the successive phrases. The pleasure may be heightened by an element of surprise, as, very grossly, in the common figure of the antithesis, or, with much greater subtlety, where an antithesis is first suggested and then deftly evaded. Each phrase, besides, is to be comely in itself; and between the implication and the evolution of the sentence there should be a satisfying equipoise of sound; for nothing more often disappoints the ear than a sentence solemnly and sonorously prepared, and hastily and weakly finished. Nor should the balance be too striking and exact, for the one rule is to be infinitely various; to interest, to disappoint, to surprise, and yet still to gratify; to be ever changing, as it were, the stitch, and yet still to give the effect of an ingenious neatness.

The conjurer juggles with two oranges, and our pleasure in beholding him springs from this, that neither is for an instant overlooked or sacrificed. So with the writer. His pattern, which is to please the supersensual ear, is yet addressed, throughout and first of all, to the demands of logic. Whatever be the obscurities, whatever the intricacies of the argument, the neatness of the fabric must not suffer, or the artist has been proved unequal to his design. And, on the other hand, no form of words must be selected, no knot must be tied among the phrases, unless knot and word be precisely what is wanted to forward and illuminate the argument; for to fail in this is to swindle in the game. The genius of prose rejects the *cheville* no less emphatically than the laws of verse; and the *cheville,* I should perhaps explain to some of my readers, is any meaningless or very watered phrase employed to strike a balance in the sound. Pattern and argument live in each other; and it is by the brevity, clearness, charm, or emphasis of the second, that we judge the strength and fitness of the first.

Style is synthetic; and the artist, seeking, so to speak, a peg to plait about, takes up at once two or more elements or two or more views of the subject in hand; combines, implicates, and contrasts them; and while, in one sense, he was merely seeking an occasion for the necessary knot, he will be found, in the other, to have greatly enriched the meaning, or to have transacted the work of two sentences in the space of one. In the change from the successive shallow statements of the old chronicler to the dense and luminous flow of highly synthetic narrative, there is implied a vast amount of both philosophy and wit. The philosophy we clearly see, recognising in the synthetic writer a far more deep and stimulating view of life, and a far keener sense of the generation and affinity of events. The wit we might imagine to be lost; but it is not so, for it is just that wit, these perpetual nice contrivances, these difficulties overcome, this double purpose attained, these two oranges kept simultaneously dancing in the air, that, consciously or not, afford the reader his delight. Nay, and this wit, so little recognised, is the necessary organ of that philosophy which we so much admire. That style is therefore the most perfect, not, as fools say, which is the most natural, for the most natural is the disjointed babble of the chronicler; but which attains the highest degree of elegant and pregnant implication unobtrusively; or if obtrusively, then with the greatest gain to sense and vigour. Even the derangement of the phrases from their (so-called) natural order is luminous for the mind; and it is by the means of such designed reversal that the elements of a judgment may be most pertinently marshalled, or the stages of a complicated action most perspicuously bound into one.

The web, then, or the pattern: a web at once sensuous and logical, an elegant and pregnant texture: that is style, that is the foundation of the art of literature. Books indeed continue to be read, for the interest of the fact or fable, in which this quality is poorly represented, but still it will be there. And, on the other hand, how many do we continue to peruse and reperuse with pleasure whose only merit is the elegance of texture? I am tempted to mention Cicero; and since Mr. Anthony Trollope is dead, I will. It is a poor diet for the mind, a very colourless and toothless "criticism of life"; but we enjoy the pleasure of a most intricate and dexterous pattern, every stitch a model at once of elegance and of good sense; and the two oranges, even if one of them be rotten, kept dancing with inimitable grace.

RICHARD M. OHMANN

PROLEGOMENA TO THE ANALYSIS
OF PROSE STYLE

The considerations of this essay are of a very primitive sort.
If they are prolegomena to the study of style, they are preliminary by several stages to the study of style in the novel. What
is more, a few decades ago they would have seemed utterly
superfluous to most rhetoricians, who were quite content to
think of style as the verbal dress of disembodied thought. Yet
now comes a school of criticism which aims to discredit the
split between form and content, a school which argues that no
two different utterances mean the same thing, and, more radically that, "every statement is a unique style of its own." [1] This
organicist position, in spite of its stringency, has appealed increasingly to critic and linguist alike.[2] In fact it has nearly attained the status of dogma, of an official motto, voiced in the
triumphant tones of reason annihilating error. Appealing as the
idea is, commonplace though it has lately become in criticism,
semantics, and linguistics, it would seem to render futile most
extant stylistic analysis, if not to undercut the whole idea of
style. For if style does not have to do with *ways* of saying
something,[3] just as style in tennis has to do with ways of hitting

[1] Andrews Wanning, "Some Changes in the Prose Style of the Seventeenth
Century" (Ph.D. dissertation, University of Cambridge, 1938), p. 20.
[2] An example of the linguist's position: "It is a well-tried hypothesis of linguistics that formally different utterances always differ in meaning. . . ."
Leonard Bloomfield, "Linguistic Aspects of Science," *International Encyclopedia of Unified Science,* I (Chicago, 1955), 253.
[3] Here, as with too many pseudo-philosophical problems, ordinary language
seems to have been the villain. Our speech makes a separation between saying
and thing said: one *says it.* And if expressing is an action that one performs
on an idea, just as hitting is an action performed on a tennis ball, why not
different *ways* of expressing an idea? The distinction works with vocal

From Style in Prose Fiction: English Institute Essays, 1958 (*New York,
1959*). *Reprinted by permission of the Columbia University Press.*

a ball, is there anything at all which is worth naming "style"? If not, most critics of style have really given us judgments about what writers mean, masquerading as judgments about manner. The critic can talk about what the writer says, but talk about style he cannot, for his neat identity—one thought, one form—allows no margin for individual variation, which is what we ordinarily mean by style. Style, then, becomes a useless hypothetical construct half way between meaning and the person who means, and the study of style would seem to be the moribund offspring of a prolific reification: the assumption that because there is a word "style," there must be a thing to match.

Confronted with this dilemma, the conscientious critic can only say, with Wittgenstein, "Whereof one cannot speak, thereof one must be silent," and rejoice at the elimination of another pseudo-discipline. The trouble with this ascetic solution is that the critic may still feel it useful to speak of style. If he *is* unwilling to see stylistics tossed into the positivist's scrap-heap, along with ethics and metaphysics, he may work out a compromise: the most common is to say that style is part of what we ordinarily call meaning,[4] that it is peripheral meaning, or subterranean meaning, or connotative meaning. Such a solution is fruitful, I think, but it leads to a new problem. If style exists, by courtesy of this redefinition, where are its boundaries? Which part of meaning is to be called style, and which is really meaning? In short, how can we tell style from not-style?

These difficulties are not, I hope, mere compliant straw men to be handily blown down. They are real, and they are crucial, for on their resolution depend answers to these questions: What is style? What kind of scrutiny will it reward? What can it show about the writer?

---

speech, for the same words can be spoken with different stress, pitch, tone, and so forth; but a moment's reflection shows that it does not apply to the written word, and that any approach to stylistics empowered by a split between form and content is in serious theoretical trouble.

[4] This is Mr. Wanning's theoretical justification for proceeding with his study.

1

LET me begin the argument, unabashedly, where so many critical arguments begin—with I. A. Richards.

Socrates is wise.
Wisdom belongs to Socrates.

Mr. Richards offers these two sentences as a capsule demonstration of the way in which we "can put one thought form into many different word patterns." [5] He does not, as he may seem to do, neatly sever form and content; he is arguing a more subtle case, and one which ends by leaving form and content neither quite joined nor totally separated—a happy compromise, seemingly, for the beleagured would-be critic of style. Let us examine it.

Mr. Richards uses the example concerning the wisdom of Socrates in a discussion calculated to refute J. S. Mill's contention that "the principles and rules of grammar are the means by which the forms of language are made to correspond with the universal forms of thought." [6] On the contrary, argues Mr. Richards, anyone who wishes to predicate wisdom of Socrates may cast his thought in one of several molds. Conversely, in English, thoughts of incompatible forms often take the same syntactical shape: for example, "I see a tiger" and "I kick a tiger." It is obvious that to kick a tiger is to act on it, whereas to see a tiger is to be affected in a complicated way by it. Mr. Richards submits that the tiger would no doubt administer a terminal lesson in logic to the man who confused sentence forms with forms of thought in this disastrous fashion.

His contention that the two sentences about Socrates express *congruent* thoughts is not, however, a contention that they express the *same idea*, or mean the *same thing*, or are *equivalent*. In one statement Socrates is the given quantity; in the other, wisdom. One sentence works by limiting the denotation of "Socrates," by eliminating possible statements such as "Socra-

[5] *Interpretation in Teaching* (New York, 1938), p. 285.
[6] *Inaugural Lecture at St. Andrews*, quoted by Richards, p. 280.

tes is stupid," and "Socrates is foolish." The other sentence focuses on a set of attributes and ways of behaving called "wisdom," and tells of one point in space-time where we can find it, namely in Socrates. One sentence belongs in a context of curiosity about Socrates; it might come in answer to the question, "What sort of mind had Socrates?" The other might satisfy someone who is looking, not for an honest, but for a wise man. The two sentences differ in the type of information given, in pattern of emphasis, in the sort of expectation they satisfy. In short, they say different things.

Rather than artificially separating idea from expression, Mr. Richards suggests that ideas fall into a finite set of categories, according to logical shape or form. His medial position between a dualism of manner and matter which is currently heretical, and a monism which is orthodox but fatal, allows to style a tenuous existence as the manner of clothing ethereal forms of thought in neatly tailored word patterns.[7] Under the aegis of this theory the study of a writer's style becomes the examination of the formal changes he works on each group of ideas, of the metamorphoses through which he puts each form of thought.

Attractive as this theory may seem to the critic who wishes to talk about style, but is hard put to see what style is, I think it must be rejected, even at the cost, possibly, of a final lesson in logic from Mr. Richards's tiger. For one thing, these shadowy forms of thought are so indistinguishable from each other, so nearly hidden by overlapping word patterns, that, rather than implementing a rigorous criticism, they would make it inhumanly difficult. Mr. Richards's distinction between seeing and kicking a tiger is easy enough to follow; one idea is of the form "*a* receives sense data from *b*," and the other is of the form "*a* acts on *b*." But what of the sentence "I feel a tiger"? To which form of thought does it belong? A new form of thought must no doubt be established to contain this sentence. But the process is endless; as rapidly as the forms multiply, borderline sentences will rise up to plague the classifier, who may eventually find, as a result of his labors, that the number of forms precisely equals the number of sentences.

In raising this objection I have tentatively accepted the notion

[7] This rescue maneuver is my inference from Mr. Richards's position; *his* main aim is to debunk the monism of Mill's grammar.

of "forms of thought," and merely questioned the practicability of their use by a critic. But the disconcerting proliferation of thought forms calls the whole theory into question. If there is a separate form for every thought, then the concept of "form" is identical with that of "thought," and we can dispense with one or the other. To look at the matter from another angle, let me press somewhat further the hypothetical meeting of man and tiger, attending to forms of thought. To an observer the tiger consists of certain sense data—color, texture, odor, shape, motion, sound—data related to each other in extremely complex ways, however simple and primitive an object the tiger may seem to the adult's highly integrated mind. The man is a similar complex. Both tiger and man are capable of receiving sensations from, say, the jungle around them, as well as from each other. And the jungle, like man and tiger, is a welter of surfaces, glints of light, disorderly movements, unmusical noises. In this tangle of sensation the man sees trees, plants, a tiger; but these *Gestalten* are not inherently *there;* they are arbitrary ways of breaking up the flux; arbitrary, that is, except that the man has in the past been rewarded for using them, to the extent that parts of his environment (e.g. the tiger) demand, with special persistence, recognition as separate things.[8] When the man kicks the tiger, an exceedingly intricate shift takes place in the arrangement of sense data, a shift which is indistinguishable *in type* from the shifts which are occurring every millionth of a second. There has been a change; something has happened, but something is always happening, and it is man who separates one phenomenon from another, both by seeing and by naming. Our habits of sorting and classifying are so ingrained that we cannot describe or imagine things as they appear to the tiger, or in the infant's "blooming, buzzing confusion." The world in itself, the infant's world, is barren of form, without order, mere raw material for man's perceptual and verbal manipulation. The forms of thought, then, are not inherent in things as

[8] This view is, to the best of my knowledge, in accord with current perception theory. For instance: "perception is never a sure thing, never an absolute revelation of 'what is.' Rather, what we see is a prediction—our own personal construction designed to give us the best possible bet for carrying out our purposes in action. We make these bets on the basis of our past experience." W. H. Ittelson and F. P. Kilpatrick, "Experiments in Perception," *Scientific American Reader* (New York, 1953), p. 581.

they are. There is no logical or ontological reason why, on some tiger-infested tropical island, a people could not see man and tiger as one entity, and give a single name to this "object." Then "I kick the tiger" might run, "The tigerman coalesces footwise," and "I see the tiger" could read, "The tigerman coalesces eyewise." Surely the two ideas are now of the same form, as are the two sentences.

In another section of *Interpretation in Teaching*,[9] Mr. Richards argues that communication depends on a sameness of experience—a uniformity offered from without and a uniformity as organized from within. His acceptance of "forms of thought" must depend on this "sameness," on a belief that experience affords common elements to all men. But if my analysis is correct, experience is not molded from without, except in so far as nature rewards certain of man's sorting responses to the passing show and punishes others. It is interesting to note that we may be led into a misconception partly by the very word "experience." A logician points out that " 'experience' itself is a relational term masquerading as a thing-name; x is an experience if and only if there is some y (the experiencer) which stands in the experience relation to x." [10] Ordinary language urges us to think of experience as a constant, offered with impartial sameness to all experiencers, rather than as an infinite series of relations of which no two need be alike.

The conception of experience as a series of relations is damaging also to Mr. Richards's claim that experience has "uniformity as organized from within," for it seems extremely improbable that any experiencer should ever stand in exactly the same relation to a field of perception as any other experiencer, or, indeed, that any man should see the same way twice. I do not wish to peddle a crippling subjectivism; communication does take place, and we must act most of the time as if there were uniformity of experience. At the same time it seems more accurate to speak behavioristically and say that men often *respond* similarly to similar fields of perception—respond similarly, that is, either in words or in action.

Neither the external world, then, nor our "experience" of it

[9] Page 68.
[10] Charles W. Morris, "Foundations of the Theory of Signs," *International Encyclopedia of Unified Science*, I, 123.

offers any ready-made forms of thought to the analyst who wishes to see style as the way in which ideas get into words. What nature does offer to experience, however, and experience to language, is a constant *formlessness*. Just as, in the existentialist view, man is confronted in his search for ethical order by the indifference of the universe, man in his search for perceptual order faces a chaotic world-stuff which gives no hints as to the proper method of sorting. But Camus calls the world's moral anarchy benign, in that it allows us to consider man the maker of his own morality, and the chaos pictured by modern psychologists has a parallel advantage: the perceiver, according to this theory, shapes the world by choosing from it whatever perceptual forms are most useful to him—though most often the choice is unconscious and inevitable. The unfriendly behavior of tigers may, to be sure, coerce him in his perceptual sorting, and his choice of perceptual forms largely governs his choice of linguistic categories, but the selections are initially free, in an important sense.

In these multifarious *ur*-choices, these preverbal and verbal pigeon-holings, style has its beginnings. If the critic is able to isolate and examine the most primitive choices which lie behind a work of prose, they can reveal to him the very roots of a writer's epistemology, the way in which he breaks up for manipulation the refractory surge of sensations which challenges all writers and all perceivers. In this Heraclitean flux, and not in the elusive forms of thought, is the common source of all perceptions, all sentences, all prose. The stream of experience is the background against which "choice" is a meaningful concept, in terms of which the phrase "*way* of saying *it*" makes sense, though "it" is no longer a variable. Form and content are truly separate if "content" is not bodiless ideas, but the formless world-stuff. And if such a hypothesis carries forward the analysis of style only a comfortless millimeter or so, at least it offers to that discipline a firm theoretical base, and a justification as well, inasmuch as it establishes an accessible and interesting connection between style and epistemology.

2

BEFORE this hypothesis can be of use, however, it requires major refinement. The most obvious barrier to a fruitful consideration of these fundamental epistemic choices is the fact that most of them are irrevocably made for any given writer by the particular language he writes in. A James Joyce or a Gertrude Stein may reshuffle linguistic forms in an attempt to draw aside the curtain that English places between us and the world of psychic and physical phenomena, but most conventional writers permit English to govern their epistemologies, as do all who merely speak the language. In other words, writers in English deal with bare experience only as it is censored by their language; they manipulate linguistically a world which is already highly organized for them.

Take, for example, the question of grammatical case. In English, a language which, compared to its neighbors, is syntatically rigid and very slightly inflected, most contemporary linguists recognize two cases [11] (as opposed to the four, five, or six of earlier grammarians). Of these two, genitives are relatively uncommon, so that nearly all occurrences of nouns are in one case. This limitation of cases means that a noun standing by itself, say "dog," calls attention merely to the animal of that name, and tells us nothing about it, not even that it is *not* a dog seen in an attitude of possession, since we have many constructions such as "hair of the dog" which express the genitive idea without recourse to the genitive case. The isolated word "dog's" names an animal *seen as owning something;* that is, it conveys a somewhat different idea. It also creates a different set of expectations; to say "dog" is probably to stimulate the question

[11] "Contemporary" in a loose sense: Otto Jespersen, whose semi-notional approach to grammar has made him seem old-fashioned to many later linguists, is one who argues against more than two cases in English: *The Philosophy of Grammar* (London, 1924), pp. 173–86. Writers of the Fries-Trager-Smith era also favor a two-case system, as for example, Paul Roberts in *Understanding Grammar* (New York, 1954), pp. 39–40, and Donald Lloyd and Harry Warfel in *American English in Its Cultural Setting* (New York, 1956), pp. 241–42.

"What about a dog?"; but the word "dog's" leads to the question "Dog's what, and what about it?" Thus English offers the speaker or writer two different notions of a certain four-footed animal; it sees the canine beast in two different ways.

In French, by contrast, there is only one form of *chien*. That word in isolation tells nothing about the dog at all. At the atomic level of meaning English has two things where French has but one. When we turn to Latin, with its six cases, the difference becomes more obvious. To translate *canis* properly, we would have to use a term such as "dog-doing-something-or-having-something-predicated-of-it" (actually, a full translation would be much more complex even than this). *Canem* might be partially rendered "dog-being-acted-upon-or-seen-as-the-goal-of-action." In Latin there is no conceivable way of expressing the English idea of "dog," untrammeled by ideas of position, agency, attitude, possession, mode of being perceived, and so forth. There is in Latin no symbol which is so free to be manipulated syntactically.

The writer in English, therefore, sees the universe through a verbal screen which divides it up less finely; classes are larger in English, because less subtly distinguished. What we conceive of as one thing, the writer of Latin must have conceived of, in some unquestioning, preverbal way, as six different things. These are the epistemic implications of case. The implications for style are equally significant: the importance of word order in English, the many possibilities of achieving emphasis in Latin by placement of a word, the greater dependence of the English writer on "function words." Epistemic differences of this sort run through the whole Indo-European family of languages, but within that family the similarities are more noticeable than the differences, and one must examine languages of other groups to find out how radically verbal environments can differ.

Benjamin Lee Whorf, a pioneer in metalinguistics, studied Western languages in juxtaposition with esoteric languages such as Hopi, and found that we treat the cosmos as much more segmented than do they—often artificially so.[12] We objectify time into a thing with boundaries and divisions instead of see-

---

[12] *Language Thought, and Reality* (Cambridge, Mass., and New York, 1956), esp. "The Relation of Habitual Thought and Behavior to Language" and "Languages and Logic."

ing it in terms of relations in lateness as Hopi does. We have "distributed nouns," such as "meat," "water," and "butter," whereas Hopi has none; nor does Hopi have abstract nouns. Evidently the Hopi language is in some sense closer to the raw material of perception than English is, with its complex and sophisticated system of categories.

It is notorious that Korzybski, Hayakawa, and other semanticists go further than Whorf, attacking Western languages for making inaccurate distinctions and concealing the functional relationships of nature.[13] Supposedly, Indo-European language structure was responsible for our long slavery to Aristotelian philosophy and Newtonian physics [14] and is to blame for a good share of our present neuroses to boot. This criticism of ordinary language seems to me even more utopian that that leveled against it by the early positivists, and logically faulty as well. The semanticists use the very language which, according to them, hoodwinks us so severely to point out the fallacies of thought which it induces. Certainly a language which permits analysis of its own artificialities—which in effect transcends its own limitations—will suffice for most ordinary thinking.

Thus I find attacks on the cosmological limitations of English beside the point. What *is* relevant to the study of style is the fact that any language persuades its speakers to see the universe in certain set ways, to the exclusion of other ways. It thereby limits the possibilities of choice for any writer, and the student of style must be careful not to ascribe to an individual the epistemic bias of his language. A writer cannot escape the boundaries set by his tongue, except by creating new words, by uprooting normal syntax, or by building metaphors, each of which is a new ontological discovery. Yet, even short of these radical linguistic activities, an infinite number of meaningful choices remain to be made by the writer. A heavy dependence on abstraction, a peculiar use of the present tense, a habitual evocation of similarities through parallel structure, a tendency to place feelings in syntactical positions of agency, a trick of underplaying casual words: any of these patterns of expression,

[13] See, for example, "What Is Meant by Aristotelian Structure of Language?," in *Language, Meaning and Maturity*, ed. by S. I. Hayakawa (New York, 1954).

[14] According to this view it is not surprising that the Hopi have produced no Newton, but it is surprising that no Einstein has risen among the Pueblos.

when repeated with unusual frequency, is the sign of a habit of meaning, and thus of a persistent way of sorting out the phenomena of experience. And even single occurrences of linguistic oddities, especially in crucial places, can point to what might be called temporary epistemologies.

Here, then, is one way in which the term "style" is meaningful, one kind of *choice* which really exists for the author. This view does not, of course, represent an entirely new departure from conventional stylistics, even though my formulation has been elicited by the chaos of past criticism. Style as epistemic choice may be what John Middleton Murry has in mind when he says that "a true idiosyncrasy of style [is] the result of an author's success in compelling language to conform to his mode of experience." [15] It probably is what W. K. Wimsatt refers to when he calls style "the last and most detailed elaboration of meaning." [16] New or not, this approach to style has the advantage of being philosophically defensible, as well as the advantage of yielding results that have to do with the literary work as a whole, not merely with its (nonexistent) window dressing. Finally, the method which I suggest saves the study of style from having to rely *only* on those impressionistic, metaphorical judgments which have too often substituted for analysis: dignified, grand, plain, decorative, placid, exuberant, restrained, hard, and the whole tired assortment of epithets which name without explaining. [17]

Yet this account of style is not complete. The naive, commonsense feeling that style is a *way* of saying *something* demands more than a cursory dismissal. For one thing, a discussion of style as epistemic choice can operate effectively only over wide areas of prose, where habitual kinds of choice become evident. There is little sense in comparing the epistemic decisions of a writer who is discussing a rowing match with those of a writer on Christian ideas of teleology. The very choice of subject mat-

[15] *The Problem of Style* (London, 1922), p. 23.
[16] *The Prose Style of Samuel Johnson* (New Haven, 1941), p. 63. Mr. Wimsatt is one critic who has fruitfully approached style in this way, both in this book and in *Philosophic Words* (New Haven, 1948).
[17] Such terms may be legitimately used to name habits of meaning which have been described specifically; see, for instance, Mr. Wimsatt's discussion of "plain" and its opposite, *Prose Style of Johnson*, p. 101. The more usual procedure, however, is to use them as if they had clear a priori meaning.

ter precludes a large number of stylistic decisions: it can force the writer to be concrete or abstract, for instance. Thus the criticism of style requires a more manageable backdrop than the entire panorama of the world. If, as Wittgenstein says, "the world is the totality of facts, not of thing," [18] perhaps individual facts, or combinations of them, will serve the purpose.

This position is the one that I propose to take, and I shall use the term "proposition" to describe what is expressed by sentences. As before, Mr. Richards's remarks will provide a convenient starting place for the argument. During a discussion of logic [19] he lists these three sentences:

> Mussolini is mortal.
> Voltaire is witty.
> Havelock Ellis is old.

A logician, he says, would claim that these sentences "express propositions of the same form," a contention which "is flagrantly not so." The first sentence, Mr. Richards says, means "Mussolini will die sometime"; the second means "Voltaire makes remarks which cause in certain people, a peculiar pleasure, and in others a peculiar annoyance"; the third, "Havelock Ellis has lived through many years." These sentences show that "the similar adjectives stand for very different forms." Mr. Richards's analysis is revealing, and the particular logician he has in mind [20] *had* made the error of assuming that syntactical structure is a key to the structure of propositions. But Mr. Richards makes precisely the same error in implying that his *translations* of the first three sentences reveal the structure of the propositions they express, for he takes the translations as showing that the propositions are of different forms. And by what superior right is the sentence "Mussolini will die sometime" a better indication of propositional form than the sentence "Mussolini is mortal"? Or for that matter, why not other sentences, such as "Mussolini's life will end," or "Mussolini will not live forever"? If the first two sentences express the same proposition, then there are many other sentences which do so,

[18] Ludwig Wittgenstein, *Tractatus Logico-Philosophicus*, trans. by C. K. Ogden (London, 1922), p. 31.
[19] *Interpretation in Teaching*, p. 370.
[20] Susan Stebbing, *A Modern Introduction to Logic* (London, 1930), p. 51.

and these sentences are of many syntactical forms. I see no way of picking one of such a group of sentences as *the* mirror of the proposition it expresses.[21]

The difficulty, of course, is that a "proposition," as Mr. Richards uses the term and as I wish to use it, has no form at all. The form of a proposition, like the forms of thought, is illusory, if I am right in what I take a proposition to be. It is the class of all sentences which are related to a fact or a cluster of facts in this way: if the fact (or cluster) exists, the sentences are all true; if the fact does not exist, the sentences are all false. In other words, they contain no parts which will not stand or fall with the fact. The process of determining, by observing facts, whether a sentence is true or false, is called "verification."[22] What may have led Mr. Richards to claim that his translations revealed the propositional forms which had been concealed by the original versions, is the fact that the restatements are more nearly descriptions of the facts which would go to *verify* the propositions involved.

[21] The truth is, I think, that most logicians would say that Mr. Richards's *sentences* are of the same form, and not the propositions they express.

[22] See A. J. Ayer, *Language, Truth and Logic*, rev. ed. (New York, 1946), pp. 13, 35, for a positivist's account of the criterion of verifiability. See also Alfred Tarski, "The Semantic Conception of Truth and the Foundations of Semantics," *Semantics and the Philosophy of Language* (Urbana, Ill., 1952), esp. pp. 15–17. According to Tarski, whose article is a classic in the field, the general definition of "truth" is a logical conjunction of all equivalences of the form "x is true, if and only if p," where "p" is any "true" sentence and "x" is the name of that sentence (i.e., that sentence in quotation marks). Tarski's definition seems to bypass propositions altogether by applying the term "true" to sentences only; and in view of the long dispute over propositions among logicians and philosophers, Tarski's move may be a wise application of Occam's razor. But it has the disadvantage of throwing out a term which is in common use by both philosophers and laymen, and the more severe disadvantage of leaving no term at all to describe that which sentences express. For these reasons I follow Ayer, *The Foundations of Empirical Knowledge* (London, 1940), pp. 100–1, in retaining the term. But I am made uncomfortable by an identification of "proposition" and "sentences which are true or false" (as in Wittgenstein, *Tractatus,* pp. 61–103), and more uncomfortable by a gentleman's agreement to use the term "proposition" while confessing ignorance as to its meaning. My own definition (which I have not seen elsewhere) is somewhat odd in that it requires us to think of a *class* of sentences as being true or false. But it jibes reasonably well with most technical usage, and has notable advantages for the study of style, the main one being that it places something between sentences and the facts, thus allowing meaningful talk of what sentences express (propositions) as well as of what they describe (facts).

Thus, for a sentence to express a proposition is for it to be a member of a group of sentences. But this class membership does not imply that a given sentence is one sub-form of a main propositional form. Rather, all members of the class have a most general form: the form "x is the case," or $f(x)$. And this form they have in common with *all* sentences, and with all propositions, for "the general propositional form is a variable.[23] This form distinguishes propositions from expletives, isolated words, commands, and so forth, none of which state that anything is the case, but it does not distinguish one proposition from another.

Propositions, then, offer a second locus for the analyst of style. Many sentences can express the same proposition; that is, they can be jointly verifiable by reference to the same fact. This is Bloomfield's contention when he states that "formally different utterances," though they always differ in meaning, may be equivalent "as to some partial phase of meaning." Equivalence covers "the phase of meaning which is observable indifferently by all persons," and "it is only the accompanying personal and social adjustments which differ." [24] These "adjustments" in language I would call "style," but it is worth noting again that they, as well as the root idea, are *meanings,* and not merely embellishment. Style is the hidden thoughts which accompany overt propositions; it is the highly general meanings which are implied by a writer's habitual methods of expressing propositions. Thus, as an aid to analyzing a writer's dissection of the entire universe, the critic may examine what the writer does with modest corners of that universe—that is, with particular facts and particular propositions.

Some theory such as the one I have been suggesting must be held by the modern critic who looks to style for insight into meaning, who believes that "the consideration of style is a consideration of complete meanings, and there is litle of any importance that can be studied that is not a consideration of meanings." [25]

[23] Wittgenstein, *Tractatus,* p. 103.
[24] *International Encyclopedia of Unified Science,* I, 253.
[25] Wanning, "Some Changes," p. 20.

3

SO far I have been outlining a theory of style which describes choices that I have called epistemic. These choices are important, for they are the critic's key to a writer's mode of experience. They show what sort of place the world is for him, what parts of it are significant or trivial. They show how he thinks, how he comes to know, how he imposes order on the ephemeral pandemonium of experience. These insights into a writer's world view are well worth pursuing, to whatever extent style can yield them. But an account of style which focuses on discursive content alone is only partial; style as it appears, for example, in the novel, I have left largely untouched. For the limits of speakable thought are not the boundaries of experience, or even of rational experience, and thoughts not included in the totality of verifiable propositions are nonetheless an integral part of style, as of knowledge. Thus argues Susanne Langer, who finds post-positivist man on "a tiny grammar-bound island" of human thought, in "the midst of a sea of feeling." [26] He wants to talk of good and evil, substance, beauty, and so forth, but whenever he does, he lapses into nonsense (according to the positivists). Mrs. Langer's method of egress from the narrow cage is well known. She calls symbolism of the sort tolerated by radical empiricists "discursive," and claims that even beyond its limits there is a possibility of genuine semantic. This semantic she calls "presentational symbolism," because its symbols "are involved in a simultaneous, integral presentation." [27] Of this sort is the symbolism of single words, or cries, or music and the visual arts. It is a symbolism of emotional configurations, Mrs. Langer contends, for feelings have contours just as do thoughts, though of a different kind. They are static, grasped in sudden gestalts, rather than formed by gradual accretions of meaning. And to presentational symbolism belongs a large part of what we call "style," a part with which I have yet to deal.

[26] *Philosophy in a New Key* (New York: Mentor edition, 1948), pp. 70–71.
[27] *Ibid.*, p. 79.

Mrs. Langer says elsewhere,[28] "A statement is always a formulation of an idea, and every known fact or hypothesis or fancy takes its emotional value largely from the way it is presented and entertained." For "idea" my term is "proposition," and this substitution brings Mrs. Langer's statement into close parallelism with my analysis of varying descriptions of facts—but with this exception: her point is that one proposition may be expressed in many different *emotional* forms. The claim is incontestable; a large portion of the submerged meaning in prose is presentational, and the constant shaping of emotions is an always audible counterpoint to the melodic line of discursive thought. The presentational part of prose does not, of course, get communicated by a special set of symbols or by a code of emotive punctuation marks. It is buried in an exceedingly complex set of relationships among the same symbols which transmit the discursive meaning. These relationships are what Bloomfield referred to as "accompanying personal and social adjustments."

Many critics see the emotional freight of literature as of primary importance, even in prose that is mainly discursive. Hence epigrams such as "Style is the man himself," or "Style is ingratiation." [29] Certainly the configurations of feeling which accompany any argument are vital in governing its reception by the reader. The writer must observe the amenities common to all human relationships, by "saying the right thing," as Kenneth Burke puts it, by showing himself a particular human being in a certain social relationship with his auditor.[30] Style adds the force of personality to the impersonal forces of logic and evidence, and is thus deeply involved in the business of persuasion. Students of rhetoric since Plato have been largely concerned, at one or another level of sophistication, with analyzing the role of emotion in inducing agreement, and with the methods of embodying it in writing.

But an analysis of tone, distance, dramatic situation, and the rest, solely as ways of persuading, is only a partial analysis, and one which can lead to the damaging distrust of rhetoric as

---

[28] *Feeling and Form* (New York, 1953), p. 258.
[29] Kenneth Burke, *Permanence and Change* (New York, 1935), p. 71.
[30] See Reuben Arthur Brower, *The Fields of Light* (New York, 1951), chap. I, for this view of tone.

tricky and insidious. Emotion enters prose not only as disguises for slipping into the reader's confidence, but as sheer expression of self. Complete honesty demands that the writer not only state his ideas accurately, but also take an emotional stance. A proposition is never held altogether dispassionately, nor can it be expressed without some indication of feeling (except in the artificial languages of logic and mathematics, where symbols and structural patterns have no connotations, no psychic contexts). This being so, the writer must either recreate in prose the emotional concomitants of his thinking, or be in some degree unfaithful to himself. To acknowledge the expressive value of tone, however, is not to say that it is isolated from the persuasive value. When a writer such as Newman creates a full picture of the frame of mind in which he approaches a problem and reader, he is being honest, certainly, but his self-revelation may have the effect of persuading the reader to follow the same emotional path. With Arnold and many other writers the two uses of tone are even more inextricably fused. Arnold argues for a temper of mind, rather than for a set of specific doctrines. In his prose, therefore, tone *is* the argument, in large measure: ingratiation and personality become one, for the case stands or falls depending on whether Arnold's feelings and attitudes are attractive to his readers.[31] His use of language is presentational in that a full understanding of his prose depends on a grasp of the emotional pattern which it presents.

Feeling enters discursive prose, then, as expression and as persuasion. In addition there is a third way, I think, which is almost beyond the power of language to describe. A sentence, at its inception, raises questions rather than answering them. The first word or two may limit the field of possible things-to-be-said, but they do not really transmit information. They may name something, or set an attitude toward something, or indicate a shift in direction from a previous sentence, but they always give rise to questions such as "What about it?" or "What am I to think of in that way?" These demands for completion of a sequence are of course subverbal; they are the vaguest sort of dissatisfaction with suspended thought, with a rational process not properly concluded. As the sentence progresses some of

[31] I am indebted for this notion to John Holloway, *The Victorian Sage* (London, 1953), p. 207.

the demands are satisfied, others deferred, others complicated, and meanwhile new ones are created. But with the end of the sentence comes a kind of balance which results from something having been *said*. There may be a new set of indefinite expectations which remain for future sentences to gratify or disappoint, but one circle is completed, one temporary equilibrium gained. The very act of predication is an emotional act, with rhythms of its own. To state something is first to create imbalance, curiosity, where previously there was nothing, and then to bring about a new balance. So prose builds on the emotional force of coming to know, of pinning down part of what has previously been formless and resolving the tensions which exist between the human organism and unstructured experience. Mrs. Langer speaks of the

> feeling that naturally inheres in studious thinking, the growing intensity of a problem as it becomes more and more complex, and at the same time more definite and "thinkable," until the demand for answer is urgent, touched with impatience; the holding back of assent as the explanation is prepared; the cadential feeling of solution, and the expansion of consciousness in new knowledge.[32]

To emotion, then, as well as to epistemic choice, the stylistic critic must turn his attention. This part of the study is and always has been particularly enticing, perhaps because the individual character of a writer emerges with special clarity in the patterns of feeling which are habitual with him. The epistemic part of style, moreover—a writer's method of dissecting the universe, as expressed by the infinite number of choices he makes—is likely to seem indistinguishable from what he overtly *says*. Yet this is all the more reason for pursuing stylistic meaning through the maze of surface meaning. That which is not immediately obvious may be just as central to the spirit of the writer, and therefore just as valuable to know, as that which starts up unbidden from the page. And, finally, it should be said that a dichotomy between thought and emotion, though useful, is artificial. A writer's characteristic way of manipulating experience is organically related to his feelings about coming to know; his attitude toward the reader and toward the process of communicating is also part of the whole.

[32] *Feeling and Form*, p. 302.

The view of style which I have been outlining clearly takes prose as a serious literary venture. What Leo Spitzer says of the purely imaginative forms is also true of good discursive prose: "the lifeblood of the poetic creation is everywhere the same, whether we tap the organism at 'language' or 'ideas,' at 'plot' or at 'composition.' " [33] This rather mystical theory makes good sense if "lifeblood" is translatable to "modes of experience and habits of feeling." Spitzer's dictum means only that a work of prose can be self-consistent just as a good poem is, its fabric all of a piece. Such a view is the direct antithesis of the older one, which saw style as sugar-coating; if my hypothesis is legitimate, style is just as useful a key to total meaning as is any other element. For this reason, and for no other, it is worth studying: to say something about style is to contribute fresh insight into the artistic contours of the work as a whole.

LEONARD LUTWACK

MIXED AND UNIFORM PROSE STYLES IN THE NOVEL

A distinction may be made between a novel in which more than one prose style is used and a novel which is written in a single, uniform style throughout. *Tom Jones* and *Ulysses* are mixed style novels, *Pamela* and *The Ambassadors* are uniform style novels. The object of this paper is to define the distinction and to work out some of the implications it may have in the study of the novel.

Tom Jones is an early specimen of a novel with mixed prose styles that originate from the author's ironical attitude towards his material and from his compartmentalized treatment of the

[33] *Linguistics and Literary History* (Princeton, 1948), p. 18.

From The Journal of Aesthetics and Art Criticism, *XVIII (1960). Reprinted by permission of The American Society for Aesthetics and the author.*

three genres of which fiction is composed: narrative, essay, and drama. At least three narrative styles are used by Fielding. Tom's rescue of Mrs. Waters from Northerton is a passage of "mere narrative":

> He had not entered far into the wood before he beheld a most shocking sight indeed, a woman stripped half naked, under the hands of a ruffian, who had put his garter round her neck, and was endeavouring to draw her up to a tree. Jones asked no questions at this interval, but fell instantly upon the villain, and made such good use of his trusty oaken stick that he laid him sprawling on the ground before he could defend himself, indeed almost before he knew he was attacked; nor did he cease the prosecution of his blows till the woman herself begged him to forbear, saying, she believed he had sufficiently done his business.

Although excrescences of abstract diction slip into these lines, they are few and do no injury to the narrative force of the style. This prose is almost purely objective, with only the slightest suggestion of authorial attitude towards its content; it is prose that takes its subject seriously. The syntax is a matter of the simple compounding of short clauses that make absolutely clear the persons, objects, and time sequence of the action.

Against this plain narrative style Fielding sets his "Homerican style," which parodies the heroic manner of narration in epic poetry and romance:

> Now the dogs of war being let loose, began to lick their bloody lips; now Victory, with golden wings, hung hovering in the air; now Fortune, taking her scales from her shelf, began to weigh the fates of Tom Jones, his female companion, and Partridge, against the landlord, his wife, and maid . . .

In Fielding's third narrative style, the formal, periodic manner of the eighteenth-century essay is used to overlay the plain narrative contents. After Tom's rescue of Mrs. Waters, the two repair to an inn where the landlady is not anxious to receive them:

> Now it required no very blamable degree of suspicion to imagine that Mr. Jones and his ragged companion had certain purposes in their intention, which, though tolerated in some Christian countries, connived at in others, and practised in all, are however as expressly forbidden as murder, or any other horrid vice, by that religion which

is universally believed in those countries. The landlady, therefore, had no sooner received an intimation of the entrance of the above-said persons than she began to meditate the most expeditious means for their expulsion. In order to do this, she had provided herself with a long and deadly instrument, with which, in times of peace, the chambermaid was wont to demolish the labours of the industrious spider. In vulgar phrase, she had taken up the broomstick, and was just about to sally from the kitchen, when Jones accosted her with a demand of a gown and other vestments to cover the half-naked woman up-stairs.

Both the essay and the heroic styles of narration, besides being amusing in themselves as burlesque and mock-heroic, are the result of Fielding's ambiguous attitude towards the material used in a novel. They also effectively point up the unsuitability in the novel of the "elevation of style" used in more traditional forms of narrative writing. By comparison the plain style is made to appear without question to be the best for the novel. The variety of narrative styles at the disposal of the novelist is succinctly illustrated by Fielding in *Joseph Andrews* on the occasion of one of the many beatings suffered by Parson Adams, whose assailant this time "belaboured the body of Adams till he was weary, and indeed till he concluded (to use the language of fighting) that he had done his business; or, in the language of poetry, 'that he had sent him to the shades below'; in plain English, 'that he was dead.' " And yet Fielding cannot take quite seriously the behavior of the "comic class" which his plain narrative style is so well calculated to report; his parodies and burlesques, like those of Joyce in *Ulysses*, exhibit the risibility of the world he is rendering and restore the ironical viewpoint of the author.

In addition to the three different narrative styles in *Tom Jones*, the style of the eighteenth-century essay is put to normal use in the well-known introductory chapters, "composed of observation and reflection," as well as in the course of the story itself when authorial comment seems appropriate. And to make the variety of styles even richer, Fielding, borrowing the principle of verisimilar speech from the drama, makes liberal use of many different speaking styles: the learned jargon of Square and Thwackum, the tiresome commonplace chatter of Mrs. Honour, the local dialects of barmaids, servants, and Squire Western.

Fielding's practice suggests the principle that the more independently the three genres composing the novel are developed, the more sharply differentiated will be the several prose styles of a novel, or the greater divergence there will be between the language that conveys the story, the language that conceptualizes and analyzes, and the language in which the characters speak. The structure of such a novel will tend to be episodic, the pattern of styles, paratactic: that is, blocks of varied material will be set beside each other without much coordination and modulation, and prose styles of sharply differing character will be juxtaposed. *Moby Dick,* even more than *Tom Jones,* is a prime example of a novel with mixed styles growing out of unassimilated genres and the divided mind of the author who regarded his material as both common whale blubber and rare mythic poetry. The narrative is presented in prose that is economical, concrete, and direct; exposition and authorial observations and reflections are presented ironically in a mixture of the "hopping," intimate style of the whimsical essay and the public style of oratory; the dialogue has the quality of heroic poetry, which Melville takes seriously as imitation, not parody, of Elizabethan blank verse. While all of these styles make a remarkable blend in *Moby Dick,* the special quality of each is preserved.

Being itself a compound of genres, each with a more fixed character than the novel and each having a different stylistic potential, the novel has always offered opportunities for a mixture of styles. And yet the novel has never imposed the necessity of being written in mixed styles. Indeed, from the very beginning, novelists have easily avoided the mixture of styles that the hybrid form and uncertain status of the novel seem to encourage. Far from being the rule, the mixed style novel has been the anomaly in the history of fiction, the kind of work that it is so difficult to justify as belonging at all to the genre.

The concentration on one of the component genres of the novel to the exclusion of the others has been one method to avoid a mixture of styles. Uniformity of style in *Clarissa* was made possible by the adaptation of the moral essay to fictional purposes; in *Tristram Shandy,* by the exploitation of that aspect of the personal essay that lends itself to facetious rhetoric and parenthesis. Concentration on the essayistic or analytic potential of prose produced uniform style in the later James and Proust, just as the scrupulous avoidance of analytic prose and an almost complete dependence upon narrative and drama yielded a uniform plain style in Hemingway.

In *The Ambassadors*, Maria Gostrey and Strether discover that they have in Waymarsh a mutual acquaintance:

> "Oh yes," he replied, "my very well-known friend. He's to meet me here, coming up from Malvern, and I supposed he would already have arrived. But he doesn't come till later, and I'm relieved not to have kept him. Do you know him?" Strether wound up.
>
> It was not till after he had spoken that he became aware of how much there had been in him of response; when the tone of her own rejoinder, as well as the play of something more in her face—something more, that is, than its apparently usual restless light—seemed to notify him. "I've met him at Milrose—where I used sometimes, a good while ago, to stay; I had friends there who were friends of his, and I've been at his house. I won't answer for it that he would know me," Strether's interlocutress pursued; "but I should be delighted to see him. Perhaps," she added, "I shall—for I'm staying over." She paused an instant, while our friend took in these things, and it was as if a good deal of talk had already passed. They even vaguely smiled at it, and Strether presently observed that Mr. Waymarsh would, no doubt, be easily to be seen. This, however, appeared to affect the lady as if she might have advanced too far. She was frank about everything. "Oh," she said, "he won't care!"—and she immediately thereupon remarked that she believed Strether knew the Munsters; the Munsters being the people he had seen her with at Liverpool.

The speeches of the characters, the motions of Strether's consciousness as it begins to play on a new phenomenon, and the author's objective record of the scene are all of a piece stylistically. There is no break from one kind of material to another; stiff-jointed syntax carries the burden of meticulous analysis. Colloquial usage gets into the recording prose of the author ("our friend took in these things"), and the formality of the author's manner gets into the speeches ("I supposed he would already have arrived").

A different kind of uniformity is achieved by Hemingway. The ambulance of Lieutenant Henry is bogged down in the mud:

> The thing to do now was to dig out in front of the wheels, put in brush so that the chains would grip, and then push until the car was on the road. We were all down on the road around the car. The two sergeants looked at the car and examined the wheels. Then they started off down the road without a word. I went after them.
>
> "Come on," I said. "Cut some brush."
>
> "We have to go," one said.
>
> "Get busy," I said, "and cut brush."

"We have to go," one said. The other said nothing. They were in a hurry to start. They would not look at me.

"I order you to come back to the car and cut brush," I said. The one sergeant turned. "We have to go on. In a little while you will be cut off. You can't order us. You're not our officer."

"I order you to cut brush," I said. They turned and started down the road.

"Halt," I said. They kept on down the muddy road, the hedge on either side. "I order you to halt," I called. They went a little faster. I opened up my holster, took the pistol, aimed at the one who had talked the most, and fired.

The same style is used for both action and dialogue and never varies throughout the book. No differentiation is made between the speeches of the narrator, an American who is presumably speaking simple Italian, and the speeches of the sergeant, a native Italian. No analysis is made of the characters' thought; it must be deduced from what they do and say: Lieutenant Henry "aimed at the one who had talked the most." There is no attempt in *A Farewell To Arms* to go beyond the plain recording of simple action and speech, except on one occasion when the mind of Lieutenant Henry is rendered as it succumbs to sleep and on another when an unspoken prayer for Catherine's recovery passes through the mind of the narrator.

Although competition among the three original genres of the novel has always been a condition in the writing of fiction, it is to be noted that in the earliest and latest years of the history of the novel this competition has been more pronounced than in the middle period, the nineteenth century. At that time the principle of assimilation prevailed: that is, the narrative, essayistic, and dramatic ingredients of the novel were not treated independently, each with a different potential fully realized, but were combined in a single genre and presented under a single aspect of language. Henry James stated the principles of assimilation when he wrote:

> I cannot imagine composition existing in a series of blocks, nor conceive, in any novel worth discussing at all, of a passage of description that is not in its intention narrative, a passage of dialogue that is not in its intention descriptive, a touch of truth of any sort that does not partake of the nature of incident. . . . A novel is a living thing, all one and continuous, . . . in each of the parts there is something of each of the other parts.

In a novel of such closely articulated parts—and the works of James's middle phase are among the best examples—the essayistic material ("a touch of the truth"), the dramatic material, and the narrative ("incident") have no existence as independent genres and are presented in a prose style that is essentially uniform. Moreover, the elements of narrative, essay, and drama are held in more or less equal proportions: there is not more essay material than dramatic, no more dramatic material than narrative. The balancing of novelistic ingredients and the presentation of all in a uniform style characterize the greatest achievements in the novel of the nineteenth century. A uniform style was thus the result of the assimilation of the component genres of the novel, and uniform style was also the means by which assimilation was helped.

Concentration on the essayistic element in fiction is likely to result in a complex prose style of a personal rather than conventional quality. Conversely, the assimilation and balancing of the novel's three component genres more readily leads to a plain style of conventional character, the language of narrative and drama acting as correctives to the tendency of essayistic prose to become syntactically complex and verbally abstract. The prose style of nineteenth-century English, French, and Russian fiction is distinguished by its plainness and by its lack of literary distinction. It was not far removed from the common style used in all sorts of contemporary writing that made a close approach to the plain facts of existence. Being close to the style of journalism, it was an easy and a popular style, well suited to the purposes of realism.

Whatever variety there was in this unspecialized and general style for fiction was gained by differentiating the speeches of characters. Such variety places most nineteenth-century fiction somewhere between the pure extremes of mixed and uniform style novels. It was of course the spirit of realism and the principle of verisimilar speech practiced in the drama that had prompted novelists as early as Fielding to contrive a mixture of speaking styles appropriate for various character types: dialect speakers, exotics like Scott's Highlanders and Cooper's Indians, and eccentrics whose peculiarities were better displayed in their speech than in their behavior. All of these speakers had numerous prototypes in Shakespeare and the contemporary stage, and most spoke in the novel "for the jest-sake," as Fielding put it, and for the purpose of injecting into the plain prose of the nineteenth-century novel a touch of "quaint," strange, or poetic language. Their varied speaking styles were not to be taken quite seriously, however, never to be accorded the same high value associated with the speaking style of the proper heroes and heroines. Since these spoke in the same style used in the essay and narrative material of the novel, the general effect of uniform style thus remained in spite of the speeches of amusing and exotic characters, whose divergent styles supplied only occasional color to the common fabric of the prose.

The normative or base style of the typical nineteenth-century novel can be described as polite, "literary," book prose, greatly relaxed and loosened by the influence of journalism—what Carlyle contemptuously labelled "ready-writing" and Thoreau "fluent writing." Undistinguished as such a style was, it served the purpose of the best fiction of the time. It had two important advantages for the novel of that time: its fluency and prolixity supported the sense of continuous and detailed existence that the novel tried to render, and its gentility constituted a valuable means of reader edification and reader identification with the point of view of the author. An equable and consistent view of reality was presented in a consistent and unpointed flow of language. Every narrative incident, every authorial comment was assured of a respectful response by reason of its being conveyed in a style common to both writer and reader. Characters of irregular habit or disposition were easily identified and evaluated according to their degree of departure from the normative style of the hero and the author.

Uniform style in fiction employing first-person narration is of course a formal requirement to reflect limited point of view. Some variety of style is secured by the narrator's total recall of the speeches of characters he encounters. When partial recall is used, as in *Huckleberry Finn,* the recorded speaking styles are accommodated to the style of the narrator, so that while there is some difference between the style of the narrator and other characters, it is not as great as in a novel like *David Copperfield,* in which the narrator preserves exactly the strikingly different qualities of Micawber and Mrs. Mowcher. Absolute uniformity of style in a first-person novel is achieved simply by making no concessions whatever to individual differences. Interest is made to center so exclusively on the narrator's particular response to reality and on a set of characters closely resembling the narrator, that no expectation of stylistic variation has to be met by the writer. Walter Shandy and his guests are rhetoricians of the same school as Tristram; the narrators of James and Hemingway present worlds that are closed to any character and any style that is not of a piece with the narrator's.

While verisimilar speech was widely used for amusing and exotic characters in novels before the last quarter of the nineteenth century, little attempt was made to have the first-person narrator deliver his fiction in a verisimilar speaking style. Convention required that the narrator "write" his account in the style generally expected in all fiction rather than "speak" it in a special personal style. The prose of a narrator like David Copperfield differs not at all from the prose used by Dickens in his third-person novels. David Copperfield's personality is of course revealed, but not through the kind of prose style he employs. The manner in which he tells his story is calculated less to individualize his character than to supply the stabilizing and evaluative function of a conventional style. *Tristram Shandy* and *Moby Dick* represent early attempts to depart from the conventional style for first-person narration by exploiting the idiosyncrasies of the narrator's language. Tristram drives traditional rhetorical devices to unconventional extremes, and Ishmael resorts to archaic essay styles. Neither uses a verisimilar speaking style, although this is speciously suggested by their addressing the reader on almost every page. In neither case is a new style for fiction developed or even intended; the striking effect in each book depends upon the highly mannered application to fiction of prose styles that are outrageously unsuited for fiction.

It was not until the latter part of the nineteenth century, when the fully developed theory of realism embraced the serious use of dialect styles, that versimilar speech was considered appropriate for first-person narrators. Mark Twain proved that a special dialect style could support a masterpiece, and Hemingway later proved that a general colloquial style is equally capable of sustaining a novel. But these are singular achievements of stylistic imitation and hold no promise either for the continued creativeness of a writer or for the novel in general.

Uniform style is characteristic of the naturalistic novel that specializes in the breadth rather than the depth of its *tranche de vie*. Since the naturalist takes no commanding view of his fiction, narrative and essay materials are presented in a style not far removed from the dull, unpointed speaking style of the characters, who are representative of average humanity. The result is a monolithic dullness of language. In the later development of naturalism, however, the limitations of simple syntax and colorless diction became an intolerable burden, and we find naturalists resorting to a modified mixed style novel. By the use of "interchapters" that range in style from the newspaper headline to the stream of consciousness, Dos Passos sought ways of varying the uniform dullness of his prose and gaining access to subjective and even poetic expression. Steinbeck, in *The Grapes of Wrath*, carries his tribe of Joads into Canaan almost entirely in the low dialect style of their speech, but, quite appropriately for a story that is a latter-day Exodus, his interchapters reflect the style of the King James Version.

The tendency towards mixed styles in the naturalistic novel proves the inadequacy of a prose style based exclusively on the low tone of ordinary speech, or what Henry James called the "unutterable depths" of the "bastard vernacular" of modern communities. An uncommon dialect speaker like Huck Finn commands interest, and his speech may even rise to heights of poetic expressiveness; a common colloquial narrator, like Frederick Henry in *A Farewell To Arms*, attracts because of his artful selection from the common store of colloquial diction and rhythm. But the unrelieved, common slush of prose characteristic of Studs Lonigan cannot fail to be dull. The naturalists as well as their critics recognized this, and their interchapters suggest the close of another period of uniform prose and the return of the novel to a mixture of styles.

In naturalistic novels that specialize in depth, the stream of consciousness technique constitutes an extreme development of the earlier principle of verisimilar speech. When the content of a character's consciousness is composed of ideas, of thought, it must be conveyed in language that approaches closer to the quality of speech than to the style of either essay or narrative. It is speech without the use of syntax, or speech in which conventional syntax is replaced by a personal rhetoric of associations employed just below the level of communication. The style of such passages must be an appropriate imitation of potential or incipient speech, just as speaking style in conventional fiction imitates actual or achieved speech. When the content of a character's consciousness is composed of sensations, however, the style cannot be modeled upon speech patterns but must depend upon the non-imitative imagination of the novelist working with the syntax and vocabulary of poetry. In either event, opportunities for mixed style novels have been immeasurably increased by the stream of consciousness technique; for in a single novel there may be as many styles as there are characters, and a single character may have more than one style assigned to him, depending upon the levels of consciousness in which he is revealed.

No historical or evolutionary principle explains the incidence of mixed and uniform styles in the novel. The possibilities of both methods were realized in the earliest novels, and both methods are in use today. The least one can safely say is that between *Moby Dick* and *Ulysses* the novel was committed to a uniform plain style. *Moby Dick* is the last specimen of the early mixed style novel, and *Ulysses* begins the return of the contemporary novel to mixed styles. In the period between these two works, the novel attained a degree of stylistic stability that made possible the perfection of the genre in that time.

Uniform style novels may result from the operation of some formal principle such as first-person narration, the assimilation of the three component genres of fiction, or the exclusive dependence upon one. Uniform style in a novel generally depends upon the writer's settled conviction of the single, unambiguous nature of his materials and of the novel's adequacy as a vehicle for their serious presentment. In so far as style is a means of shutting out many possible views on a subject and directing attention to a few selected views, a uniform style has the effect of better narrowing the scope to a single, unified view of reality. A uniform style is assimilative in that it helps to create under a single aspect of language a single vision of the multiplicity of reality; it is a bond between author and reader, insuring that no different adjustment to language and viewpoint will be demanded from the reader than that established at the outset. In the nineteenth century it was confidently expected—and sometimes rigorously demanded as in the case of Melville and James—that every work of a novelist be in the same style as his first success. Our contemporary taste is just the reverse: it finds fault with a writer like Hemingway because his style repeats itself from one work to another, while nothing now creates more respect and attention than a change of style, as was evidenced in the recent stir in critical circles over Cozzens' *By Love Possessed.*

A mixed style novel may proceed from the variety that can be gained from exploiting the different potentials of the three genres composing the novel. It is the ideal vehicle for the writer who is motivated by the spirit of irony and parody and who finds it impossible to remain committed to a single vision of reality. A mixture of styles has the effect of making the reader pass through a succession of contradictory and ambiguous attitudes; it offers no sure stylistic norm by which the reader may orient himself permanently to the fiction and to the point of view of the author. He is conditioned to expect to change his position of witness as the style changes. Instead of being assimilative, the mixed style method is mimetic, or imitative of the inherent qualities of things and of the diverse attitudes with which reality may be viewed.

6

CHARACTER

Critical theory has its fashions, like anything else. Through the nineteenth century, until well into the twentieth, the fashionable way of responding to a novel was to consider its characters, to analyze their motives, to remark on the cleverness of their portrayal, and quite often to declare one's love for them. Both Don Quixote and Sancho, Sterne's Uncle Toby, Scott's Jeanie Deans, and a whole gallery of Dickens' characters were perennial objects of such an approach. It was that method of discussing novels which transformed the ironic and extremely intelligent Jane Austen into the bland and genial chronicler she was largely taken to be for so long. The drama, too, was often approached in a similar way. Shakespeare studies throughout the nineteenth century, like studies of the novel, are heavily weighted with analysis of character. The reaction to a central concern with character is easier to chart in respect to the drama than the novel. The long reaction to the former reaches a climax in L. C. Knights' attack, somewhat unfair it must be said, upon the premises of the Shakespearean critic A. C. Bradley in Knights' essay "How Many

Children Had Lady Macbeth?" If the reaction against character in the criticism of novels is somewhat more diffuse, it is no less forceful. Any amount of critical work on the novel in the '30's and '40's, especially that associated with F. R. Leavis and the British journal Scrutiny, begins by aggressively denying any interest in character. Thus the fashion, by mid-century, had shifted so completely that it had become virtually impossible, in serious critical circles, to say anything at all about character as such.

E. M. Forster's Aspects of the Novel is so personal and original a book that it tends to stand outside of these patterns of fashion. In its independence, it goes some ways toward demonstrating that whether criticism of character is fashionable or not, whether the bulk of criticism that deals with character is incisive or fatuous, individual readers will continue to respond to novels because their curiosity and their sense of common humanity is engaged by the portrayals of human beings which they find there. Character, of course, is only one of the topics treated by Forster, but it is probably the best known, largely because his treatment of character has given to the critical vocabulary of the novel the terms "round and flat characters." The terms have often been applied badly; at worst, "flat characters" has become a club with which one may beat Dickens. It goes without saying that a responsible use of the terms implies a knowledge of what Forster said when he invented them.

If Forster stands outside of the flow of fashion, W. J. Harvey's Character and the Novel is very much a part of it—in its own modest way, a notably anti-fashionable book. It is hardly a revival of that much despised interest in character that led critics to speculate about Hamlet's student days before the action of the play begins. Rather it is a thoughtful attempt to give an account of what one means by such words as "real," "probable," and "true to life," to illuminate the idea of fictional character by the categories of Time, Identity, Causality, and Freedom, and, in the section reprinted here, to relate the nature and purpose of fictional characters to the web of other characters that surrounds each of them. Implicitly the book is a defense of the importance of character and—it is not too audacious a conjecture—the beginning of a revival on its own terms.

E. M. FORSTER

FLAT AND ROUND CHARACTERS

We now turn from transplantation to acclimatization. We have discussed whether people could be taken out of life and put into a book, and conversely whether they could come out of books and sit down in this room. The answer suggested was in the negative and led to a more vital question: can we, in daily life, understand each other? Today our problems are more academic. We are concerned with the characters in their relation to other aspects of the novel; to a plot, a moral, their fellow characters, atmosphere, etc. They will have to adapt themselves to other requirements of their creator.

It follows that we shall no longer expect them to coincide as a whole with daily life, only to parallel it. When we say that a character in Jane Austen, Miss Bates for instance, is "so like life" we mean that each bit of her coincides with a bit of life, but that she as a whole only parallels the chatty spinster we met at tea. Miss Bates is bound by a hundred threads to Highbury. We cannot tear her away without bringing her mother too, and Jane Fairfax and Frank Churchill, and the whole of Box Hill; whereas we could tear Moll Flanders away, at least for the purposes of experiment. A Jane Austen novel is more complicated than a Defoe, because the characters are inter-dependent, and there is the additional complication of a plot. The plot in *Emma* is not prominent and Miss Bates contributes little. Still it is there, she is connected with the principals, and the result is a closely woven fabric from which nothing can be removed. Miss Bates and Emma herself are like bushes in a shrubbery—not isolated trees like Moll—and anyone who has tried to thin out a shrubbery knows how wretched the bushes look if they are transplanted elsewhere, and how wretched is the look of the bushes that remain. In most books the characters cannot spread themselves. They must exercise a mutual restraint.

The novelist, we are beginning to see, has a very mixed lot of ingredients to handle. There is the story, with its time-sequence of "and then . . . and then . . ."; there are ninepins about whom he might tell the story, and tell a rattling good one, but no, he prefers to tell his story about human beings; he takes over the life by values as well as the life in time. The characters arrive when evoked, but full of the spirit of mutiny. For they have these numerous parallels with people like ourselves, they try to live their own lives and are consequently often engaged in treason against the main scheme of the book. They "run away," they "get out of hand": they are creations inside a creation, and often inharmonious towards it; if they are given complete freedom they kick the book to pieces, and if they are kept too sternly in check, they revenge themselves by dying, and destroy it by intestinal decay.

These trials beset the dramatist also, and he has yet another set of ingredients to cope with—the actors and actresses—and they appear to side sometimes with the characters they represent, sometimes with the play as a whole, and more often to be the mortal enemies of both. The weight they throw is incalculable, and how any work of art survives their arrival I do not understand. Concerned with a lower form of art, we need not worry— but, in passing, is it not extraordinary that plays on the stage are often better than they are in the study, and that the introduction of a bunch of rather ambitious and nervous men and women should add anything to our understanding of Shakespeare and Chekov?

No, the novelist has difficulties enough, and today we shall examine two of his devices for solving them—instinctive devices, for his methods when working are seldom the same as the methods we use when examining his work. The first device is the use of different kinds of characters. The second is connected with the point of view.

WE may divide characters into flat and round. Flat characters were called "humorous" in the seventeenth century, and are sometimes called types, and sometimes caricatures. In their purest form, they are constructed round a single idea or quality: when there is more than one factor in them, we get the beginning of the curve towards the round. The really flat character can be expressed in one sentence such as "I never will desert Mr. Micawber." There is Mrs. Micawber—she says she won't desert Mr. Micawber, she doesn't, and there she is. Or: "I must conceal, even by subterfuges, the poverty of my master's house." There is Caleb Balderstone in *The Bride of Lammermoor*. He does not use the actual phrase, but it completely describes him; he has no existence outside it, no pleasures, none of the private lusts and aches that must complicate the most consistent of servitors. Whatever he does, wherever he goes, whatever lies he tells or plates he breaks, it is to conceal the poverty of his master's house. It is not his *idée fixe,* because there is nothing in him into which the idea can be fixed. He is the idea, and such life as he possesses radiates from its edges and from the scintillations it strikes when other elements in the novel impinge. Or take Proust. There are numerous flat characters in Proust, such as the Princess of Parma, or Legrandin. Each can be expressed in a single sentence, the Princess's sentence being, "I must be particularly careful to be kind." She does nothing except to be particularly careful, and those of the other characters who are more complex than herself easily see through the kindness, since it is only a by-product of the carefulness.

One great advantage of flat characters is that they are easily recognized whenever they come in—recognized by the reader's emotional eye, not by the visual eye, which merely notes the recurrence of a proper name. In Russian novels, where they so seldom occur, they would be a decided help. It is a convenience for an author when he can strike with his full force at once, and flat characters are very useful to him, since they never need reintroducing, never run away, have not to be watched for development, and provide their own atmosphere—little luminous disks of a pre-arranged size, pushed hither and thither like counters across the void or between the stars; most satisfactory.

A second advantage is that they are easily remembered by the reader afterwards. They remain in his mind as unalterable for the reason that they were not changed by circumstances; they moved through circumstances, which gives them in retrospect a comforting quality, and preserves them when the book that produced them may decay. The Countess in *Evan Harrington* furnishes a good little example here. Let us compare our memories of her with our memories of Becky Sharp. We do not remember what the Countess did or what she passed through. What is clear is her figure and the formula that surrounds it, namely, "Proud as we are of dear papa, we must conceal his memory." All her rich humour proceeds from this. She is a flat character. Becky is round. She, too, is on the make, but she cannot be summed up in a single phrase, and we remember her in connection with the great scenes through which she passed and as modified by those scenes—that is to say, we do not remember her so easily because she waxes and wanes and has facets like a human being. All of us, even the sophisticated, yearn for permanence, and to the unsophisticated permanence is the chief excuse for a work of art. We all want books to endure, to be refuges, and their inhabitants to be always the same, and flat characters tend to justify themselves on this account.

All the same, critics who have their eyes fixed severely upon daily life—as were our eyes last week—have very little patience with such renderings of human nature. Queen Victoria, they argue, cannot be summed up in a single sentence, so what excuse remains for Mrs. Micawber? One of our foremost writers, Mr. Norman Douglas, is a critic of this type, and the passage from him which I will quote puts the case against flat characters in a forcible fashion. The passage occurs in an open letter to D. H. Lawrence, with whom he is quarrelling: a doughty pair of combatants, the hardness of whose hitting makes the rest of us feel like a lot of ladies up in a pavilion. He complains that Lawrence, in a biography, has falsified the picture by employing "the novelist's touch," and he goes on to define what this is:

> It consists, I should say, in a failure to realize the complexities of the ordinary human mind; it selects for literary purposes two or three facets of a man or woman, generally the most spectacular, and therefore useful ingredients of their character and disregards all the others. Whatever fails to fit in with these specially chosen traits is eliminated—must be eliminated, for otherwise the description would not hold water. Such and such are the data: everything incompatible with those data has to go by the board. It follows that the novelist's touch argues, often logically, from a wrong premise: it takes what it likes and leaves the rest. The facets may be correct as far as they go but there are too few

of them: what the author says may be true and yet by no means the truth. That is the novelist's touch. It falsifies life.

Well, the novelist's touch as thus defined is, of course, bad in biography, for no human being is simple. But in a novel it has its place: a novel that is at all complex often requires flat people as well as round, and the outcome of their collisions parallels life more accurately than Mr. Douglas implies. The case of Dickens is significant. Dickens' people are nearly all flat (Pip and David Copperfield attempt roundness, but so diffidently that they seem more like bubbles than solids). Nearly every one can be summed up in a sentence, and yet there is this wonderful feeling of human depth. Probably the immense vitality of Dickens causes his characters to vibrate a little, so that they borrow his life and appear to lead one of their own. It is a conjuring trick; at any moment we may look at Mr. Pickwick edgeways and find him no thicker than a gramophone record. But we never get the sideway view. Mr. Pickwick is far too adroit and well-trained. He always has the air of weighing something, and when he is put into the cupboard of the young ladies' school he seems as heavy as Falstaff in the buck-basket at Windsor. Part of the genius of Dickens is that he does use types and caricatures, people whom we recognize the instant they re-enter, and yet achieves effects that are not mechanical and a vision of humanity that is not shallow. Those who dislike Dickens have an excellent case. He ought to be bad. He is actually one of our big writers, and his immense success with types suggests that there may be more in flatness than the severer critics admit.

Or take H. G. Wells. With the possible exceptions of Kipps and the aunt in *Tono Bungay*, all Wells' characters are as flat as a photograph. But the photographs are agitated with such vigour that we forget their complexities lie on the surface and would disappear if it were scratched or curled up. A Wells character cannot indeed be summed up in a single phrase; he is tethered much more to observation, he does not create types. Nevertheless his people seldom pulsate by their own strength. It is the deft and powerful hands of their maker that shake them and trick the reader into a sense of depth. Good but imperfect novelists, like Wells and Dickens, are very clever at transmitting force. The part of their novel that is alive galvanizes the part that is not, and causes the characters to jump about and speak in a convincing way. They are quite different from the perfect novelist who touches all his material directly, who seems to pass the creative finger down every sentence and into every word. Richardson, Defoe, Jane Austen, are perfect in this particular way; their work may not be great but their hands are always upon it; there is not the tiny interval between the touching of the button and the sound of the bell which occurs in novels where the characters are not under direct control.

For we must admit that flat people are not in themselves as big achievements as round ones, and also that they are best when they are comic. A serious or tragic flat character is apt to be a bore. Each time he enters crying "Revenge!" or "My heart bleeds for humanity!" or whatever his formula is, our hearts sink. One of the romances of a popular contemporary writer is constructed round a Sussex farmer who says, "I'll plough up that bit of gorse." There is the farmer, there is the gorse; he says he'll plough it up, he does plough it up, but it is not like saying "I'll never desert Mr. Micawber," because we are so bored by his consistency that we do not care whether he succeeds with the gorse or fails. If his formula were analysed and connected up with the rest of human outfit, we should not be bored any longer, the formula would cease to be the man and become an obsession in the man; that is to say he would have turned from a flat farmer into a round one. It is only round people who are fit to perform tragically for any length of time and can move us to any feelings except humour and appropriateness.

So now let us desert these two-dimensional people, and by way of transition to the round, let us go to *Mansfield Park,* and look at Lady Bertram, sitting on her sofa with pug. Pug is flat, like most animals in fiction. He is once represented as straying into a rosebed in a cardboard kind of way, but that is all, and during most of the book his mistress seems to be cut out of the same simple material as her dog. Lady Bertram's formula is, "I am kindly, but must not be fatigued," and she functions out of it. But at the end there is a catastrophe. Her two daughters come to grief—to the worst grief known to Miss Austen's universe, far worse than the Napoleonic wars. Julia elopes; Maria, who is unhappily married, runs off with a lover. What is Lady Bertram's reaction? The sentence describing it is significant: "Lady Bertram did not think deeply, but, guided by Sir Thomas, she thought justly on all important points, and she saw therefore in all its enormity, what had happened, and neither endeavoured herself, nor required Fanny to advise her, to think little of guilt and infamy." These are strong words, and they used to worry me because I thought Jane Austen's moral sense was getting out of hand. She may, and of course does, deprecate guilt and infamy herself, and she duly causes all possible distress in the minds of Edmund and Fanny, but has she any right to agitate calm, consistent Lady Bertram? Is not it like giving pug three faces and setting him to guard the gates of Hell? Ought not her ladyship to remain on the sofa saying, "This is a dreadful and sadly exhausting business about Julia and Maria, but where is Fanny gone? I have dropped another stitch"?

I used to think this, through misunderstanding Jane Austen's method—exactly as Scott misunderstood it when he congratulated her for painting on a square of ivory. She is a miniaturist, but never two-dimensional. All her characters are round, or capable of rotundity. Even Miss Bates has a mind, even Elizabeth Eliot a heart, and Lady Bertram's moral fervour ceases to vex us when we realize this: the disk has suddenly extended and become a little globe. When the novel is closed, Lady Bertram goes back to the flat, it is true; the dominant impression she leaves can be summed up in a formula. But that is not how Jane Austen conceived her, and the freshness of her reappearances are due to this. Why do the characters in Jane Austen give us a slightly new pleasure each time they come in, as opposed to the merely repetitive pleasure that is caused by a character in Dickens? Why do they combine so well in a conversation, and draw one another out without seeming to do so, and never perform? The answer to this question can be put in several ways: that, unlike Dickens, she was a real artist, that she never stooped to caricature, etc. But the best reply is that her characters though smaller than his are more highly organized. They function all round, and even if her plot made greater demands on them than it does, they would still be adequate. Suppose that Louisa Musgrove had broken her neck on the Cobb. The description of her death would have been feeble and ladylike—physical violence is quite beyond Miss Austen's powers—but the survivors would have reacted properly as soon as the corpse was carried away, they would have brought into view new sides of their character, and though *Persuasion* would have been spoiled as a book, we should know more than we do about Captain Wentworth and Anne. All the Jane Austen characters are ready for an extended life, for a life which the scheme of her books seldom requires them to lead, and that is why they lead their actual lives so satisfactorily. Let us return to Lady Bertram and the crucial sentence. See how subtly it modulates from her formula into an area where the formula does not work. "Lady Bertram did not think deeply." Exactly: as per formula. "But guided by Sir Thomas she thought justly on all important points." Sir Thomas' guidance, which is part of the formula, remains, but it pushes her ladyship towards an independent and undesired morality. "She saw therefore in all its enormity what had happened." This is the moral fortissimo— very strong but carefully introduced. And then follows a most artful decrescendo, by means of negatives. "She neither endeavoured herself, nor required Fanny to advise her, to think little of guilt or infamy." The formula is reappearing, because as a rule she does try to minimize trouble, and does require Fanny to advise her how to do this; indeed Fanny has done nothing else for the last ten years. The words, though they are negatived, remind us of this, her normal state is again in view, and she has in a single sentence been inflated into a round character and collapsed back into a flat one. How Jane Austen can write! In a few words she has extended Lady Bertram, and by so doing she has increased the probability of the elopements of Maria and Julia. I say probability because the elopements belong to the domain of violent physical action, and here, as already indicated, Jane Austen is feeble and ladylike. Except in her school-girl novels, she cannot stage a crash. Everything violent has to take place "off"—Louisa's accident and Marianne Dashwood's putrid throat are the nearest exceptions—and consequently all the comments on the elopement must be sincere and convincing, otherwise we should doubt whether it occurred. Lady Bertram helps us to believe that her daughters have run away, and they have to run away, or there would be no apotheosis for Fanny. It is a little point, and a little sentence, yet it shows us how delicately a great novelist can modulate into the round.

All through her works we find these characters, apparently so simple and flat, never needing reintroduction and yet never out of their depth—Henry Tilney, Mr. Woodhouse, Charlotte Lucas. She may label her characters "Sense," "Pride," "Sensibility," "Prejudice," but they are not tethered to those qualities.

As for the round characters proper, they have already been defined by implication and no more need be said. All I need do is to give some examples of people in books who seem to me round so that the definition can be tested afterwards:

All the principal characters in *War and Peace,* all the Dostoevsky characters, and some of the Proust—for example, the old family servant, the Duchess of Guermantes, M. de Charlus, and Saint Loup; Madame Bovary—who, like Moll Flanders, has her book to herself, and can expand and secrete unchecked; some people in Thackeray—for instance, Becky and Beatrix; some in Fielding—Parson Adams, Tom Jones; and some in Charlotte Brontë, most particularly Lucy Snowe. (And many more—this is not a catalogue). The test of a round character is whether it is capable of surprising in a convincing way. If it never surprises, it is flat. If it does not convince, it is a flat pretending to be round. It has the incalculability of life about it—life within the pages of a book. And by using it sometimes alone, more often in combination with the other kind, the novelist achieves his task of acclimatization and harmonizes the human race with the other aspects of his work.

W. J. HARVEY

THE HUMAN CONTEXT

The last chapter will at least have demonstrated the complexities inherent in even the simplest of human relationships. It would be tedious to analyse many contexts in such detail; cumu-

From Character and the Novel, *1965; reprinted by permission of Cornell University Press and Chatto and Windus Ltd.*

latively they support the point made by Kenneth Burke in an essay called *Four Master Tropes*:

> It is customary to think that objective reality is dissolved by such relativity of terms as we get through the shifting of perspectives (the perception of one character in terms of many diverse characters). But on the contrary, it is by the approach through a variety of perspectives that we establish a character's reality.[1]

Burke is here writing of metaphor and the word *character* has a special meaning for him; but if we reinterpret this passage to suit our own interest it still remains relevant and stimulating. For if we compile a list of all those relationships which make up our contextual knowledge of others and if we then try to recreate our sense of these relationships overlapping, interacting and developing in time, what we achieve is precisely that "variety of perspectives" whereby "we establish a character's reality." It is precisely because the novel can establish a greater range and variety of perspectives than any other art-form—indeed, a greater variety of viewpoints than we usually have of most other people in actual life—that we may legitimately talk of the reality of fictional characters.

By far the most important of contexts is the web of human relationships in which any single character must be enmeshed. So much of what we are can only be defined in terms of our relations with other people; indeed, if we wish to be rigorous, we can say with the philosophers that other people must exist if only to show us what we ourselves are not. Thus, for example, one aspect of Strether's reality for us in *The Ambassadors* lies in his relation to Waymarsh. Waymarsh represents one possible line of development, or rather regression, for Strether. Again, little Bilham is not simply the Complete European displayed for the benefit of the American visitor, nor yet simply a politely uncomprehending audience for Strether's mature views on life; he also illuminates aspects of Strether not directly revealed in the book but which we feel as part, perhaps, of Strether's past and as such, which we can check against James's recapitulation of Strether's history. Of course, what these characters do not share is more important than what they have in common and equally there are some alternatives for Strether which we feel are just

[1] K. Burke, *A Grammar of Motives,* p. 504. New York: Prentice Hall, 1945.

not possible. Thus he might *just* become a kind of Waymarsh but we feel he could *never* become a Jim Pocock.

The first thing to notice about this network of relationships—obviously very simplified in my account of *The Ambassadors*—is that *we* perceive it, not any of the characters. They may be more or less perceptive, and again we distinguish them as such, but none of them can aspire to our wholeness of vision. What we are offered is an exercise in contrast and comparison, a variation on the old theme of unity in variety, of similitude in dissimilitude, which is one of the major formal pleasures of art. But the pleasure is more than merely formal; we are also aware of a real analogy between our responses as readers of fiction and the process whereby in actual life we establish a person's reality by considering his many relationships, by viewing him through many perspectives. The only difference is that the fictional character offers a challenge that is perhaps more clear-cut, disciplined and subtle. If he offers no such challenge what do we call him? Probably an unreal stereotype; we can all think of creative failures which render such a verdict just. But we should also realize that too often we live by standards we condemn in art. In real life our perspectives are often extremely artificial and limited; for example, we often impose our own created stereo types on others because we are too tired or too timid for anything else. This man is a bore, that man a hypocrite, we say—as though that were the whole truth of the matter. The bore bores us, the hypocrite disgusts us—life is that simple. But in fiction the bore delights us, the hypocrite fascinates us; for in fiction they become interesting and complex characters. A good novel, by its various strategies, breaks down our stereotypes and enforces its own perspectives. If we read well we shall attend to these; the effort of so attending—which implies understanding, sympathizing, judging, etc.—is a *real* effort, a real psychological adjustment on our part. This effort on our part we impute, by a confusion of cause and effect, to the characters themselves; thereby we call them real.

The variety of perspectives thus established by fiction depends upon a double awareness on our part:

(*a*) Our awareness that the world is humanly diverse and abundant. This I shall take for granted; the range of individual variety is an obvious criterion by which we judge the greatness of most great novels. Even where experience is concentrated and focused by the lens of a single consciousness—a Tristram Shandy, a David Copperfield, even a Stephen Dedalus—we are still as much interested in the various human worlds thus revealed, however distorted or partial they may be, as in the consciousness itself.

(b) Our awareness that we experience the world in differing degrees of depth, that the quality of our various relationships depends especially on the degree of intimacy, insight and knowledge in our contact for others. For example with some people we communicate well, with others badly. Generally it is probably fair to say that in real life we transmit or receive on pretty insensitive instruments, covering a wide and blurred waveband; there is always plenty of static, plenty of merely human *noise*, against which our messages sometimes emerge loud and clear, sometimes as a jumbled code. A good novelist will generally pay tribute to this variety in the quality of our human communication; perfect communication if prolonged is implausible. Some of James's characters, for example—those who perceive every nuance, every implication, who read brilliantly not only the lines but between the lines—sometimes irritate us on this account. Of course James, like most great novelists, can exploit miscommunication between characters, and of course miscommunication between characters may often be part of the author's strategy in communicating to the reader. The important point to stress is the variety of quality in human relationships. Thus this person we know almost as well as ourselves, that one is interesting or intriguing but elusive and shadowy, a third only occasionally impinges on us so that we can fit him into one of those stereotyped categories by means of which, as I have said, we simplify and make convenient our lives.

Granted this, we can discover two sets of perspectives in fiction. This first set we may call perspectives of range and these derive from the greater knowledge bestowed on us as readers; thus we can make connections inaccessible to individual characters, we can spot motives hidden from them, we may even know the future towards which they move in their dramatic present. Anything that we label "dramatic irony" derives from this kind of perspective. But there is a second kind—we may call it the perspective of depth—in which certain characters become important because they stand out from, or are immersed in, a world of other human beings seen briefly, shallowly or in fragments. This kind of perspective corresponds to the varying quality of our relationships in the real world and like them, it is fluid and unstable. A face that is no more than a blur in the crowd may for a moment be focused sharply and significantly before fading away again; a stranger briefly met and almost totally unknown may illuminate a new possibility of life for us. So also in fiction; a background figure, a mere stereotype, may be granted a moment of dramatic intensity in which he achieves fullness as a human being. Dostoievsky and Proust are supreme in their mastery of this technique whereby we are suddenly plunged from shallows to depths, but the trick is not uncommon. This brief illumination of an otherwise sketchily realized character is one of the many ways in which the novelist legitimately provokes the reader to speculate about, and thereby give substance to the character; what we are offered, so to speak, is only one arc of the circle that if fully drawn would make up the rounded character. But the arc is so curved that we can, if we wish, extend it full-circle in our imagination.

This kind of perspective in depth, then, is a fluid and shifting affair in art as well as in life. Some characters stand in a full light, others remain shadowy, still others advance and retreat in our consciousness as readers. Nevertheless, for convenience we can group most characters into three categories. The most important are clearly the protagonists—those characters whose motivation and history are most fully established, who conflict and change as the story progresses, who engage our responses more fully and steadily, in a way more complex though not necessarily more vivid than other characters. They are the vehicles by which all the most interesting questions are raised; they evoke our beliefs, sympathies, revulsions; they incarnate the moral vision of the world inherent in the total novel. In a sense they are end-products; they are what the novel exists for; it exists to reveal them. Because of this it is unwise to generalize about them; each exists as an individual case and demands special consideration.

At the other end of the scale are those many different kinds of creation we may lump together as "background" characters. These may, as I have said, be allowed a moment of intensity and depth, but equally they may be almost entirely anonymous, voices rather than individualized characters. Singly they may be merely useful cogs in the mechanism of the plot, collectively they may establish themselves as a chorus to the main action— one thinks, for example, of Hardy's rustics—or may exist simply to establish the density of society in which the protagonists must move if they are to have any depth of realization. Clearly this social setting is one of the most important of all human contexts, and while the novelist can do a great deal by way of direct description and analysis, society must also be seen as a complex web of *individual* relationships. This is most economically achieved by establishing a range of background characters whose individuality need be no more than is adequate to typify social trends or pressures; without them society will tend to become hopelessly abstract and external. One thinks, for instance, of the weakness of those inter-chapters in *The Grapes of Wrath* in which Steinbeck attempts to convey the vast impersonal forces of a complex society determining the destinies of the Joad family. When he works in the opposite direction and allows us to take the family as the representative focus of a particular kind of society, he is much more successful.

So much, of course, depends on the society to be depicted. With a relatively simple and static world the novelist may easily convey a sense of the whole community in action—the village of Hayslope, for example, in *Adam Bede*. The same holds true of any society which is isolated or artificially delimited and which lives according to a traditional code of its own—one thinks of the ships' crews in *Moby Dick* or *The Nigger of the Narcissus* or the isolated communities, white and Indian, of a novel like *The Prairie*. In a more complex society the problems are correspondingly greater but in either case human relationships must be felt to merge into social relationships without too abrupt a change from dramatic realization to external analysis and commentary.

Indeed, one can think of remarkably few novels in which the protagonists achieve reality while remaining isolated from some social context. On the other hand, many novels may approach if not achieve greatness by realizing through a host of background characters a sense of society in action. *Germinal* is here a relevant example. Surely there is no single character in this novel who remains powerfully in the mind as an individual. Étienne is a mere dummy with the same status, say, as Felix Holt. Souvarine's inadequacy can be seen by contrasting him with his equivalent in *The Possessed*. Perhaps the character nearest to achieving individual status—and even this is peripheral—is the tormented Hennebeau. This lack prevents *Germinal* from being a truly great novel but it is still a very good one. What, then, does one remember as the source of the novel's power? First, there are individual *gestures* as distinct from individual characters—Moquette flaunting her bum in derision. Then there are superbly melodramatic scenes—Chaval's corpse bumping against Étienne and Catherine in the flooded mine. Above all there is the symbolic power of the book—the mine, for example, seen as an animal, finally wounded and collapsing in its death throes; counterpointing this, the miners seen as animals, the human figure almost being submerged into the natural. The symbolism is gross, face-slapping; the delicate tools of critical analysis would be as out of place here as a pick and shovel in a surgery. All these things derive from Zola's control of the mass; nowhere is he finer than in his mob scenes, where he is only equalled by Dickens at his best. Here is a community in action; the coarse vigour of the book is appropriately channelled through a number of characters who hardly ever achieve more than a background status; indeed, more complex characterization or greater psychological subtlety would have compelled a different kind of interest, quite fatal to the book's distinctive achievement.

Between the protagonists and the background characters fall a wide variety of intermediate figures; I wish to concentrate on two of them. The first we may call, after James, the ficelle, the character who while more fully delineated and individualized than any background character, exists in the novel primarily to serve some function. Unlike the protagonist he is ultimately a means to an end rather than an end in himself; the novelist's success in treating him will often reside in the function being so disguised that it may be performed unobtrusively. But before

I consider the various functions of the ficelle, I wish to consider another type of intermediate creation—the Card, the character who is a "character."

II

ONE fairly common use of the word *character* occurs in a phrase like "What a character!" When we describe a person in such terms we often have at the back of our minds the notion that life may here be imitating art, that such a person is "larger than life" or is distinguished by some fiction-like idiosyncrasy. Of course, in a sense we all know that life is weirder and richer than fiction, that what seems phantasmagoric may often turn out to be sober and even underplayed realism. Los Angeles is *in fact* stranger than anything in *The Loved One*; most English universities are *in fact* much odder than anything in *Lucky Jim*. Of course, the oddness of real life is diluted with a good deal of dreary ordinariness. And, of course, one must have been a don or have lived in Los Angeles to know the difference; the fictional representation of these states and places seems cardish only to outsiders. Can we say, then, that what seems odd is the result of our limited view, that if we lived inside the situation the sense of strangeness, the "larger than life" quality, would erode and crumble? Are characters who are Cards merely the result of the novelist forcing us to take an outside, objective view of them? Mary McCarthy would seem to think so; I quote at some length from a characteristically provocative essay of hers. She has just pointed out that the "real people" in novels tend not to be the "straight" characters, the heroes and heroines, but rather the minor and comic characters:

> In what does this "reality" consist? In the incorrigibility and change-lessness of the figure. Villains may reform, heroes and heroines may learn their lesson, like Emma or Elizabeth or Mr. Darcy, or grow into the author, like Stephen Dedalus and David Copperfield, but a Lady Catherine de Bourgh or a Molly Bloom or a Mr. Dedalus, regardless of resolutions, cannot reform or change, cannot be other than they are. . . . Real characterization, I think, is seldom accomplished outside of comedy or without the fixative of comedy: the stubborn pride of Mr.

Darcy, the prejudice of Elizabeth, the headstrongness of Emma. A comic character, contrary to accepted belief, is likely to be more complicated and enigmatic than a hero or a heroine, fuller of surprises and turnabouts; Mr. Micawber, for instance, can find the most unexpected ways of being himself; so can Mr. Woodhouse or the Master of the Marshalsea. It is a sort of resourcefulness. . . . The comic element is the incorrigible element in every human being; the capacity to learn, from experience or instruction, is what is forbidden to all comic creations and to what is comic in you and me. The capacity to learn is the prerogative of the hero or the heroine: Prince Hal as opposed to Falstaff. The principle of growth in human beings is as real, of course (though possibly not so common) as the principle of eternity or inertia represented by the comic; it is the subjective as opposed to the objective. When we identify ourselves with the hero of a story, we are following him with all our hopes, i.e., with our subjective conviction of human freedom; on the comic characters we look with despair, in which, though, there is a queer kind of admiration—we really, I believe, admire the comic characters *more* than we do the hero or the heroine, because of their obstinate power to do-it-again, combined with a total lack of self-consciousness or shame.[1]

This account, which has much in common with an existentialist conception of character and human relationships, raises some important points. But it is full of semantic dodges; some characters, like Emma or Mr. Darcy, figure on both sides of the ledger; *subjective* and *objective* are notoriously tricky words, while to say that such characters are more complicated and enigmatic than most protagonists is simply to use a common set of terms to describe two very different sets of phenomena. Nevertheless I feel that the truth is on Miss McCarthy's side rather than, for example, on the side of Chesterton and Santayana when they try to defend Dickens's card-like characters. Chesterton and Santayana maintain that such characters are in fact realistic and true to life, that the reader mistakes them for flat caricatures only because he has such a limited and stereotyped view of reality. In other words, this is the life-is-richer-than-art theory all over again. One cannot prove Chesterton and Santayana to be wrong; indeed one knows that their root proposition is true and I have already invoked it in this chapter. Yet the effect of their argument is to assimilate very different kinds of characters—Pip and Wemmick, for example—into one kind

[1] M. McCarthy, "Characters in Fiction", *On the Contrary*, pp. 288–9. London: Heinemann, 1962.

of realism and this one knows to be wrong. Pip and Wemmick *are* both "real"; yes, but in different senses of the word. Whether or not one agrees entirely with Miss McCarthy, she at least perceives a distinction does exist. Can we do more to clarify the ambiguities lurking in the word *real*, when applied to card-like characters? Let me start with some simple assertions:

(*a*) Most Cards—however large they bulk in the reader's imagination—are not the nominal heroes of the novels that contain them. Few novels make the Card a protagonist and these few, although they may be very good, do not approach real greatness. Most of them stay on the level, say, of *Oblomov* or *Babbit*. The one possible exception to this—though I am doubtful whether any category can possibly contain the example—is *Don Quixote*.

(*b*) The distinguishing feature of the Card—we may agree with Miss McCarthy—is his relative changelessness, combined with a peculiar kind of freedom; the joker is always wild. The Card is triumphantly himself; he is like the child's toy, its base filled with lead, which always bobs upright no matter how far it is pushed over. Part of the joy of these characters lies in their immunity to the knocks and buffets doled out to them, in their ultimate reassertion of their own natures. This is not a truth of the world as we know it in terms of sober, everyday realism; but it *is* a truth of the imagination. Man dreams of freedom from time and the world of circumstance, he dreams of innocence, integrity, invulnerability. Such a dream, such a holiday from existence as is incarnate in the Card, is no less real than our sad, open-eyed recognition of our manifold limitations. It is a part of empirical reality, part of the total complex of hopes, fears, desires, decisions that make us what we are.

(*c*) But, given this, the Card is not necessarily simple; in particular, he is not simply comic. He is often comic and pathetic at the same time or—as so often in Dickens—comic and sinister. If he is pictured as a fool then we know also that the fool can speak wisdom. Krook, Quilp, Miss Flite, Miss Mowcher—they all arouse mingled responses. But such complexity exists only in the reader's response; the character himself is not aware of it. This is one of the prime differences between the Card and the protagonist who shares in our common knowledge of internal conflict. This is why Ahab, for all his concentration and single-ness of will, is a protagonist and not a Card; he has locked him-self in his own monomania and he knows it; sometimes we can feel him beating his fists against the walls of his prison.

(d) Moreover, the Card's freedom is only relative. Here, I think, I disagree with Miss McCarthy. Cards are not absolutely immune from change and growth; of the examples she quotes, even if we discount Micawber's Australian career, we are still left with Mr. Dorrit. Dorrit's freedom as a card-like character coincides with his imprisonment in the Marshalsea; when he is offered the very different freedom of the world he begins to change. Such change presents very tricky problems for the novelist. The reader is reluctant to forego the peculiar consola-tion he finds in this kind of character; he wants Don Quixote to continue in his dream. So, very often, does the novelist. An interesting example is Denry Machin, hero of Bennett's *The Card*. In the first few chapters of the sequel to this novel, *The Regent*, Bennett seems to be nerving himself to break down his hero and make him vulnerable to the world; he comes near to creating an anti-hero. And although he changes his mind and Denry continues his triumphant antics, something has gone wrong; the balloon of invention sags a little and the sequel has nothing of the original's élan and buoyancy.

Nevertheless, although the sharp demarcation between the Card and the protagonist may sometimes be blurred, the essen-tial distinction remains. And because the Card is free in his captivity—or equally, captured in his freedom—the novelist can frequently release through him a vividness, an energy, an abundance that would submerge and obscure the more intricate contours of the protagonist. Card-like characters are, so to speak, chemically pure; that is why they are so often tonic, even intoxicating. Their realism is one of intensity, singleness, vi-vacity; the realism of the protagonist is that of dilution, com-plexity and process. Who is to say that one or other of these is the "really real"? Fiction—and indeed, life—would be impov-erished if the critic sought to pass an Act of Exclusion.

III

AT first glance the Card and the ficelle might seem to be diametrically opposed types of character. Despite the Card's difference from the protagonist, he too is an end-in-himself in the novel; any function he serves is a by-product. The danger of allowing a Card into a novel is that so exuberant is he in his autonomy, so sheerly gratuitous and in excess of what the theme or vision of the novel may demand, that he is liable to grow out of all proportion, become mutinous and anarchic in his creator's hands and destroy the structure of the total work. Beside a Charlus or a Micawber it may seem that Marcel or David Copperfield are dwarfed and dim; we may forget that it is only in the story of the pale narrator that ultimately these vivid characters have any significance. The danger of the ficelle, on the other hand, is that he may seem merely a function, serving his purpose without that margin of gratuitous life which changes a schematic figure into an interesting character. Only the greatest novelists can fuse these two types, can so blend freedom and discipline that the categories no longer apply.

The ficelle has many functions, some of which are too obvious to merit much discussion. Like the background character he too may serve a purely mechanical role in the plot or act as chorus. He may become a transitional agent between protagonist and society; he may afford relief and contrast of the simplest kind. Like the Card he may allow us the pleasurable relaxation of recognizing the limited and familiar after our struggle with the involvements or complexities of the protagonist. In innumerable ways he may act as foil to the protagonist, creating what I have called the perspectives of depth. By his misunderstanding and partial view he may focus the protagonist's dilemma more clearly. Alternatively, by a flash of insight or simply by being the spokesman of sober reality and common sense, he may illuminate the protagonist's blindness and folly. He may stand as a possible alternative to the protagonist, incarnating what the character might have been—so stands Banquo to Macbeth. Or he may embody in a simpler form some analogue, positive or negative, to the hero's experience—so stands Gloucester to Lear. He may be the moral touchstone by which we judge the aberrations of others; he may, by being simple and static, become the point of reference by which we measure change and growth elsewhere. Examples of these, and no doubt of many other functions, will readily occur to the reader; I will isolate only two typical points for more detailed discussion.

The more exceptional the experience embodied in the protagonist. the greater become the problems of mimetic adequacy and hence the more important are the mediating and choric functions of the ficelle. He becomes, so to speak, the springboard from which we launch ourselves into the turbid depths of the central figure. *Exceptional* can here mean one of two things. The experience may be remote from the reader because it is beyond the range of his normal experience—the protagonist, for example, who happens to be a saint or an artistic genius. Alternatively, the experience may be within the range of the reader but beyond his depth. That is, the reader may discover analogues for the experience within himself, but it may still be exceptional by reason of its extreme intensity and purity. We have all sinned and felt guilt, but we are still a long way from being Macbeth.

A single illustration of exceptional experience will suffice. One of the distinguishing features of much modern fiction is its concern with the epiphany, the Wordsworthian "spot of time," the moment of intense vision which yields a significance far beyond the mundane world of common experience. In different forms we find it in Forster, Joyce, Proust, Lawrence, Virginia Woolf and many other novelists. It is an essentially post-Romantic concern and—with the possible exception of Proust—quite different from the Aristotelian moment of anagnorisis or self-recognition which we should normally expect as a climax of any interesting moral process. But clearly it will, like anagnorisis, have implications for the creation of character; to put it at its crudest, some characters will be capable of the moments of vision, others not. This capability is indeed often made the basis of moral judgment and discrimination.

As I say, a similar concern is central to Romantic poetry. If the visionary moment is expressed quintessentially, asserted as a value of its own, it may properly form the basis of a lyric poem. But the epiphany cannot thus be isolated in a novel; it must in one way or another be related to a context of life stretching before and after. Such also is the concern of many Romantic poets, notably of Wordsworth in *Tintern Abbey* and *The Prelude*. How is the epiphany to be related to the ordinary, day-to-day concerns of the moral life; how, in Wordsworth's formulation, is the moment when:

> We are laid asleep
> In body, and become a living soul:
> While with an eye made quiet by the power
> Of harmony, and the deep power of joy,
> We see into the life of things.

How, precisely, do we connect this moment with "the din/ Of towns and cities," so that it becomes for us,

> The anchor of my purest thoughts, the nurse,
> The guide, the guardian of my heart, and soul
> Of all my moral being?

The problem of bridging the gap, of modulating without obvious strain or incongruity from the intense to the relaxed, the exceptional to the mundane, might seem to be primarily one of style. And here poetry scores; the language of prose which might seem more flexible and various is in fact in serious danger of achieving no more than an isolated purple patch when it attempts to render the intensity of the epiphany. In the novel, therefore, modulation must be in terms of structure and particularly in terms of character relationships. Take, for example, Mrs. Moore's epiphany in the Marabar Caves; a moment, as it happens, of negative vision:

If they reached the big pocket of caves, they would be away nearly an hour. She took out her writing-pad, and began, "Dear Stella, Dear Ralph," then stopped, and looked at the queer valley and their feeble invasion of it. Even the elephant had become a nobody. Her eye rose from it to the entrance tunnel. No, she did not wish to repeat that experience. The more she thought over it, the more disagreeable and frightening it became. She minded it much more now than at the time. The crush and the smells she could forget, but the echo began in some indescribable way to undermine her hold on life. Coming at a moment when she chanced to be fatigued, it had managed to murmur, "Pathos, piety, courage—they exist, but are identical, and so is filth. Everything exists, nothing has value." If one had spoken vileness in that place, or quoted lofty poetry, the comment would have been the same—"ou-boum". If one had spoken with the tongues of angels and pleaded for all the unhappiness and misunderstanding in the world, past, present, and to come, for all the misery men must undergo whatever their opinion and position, and however much they dodge or bluff—it would amount to the same, the serpent would descend and return to the ceiling. Devils are of the North, and poems can be written about them, but no one could romanticize the Marabar because it robbed infinity and eternity of their vastness, the only quality that accommodates them to mankind.[1]

To relate the radical negation of this moment to the multi-farious concerns of the novel, to show its effects radiating through time until it results if not in affirmation—for Godbole is the only character who can face and contain Mrs. Moore's vision in his own—then at least in the tentative note of the novel's ending; all this requires that the moment diffuses itself through many characters and many relationships. It is quite possibly this fact that dictates Mrs. Moore's departure and death; for had she lived she would have had to work out the consequences of her vision in her own terms and this might well have thrown the rest of the novel out of balance. The moment itself must be gradually connected with the disparate and com-monplace concerns of everyday life, through a careful gradation of characters from those who are able in greater or lesser degree to comprehend Mrs. Moore's experience to those who, all un-knowing, are brushed by the events which stem from the scene in the Marabar Caves. The moment and the subsequent events are refracted, echoed, distorted through a range of characters from Godbole to Dr. Panna Lal and the punkah-louvre wallah; together they form the complex prism which breaks up the pure light of this remote epiphany into the various and interesting colours of a human world which we can share and understand.

In this process a crucial role is obviously played by Adela Quested. On my reading of the novel she shares Mrs. Moore's vision in the caves, but unlike Mrs. Moore she cannot realize it for what it is. In Eliot's phrase she, like most of human kind, "cannot bear very much reality"; consequently she retreats to an explanation which is false but which at least can be com-prehended and endured in terms of the everyday world. In

[1] E. M. Forster, *A Passage to India*, Chapter 14.

Eliot's play, *Murder In The Cathedral,* one of the Four Knights (corresponding to the Fourth Tempter?) tempts the audience into believing that Becket's maryrdom can be explained away in terms of a death-wish leading to suicide. We are asked to accommodate the intense moment of truth to our own more comfortable and familiar categories. This is what Miss Quested initially tries to do. In other words her experience of the inhuman and the absolute in the Caves is transmuted into a moral process which reaches its climax in her recantation at the trial of Aziz.

But Miss Quested is not the only agent of modulation; she is backed by many other intermediate characters who play a humble but important part. They are *our* representatives, members of the ordinary, bread-and-butter life in which the otherwise remote experience of the novel is set. The Marabar Caves and what happens there are extraordinary—Forster hammers home this point—but we can only judge how extraordinary by being planted vicariously in the ordinary life of Chandrapore. Sometimes this spectrum of human understanding assumes the structure of a formal hierarchy; thus Melville in *Moby Dick* makes use of the chain of command of a ship's crew. Starbuck, Flask and Tragg, according to their rank, have almost ritualistically a greater or lesser degree of insight into Ahab's passion. Sometimes the spectrum is less schematic but even more important; thus it is only through the limited narration of the foppish Lockwood and the earthbound Nelly Dean that we can grasp and measure the transcendental relation of Heathcliff and Cathy.

Because he is, so to speak, the reader's delegate within the story, the ficelle can often take on a generalized and representative value. He is so often a type because the reader needs precisely the comfortable recognition of the typical. Because of this the ficelle may often bear the weight of a good deal of symbolic value which can in various ways extend the story of the protagonist. To load the protagonist with a great deal of generalized, representative value is always a tricky business since what we attend to in his story is the individual, the unique and particular case. It is *his* story and his alone; we can easily think of alternative equivalents for Starbuck but change Ahab and the whole of *Moby Dick* is changed. We quickly feel uneasy if the protagonist is made to stand for something general and diffused; the more he *stands for* the less he *is* and we may soon end up with an allegorical figure, an Everyman. Of course, many protagonists are in a sense Everyman but only because they are in the first instance a particular man; if the protagonist is in some way a universal value or meaning, he is primarily a *concrete* universal. Consequently the intermediate character can usefully act not just as a foil, creating perspective, but also as a buttress, supporting and extending the central meaning. Behind the type we can easily sense a representative mass; thus Isabel Archer can say of Henrietta Stackpole:

> "She's a kind of emanation of the great democracy—of the continent, the country, the nation. I don't say that she sums it all up, that would be too much to ask of her. But she suggests it, she vividly figures it."

Thus Millicent in *The Princess Casamassima* is "the muse of Cockneydom" and Mrs. Lowder in *The Wings of The Dove* is the "Britannia of the Market Place—Britannia unmistakeable, but with a pen in her ear."

These we can accept where we would worry about the same technique being employed on Isabel Archer or Hyacinth Robinson or Milly Theale. To load them so would be to detract from their individuality, and it is an important part of that reality that we should feel them simply to be there, autonomous and unique. The ficelle is a chief means to this end; on him can be loaded the weight of the typical and the representative; through him the world in which the protagonist gains his individual contours can be given the necessary mass and density, that "solidity of specification" which James felt was so essential to successful representation.

IV

These categories—protagonist, background, Card, ficelle —are, of course, only approximate; they must be, in so far as the novelist captures the fluidity of what I have called perspectives of depth. These are linked to one further important difference between fiction and life which is the source of many critical difficulties. If I maintain that a fictional character is functionally flat or stereotyped, what answer can I give the critic who argues that on the contrary, such a character is the result not of deliberation but of the failure to create a "rounded" protagonist? While we cannot appeal to the author's intention and while, of course, each case must be argued on its merits, it is surely true that any argument will include an appeal to the whole work, as a structure of relationships. Here fiction differs from life in that consideration of the aesthetic strength—that is, the successful realization—of any one character will involve consideration of the aesthetic strength of other characters with whom he is brought into relation. For example, in *Middlemarch* Dorothea is a much more successful creation when seen in relation to Casaubon, another strongly realized character, than she is when linked to the relatively sketchy figure of Will Ladislaw. Again, the reality of Isabel Archer depends vitally on the reality of Osmond. If one examines *The Portrait of A Lady* with care one realizes that Osmond's charm and attraction for Isabel, and the whole process of seducing her into marriage, is asserted rather than dramatically realized. If this relationship were shown in isolation I believe we should feel a gap or blur in the developing human spectrum at this point. The gap is partly closed by James's stressing those points of Isabel's character which make her vulnerable to attack, and partly by his evocation of the diffused glamour of Italy. But more important, Osmond— and James—find a ready ally in Madame Merle; her success as a strongly realized character conceals and compensates for a lacuna in the total human pattern. So one could go on, complicating this network of relationships, until the whole was encompassed.

The human context, then, is primarily a web of relationships; the characters do not develop along single and linear roads of destiny but are, so to speak, human cross-roads. It is within this pattern, this meshing together of individualities, that they preserve their autonomy, yet through our perception of the pattern their significance extends beyond themselves into a general comment on the world. No one has illustrated the point better or more succinctly than Germaine Brée in her study of Proust:

> No Proustian character is isolated or unique. Each is bound to other characters who surround him, and who reflect certain aspects of his

personality. But these families of characters are as numerous for each individual as are the aspects of his own character, so that none is ever enclosed within a "type." A secondary character like Legrandin, for example, takes his place with the Proustian "snobs,' a pale reflection of Swann, of the narrator, of Bloch, and of so many others; through his homosexuality he joins Saint-Loup whom he resembles outwardly, the Baron de Charlus, and indeed, a whole Proustian population; through his literary vocation he is part of a whole company of would-be artists who are, failures, or incomplete artists; Ski, the baron, Swann. Each principal character is thus doubled, tripled, quadrupled by a whole series of secondary Legrandins, as well as many others paler than he. . . . This play with mirrors gives for each character a series of reflections, each a little distorted, which are variations of his own species. In this way the individual goes beyond his own individuality, and is related to a general type. But he is never merely an example of that type, for he always evokes in addition a multitude of other characteristics. Charlus is not the prototype of the homosexual. He is the Baron de Charlus, a great lord like his brother, the Duc de Guermantes, or like Monsieur, the brother of Louis XIV; he is a scholar and an artist, like Swann. No Proustian character entirely exemplifies one species. He suggests several, and Proust gathers about him other individuals of the various species to which he belongs, who again are never simply doubles. Each character has infinite possibilities; he remains enigmatic and complex by virtue of all the ties which link him, quite humanly, to a great many other people. The Proustian vision is determined here by Proust's marked conviction that in every individual there exists a general humanness which is greater than he, but of which he is a unique specimen.[1]

Within such a pattern the characters themselves may make or mistake connections; but the pattern itself is the result of a real process in the reader's response. His knowledge and insight encompass those of any single character; hence because of his greater range and lucidity, all the effects of dramatic irony. And hence, as I have already said, because the reader does the work, reality is imputed to the raw material on which the work has been done.

In doing the work the reader enriches his knowledge of the world; that is his reward. He begins, as he probably does in life, by assimilating what is familiar to him; this he then uses as a base from which to explore the unknown. In many cases he will never complete his exploration; there will still remain a heart of darkness in the character, a central mystery which is never quite

[1] G. Brée, *Marcel Proust and Deliverance from Time*, pp. 242–3. London: Chatto and Windus, 1956.

penetrated. In aesthetic terms this is often what we mean when we praise the inexhaustibility of great art; but it is also a truth of life which may form part of the mimetic substance of the novel. There are dangers in the reader's lucidity becoming *too* great; we all know the novel which is suspiciously neat and satisfying in the way it clicks together. Dramatic irony, for example, easily becomes oppressive, obvious or over-schematic. Such irony results from the reciprocal ignorance of the characters; they are opaque to each other as we are to each other in real life. But to some extent, perhaps, they should also retain a core which remains opaque to the reader as well? Several of Dickens's characters, for example, have been condemned as melodramatic stereotypes; yet they have an excess of energy which suggests a residual heart of darkness far more profound than the merely queer or sinister. I am thinking here of such figures as Carker or Tulkinghorn. However well one gets to know them, however much Dickens explains them, they remain ultimately concealed and mysterious. Since we cannot explain them we often explain them away. But perhaps it is part of any character's mimetic adequacy that he should resist the encroaching lucidity of the reader. One of the novelist's greatest problems is thus to reconcile transparency and density.

The fascination of this problem is one reason, I believe, for much of the characteristic ambiguity of modern fiction. No man is an island; yet no man is to be thoroughly explored and charted. How is the novelist to convey this sense that there will always remain an unknown factor in the human equation? Dramatic irony, we have seen, results from the reader's superior perspective, but there are many other kinds of irony which involve and attack the reader himself so that he, too, is asked to recognize his fallibility and limitations. The reader will forgive me if I offer an unashamedly subjective example, but where the novel implicates each one of us as individuals, all testimony must be personal and variable.

My example is *Death In Venice* and I am concerned here not so much with the meaning of the novel as with the process of getting to understand it; my point, of course, is that this process is part of the meaning. How we travel determines our destination. Even a first, naïve reading of *Death In Venice* cannot but reveal the obvious nature of its extreme artifice—the accumulation of symbols, the reverberation of echoes, the parallelisms, contrasts and anticipations. The artifice is quite overt; it is not concealed but is so deliberately emphasized that one soon feels it become oppressively schematic. This, for some time, was my own judgment of the novella; a clever—indeed, over-clever—piece of work, the explicator's paradise, but ultimately claustrophobic and repugnant. A further reading contradicted this initial impression by offering the explanation that the oppressively schematic nature of the work is deliberately expressive of its theme. The theme now becomes a paradox; here is a novella which conquers life into order to show, through Aschenbach, that art can never conquer life; *Death In Venice* thus becomes a work of art devoted to destroying its own claims. This realization is then merged in a final paradox; *Death In Venice, because* it is successful, denies its self-destructive assertion *at the same time* that it affirms it. Art can never subdue life; this is what the novella says while it is engaged in the very process of subjugation. We can put it this way; *Death In Venice* is a story about Aschenbach *by* Aschenbach—but with a difference. Aschenbach tries to assimilate his experience of chaos and fails, whereas disorder in the novella is successfully given form. The extreme artifice of the work is now explained; it is expressive ultimately of the immense effort needed to control the jungle and the abyss into which Aschenbach plunges to destruction. And the difference between Aschenbach and the controlling narrator is this—that Aschenbach rejects irony whereas the novella depends upon it. But this irony is not simple dramatic irony; it derives rather from the complicated interplay of the reader's mind as the work impels him through some such developing process of perception and adjustment as I have tried to describe.

This process is also the reason why we can grant reality to a work which is, in one sense, so obviously contrived and artificial. For we are made not merely to understand the work but also to understand ourselves in relation to the work. It has forced us to the effort of self-exploration and if we deny its reality, then we deny our own. In this process the role of the narrator is clearly crucial. The narrator—and behind the narrator, the author himself—is clearly part of the total network of relationships between character and reader which make up the human context. So important is he, indeed, that he deserves a chapter to himself.

7

TIME AND PLACE

Lewis Mumford has remarked that the most significant, most characteristically modern invention is the clock. It is true that one can understand a way of life without mechanical power or medical sophistication or even without printing more easily than one can understand a way of life without clocks, with their implication of an acute consciousness of the passing of time. Tristan and Iseult exist in a timeless world, and to that extent the romance that narrates their story is strange and remote from us. Robinson Crusoe, alone on his island, invents a calendar, and it seems entirely natural to us that he should do so. Insofar as the novel is a quintessentially modern genre, it is inevitable that it express modern modes of time consciousness; and insofar as the novel exhibits experience at length, governed by most of the conditions which operate in experience at large, it inevitably renders a consciousness of time in a detailed and integral way.

Ian Watt, in The Rise of the Novel, has described the significance of time in the novels of the English eighteenth century along with the philosophical assumptions which made the presentation of time so necessary. The breadth of Watt's discussion suggests the breadth of the problem of time in any fiction of any period. For to inquire into the time sense of a novel is to inquire into the novelist's metaphysic, his psychology, and his craftsmanship. And it is to inquire as well into the network of relationships involving the novelist, his own world of experience, his created world of the novel, his contemporary readers, and his readers ever since, who must approach his novel from a temporal distance which the novelist could not have anticipated and provided for. The section from A. A. Mendilow's Time and the Novel which follows explores these latter relationships along with the questions of craft and credibility implied in them. It is worth noting that Mendilow, approaching the question of the intrusive author as a part of the larger question of how the novelist creates the illusion of passing time, is much less charitable than Wayne Booth, who, in the earlier essay in this collection, takes the intrusive author (Booth would deny that any discrete distinction exists between those authors who intrude and those who do not) to be a technique, often an altogether rich one, associated with a particular degree of distance. The essay by Father Noon explores the values of time in more general and philosophical directions, considering the anxieties of a secular literature which plays upon a time sense derived to a considerable extent from Christian theology. The two sections together imply something of the scope of a very difficult area of fictional theory, all the more difficult because those generalizations one forms about Richardson apply rather badly to Thackeray, one's observations on the time sense of Thackeray have little relevance to Proust, and what one says about time in Proust has nothing to do with time in Beckett.

Specificity of location, like time, tends to be irrelevant before the novel. "A forest" or "a castle" is enough to locate the action in most romance. Again, Ian Watt has described the importance of place in the English eighteenth-century novels, along with the assumptions that underlie that importance. That place in fiction continued to be significant is graphically demonstrated by those "literary maps of England" that used to hang in school rooms, locating "the Jane Austen country," "the Brontë country," "the Hardy country," and so on. Place, of course, functions in different ways in Bennett and Hardy, Hawthorne and Faulk-

ner. It is the purpose of D. S. Bland's essay to differentiate some of these ways in which background description is important to the total effect of different kinds of novels.

A. A. MENDILOW

THE POSITION OF THE PRESENT IN FICTION

THE TIME LOCUS OF THE READER

THE reader of a novel occupies an extended position in time, and within this falls the date of his reading the novel. This date may not correspond closely with the date of the events he is reading about. Where the difference is considerable, as in reading a historical novel, a strong effort of the imagination may be required of him if he is to project himself into the period treated and enter closely into the spirit of those distant times. An even greater effort is needed when he reads an early novel whose style and subject were once contemporary but are now become with the lapse of time 'dated'; in short, when the novel has become historical in effect though it was contemporary in intention. The twentieth century reader of a historical novel has certain initial difficulties to overcome: the change of perspective and the strangeness of atmosphere. But even in such novels as enter deeply into the spirit of the periods treated, George Moore's *Brook Kerith* or Robert Graves's *I Claudius* or Thomas Mann's *Joseph and his Brethren*, he is helped in his understanding of those far-off events by reading a rendering of them made by a co-eval; he sees through the eyes of one of his own age who in effect is interpreting the past for him. On the other hand, a greater strain may be felt in reading Richardson's *Clarissa* or Defoe's *Moll Flanders*, where the events are portrayed by a

From Time and the Novel (*London, 1952*). *Reprinted by permission of the author.*

writer who had no need to make concessions to his first readers such as would be required if a modern writer wrote about the same period. A further complication enters when we read an early novel dealing with a historical subject, for it then becomes doubly historical, both in effect and in intention.

Reactions to historical events vary with the ages. We do not, in all probability, bring to bear the same emotional attitude today, the same predilections and prejudices and fears, upon a story dealing with the French Revolution as a reader in 1800. The first readers of *Henry Esmond* or *Vanity Fair* or a *Tale of Two Cities* might well have felt very differently from us on such subjects as colonisation or revolution or the Napoleonic Wars. Writers, being themselves men of their time and writing for audiences of their time, tend to write in the terms and with the attitudes of their times. The same problem is present in drama. Shakespeare's audiences projected into the historical plays a fear of internecine warfare that had been strong since the Wars of the Roses and was accentuated by contemporary dangers and the approaching end of a dynasty. The ordinary modern audience is incapable of coming to the plays with the same atmospheric approach; its emotional charge is lower and the appeal is therefore less. The enforced abdication of Richard II would have a different value, moreover, when it was regarded as a contravention of a natural law that was cosmic in its application and involved theological no less than political principles. By way of contrast, though the circumstances were, it is true, vastly different, the abdication of Edward VIII aroused little more than social embarrassment and a general feeling of regret. The later the reader, the more knowledge is demanded of him and the greater is the imaginative effort required fully to savour the novel and to do justice to the reactions of the characters and the significance of the theme.

THE TIME LOCUS OF THE WRITER

IF the average writer is limited by the limitations of his age and reflects its views, the great writer stands above his, and sees it *sub specie aeternatis*. For the great writer always writes more truly than he knows, and under the surface of his subjects and through the restrictions of his medium and treatment glows a universal humanity in the light of which contemporary distortions of perspective vanish or become of no significance.[1] The fashions diminish in importance, the permanent element remains. 'The stream of time, which is continually washing the dissoluble fabricks' of lesser writers 'passes without injury by the adamant' of the greater ones. Nevertheless, the greatest of authors is still related to his age, and even in dealing with historical events his views are modified by the outlook of his contemporaries.

> The historical novel, though it deals with the names and perhaps with the facts, of a bygone period, describes only the virtues and vices of the day.[2]

The work of every novelist, whether it treats of the contemporary situation or leads one to escape from it into an ivory tower, is explicitly or implicitly a social commentary on the time in which it is written. Even the Utopian novel is essentially a negative taken from the print of reality and indicates what the author regards as evil in the world of his day. The most independent writer is grappled to the soul of his times with hoops of steel. The story of Effie Deans in Scott's *Heart of Midlothian* shows differences in emphasis and understanding when comcompared with Hardy's treatment of a similar theme in *Tess of the Durbervilles* that are to be ascribed not only to the differences of their genius but also to the times in which they wrote and the audiences for whom they wrote. Scott and Stevenson might write of the '45 rebellion, but they see it in a very different light. Pater and Graves and Baron Corvo may deal with similar periods of history, but they do so in a vastly different spirit. The dissimilarity lies not merely in the selection and treatment of detail or the placing of emphasis but in the conception of a central situation and the attitude to it.

If most writers keep abreast of their times, it sometimes happens that one is in advance of his, so that a time-lag elapses

---

[1] See Sorel: *De la Connoissance des Bons Livres,* 1671, pp. 22–4, for a discussion of the point "Que tous les livres ont leur Temps."
[2] A. Trollope: *On English Prose Fiction as a Rational Amusement.* A lecture first delivered in 1870.

before the public can catch up with his ideas or forms of expression. This is a truism of Blake and Hopkins and numerous other poets, and the same claim has often been put forward for Henry James, James Joyce, D. H. Lawrence and many other novelists. It is of course undeniable that

> every author as far as he is great and at the same time *original*, has had the task of *creating* the taste by which he is to be enjoyed.[3]

In this sense, he writes for posterity; but the greatest writers of all have not been too fastidious to direct their appeal to their contemporaries as well. While it is an exaggeration to hold with Trollope that

> the novelist is bound to adapt himself to his age; and is almost forced to be ephemeral," [4]

he nevertheless is set in his times even when he transcends them. The most original mind does not work in a vacuum.

THE TIME LOCUS OF THE PSEUDO-AUTHOR

THIS aspect of time is peculiar to novels written in the first person, whether in the form of letters, journals, memoirs or autobiography. By it is meant the time of writing of the assumed author in relation to the time when the events recorded are given as having occurred.

The question of the double focus fascinated Sterne who made great play with it in *Tristram Shandy*. It also intrigued Thomas Mann:

> I do not know why this double time-reckoning arrests my attention or why I am at pains to point out both the personal and the objective, the time in which the narrator moves and that in which the narrative does so. This is a quite extraordinary interweaving of time-units, destined, moreover, to include even a third: namely, the time which one day the courteous reader will take for the reading of what has been

---

[3] Wordsworth: Lyrical Ballads. *Essay Supplementary to the Preface*, 1815–1845.
[4] *vid. sup.*

written; at which point he will be dealing with a threefold ordering of
time: his own, that of the chronicler, and historic time.[5]

Richardson was at great pains to justify his technique of presenting 'instantaneous descriptions and reflections' [6] through the
medium of

> familiar letters, written, as it were, to the moment, while the heart is
> agitated by hopes and fears, on events undecided.[7]

> *Much more* lively and affecting . . . must be the style of those who
> write in the height of a *present* distress; the mind tortured by the pangs
> of uncertainty (the events then hidden in the womb of fate;) *than* the
> dry, narrative unanimated style of a person relating difficulties and
> danger surmounted, can be . . . the relater perfectly at ease; and if
> himself, unmoved by his own story, not likely greatly to affect the
> reader.[8]

There is another difference of effect between the novel where
the events are recorded immediately after they have taken place
and that where they are related long after. In the latter, his life
is seen by the pseudo-author as falling into a pattern or sub-
serving some great end or proving a thesis. By a sort of prophecy
after the event, Defoe in his anticipatory flashes shows, before
anything of much account has happened, that the event will
prove the truth of the ethical opinions held by *Robinson Crusoe*
in later years and give substance to the warnings of his parents.
He constantly projects his later writing self on to his earlier acting self, and one is in doubt whether the morals he draws from
his life really derive from it or whether he has coloured his de-
piction to accord with his subsequent views.

A further complication arises where the pseudo-author is
separated from the events he narrates by a long space of time.

> The author has all along two characters to support, for he has to con-
> sider how his hero felt at the time of the events to be related, and how
> it is natural he should feel them at the time he is relating them; at a
> period, perhaps, when curiosity is extinguished, passion cooled, and

[5]   *Dr. Faustus*, p. 114.
[6]   Preface to *Clarissa*.
[7]   Preface to *Sir Charles Grandison*.
[8]   Preface to *Clarissa*.

when, at any rate, the suspense which rendered them interesting is over.[9]

Proust resolved the problem by making it almost his theme, and his lengthy discussion of the many selves within each person in *Time Regained* forms the climax and rounds off the entire series of *Remembrance of Things Past*. In Defoe's *Moll Flanders* one often senses the gap between the action and its record. The repentant Moll colours the record of her sins in deeper hues and attributes to herself at the time of committing them, evil reflections and motives, in the interest not of truth of naration, but of the morals she acquired at a much later date.

Conversely, Roxana warns the readers:

> Let nobody conclude from the strange success I met with in all my wicked doings, and the vast estate which I had raised by it, that therefore I either was happy or easy. No, no, there was a dart struck into the liver; there was a secret hell within, even all the while when our joy was at the highest.[10]

This feeling of remorse at the time of her misdeeds does not ring true, and is indeed belied by the numerous comments of self-satisfaction made at each iniquitous transaction, incidents which are rebuked by the writing Roxana:

> no woman ever lived a life like me, of six and twenty years of wickedness, without the least signals of remorse, without any signs of repentance, or without so much as a wish to put an end to it.[11]

One cannot at any time accept her analysis of her motives or of her frame of mind unless we discount her subsequent desire to turn her evil doing to good account by saving others from similar lapses. As with Moll Flanders, two characters are superimposed one upon the other, and the impression of the one who acts is coloured and distorted by the interpretation of the one who narrates. If one can imagine Moll Flanders or Roxana keeping a journal, it would be far different from the memoirs as set down in contrite old age when the pleasures of vice can at best, or at worst, be but of academic interest to the most hardened of sinners. As it is, even in the statement of bare facts, let alone in

---

[9] Mrs. A. L. Barbauld: *The Correspondence of Samuel Richardson*, 1804, from the prefatory *Biographical Account of that Author and Observations on his Writings*. Vol. I, pp. XXV–XXVI.
[10] *Abbey Classics* edn. p. 253.
[11] *ibid*. p. 182.

the narration of the contemporary feelings aroused by the facts, one feels the double self, the woman as she was and the woman she later imagined or wished to imagine she must have been.

Defoe himself had an occasional twinge of artistic conscience, when he became uneasily aware of the double focus in the character and in himself. Like Richardson, he enjoyed writing about certain subjects, and, as in the seduction of Roxana's servant Amy in her mistress's presence, went sometimes far beyond the needs even of his plot. He tried to cover himself *vis à vis* his readers by claiming that Roxana

> makes frequent excursion, in a just censuring and condemning her own practice. How often does she reproach herself in the most passionate manner, and guide us to just reflections in the like cases! [12]

But one is not quite convinced that he undertook to describe such crimes and in such circumstantial detail too, in a spirit of self-sacrifice for the spiritual enlightenment of his fellow-beings. In *Moll Flanders*, he falls into a similar deception with regard to his central character. He states that Moll is a reformed character as is shown by the manner of her narration:

> There is not an ill thing mentioned but it is condemned, even in the relation, nor a virtuous just thing but it carries its praise along with it.

Yet elsewhere in the same preface he admits that he, the 'editor' of Moll's memoirs, had to doctor the story on account of

> the copy which came first to hand, having been written in language more like one still in Newgate, than one grown penitent and humble, as she afterward pretends to be.

In the first person novel that purports to be written long after the event, the principle of selection has of necessity to be ruthlessly applied.

> Seen from afar, my life appears to contract by some mental process. That long, slow agony of ten years' duration can be brought to memory today in some few phrases. [13]

The journal or the epistolary novel, on the other hand, can introduce more of the random nature of life which has little or

[12] Preface to *The Fortunate Mistress or . . . the Lady Roxana*, 1724.
[13] Balzac: *The Wild Ass's Skin*. Opening of Part II. *Everyman* edn. p. 73.

no apparent bearing at the time on the main incidents. One follows the events as they evolve; there is no time-lag between the event and its recording as one feels when a pattern is imposed on them subsequently, after their immediate repercussions have passed.

> These novels—wrote Whately, analysing the epistolary technique—are apt to become excessively tedious; since, to give the letters the appearance of reality, (without which the main object proposed would be defeated), they must contain a very large proportion of matter which has no bearing at all upon the story.[14]

Richardson, justifying his practice in the face of the criticism directed against the slow tempo of the first two books of *Clarissa*, insisted that

> there was frequently a necessity to be very circumstantial and minute, in order to preserve and maintain that air of probability, which is necessary to be maintained in a story designed to represent real life.[15]

and he quoted with satisfaction a contemporary review which related these

> minute particulars of events, the sentiments and conversations of the parties

to the

> warmth and spirit that the passion supposed to be predominant at the very time could produce, and with all the distinguishing characteristics which memory can supply in a history of recent transactions.[16]

THE TIME LOCUS OF THE THEME OF THE NOVEL

THE theme of the novel has its own date and temporal setting. The subject may be contemporary with the author as in *Tom Jones* or *Clarissa*, or it may be historical, anteceding author

[14] Review of *Northanger Abbey* and *Persuasion* in the *Quarterly Review*, Jan. 1821.
[15] Postscript to *Clarissa*.
[16] *ibid.*

and reader as in *Quentin Durward* and *Henry Esmond;* or it may deal with the future as in Utopian novels like *Brave New World* and *News from Nowhere;* or it may become historical only in the course of time, though written by the writer as of contemporary events, as it recedes further into the past. There may even be combinations of several types as in Cabell's *Jurgen,* Virginia Woolf's *Orlando* and Henry James's *Sense of the Past,* written simultaneously on historical and contemporary planes, or as in Morley's *Thunder on the Left,* written on future and contemporary planes, requiring divided attention together with simultaneous apprehension. The 'saga' novels of Zola and Galsworthy deal with what is in part virtually historical material proceeding progressively to the contemporary situation. Novels like *Ulysses* and Stella Benson's *Tobit Transplanted* are written as of the contemporary scene but derive their significance from being projected step by step against an ancient theme, itself not treated but constantly implied.

The common run of novels too contain different degrees of pastness. Mostly the past tense in which the events are narrated are transposed by the reader into a fictive present, while any expository matter is felt as a past in relation to that present. The 'stream of consciousness' novels which are concerned mainly with the past of the characters *qua* past, nevertheless reveal that past as present in the immediate, that is, ficitonally present, consciousness of those characters. This reminds us of T.S. Eliot's well-known view of tradition in the literature of Europe which

has a simultaneous existence and composes a simultaneous order.[17]

It seems to derive from the Bergsonian conception of *durée.* Novels which use the device of the 'time-shift' to any large degree constantly change their locus; each episode is treated as a fictional present, or as Henry James preferred to call it 'a discriminated occasion,' without reference to the temporal position it occupies when related to any other episode.

The straight historical novel has its own temporal varieties. It may be written as by a pseudo-contemporary, the assumed writer of memoirs or a journal; or else omnisciently, that is, not seen through the limited vision of a contemporary but with the

[17] *Tradition and the Individual Talent,* 1917.

wider historical sense of a later age, in the light of what has happened since.

The Utopian novel presents special difficulties, for the implied writing of it is even further in the future than the action described, so that the events occur in the relative past of the pseudo-writer, though in the future of the reader. While readers are accustomed to making an imaginative transfer from the past in which all novels are written into a 'fictive present,' to transfer the past tense into a chronological future, felt imaginatively as a fictive present is a little excessive; the full illusion of the future is rarely conveyed, and perhaps that is why so many of these novels start off from the contemporary scene and recur finally to it at the climax of the narrative.

The time-loci of the reader, the writer and the theme are important as indicating and affecting changing aspects of culture, taste, education and society; they are interesting because they may demand the use of so many unusual techniques and conventions.

Verisimilitude of period has not always engrossed the historical novelist to the degree that it does now. Shakespeare felt no qualms of artistic conscience when he allowed so many anachronisms to slip into his plays. Similarly, in the early French and English romances, no attempt was made to present the historical heroes in keeping with their times; the classical themes were frankly handled in terms of the behaviour and attitudes of the sixteenth and seventeenth centuries. This proved of course a godsend to the satirists, and writers like Sorel and Boileau directed their most penetrating shafts at the loopholes so temptingly offered.

IDENTIFICATION AND TEMPORAL TRANSFER

IN contrast with the acted play, the novel can at best create only the *illusion* of immediacy and directness in the mind of the reader. This illusion can, however, be extremely vivid, conveying the impression of actual participation in the action. While the attitude of the spectator in the theatre is that of an observer of an action proceeding before his eyes in real life, the reader who is engrossed in a work of fiction is a participator in what is going on, and feels not merely sympathy for the hero as in the play, but may identify himself with the hero, *be* the hero in imagination, and himself suffer and do, to an extent uncommon in a play. This is possible in spite of his following the action at second hand through a symbolic and even distorting medium, not directly through the senses of sight and hearing; in spite of his not being physically present; and furthermore, in spite of the fact that, apart from passages in dialogue, that is, dramatically presented passages, most novels are written in the past tense and in the third person.

As stated earlier, the past in which most novels are written represents not a simple value of pastness but a complex of different degrees of it. There is as a rule one point of time in the story which serves as the point of reference. From this point the fictive present may be considered as beginning. In other words, the reader if he is engrossed in his reading translates all that happens from this moment of time onwards into an imaginative present of his own and yields to the illusion that he is himself participating in the action or situation, or at least is witnessing it as happening, not merely as having happened. Everything that antedates that point, as for instance exposition, is felt as a fictive past, while all that succeeds it, as for instance those premonitions and anticipatory hints that novelists find so useful for directing the attention forward to the climax or evoking a feeling of suspense, are felt as future. Verbally, all may be equally past; psychologically, once the point of reference has been established, each event presented in its time-order constitutes a point in the past series considered as a now, and whatever is out of sequence in relation to that series of points is considered as relatively past or future.

A good description of the way this illusion of immediacy operates in the reader is provided by Faulkner in his novel *Go Down, Moses.*[18] Young Mc Caslin is listening to Sam Fathers who is relating to him the story of his Indian forefathers:

And as he talked about those old times and those dead and vanished men of another race from either that the boy knew, gradually to the boy those old times would cease to be old times and would become a

[18] 1942, pp. 122–3.

part of the boy's present, not only as if they had happened yesterday but as if they were still happening, the men who walked through them actually walking in breath and air and casting an actual shadow on the earth they had not quitted. And more: as if some of them had not happened yet but would occur tomorrow, until at last it would seem to the boy that he himself had not come into existence yet.

Not only then is the reader's actual present, his own time-locus, absorbed into the fictive present of the action, but that fictive present itself constitutes an imaginative shift from the past tense in which it is recorded. To put it more concretely, someone may today be reading a novel written in the past tense about events that took place on a certain day in the year 1789, and feel as though they were happening now at his moment of reading, in his presence and presentness. The relation of the tenses used in the novel to those felt by the reader, that is, of the chronological past of the action to the fictive present felt by the reader is that of *oratio obliqua* to *oratio recte:* the past of the narration—*he went*—is translated in imagination into *I am going* or *I go;* the pluperfect—*he had gone*—into the present perfect—*I have gone* or the past—*I went;* and the conditional—he *would go*—into the future—*I shall go.*

An experiment unusual in a novel not based on 'interior monologue' was made in the best-seller translated as *The Street of the Fishing Cat*,[19] where only the present sequence of tenses is used. One is reminded of the style of speech adopted by the American heroes of Damon Runyon and by the Cockney who regularly try to give reality and vividness to past events by relating them in the present tense, as thus: "So I goes up to him and tells him what I thinks of her" etc. The 'historic present' and the common use of the present tense for the future (I leave tomorrow at nine; I am going away next year), may well derive from a similar intention.

One of the reasons for the feeling of pastness is that we are familiar with the things or events that we recognise as past. But it remains true that

this feeling of familiarity is a *present* experience, and therefore logically should not arouse a concept of the past. On the other hand, a present impression (or memory) of something which is past is different from

[19] Jolán Földes, 1937.

a present impression of something which is present but familiar from the past.[20]

Without attempting a solution of this psychological crux, it may be suggested that the reader feels the past of the novel as present, even if he is familiar with the story or has read it before, because he transfers to himself the absence in the minds of the characters of the sense of familiarity which, as stated above, is one of the elements that give rise to the idea of pastness.

THE INTRUSIVE AUTHOR

THE discrepancy between the reader's absolute or actual *now*, his present moment of reading, and the time-locus of the fictional protagonists, the dates on which they are and do, is one that constantly confronts the historical novelist and taxes his skill to the utmost. But the novelist dealing with contemporary themes is no less faced by the same problem: how to make the reader forget his own present and sink himself into the fictive present of the story. Lamb refers to the difficulty of harmonising different presents in another connection which is nevertheless appropriate here:

> Our mutual friend P. is at this present writing—*My Now*—in good health, and enjoys a fair share of worldly reputation . . . But at your present reading—*Your Now*—he may possibly be in the Bench, or going to be hanged . . . This confusion of tenses, this grand solecism of *two presents*, is in a degree common to all postage.[21]

The beautiful opportunities for classical irony in the first person novel offered by the exploitation of 'this grand solecism' were not taken up by the writers of epistolary fiction though Sterne used it effectively on occasion in *Tristram Shandy*. It is, however, common in a rather different sense in most novels. Many modern readers find themselves distracted by the way

[20] M. Sturt: *Psychology of Time*, 1925, pp. 20–1.
[21] *Distant Correspondants*. cf. his letter to Barron Field, August 31, 1817; "Your 'now' is not my 'now'; and again, your 'then' is not my 'then'; but my 'now' may be your 'then,' and vice versa. Whose head," he continues pathetically, "is competent to these things?"

certain novelists, particularly the earlier novelists, jolt them out of the fictive present into their actual present. By stepping out from behind the imaginary frame of the novel to address the reader in person, they recall him from the 'Relative Now' of the characters to his own 'Absolute Now.' He is jerked from the battlefield of long ago where he was witnessing or performing superhuman feats of valour back to the armchair before the fire with a ripe November fog pressing against his windows. There is a breaking of his suspension of disbelief to which he must be induced to yield if he is to abandon himself to the illusion of reality. The sense of immediacy and presentness which the reader enjoys on the plane of 'fictional time' is destroyed by the implied reference to his chronological time, his moment of present sensation. He becomes conscious of the 'solecism of the two presents.'

The convention of the omniscient author is the commonest in fiction. The slightest hint by the author of his being omniscient is, however, enough to brush away the carefully created illusion of the fictive present.

> . . . the object of the novelist is to keep the reader entirely oblivious of the fact that the author exists—even of the fact that he is reading a book. This is of course not possible to the bitter end, but a reader *can* be rendered very engrossed, and the nearer you can come to making him entirely insensitive to his surroundings, the more you will have succeeded.[22]

Two of the most flagrant sinners against the principle that the author should not obtrude himself *qua* author into the body of the novel are Thackeray and Trollope. A typical example from *Vanity Fair* will show how completely the reader's illusion of participating in the time and place of the action is shattered:

> If, a few pages back, the present writer claimed the privilege of peeping into Miss Amelia Sedley's bedroom, and understanding with the omniscience of the novelist all the gentle pains and passions which were tossing upon that innocent pillow, why should he not declare himself to be Rebecca's confidante too, master of her secrets, and sealkeeper of that young woman's conscience?[23]

*   *   *

[22] Ford: *Joseph Conrad: A Personal Remembrance*, 1924, p. 186.
[23] Chap. 15.

PRELIMINARY AND DISTRIBUTED EXPOSITION

EPIC theory had long demanded that the narrative should begin in the middle or towards the end of the action, then break off to recount what had happened before the poem began, and finally continue with the main issue from the point of interruption to the end. This epic structure was taken over in the pastoral and heroic romances of the sixteenth and seventeenth centuries; these further elaborated it by inserting further expositions into the major intercalated exposition, till the main thread of the story became inextricably tangled. Almost all the early critics of fiction in France and England accepted the convention, and it persisted as one of the central 'rules' till quite late in the history of the novel.

Another convention common in many novels of the eighteenth and nineteenth centuries arose out of the division of the novel into virtually self-contained sections. This practice derived from the structure of the epic and was further supported by publication in instalments in journals and magazines. Fielding, for example, would often devote a separate book or even a chapter to an episode or linked group of episodes. The action within this unit was inset into expository matter of its own, with explanation and comment preceding and following the narration. The novel has assumed the form of a Lord Mayor's pageant: each tableau is separate and distinct, but altogether when regarded in their broad sequence and their mutual relations contributing to the development of one extended theme.

Balzac had a particular weakness for long and detailed expositions, and often as good as notified the reader at which point the story proper, or in other words the fictive present, was to be considered as beginning. Zola objected very strongly to this practice as crude and inartistic; he applauded Flaubert for reducing

to strict necessity the long appraiser's enumerations with which Balzac lumbered up the beginnings of his novels.[24]

[24] *The Experimental Novel*, transl. B. M. Sherman, 1893, p. 235. [The numbering of this and subsequent footnotes in this article varies from the original by reason of the preceding ellipsis—*Editor's Note*.]

The modern tendency is against presenting the exposition in one continuous passage after the preliminary introduction of the chief character or after the first constituted scene. Instead, writers today prefer to interweave the exposition with the main line of action in the form of short alternating or even intermingling retrospective and anticipatory flashes. Ford Madox Ford has analysed at length the nature and *raison d'être* of the technique which he and Conrad called 'the chronological looping method,' more commonly known as 'the time-shift technique.' Their practice was to

> get in the character first with a strong impression, and then work backwards and forwards over his past.[25]

The novelty of this technique lies in the exposition being treated as part of the main action, not as a subordinate adjunct to it. The focus of presentness shifts continually; the relative pastness and presentness are deliberately dissolved; the tenses are confused or rather fused, so that the past is felt not as distinct from the present but included in it and permeating it. Every moment is conceived as the condensation of earlier history, and the past is not separate and completed but an ever-developing part of a changing present.

> Whoever has approved this idea of order . . . will not find it preposterous that the past should be altered by the present as much as the present is directed by the past.[26]

There is no place in the modern novel except the end at which the reader can say: 'The story has now reached such and such a point.' Similarly, the characters do not proceed in regular progression through time from one point to another, beginning here, pausing there and ending somewhere else. Their actions, thoughts and feelings are not looked upon as stationary milestones that mark off what is past; for the whole of their experience is implicit in any moment of their present. Their progress

[25] *Joseph Conrad: A Personal Remembrance*, 1924, p. 130. cf. "For an historigrapher discourseth of affairs orderly as they were done, accounting as well the times as the actions; but a Poet thrusteth into the middest, even where it most concerneth him, and there recoursing to the things forepast, and divining of things to come, maketh a pleasing analysis of all." (Spencer to Raleigh, 1590.)
[26] T. S. Eliot: *op. cit.*

through life is not to be viewed like that of a point moving along a line but that of a wave increasing and swelling with every instant of its movement. In fact, for such writers, and they include most of the 'stream of consciousness' school, there is no past as such at all, only a growing present, for no part of the past has an independent identity; the whole grows and alters as the present shifts.

> I am—says the hero of one modern novel—a part of all that I have touched and that has touched me, which, having for me no existence save that which I gave to it, became other than itself by being mixed with what I then was, and is now still otherwise, having fused with what I now am, which is itself a cumulation of what I have been becoming.[27]

This view of an eternal present in which the past is fused is essentially a modern one.

> . . . the philosophy of being present is also, in a perfectly real sense, the philosophy of our contemporaries.[28]

In modern fiction, it implies the discarding of straight sequence which suggests the immutable pastness of the past; it does away with the epic technique of intercalated exposition which adds further emphasis to the distinction between past and present; it is fundamental to the technique of Joyce, Dorothy Richardson and all the impressionist novelists. They have carried to its logical conclusion the dictum of Henry James:

> A novel is a living thing, all one and continuous, like any other organism, and in proportion as it lives will it be found, I think, that in each of the parts there is something of each of the other parts.[29]

The effect of reading is similar to that of watching a picture being painted. The artist need not proceed regularly from one corner of the canvas to another; he is under no obligation to finish one section before beginning on another, but is at liberty to distribute the strokes of his brush wherever he thinks fit. The order and precedence of his work is determined by him and him

[27] Thomas Wolfe: *Look Homeward, Angel*, 1929, p. 192.
[28] Prof. Murphy's introduction to Prof. Mead: *The Philosophy of the Present*, 1932, p. XI.
[29] *The Art of Fiction*, O.U.P. 1948, p. 13.

alone, just as the order and precedence of the act of seeing the picture, the movements of the eye of the viewer, follow no fixed rule, The effect of the whole picture is felt when the whole is seen, not in a fixed order of succession but in what psychologists call 'a specious present'—a present that has a narrow temporal spread. Something of the same effect is created by distributed exposition, if the term 'exposition' can any longer apply at all. The ultimate synthesis and the organisation of the parts into a satisfying whole are left to the reader.

TEMPORAL TRANSFER IN THE AUTOBIOGRAPHICAL NOVEL

CONTRARY to what might be expected, a novel in the first person rarely succeeds in conveying the illusion of presentness and immediacy. Far from facilitating the hero-reader identification, it tends to appear remote in time. The essence of such a novel is that it is retrospective, and that there is an avowed temporal distance between the fictional time—that of the events as they happened—and the narrator's actual time—his time of recording those events. There is a vital difference between writing a story forward from the past, as in the third person novel, and writing one backward from the present, as in the first person novel. Though both are equally written in the past, in the former the illusion is created that the action is taking place; in the latter, the action is felt as having taken place.

The reader of the autobiographical novel finds it therefore more difficult to sink his own actual present into a fictive present. Nor can he sink his own personality into that of the narrator. Another person is felt to be interposed between the *I* of the novel and the reader's *I*. The presence of the narrator obtrudes itself. A narrative in the first person and written throughout in the present tense would, if it were possible at all, appear so artificial as to make any identification impossible. It would obviously be limited to sensations and thoughts and exclude all action. It would also obtrude the act of writing itself, and by specifying itself so closely in time would appear even more remote to the reader, for it would impress on him constantly the fact and the

act of communication. The nearest natural approach to presentness and immediacy is to be found in the diary and epistolary
forms of the novel, but they seldom overcome the loss of intimacy
that the omniscient author technique can convey.

> it is highly fictitious; it is the most natural and the least probable way
> of telling a story.[30]

There is a good deal of truth in the French 'critique' of *Pamela*
and *Clarissa* which Richardson quoted so complacently:

> both are related in familiar letters by the parties themselves, at the
> very time in which the events happened: and this method has given the
> author great advantages, which he could not have drawn from any other
> species of narration. The minute particulars of events, the sentiments
> and conversations of the parties, are, upon this plan, exhibited with
> all the warmth and spirit that the passion supposed to be predominant
> at the very time could produce, and with all the distinguishing charac-
> teristics which memory can supply in a history of recent transactions.
> Romances in general . . . are wholly improbable; because they suppose
> the history to be written after the series of events is closed by the
> catastrophe: a circumstance which implies a strength of memory beyond
> all example and probability in the persons concerned, enabling them,
> at the distance of several years, to relate all the particulars of a transient
> conversation: or rather, it implies a yet more improbable confidence
> and familiarity between all these persons and the author.[31]

What has been missed in this criticism is the fact that, where
absolute realism is impossible and arbitrary conventions are inevitable, illusion may sometimes be stronger than a close ap-
proximation to reality. Moreover, exposition becomes an awkward factor to handle in a series of letters. Richardson was reduced to such lumbering devices as the following letter contains:

> In order to set this matter in a clear light, it is necessary to go a little
> back, and even perhaps to mention some things which you already
> know . . . I will give you the substance of this communicated con-
> versation after I have made a brief introductory observation or two,
> which however I hardly need to make to you who are so well acquainted
> with us all, did not the series or thread of the story require it.[32]

[30] Mrs. A. L. Barbauld: Preface to *The Correspondence of Samuel Richardson,* 1804, Vol. I, p. XXVII.
[31] Postscript to *Clarissa.*
[32] *Clarissa, letter* XIII.

Such a barefaced betrayal of the artistic conscience is far more reprehensible than Fielding's equally clumsy practice:

> Now, as this was a discovery of great consequence, it may be necessary to trace it from the fountainhead. We shall therefore very minutely lay open those previous matters by which it was produced; and for that purpose we shall be obliged to reveal all the secrets of a little family with which my reader is at present entirely unacquainted.[33]

Obstacles like these in the way of creating the illusion of immediacy and of introducing exposition, when taken in conjunction with all the other limitations that restrict the first person novel, sufficiently explain why the technique of writing novels in, to appropriate a pleasantly alliterative phrase, 'large, lauishe, laxative letters'[34] became so soon obsolete.

> . . . the first person, in the long piece, is a form foredoomed to looseness[35]

wrote Henry James explaining why he refused to make his heroes the historians of their own actions and thoughts. There are bounds which the *I* of the autobiographical novel cannot, except by means of unlikely and artificial tricks, overstep. He cannot present his own character or analyse his unconscious reactions and prejudices convincingly, though in a story where the emphasis is on action and adventure, this may not be the drawback it is in the novel where the accent is placed on character and psychology. There are furthermore other difficulties of knowing what other characters feel, or what is going on outside the actual knowledge and presence of the narrator. These gaps can only be filled by the report of others, a device which further hinders the conveying of the sense of immediacy. In the past tense, third person novel, the author, being omniscient about the characters and all their actions and feelings, suffers from no such restrictions, though he may, for other reasons, prefer to limit his omniscience to one character only. Most novelists, therefore, prefer the 'omniscient author' to the autobiographical form.

[33] *Tom Jones,* Book II Chapter 2.
[34] Gabriel Harvey: Letter to Spenser.
[35] Preface to *The Ambassadors.*

THE DRAMATIC METHOD

WHERE the omniscient author refrains from obtruding himself or his comments into his work, the illusion of presentness and immediacy may persist very strongly in the mind of the reader. The modern novelist will usually use one or more of three ways for cheating the reason of the reader and encouraging his imagination to lose itself in time: the dramatic method, the lavish use of dialogue, and the restricted point of view.

The dramatic method aims at conveying

the psychological equivalent of the dramatic present,[36]

and has been thus defined:

The dramatic method is the method of direct presentation, and aims to give the reader the sense of being present, here and now, in the scene of the action. That is why those elements are undramatic which make us aware of an author explaining things.[37]

Ex cathedra reflections and comments, and short guides to the reader on how to judge or how much to like the various characters are obvious evidences of the intrusive author. Exposition, and description as seen not through the characters' minds but through the author's reflect the same 'betrayal of a sacred office' [38] in more subtle guise. There is a clear difference in the effect produced by the author's exposition, so common in Balzac, for example, whereby anterior events are narrated with a view to setting up a convenient framework into which to fit the novel proper, as against the reflections on the past as they arise in a character's mind; or the rendering of associative links with earlier events as they derive from his present. Exposition should in short be an integral part of the narrative, built into the structure. As an extraneous piece tacked on to the main novel,

[36] Beach: *The Twentieth Century Novel*, 1932, p. 148.
[37] *ibid.* p. 181.
[38] *vid. sup.* page 134.

it hinders the reader from losing himself in the time and place of the novel.

Similar to the author's exposition and equally undramatic and intrusive is nature description by the author as author. Here he puts up backgrounds and settings to provide the reader with atmosphere or show his powers of fine writing. Quite different is the effect where a scene as it appears to a character forms part of his reactions at a specific moment and serves as an element in the process of his development or in his emotional make-up. In the first case the author is felt to be working out his characters in full view of the reader, in the second they work themselves out themselves.

As regards comments on and analyses of character, interpretation of action, in short the attaching of values to ideas, facts or feelings, a distinction must be made between the views of an observer-within-the-novel and those of the novelist-outside-the-novel, between say Lockwood in *Wuthering Heights* and Trollope in *Barchester Towers*.

The dramatic method is then entirely incompatible with the intrusive author; when successfully pursued, it enables the reader to merge himself into the fictive present and fictional time of the book, and creates in him the illusion of being present at the action, in both meanings of the word 'present,' as he is when seeing a play on the stage. It achieves these effects by the direct presentation of scenes, where the fullness of detail, the limitation of time and the exclusion of extraneous comment as explanation, all help to give the feeling of what Beach calls 'the continuous dramatic present.'

THE USE OF DIALOGUE

THE greater vividness accruing to the direct method of presentation was realised in very early times. Euclid, reporting to Terpsion the narration by Socrates of conversations the latter had held with various persons, says:

I may observe that I have introduced Socrates, not as narrating to me, but as actually conversing with the persons whom he mentioned . . .

I have omitted, for the sake of convenience, the interlocutory words 'I said,' 'I remarked,' which he used when he spoke of himself, and again, 'he agreed' or 'disagreed,' in the answer . . . .[39]

Here, as in the novel, the illusion of presentness is considerably strengthened by the extensive use of dialogue which produces an effect similar to that felt in the theatre where the spectator is indeed present, though as far as the play is concerned, he is assumed not to be there at all. The comparison holds only for the modern stage. It does not hold for the Elizabethan theatre where the audience collaborated in the play, and was addressed by the actor in asides or soliloquies on set themes, and was kept informed of events or guided in its views by means of choruses and expository and explanatory prologues. This is the equivalent of the Scott, Thackeray, Meredith type of novel, where the author as author continually addresses the reader as reader.

The lavish use of dialogue is an important element in the dramatic method, and is perhaps the most obvious means of producing the illusion of immediacy and presentness in the reader. It has its limitations, however, for a novel can hardly be wholly or even mainly in dialogue without losing much of its flexibility. Such a novel would in fact approximate so closely to a play as to lose its character as a novel.[40] There is an intermediate form between dialogue and narrative, represented speech:

He had left the letter upon the table in the Auberge—he would run for it, and be back with it in three minutes.[41]

That she was very well: that there were many women deemed passable who were inferior to herself: that she was always thought comely; and comeliness, let her tell me, having not so much to lose as beauty had, would hold . . . Nothing, in short, to be found fault with, though nothing very engaging she doubted—was there, Clary?[42]

---

[39] Plato: *Theaetetus.* Jowett's translation. *The Dialogues of Plato*, 3rd edn. 1892, Vol. 4, p. 194. cf. B. Franklin's comment on Bunyan in his *Autobiography, Harvard Classics* edn. p. 23: "Honest John was the first that I know of who mix'd narration and dialogue, a method of writing very engaging to the reader, who in the most interesting parts finds himself, as it were, brought into the company and present at the discourse."

[40] The experiment was tried in *The Disguise, A Dramatic Novel*, 1771. For the anonymous author's justification, see the preface, p.x. cf. also Mabbe's translation of *Celestina*, 1631.

[41] Sterne: *Sentimental Journey*, Macdonald edn. 1948, p. 94.

[42] *Clarissa*, Book I, letter 2.

This compromise of direct and reported dialogue has the effect of identifying the characters, author and reader more closely, bringing them all into a unity in which their separateness is less marked.

There are two other ways of preserving the directness of dialogue without sacrificing the advantages attendant on the omniscience of the author. These are the mental soliloquy in its developed form—the interior monologue, and the stream of consciousness. At the verbal level of consciousness they are almost as old as the novel itself, but a new turn was given to them by Meredith in *Rhoda Fleming* and was developed to its furthest limits by Henry James. The attempt to suggest the workings of the lower strata of the mind was first made in England by Dorothy Richardson, and she was closely followed by Joyce. These two were not satisfied with depicting the ratiocination of the mind for which a fair degree of verbal equivalence can be found. Rather they aimed at evoking the sub-verbal levels of consciousness by breaking up the fixed categories of linguistic forms and so creating the effect of unbroken continuity. Since them, Virginia Woolf, Faulkner and a host of others have taken up these solipsistic techniques. They constitute, as it were, the picture-frame play transferred to a mental plane; we see a mind open to view and watch its inner processes at work. Eugene O'Neill has in fact tried to apply this technique to the drama, where it provides a modern variant of the soliloquy and aside of earlier drama. The basic convention of the omniscient author is not eliminated, but on the contrary is exploited to an even greater degree. The principle of selection likewise still operates, though it aims at being far less arbitrary. Similarly, the translation of mental processes into verbal forms still obtains, though the language is so unusual.

One explanation of the vividness that this technique is capable of achieving lies in the effect of presentness produced by the fact that such writing is in the present tense; it gains thereby in immediacy what it loses for most readers by its use of private and esoteric forms of expression, associations and symbols which hinder easy identification with the protagonists.

An interesting anticipation of these developments in the novel was made by Stendhal who hints at the modern methods nearly a hundred and fifty years ago:

Supposons qu'un sténographe pût se rendre invisible et se tenir tout un jour à côté de M. Petiet, qu'il écrivît tout ce qu'il dirait, qu'il notât tous ses gestes, il est évident qu'un excellent acteur muni de ce procès-verbal pourrait nous reproduire M. Petiet tel qu'il a été ce jour-là . . . Il y aurait un autre procès-verbal de la même journée bien plus intéressant, ce serait celui que nous donnerait un dieu qui aurait tenu un compte parfaitement exact de toutes les opérations de sa *tête* et de son *âme*. C'est-à-dire de ses pensées et de ses désirs dans l'ordre avec lequel ils se sont mutuellement suivis ou causés.[43]

THE RESTRICTED POINT OF VIEW

THE dramatic method and the extensive use of dialogue are commonly, and the stream of consciousness technique is almost invariably associated with the third method, the restricted point of view. The author presents everything through the mind of a single character, or at least of one character at a time for a considerable part of the book. The other characters are judged from the outside, from their acting and behaviour as viewed by the central character. This method is by way of a compromise between the omniscient and the autobiographical methods; the artificial convention of the omniscient author is limited to one person only in the novel; on the other hand, the inflexibility and the various disadvantages attendant on the first-person novel are avoided.

The use of the restricted point of view not only renders the reader-character identification more easy; it also conveys directness of presentation and immediacy because it resembles the way people react in real life. We do not see ourselves as others see us. We are aware in ourselves of the whole pressure of the past on our present, of the tug and clash of forces that may or may not express themselves in terms of action. We know ourselves from the inside; we are to a greater or lesser extent omniscient about ourselves. As regards others, however, we are mere spectators; we can only guess at their motives from their actions and behaviour; direct evidence of the interior of their minds we cannot have. That is why other people are so much more simple to us than we ourselves. We know only the resultant

[44] *Pensées, Filosofia Nova*, written 1804, edn. *Le Divan*, 1931, Vol. 2, pp. 179–180.

of the forces that work in them as it expresses itself in outward behaviour; in ourselves, we are aware of the complex and ever shifting equilibrium of conflicting forces as well, before they reach their expression in action.

WILLIAM T. NOON

MODERN LITERATURE AND THE SENSE OF TIME

> *"Tymes go by turnes and chaunces chang by course,*
> *From foule to fayre, from better happ to worse."*
> —Blessed Robert Southwell.

Time and history, the two most distinctively characteristic literary themes of this century, have arrested the attention of our imaginative writers in a manner wholly compelling and unique. The basic intellectual problem raised by so deep and unparalleled a concern with these two themes, or two aspects of the one theme, calls for the resources of the historian, the philosopher, the theologian, the political economist as well as of the literary critic and man of letters. Ideally, even an initial approach toward a clear definition of the problem would require a long collaborative effort. Roger Mehl, professor in the Protestant Faculty of the University of Strasbourg, has called the philosophy of history at the level of mythology, of secularized theodicy, "the spiritual adventure of our generation"; [1] Josef

---

[1] Roger Mehl, "Philosophy of History or Theology of History?" tr. Joseph E. Cunneen, *Cross Currents*, 3 (Winter, 1953), 165. Cf. Charles P. Loughran, S.J., "Theology and History, A Bibliography," Thought, 29 (Spring, 1954), 101–15. See also *Man and Time*, Papers from the *Eranos Yearbooks*, III, ed. Joseph Campbell, Bollingen Series XXX (New York, Pantheon, 1957). Twelve distinguished European scholars from eight countries are represented in this collection, which is drawn from the Eranos meetings at Ascona, Switzerland, 1949, 1951.

From Thought, *XXXIII (1958). Reprinted by permission of* Thought *and the author.*

Pieper, German Catholic lay apologist, has asserted that "the philosophy of history has ceased to exist, its place has been taken by the sociology of culture." [2] Pieper adds that a Christian philosophy of history is "the most intellectually arduous task" of our times, indeed, "in the whole domain of philosophy." [3] The Anglo-Catholic C. S. Lewis, better known, perhaps, than these others to readers of English fiction and criticism, has described as "Historicism" the human effort, unaided by grace and revelation, to provide such a philosophy, to "discover an inner meaning in the historical process," and has contended that the effort is "atheo-logical," and that the "Historicists are wasting their time": "We ride with our backs to the engine. We have no notion what stage in the journey we have reached. Are we in Act I or Act V?" [4] It is an "illusion," on Lewis' grounds, to imagine that history can provide a key to life's mysteries. H. Butterfield, Professor of Modern History at the University of Cambridge, likens the human story to "a piece of music that we are playing over for the first time. In our presumption we may act as though we were the composer of the piece or try to bring out our own particular part as the leading one. . . . None of us can know what the whole score amounts to. . . . And no single person in the orchestra can have any idea when or where this piece of music is going to end." [5] Christopher Dawson's position is well known: religion alone is the key to history itself.[6] In widely analogous senses, Arnold Toynbee and T. S. Eliot, as analysts of our culture, have taken a similar position. Though Jacques Maritain entitles his recently published discourses, lectures "On the Philosophy of History," most readers, especially non-Catholic ones, are likely to feel that Maritain is much too deeply committed to Christian revelation to illuminate the meaning of history in any other than a profoundly Christian theological sense. As he himself readily admits, "There is no

[2] Joseph Pieper, *The End of Time: A Meditation on the Philosophy of History*, tr. Michael Bullock (London: Faber and Faber, 1954), pp. 28–9.
[3] *Ibid.*, p. 32.
[4] C. S. Lewis, "Historicism," *Month*, New ser. 4 (Oct., 1950), 230, 234, 236.
[5] H. Butterfield, *Christianity and History* (New York: Scribner's, 1949), p. 94.
[6] See, for example, *Progress and Religion* (New York: Sheed and Ward, 1929), p. 23: "As the rationalists had destroyed men's faith in Reason, so it was the work of the historians to undermine men's belief in the unity of History."

complete or adequate philosophy of history if it is not connected with some prophetic or theological data." [7] Oswald Spengler's myth of man's nonethical, nonrational development, so popular in the thirties, is little honored intellectually today. In his *Essay on Rime*, the American poet Karl Shapiro has noted with concern the unparalleled currency of *history* in our rhetoric, and has, furthermore, reminded us in the same context that today's fashion of viewing "art as the supreme/Criterion of experience is as new/As the electric light." [8]

So far as our works of literature imaginatively record, evaluate, and interpret our twentieth-century concern with this obsessive time-and-history theme, they provide the literary commentator with no special solution to the problem. Literature reveals belief or lack of belief, witnesses to our failures and fears, voices our concerns, embodies our attitudes; it cannot, of itself, constitute our beliefs nor account for their validity; it does not as literature resolve fundamental inconsistencies between belief and human experience. So it is that the literary-minded man today is faced as never before with the need, out of his accumulated intellectual and spiritual resources, to bring into some kind of order, or focus, his own reflections on this time-and-history question, one which most urgently and insistently confronts him under so many guises in modern poetry, drama, and fiction.

Literature has its own autonomy, the imagination has its own vitality and validity in its seizure of and re-presentation of reality; the approach of literature is not that either of theology or of philosophy. Theology explores reality so far as reality is presented by God's revelation and accepted by faith, a supernatural virtue, energized by divine grace; philosophy explores reality so far as reason can discern it in virtue of its natural powers, especially as these are aided by the inherited traditions of reasoning which have been transmitted to us from the past. Literature is not, primarily, an effort either of faith or of reason; essentially, it is rather an effort of the creative imagi-

[7] Jacques Maritain, *On the Philosophy of History*, ed. J. W. Evans (New York: Scribner's, 1957), p. 170.
[8] Karl Shapiro, *Essay on Rime* (New York: Reynal and Hitchcock, 1945), pp. 42–3, ll. 1191–1205; p. 52, ll. 1453–6.

nation to discover reality and, through the resources of language, to interpret our encounter with it, our affective appraisal of it, in as fully engaged a human way as our language resources (for example, our insight into metaphor, our feeling for verbal rhythms, our sense of syntactical relationships, our appreciation of words as signs or symbols of another level or reality) can make possible. Literature, itself a symbol, has never before so self-consciously set itself the task of explaining under the rubric of time the *theoria,* or symbolic meaning, of human actions and gestures (personal, interpersonal) which the creative imagination has discovered in men's historical, or spatio-temporal, relationships with each other. Is time itself comprehensible, or has the fortune-teller in Thornton Wilder's *The Skin of Our Teeth* spoken the last word on the subject? "Think! Think! Split your heads. I can't tell the past and neither can you. If anybody tries to tell you the past, take my word for it, they're charlatans." [9]

Can a man hope today to salvage his identity, to say nothing of his human dignity, from what T. S. Eliot has called this "drifting wreckage" of time?

And the way up is the way down, the way forward is the way back.
You cannot face it steadily, but this thing is sure,
That time is no healer: the patient is no longer here.[10]

Does the past have a meaning? our own past? the past of our race? If so, may we read it, and how do we find it out? "Have you not done tormenting me with your accursed time!" exclaims one of the characters in Samuel Beckett's *Waiting for Godot.* "When! When! One day, is that not enough for you, one day like any other day, one day he went dumb, one day I went blind, one day we'll go deaf, one day we were born, one day we shall die, the same day, the same second, is that not enough for

---

[9] Thornton Wilder, *The Skin of Our Teeth* (New York: Harper, 1942), Act II, p. 64. See Malcolm Cowley, "Thornton Wilder and the Spirit of Anti-History." *Saturday Review,* Oct. 6, 1956, pp. 13–14ff. Cowley notes (p. 50) that Wilder "is our great unsocial and antihistorical novelist, the artist of the anachronism. In all his work I can think of only one event that marks an absolute change; it is the birth of Christ."

[10] T. S. Eliot, *Four Quartets* (London: Faber and Faber, 1944), "Dry Salvages," III, p. 30.

you?" [11] What was the past trying to tell us? What was the Holy Spirit through the past trying to say? May history yet be redeemed, or rehabilitated? May the past again be recovered, or, as Marcel Proust would have it, is the search for it in the long run to be abandoned to chance? "And so it is with our own past. It is a labour in vain to recapture it: all the efforts of our intellect must prove futile. The past is hidden somewhere outside the realm, beyond the reach of intellect, in some material object (in the sensation which that material object will give us) which we do not suspect. And as for that object, it depends on chance whether we come upon it or not before we ourselves must die." [12]

What is the special quality, and value, if any, in the present fleeting moment? What are its enduring links with what has gone before, and with what is yet to come? "Time is the echo of an axe / Within a wood," Philip Larkin writes in one of his many time poems. In another, he tells us: "Truly, though our element is time, / We are not suited to the long perspective / Open at each instant of our lives." [13] Father Daniel Berrigan has entitled his prize-winning volume of poetry *Time Without Number*. Is time leading us to any goal? Or are we headed for another blind alley, another impasse, another cul-de-sac? In the "risible universe" of James Joyce's *Finnegans Wake*, the song which the grasshopper, or "Gracehopper," sings to the busy "Ondt" (or "evil one") concludes:

> Your genus its worldwide, your spacest sublime!
> But, Holy Saltmartin, why can't you beat time? [14]

Father William Lynch has already convincingly argued in the pages of *Thought* that the literary imagination is a most sharp

[11] Samuel Beckett, "Waiting for Godot," Act II (London: Faber, 1956), p. 89. See also Beckett's 1931 monograph, *Proust* (London: Chatto and Windus), p. 4: "But the poisonous ingenuity of Time in the science of affliction is not limited to its action on the subject, that action . . . resulting in an unceasing modification of his personality, whose permanent reality, if any, can only be apprehended as a retrospective hypothesis."
[12] Marcel Proust, "Overture," *Swann's Way,* in *Remembrance of Things Past,* tr. C. K. Scott Moncrieff (New York: Random House, 1934), I, 34.
[13] Quoted by John Wain, "English Poetry: The Immediate Situation," *Sewanee Review,* 65 (Summer, 1957), pp. 363, 365. See also, the poems in *The Less Deceived* (Hessle, East Yorkshire: Marvell Press, 1955).
[14] James Joyce, *Finnegans Wake* (New York: Viking, 1947), p. 419.

and luminous expression of the attitudes of the ordinary modern man. I do not see how anyone could wish to dispute his conclusion: "The time is coming when the theologian and the poet or critic will stop confronting each other in potentially hostile attitudes on the outside of the literary organism. . . . Someday they will and must meet at the inside of the poem." [15] If so, they may scarcely evade this question of the effort of the contemporary imagination to explain to itself its overriding consciousness of history under the aspects of time. If literature is to man what Cardinal Newman claimed it to be, "in some sort what autobiography is to the individual," [16] no contemporary study of man, "his mind and his heart," may be complete so long as it leaves out of literary account this psychological and philosophical time-consciousness of modern man.

In stating that modern literature is most urgently and centrally concerned with this acute, humanly felt experience of time, we need, of course, to recognize that this theme, "the lament of mutability," has been a major one in every literature since, indeed, literature began. As a mode of poetic consciousness it seems least of all to be altered even by translations of our literary classics. We recognize it in Achilles' lament to Priam over the ravaged body of Hector as the two old men grieve at the "woven sorrow" of their lives; we recognize it in Virgil's unforgettable symbolic insight into the whole historical process when he represents Aeneas, in his flight from Troy, carrying his father, Anchises, the past, on his back, leading his son, Ascanius, the future, by the hand, and carrying with him his household gods, who do not change. On another journey, Dante, with Virgil for his guide, is scarcely less concerned with the contingencies of history and the senses or significations which may be discerned for the spacious future of eternity in the once mutable, time-dimensional, passionately purposeful choices of the past.

It is natural, most of all, that in English literature we should everywhere overhear this refrain of mutability, for English literature came into its maturity during the Renascence; this was

---

[15] William F. Lynch, S.J., "Theology and the Imagination," *Thought*, 24 (Spring, 1954), 86.
[16] Cf. Discourse IX, "Duties of the Church Towards Knowledge," in *The Idea of a University*.

a period when the medieval orientation of man to eternity began to be radically questioned, his hope of a personal immortality to be much muted on any intellectually perceived or realizable score. Shakespeare's sonnets, for example, more often than not come to a focus in the poetic effort to salvage something from the remorseless flow of time: life is short, art is long, and human love is somewhere in between. This same theme is sounded repeatedly in Shakespeare's plays, sometimes in the cadences of song, sometimes in the tragic perceptions and reversals of the action:

> When that I was and a little tiny boy,
> With hey, ho, the wind and the rain . . . .

> To-morrow, and to-morrow, and to-morrow,
> Creeps in this petty pace from day to day,
> To the last syllable of recorded time . . . .

The very titles of Spenser's poems suggest sufficiently his preoccupation with this theme: "The Ruines of Time," "Mutability Cantos":

> But time shall come that all shall changèd bee,
> And from henceforth none no more change shal see.

With Milton we are aware from the start with the Nativity Ode of an ambitiously renewed attempt, not yet doomed by any apocalyptic vision of darkness (as W. B. Yeats's attempts later on would be) to resolve the discord between the past and the present into a timeless concord of eternity. *Paradise Lost*, itself, from its first invocation of the Holy Spirit, sets out to span "the vast abyss" of created history (angelic and human) with the arch of poetry, the immediate, imaginatively experienced consciousness of our fall and restoration in "this frail World" of time. Though it is probably true to say that most modern readers conceive of fall and restoration only as part and parcel of Milton's over-all mythological texture, the pattern of the poem, especially at its ending, suggests even to the modern mind that the real paradises are not lost irretrievably—in spite of what Marcel Proust has said.

This "lament for mutability" so characteristic of our literature in the past is not precisely nor dominantly what we find in twentieth-century literature. Formerly it would have been easy to equate poetry's time-concern with a concern or avowal of the poet's human finiteness, his awareness of the essential instability of his body-and-soul's hold on reality in a world forever undergoing change. The most human of all human regrets at the loss of a past, perhaps not humanly responded to, and perhaps not even adverted to, has manifested itself most characteristically in art as an effort either to recover, to reconstitute its meaning in the symbols of poetry itself, or to find philosophically some "more abundant recompense" in memory for the time that can be no more. The poet of the past thought of himself as existing like other men "in time's covenant." The imaginative pilgrimages of the individual or of the human race through history have followed until quite recently a course marked all the way by the landmarks of time. This archetypal metaphor of the journey suggests, too, that the pilgrimages of the past, however profound their consciousness of loss, have had a journey's end in view. Such a sense of direction is notably absent from much of the most significant literature of the twentieth century; its absence seems symptomatic of a general dissolution of meaning:

> Turning and turning in the widening gyre
> The falcon cannot hear the falconer;
> Things fall apart; the centre cannot hold;
> Mere anarchy is loosed upon the world . . . .[17]

No other literature has ever so self-consciously and deliberately undertaken, albeit with a sense of hopelessness, to search for "the figure in the carpet," "the beast in the jungle" of time. None has so deeply committed itself to a global world view of history, grand, epic, and metaphysical in its refusal to accept the ordinary indices which men have used to place events in time. The originality and influence of Bergson, as Georges Poulet argues in his *Studies in Human Time*, has been nowhere greater than in his affirmation that duration is a free creation, the intuited succession of our conscious states all felt at once. In *Time and Free Will*, Bergson says, "It is the same self which perceives distinct states at first, and which, by afterwards con-

---

[17] *The Collected Poems* of W. B. Yeats (New York: Macmillan, 1951), "The Second Coming," p. 184.

centrating its attention, will see these states melt into one another like the crystals of a snow-flake when touched for some time by the, finger"; though Bergson grants that "a superficial psychology" and "the requirements of social life" may be contented by "an inner life with well distinguished moments," he adds that it is an intellectual "absurdity," in thinking about time, to put "succession at the very centre of simultaneity." [18] The poets of our day tend to think of the imagination as generative of the act of time. Such a development would seem to be conditioned, too, at least atmospherically, by Kant's transcendental aesthetic, which conceives of time as purely an *a priori* subjective condition, "nothing else than the form of the internal sense, that is, of the intuitions of self and of our internal state." [19] Space and time, as Kant describes them, are "mere creations of the imagination." [20] In James Joyce's *A Portrait of the Artist as a Young Man,* Stephen Dedalus views his rupture with Christianity as freeing his creative powers to operate more triumphantly in the timeless world of art: "So timeless seemed the grey warm air, so fluid and impersonal his own mood, that all ages were as one to him." [21]

The "suttle theef" of Milton's youth has been metamorphosed into a kind of transcendent abstraction: time is conceived of as a thought category which may and must be surmounted; the boundaries of past, present, and future are blurred in the timeless, privileged "epiphanies" of poetry. "A people without history / Is not redeemed from time, for history is a pattern / Of timeless moments," writes Eliot in the concluding section of "Little Gidding," the last of the *Four Quartets.* Stephen Dedalus, in the Library chapter of *Ulysses,* thinks of himself as remembering the future. Throughout the novel he despairs of either finding or changing the meaning of time: "Time surely would scatter all. . . . History, Stephen said, is a nightmare from which I am trying to awake. . . . A whirring whistle:

[18] Henri Bergson, *Time and Free Will,* tr. F. L. Pogson (New York: Macmillan, 1928), pp. 138–9.
[19] Immanuel Kant, "The Critique of Pure Reason," tr. J. M. D. Meiklejohn, in *Great Books of the Western World,* no. 42 (Chicago: Encyclopaedia Britannica, 1952), p. 27.
[20] *Ibid.,* p. 29.
[21] James Joyce, *A Portrait of the Artist As a Young Man* (New York: Modern Library, 1928), p. 196.

goal. What if that nightmare gave you a back kick?" [22] The
"Great Wheel" of Yeats's *A Vision*, so elaborately described in
its gyres, circuits, and emanations, is presented as the uniquely
valid time-symbol of reality; together with Yeats's complex
mythology of the ever-recurring twenty-eight phases of the
moon, the wheel is described as the central image of man's unstable place in history, the unique satisfactory clue imaginatively
to the labyrinth of his mind.

This temporalized poetic consciousness which questions or
denies value-charged aspects of time ("the science of affliction") [23] and of history (" that double-headed monster of damnation"), [24] though it is the bitter fruit of the secularization and
mythologizing of the traditional Christian theological sense, has
roots also in the characteristically modern philosophical reluctance to distinguish between what Hans Meyerhoff has called
psychological and *physical* time. Though Bergson would dismiss
such a distinction as meaningless in any nonmechanistic account
of reality, it seems unavoidable so soon as we attempt to define
the problem of time realistically in its relation to man. Meyerhoff, among others, casts much light, therefore, on the problem
by distinguishing between what he calls psychological time,
which is personal and subjective (*le temps humain*), and physical time, which is impersonal and objective, what we mean in
science when we measure the rate of change, the "number of
motion" (*numerus motus secundum prius et posterius*) of one
finite object in terms of that of another, and in virtue of which
comparison we derive, for example, our notions of lunar, stellar,
or sidereal time, and in accordance with which we set our
watches and our clocks. [25] It is along these latter cosmological
lines, in general, that the Scholastic (Aristotelian) description
of time has been, at best obliquely, worked out, an *ens rationis
cum fundamento in re*. Though proof is scarcely needed to show
that the time theme in literature has always been preeminently
personal and subjective, it has only been in our modern age
that literary time has resigned itself, at least in theory, to be
without public reference, a kind of purely private and personal

[22] James Joyce, *Ulysses* (New York: Modern Library, 1946), p. 35.
[23] Beckett, *Proust*, p. 4.
[24] *Ibid.*, p. 1.
[25] Hans Meyerhoff, *Time in Literature* (Berkeley: University of California
Press, 1955), pp. 4–5, 12–13.

"epiphany," or illumination, of consciousness without any public temporal index whatsoever attached.

St. Augustine may have been the first, as Meyerhoff says, who "recognized the nature of memory as a key to the structure of time and the self," [26] but to say nothing of St. Augustine's conviction that eternity alone could provide the most necessary clue, "transhistorical" in its intelligibility, to this "most entangled enigma of time," St. Augustine attempts always to give to memory, to time as a measuring activity of the soul in its quest for continuity and unity, an objective basis in the succession of physical motion, what goes on in the changing "outside" world. He would certainly not have accepted Spengler's counsel of cyclic despair: "We ourselves are time." Without some basis other than a mental act of the memory, the "recovery of the self" would prove to be not merely a "flight" from time but a betrayal and turning away from reality. Such a falsification of the temporal structure of nature and of history would leave our subjective experiences without any meaningful cohesion at all.

Some sort of psychic control is called for to face the past as well as the future. Like the imagination of the literary artist, St. Augustine's memory relies on the conscious powers of the mind to cope with change, especially as a realized restriction on the psychic energy of one's own unconscious hopes.[27] Without some such implicit acknowledgment of one's own position in an extra-subjective realm of change, the mind could neither recover for a moment the memory of the past nor project either hope or apprehension of the future. "So," ultimately admits Proust, "it is with Time in one's life." [28] Until one has faced the full horror of it, adds Proust, one can never know the joy of escape. No major artist in recent literature, whatsoever his putative time metaphysics or temperamental intolerance of time may have been, has completely succeeded in eliminating the public referents of time. Quite the contrary! For all the poetic value which Proust's great masterpiece, *Á La Recherche du Temps Perdu*, may have enduringly achieved in the genre of

[26] *Ibid.*, p. 42.
[27] Cf. St. Augustine's prayer, Ch. 22, Book XI, *The Confessions*, tr. J. G. Pilkington, in *Basic Writings of St. Augustine*, ed. Whitney J. Oates (New York: Random House, 1948), I, 196, and his famous text on "this most entangled enigma of time" given in Ch. 14 of the same book (191).
[28] *Remembrance of Things Past*, I, "Swann's Way," p. 369.

"timelessness," few men today would care to argue that even so magnificent an artistic achievement was for Proust personally a perfectly satisfactory human reintegration of his self or of his life. As W. B. Yeats has memorably said, "The intellect of man is forced to choose / Perfection of the life or of the work." It may be that certain works of art are brought to completion only with the sacrifice of well-nigh every other human value, personal, religious, and humane, but it does not help our critical discourse to pretend that such other human values have not in truth been sacrificed. "The viewless wings of Poesy" cannot always bear so great a freight, as Keats for his part well enough understood. Furthermore, the reason why men continue to read Proust's masterpiece is not that it is a kind of timeless surrogate for the clinical rehabilitation of the author's personality, but that in portraying the decline of a certain way of life, the Guermantes way, at a certain point in public time, it still continues, perhaps too well, to possess a meaningful relevance for our own experiences and our own way of life.

All great art is "timeless" in this sense, if you will, but such a view of its timelessness, of that which, like the bee in amber, the temporal in the eternal, survives the changes of time would appear to be a bankrupt notion if for the enduring consciousness there were no changes to be survived, to be transcended and understood. The Proustian duration, as Poulet says, "is a simple plurality of isolated moments remote from each other." [29] St. Augustine's intellectual memory, unlike the affective memory of Proust, never undertook to play the supernatural role of grace. He supposed that some ground of being other than the past conferred on the present its authentic existence. Time is not an absolute. We are not always spectators remembering; willingly or unwillingly, all of us, and especially our artists, are compelled on occasion to act, to make choices. Time (inner or outer) is not exclusively a construct of the memory. It may be that the Proustian "involuntary" memory provides us our most vivid experience of discontinuity and mutability; there is, to be sure, an incommunicability and impenetrability about this kind of experience of our unconscious states of sensation. This incommunicable, impenetrable experience is exactly what the

[29] Georges Poulet, *Studies in Human Time*, tr. Elliott Coleman (Baltimore: Johns Hopkins Press, 1956), p. 316.

artist like Proust must penetrate and communicate. Energetically he must articulate it, consciously and voluntarily, in language, if he is to succeed, as Proust does, in having us mime, or re-enact, in our own consciousness his private experience of discontinuity. The technical problem of what to do with time in a narrative—foreshortening, perspective, acceleration, tempo, and so forth—permits of many complex and sophisticated resolutions by poets and novelists.[30] The technical resolution of this literary time problem is not, in itself, however, a metaphysical resolution of the time enigma, nor does it commit one to any single supra-historical metaphysics of time. Proust's bifocal vision of past and present fusing in a moment of ecstatic restoration is one notable literary technique for managing the time perspective, but one may still choose to bargain with time on other terms. His technique does not oblige us to accept a quasi-magical view of time as hostile transformer and falsifier of all in reality that is valuable and dear. Another novelist might care to use the same technique, but with, at least, one different lens. Time is not necessarily an archenemy to be defeated in memory. To some extent, certainly, it is, in Allen Tate's phrase, a "gentle serpent," and it depends on us whether the work of time will be for us or against us when memory sits either to contemplate or to judge. In his poem, "Looking into History," Richard Wilbur has said of our effort to "father the waiting past":

> The dead give no command
> And shall not find their voice
> Till they be mustered by
> Some present fatal choice.[31]

Hans Meyerhoff has suggested three causes, intellectual and cultural, to account for "the heightened and perhaps excessive consciousness of time in the modern world": (1) the "sharp decline or virtual collapse of the dimension of 'eternity' which had been an integral part of the ancient and medieval picture of the world and man"; (2) "the adoption of the quantitative metric of time in modern science: the familiar units of clocks

---

[30] These technical resolutions of style in "an attempt to beguile time with an artificial version" are admirably examined in David Paul's "Time and the Novelist," *Partisan Review,* 21 (Nov.–Dec., 1954), 636–49.

[31] *Things of This World* (New York: Harcourt, 1956), p. 25.

and chronometers"; (3) the tendency to view truth itself as "a function of time, or the historical process." [32] It has often been stated that Christianity alone rescued Western thought from the fatalistic cyclic time theories of the East, and substituted a linear movement of free progress for the deterministic Greek notions of perpetual emanations and returns. Roy W. Battenhouse, for example, in a notable modern reading of *Hamlet*, thus contrasts Hamlet's speech, "The readiness is all" with Edgar's "Ripeness is all" in *King Lear:* "Edgar's phrase with its context of 'coming hither' and 'going hence' takes time seriously and maintains for man a purpose in history, whereas Hamlet's —like Stoic and also like modern Existentialist thought—collapses history within a present moment empty of recall of the past or of anticipation of the future, of any sense of preparation behind or of consummation ahead. . . . It makes of history a treadmill rather than a schoolhouse." [33]

If this were the whole story, one might attempt defensibly to ascribe time's strangle hold on our imaginations, in terms of Meyerhoff's three causes, to an accelerated rate of dissipation in our days of the Christian theological sense. It is not altogether clear, however, that Christianity alone introduced a positive orientation toward time in our Western consciousness; as C. S. Lewis has reminded us, the pagan gods of the Norse epics are "rooted in a historical process," and the time sense of the ancient Romans (unlike that of the Greeks, of the Norsemen) seems on the whole progressive and positive.[34] In *Four Views of Ancient Time*, John F. Callahan has demonstrated that for Plato, Aristotle and Plotinus, as well as for St. Augustine, the time sense of these ancients, in spite of greatly varying dialectical emphases, had a generally optimistic psychological vitality.[35] We may surmise that something of this vitality, in no way in opposition to Christianity, carried on over into the medieval attitude toward time as an image or intimation of eternity, a kind of unity of consciousness which for all of its naiveté as scientific history disposed men to view history as possessing pur-

[32] Meyerhoff, *Time in Literature*, pp. 87–94.
[33] Roy W. Battenhouse, "Hamlet's Apostrophe on Man: Clue to the tragedy," *PMLA*, 66 (Dec., 1951), 1101.
[34] C. S. Lewis, "Historicism," *Month*, New ser. 4 (Oct., 1950), 233.
[35] John F. Callahan, *Four Views of Ancient Time* (Cambridge: Harvard University Press, 1948).

pose and meaning in the Christian sense. Nor has it been established that every theory of cyclic recurrence, Giambattista Vico's *New Science,* for example, must be without a providential significance for interpreting men's free actions transacted in a Christian context of time. The distortion of the time sense to which our modern literature witnesses owes as much to loss of confidence in reason, in idea, as it does to lack of nerve in our faith. The imagination staggers under burdens too heavy for it to carry.

With all due allowance for the prophetic messianism of Marxism, it has not been a characteristic quality of twentieth-century thought to conceive of time under the image of a straight line toward some end or goal. *The Education of Henry Adams* has been available since 1907 as a record of one distinguished American historian's despair of the whole historical process. Both in this autobiography and in "A Letter to American Teachers of History," 1910, Adams sets forth a theory of history (a physics in its analogues rather than a metaphysics) in which he predicts that our universe is now approaching complete dissolution, and in which he counsels us to find in art what poise we can as we await the end. Appalled by the increasing mechanization and fragmentation of human life into senseless multiplicity, Adams chose the dynamo as the most apt symbol of our modern, desperate plight: "He began to feel the forty-foot dynamo as a moral force, much as early Christians felt the Cross." [36] However we may judge Adams' suggestion for a dynamic theory of history (most American historians, most Christian theologians, have not judged it favorably), the terms in which it is set forth reveal a disillusionment with meaningful historical sequence which has become increasingly persuasive as the century has gone on, even beyond the limits predicted by Adams for complete extinction.

Overwhelmed with a sense of advancing doom, men's hopes, so far as our literature expresses them, no longer focus today, as they may have once in the past, on imaginary countries like Plato's "ideal" Republic or More's Utopia, where with the resolution of every human conflict time has ended and society

---

[36] *The Education of Henry Adams* (New York: Modern Library, 1931), p. 380. See, also, page 500: "The two-thousand-years failure of Christianity roared upward from Broadway, and no Constantine the Great was in sight."

has been frozen into permanent patterns according to some gigantic dialectical plan. Like Jonathan Swift's two-edged satire in *Gulliver's Travels* on the Utopian universe of Houyhnhnm land as well as on the actual universe of the eighteenth century, the Utopias-in-negative of our present anti-Utopian minded century—for example, Aldous Huxley's *Brave New World* and George Orwell's *1984*—manifest a total abandonment of hope in any organizational plan for society. Our vision has been too horrible, in its pessimism as well as in its immediacy, of what the blueprints of Utopia have looked like when they have actually been translated into facts: "Progress in our world will be progress toward more pain. . . . In our world there will be no emotions except fear, rage, triumph, and self-abasement. . . . If you want a picture of the future," O'Brien tells Winston Smith, the "hero" of *1984*, "imagine a boot stamping on a human face—forever." [37] Winston Smith's successive falsifications of the past have failed, to be sure, to atrophy his own sense of time: " 'Who controls the past,' ran the Party slogan, 'controls the future: who controls the present controls the past.' And yet the past, though of its nature alterable, never had been altered." [38] Our literature is antiteleological not simply in an un-Christian sense, as, for example, is Voltaire's *Candide* or Shelley's *Prometheus Unbound*. Often enough it seems to have lost faith in any rational grounds, however secular, for meaning or purpose in existence. Thomas Hardy and Herman Melville are the novelists of the recent past whose revivals have mattered most for the temper of our age, as if Captain Ahab's quarrel with God were our own, as if like him we too felt "deadly faint . . . as though I were Adam, staggering beneath the piled centuries since Paradise." [39] Our reaction to the discredited rationalistic progressivism of the past two centuries has not carried any notable portion of this century's writers to a new affirmation of the pristine Christian values, as it so carried Dostoevsky and Tolstoy a century or so ago. Our historical relativism has not been able to cure itself: to tell us why things happen, why men act as they do.

[37] George Orwell, *1984* (New York: Harcourt, 1949), pp. 270–1. Cf. George Woodcock, "Utopias in Negative," *Sewanee Review,* 64 (Winter, 1956), 81–97.
[38] *1984,* p. 35.
[39] Herman Melville, *Moby Dick* (New York: Rinehart, 1948), p. 534.

William Faulkner, in accepting the Nobel Prize award for literature in 1950, said at Stockholm that he refused to accept the end of man: "I believe that man will not merely endure: he will prevail. He is immortal, not because he alone among creatures has an inexhaustible voice, but because he has a soul, a spirit capable of compassion and sacrifice, and endurance." [40] Yet as one studies the text of this speech, and more significantly, as one reads its dramatic restatement in the context of *A Fable*, it seems that the kind of immortality which Faulkner has in mind when he links the dark narrative of man's sufferings today to the luminously clear narrative of Christ's Passion is at most a racial, not a personal, immortality. Mankind will prevail, Faulkner seems to be saying, but always and everywhere the individual man goes down defeated forever into the night. In defining his own relation to the time theme in literature, Meyerhoff has admitted: "Nothing is said (nor can be said, I think) about the meaning of eternity beyond the mortality of memory." [41] Today's most characteristic literary insights into our own mortality are likely to be tuned to the Prince's words to Maggie Verver in *The Golden Bowl:* "Everything's terrible, *cara* —in the heart of man." [42]

So traumatic has been the common experience of a loss of meaning in history, personal and collective, that a sense of the nightmare of time has become almost a staple of modern literature. "There's a great devil in the universe, and we call it Time," remarks one of the characters in hopelessness at the end of the second act of one of J. B. Priestley's time plays, *Time and the Conways:* "If things were merely mixed—good and bad— that would be all right, but they get worse. We've seen it tonight. Time's beating us. . . . As if we were all in panic on a sinking ship." [43] Mrs. Ramsay, the central consciousness of Virginia Woolf's *To the Lighthouse,* tries valiantly to find a clue to coherence, to stability: "Something, she meant, is immune from change, and shines out (she glanced at the window with its

[40] William Faulkner's Nobel Prize Award Speech, *Saturday Review*, Feb. 3, 1951, pp. 4–5.
[41] Meyerhoff, *Time in Literature*, p. 55.
[42] Henry James, *The Golden Bowl* (New York: Grove Press, 1952), Part II, p. 357.
[43] J. B. Priestley, "Time and the Conways," in *Three Time Plays* (London: Pan Books, 1949), pp. 152–4.

ripple of reflected lights) in the face of the flowing, the fleeting, the spectral, like a ruby; so that again tonight she had the feeling she had had once today, already, of peace, of rest. Of such moments, she thought, the thing is made that endures." Yet, in the end, Mrs. Ramsay is also defeated. She is no longer alive when the trip to the lighthouse, projected in joy, after many years comes disappointingly to pass: "So it was like that, James thought, the Lighthouse one had seen across the bay all these years; it was a stark tower on a bare rock." At the end when James, Mrs. Ramsay's son, arrives at the lighthouse, it seems to him as if his father, for all the world, were saying, "There is no God." [44] Michael Moloney has already ably demonstrated, in the pages of *Thought* that whereas "Proust's long novel tracing the unrelenting search for the key to the meaning of time ends in apparent triumph," Mrs. Woolf's novels are the record of "a gallant effort" vanquished.[45]

So it is that our symbolic efforts to portray the perceived reality of time more often than not seem to carry us to a frontier of moral futility and of religious doubt: "Thoughts of a dry brain in a dry season." What sense, the modern secularist imagination asks itself, may the human mind make out of its own finite existence? How can modern man compare himself or his existence significantly with other men, with other times? "After such knowledge, what forgiveness? Think now / History has many cunning passages, contrived corridors. . . ." [46] Without some meaningful objective basis of comparison of our finite existence with the existence of other finite beings, the time concept cuts its links with the physical world of nature and of men, retreats to a purely private citadel impregnable to history. A kind of restless angelism ensues. Elliott Coleman significantly entitles his published papers on Proust *The Golden Angel*. There is a tendency to evade the limited, finite human situation as it exists in its recalcitrant complexity, to substitute for the notion of collective solidarity in redemption a purely private and personal salvation beyond the "captivity" of time. As Henri-

---

[44] Virginia Woolf, *To the Lighthouse* (New York: Harcourt, 1927), pp. 158, 301, 308.

[45] Michael F. Moloney, "The Enigma of Time: Proust, Virginia Woolf, and Faulkner," *Thought*, 32 (Spring 1957), 81.

[46] T. S. Eliot, "Gerontion," *The Complete Poems and Plays* (New York: Harcourt, 1952), p. 22.

Charles Puech has ably argued, in his *Eranos Yearbook* discourse, "Gnosis and Time," this sense of revulsion against time, this passionate striving to negate it, as a taint, an anguish, a horrible instrument of servitude which must inspire loathing and revolt, this hostility to history is at the heart of gnosticism: the "transcendent God" is seen as "alien to both the world and its history: he is . . . the alien God." [47]

In sober fact, however, the dialogue of modern poetry proves, if it proves anything, that the human imagination resists this gnostic tendency, that it can never accept as more than a metaphor any view which asserts "all time is always present," "all ages are contemporaneous," which sets out to obliterate under the rubric of "timelessness" the boundaries between the future, the present, and the past. Howsoever sophisticated its own dialectical theory of time may be, the voice of poetry, so long as poetry re-enacts or mimes the action of the modern mind, continues to affirm under the pressures of change an abiding personal identity for the soul of man. Sensing in common experience that there is an area of freedom, it does not feel itself compelled to say that all history, personal, interpersonal, is already somehow badly written in advance. To this extent, at least, there is a survival of the Christian sensibility, a sensibility which every secular literature, indeed, might be said in some manner "tropologically" to announce: the poetic effort to find meaning (if only a hard one) is in itself a refusal of the ultimate horror of meaninglessness. Time's role in our drama, like that of the Chorus Time in *The Winter's Tale*, may be to reveal error, to heal, and to restore; there is the possibility of undoing what has been done if we keep time on our side. "But this, this is out of life, this is out of time," chants the Chorus of *Murder in the Cathedral* at the moment of St. Thomas' martyrdom. If so, the words of Eliot's subtle Fourth Tempter are right when he predicts that "men shall declare that there was no mystery about this man who played a certain part in history." It is only in history, and in time, not out of it, that the poetic fact like the religious one becomes "sensible" in more senses than one: "Only through time is time conquered," as Eliot, later, in "Burnt Norton," would say. The more traditional Christian

[47] Henri-Charles Puech, "Gnosis and Time," tr. Ralph Manheim, *Man and Time*, p. 57.

idiom to use here, however, in speaking of insight into our
most privileged moments of flawless joy, of deep distress, in or
out of Eliot's rose-garden of memory, would be that of time's
"fulfillment" rather than of its "conquest."

As Eliot's language suggests, literature is bilingual; it speaks
the language of St. Augustine's two cities, and it tends to oscil-
late between two time poles, two attitudes about history: (1)
a latent, residually theological view, hinted at in all our sym-
bolisms, that there is an underlying hidden meaning, a kind of
unity and direction, grounded in reality—or, if you will, a kind
of "overplot" of anagogic meanings—behind and beyond the
events that take place in time; (2) a far more strictly secular
view which takes over the theological notion of *saeculum* and
tries to find time or "timeless" equivalents for it exclusively
within the resources of its own creative act. This may be only
a roundabout way of saying that for poetry there are two kinds
of history, sacred and profane. Lacking the *kerygma* of divine
inspiration, poetry tends, furthermore, to blur the two *saecula*,
time and eternity, into one symbol, and to transpose the don-
nées of the two histories into as complex a single myth as its
own immanent power to organize experience will permit.

For this reason, the many-sided effort of our twentieth-century
theologians to rethink, restate traditional Christian theology
within a time-and-history context has not had any clearly definable influence to date on the development of our imaginative
literature. The contemporary answers which Christian theology
has attempted to provide to our unprecedented uncertainties
about the drift of history, our obstinate, self-conscious questions
about "the dark backward and abysm of time," have not much
altered the sensibilities of modern poets, nor entered except,
perhaps, in a kind of underground way into the plotted texture
of their novels, poems, and plays. Paul Tillich has called time
the central category of finitude: "As experienced in immediate
self-awareness, time unites the anxiety of transitoriness with the
courage of a self-affirming present." [48] The major Protestant
problem of theology in this century (in Bultmann, Schweitzer,
Barth, Cullman, and to some extent Tillich) has been the so-
called eschatological one, which manifestly is a concern less

[48] Paul Tillich, *Systematic Theology* (Chicago: University of Chicago Press,
1951), I, 193.

about the present, more about the limits of history and time: Does the Kingdom of God, in the perspective of the New Testament, sovereignly transcend the category of time? Is it essentially independent of history, or does its manifestation in some very real sense begin through our efforts in the limited Now? "We should not say," writes Cullman in his now classical exposition *Christ and Time,* "that with Christ calendar time is abolished, so that past and future no longer have their normal calendar sense. . . . It is not 'a new time' which is created after Christ, but a new division of time." [49] When one reads Cullman on the Incarnation, one suspects that his difference from T. S. Eliot, for example, is not merely a verbal one:

> Here the impossible union
> Of spheres of existence is actual,
> Here the past and future
> Are conquered and reconciled. . . .[50]

So far Eliot. Cullman writes, "It is not correct to say that in Christ '[timeless] eternity invades time,' 'conquers time'." [51] Eliot, articulating finely the affection of the modern sensibility for the privileged moment of isolated ecstasy, the detached, fortuitous moment of intermittent insight, writes, again in *Four Quartets:*

> Here, the intersection of the timeless moment
> Is England and nowhere. Never and always.[52]

Culman states, "The Church is the earthly center from which the full Lordship of Christ becomes visible." [53]

It would not be fair, however, to call Eliot an "eschatological" poet indifferent to time. As far back as his 1931 essay "Thoughts after Lambeth," he committed himself memorably on the enduring temporal presence of Christ through His visible Church on earth, and in one of the 1934 Choruses from *The Rock,* his counsel "not to count the future waves of Time"

---

[49] Oscar Cullman, *Christ and Time: The Primitive Christian Conception of Time and History,* tr. Floyd V. Filson (Philadelphia: Westminster Press, 1950), p. 92.
[50] "Dry Salvages," *Four Quartets,* p. 33.
[51] *Christ and Time, p.* 93.
[52] "Little Gidding," *Four Quartets,* p. 37.
[53] *Christ and Time,* p. 154.

supports Cullman's view that "time is not a thing opposed to God, but is rather the means of which God makes use in order to reveal his gracious working": [54]

> Then came, at a predetermined moment, a moment
>   in time and of time,
> A moment not out of time, but in time, in what we call
>   history. . . .[55]

The pressures of Protestant eschatological theology have not worked, on the whole, to orient the modern sensibility, Eliot's or our own, to any such positive view of historical process. The impending sense of disaster, expressed, for example, in Eliot's 1925 "The Hollow Men,"

> This is the way the world ends
> Not with a bang but a whimper. . . .

has been most characteristically countered in advanced Protestant theology by an apocalyptic hope that only in the catastrophic end-situation of history, discontinuous with time, can the absolutely valid goal of man be reached. Such a theological view accepts it as inevitable that Henry Adams' clock or dynamo should run down, that our "botched civilization," in the words of Ezra Pound, should be "an old bitch gone in the teeth." [56] Having projected its hope of salvation into the future, beyond "time's covenant," this view assumes as an ultimate that only some inward or outward cataclysm can provide the occasion for man to make an honest appraisal of his nothingness through the abolition of history and the elimination of time. In such a context, the most that may be said for the present moment is that it is in some providential sense a delay of grace: "The Time Being is, in a sense, the most trying time of all." But as the dramatic organization of W. H. Auden's Christmas Oratorio, *For the Time Being*, suggests, the time being may be redeemed from insignificance only if its actual vision of an "Otherness that can say I" may be actualized dramatically in the here and now. The words ascribed to Simeon in Auden's poem, "The emancipa-

[54] *Christ and Time*, p. 51.
[55] T. S. Eliot, *Complete Poems and Plays*, p. 107.
[56] "Hugh Selwyn Mauberley," V, text in John J. Espey's *Mauberley* (Berkeley: University of California, 1955), p. 122.

tion of Time from Space had first to be complete," [57] seem self-defeating unless Auden himself is prepared to admit that his own poem has sought from the outset no valid insight into the Christmas mystery, and that it might now best be dismissed, along with the rest of poetry, as an example of the unredeemed imagination's "promiscuous fornication with her own images" (as the Simeon of the poem is prepared with the familiar Platonic gesture so to dismiss it).

It is true enough that the Christian conscience has never been able to find the ultimate reality of the Christian hope either in secular literature, or in the immanent workings of historical processes. In one of the most rewarding of the recent inquiries into the theological implications of history, *Meaning in History,* the Protestant theologian Karl Löwith has already observed: "History as such has no outcome. There never has been and never will be an immanent solution of the problem of history, for man's historical experience is one of steady failure." [58] Such a view is understandable by way of reaction to the modern tendency to substitute literature for revelation, myth for theology, to read our dialectical and symbolical maneuvers as clues to the ultimate, comprehensive sense of history and time. The opposition between the *saeculum* of this world, the profane, the "secular," and the *saeculum* of the Gospel is an old one; the Christian who would try to blur it would do a disservice to theology and poetry.

It seems that one might question Löwith's assertion that the Gospel scheme of redemption through Christ involves of necessity a "redemption . . . from profane history." [59] Dom Gerard Ellsperman, in his admirable study *The Attitude of the Early Christian Latin Writers Toward Pagan Literature,* has pointed out that the reading of pagan literature did not become a problem for the Christian conscience until the fourth century, and that it seemingly would not have become crucial even at that relatively late date, had it not been that the unprovoked and bitterly hostile animosity of Julian the Apostate's totalitarian regime had forced the Christians to accept the defensive and

[57] W. H. Auden, "For the Time Being," *Collected Poetry of W. H. Auden* (New York: Random House, 1945), p. 449.
[58] Karl Löwith, *Meaning in History: The Theological Implications of the Philosophy of History* (Chicago: University of Chicago Press, 1949), p. 191.
[59] *Ibid.*

retreat.[60] The poetic imagination has no other way of expressing itself than to cast about in its historical, time-bound experience in its search for apt symbols; thus it seeks to embody its faith in the invisible as well as to articulate its *theoria* (or vision) of what it has already seen. Since time is a central category of our finitude, it should not surprise us if the weight of the poet's testimony should seem to fall, as it certainly does in modern literature (though it does as well, also, though less desperately, even in Spenser's "Mutability Cantos") on the stresses and distresses of our human experience of impermanence, loss, instability, and change. A fully Christian commitment, it would seem, ought meaningfully to confront this experience as we know it in our literature, in our lives, rather than to transmit it to some eschatological realm beyond human existence, howsoever secularized, or profane, our existence may have become.

Contemporary Catholic theologians, though not always in agreement with one another, have followed the lead, it would seem, of their Protestant colleagues in focusing much attention on the significance of eschatology as a key to the meaning of history and the mysteriousness of time. For example, Jean Daniélou, though he has written eloquently on the Christian's vocation to shape the course of history so as to hasten the Parousia, tends to stress the end of time as a deliverance from our present historical process and plight: ". . . eschatology has become again for us, as it was for the writers of the New Testament, the perspective in which the Christian message is seen and understood." [61] His fellow Jesuit Paul Henry is unwilling to accept so sharp a contrast between time and eternity. Henry argues instead for what has been called the view of the "Incarnationists" ("I range myself among them") who discern a misunderstanding of Christian humanism in the Barth, Daniélou and Pieper perspectives of the temporal and eternal standing over against one

---

[60] Gerard L. Ellsperman, O.S.B., *The Attitude of the Early Christian Latin Writers Toward Pagan Literature and Learning*, Dissertation (Washington, D. C.: Catholic University of America Press, 1949), p. 3: "When Julian, on June 17, 362 A.D., excluded all Christian teachers from pagan schools, . . . the question whether there was a total incompatability between the Christian ideal and pagan studies was thus openly brought to the attention of all. *For the first time,* public opinion was alerted" (emphasis added).

[61] Jean Daniélou, S.J., "The First Thing and the Last," *Month*, New ser. 2 (Nov., 1949), 333. Cf. Father Daniélou's "A Dialogue with Time," tr. Bernard Gilligan, *Cross Currents*, 1 (Winter, 1951), 78–90.

another in isolation. The Incarnationists, holding that the two orders can and ought to interpenetrate, assert their own confidence in reason, in thought, in human action as a prolongation of Christ's action unfolding in time. A third Jesuit, Robert Johann, in an article of great original perception, "Charity and Time," has argued persuasively for the theological virtue of charity as alone "the adequate orientation of temporalized consciousness," since it alone engenders in the now of the soul's "spiritual extension, a sort of simultaneous existence in past, present, and future." [62] Whether or not we decide at this point that today's theologians, Catholic or Protestant, have shed much light on the philosophy of history as distinct from its theology does not from the point of view of modern imaginative literature seem greatly to matter. The secularist orientation of most of this modern literature, on the whole negative in its response to time, would suggest that only obliquely, if at all, has the parallel theological concern with time impinged significantly on the literary consciousness. Such interaction as there has been would seem to have been initiated mostly in reverse.

As some of the examples introduced into this discussion may have already suggested, the notion of history, as we meet it in modern poetry, is in spite of its unparalleled currency, a rather hazy one. Karl Shapiro tells us in his *Essay on Rime:*

> I won a wager once that opening
> A magazine of verse at random, one
> Could put his finger on this word, and used
> Moreover in some sense of mystery
> Which would defy interpretation.[63]

The mystery in part rises from a secularist-minded effort, more or less unconscious with our poets, to find in History hypostatized a lay equivalent for the lost resonances of the theological notion of eternity, or, indeed, of God. With jeering laughter, Bildad,

---

[62] Robert O. Johann, S.J., "Charity and Time," *The Theologian,* 9 (Winter, 1953), 34–5. (*The Theologian* is a review of restricted circulation, published at Woodstock College, Woodstock, Maryland.) For Father Paul Henry's admirable survey of theological opinion, Catholic and non-Catholic, on this subject, see "The Christian Philosophy of History," tr. from French text of the Philip Maurice Deneke Lecture, Oxford, *Theological Studies,* 13 (Sept, 1952), 419–32.

[63] *Essay on Rime,* p. 43, ll. 1201–05.

the secularist tempter of Job, in Archibald MacLeish's current play, *J.B.*, tells J. B. for his "comfort": "God is History. If you offend Him/Will not History dispense with you? History has no time for innocence." [64] The total content of the past is not available to us; there is much that is lost irretrievably; much which survives is yet only potentially discoverable, and, when discovered, is often indecipherable because we lack the essential clues. Since the classics of our literature have long enjoyed a privileged priority as a most meaningful part of the surviving record, it is not surprising that contemporary poets and artists should tend to think that their own achievements in reconstructing on some symbolic basis their personal, transpired past should have a kind of universal significance. On the relatively scanty evidence of the uniquely personal experiences of their own lives, they tend to generalize in a most metaphysical and absolute sense about the universal purposes of history. No mind can cope with all of history's complexities; the modern mind's attempt to universalize often ends too abruptly in a cosmic gesture of despair. Flaubert notwithstanding, it is true that the poet may make a philosophical statement, though if he so chooses, he must make it in some mode of the historically singular event. Our new poetic rhetoric, however, tends to an absolutizing of this history in some exclusively monistic sense. Are we really prepared to say that poetry is more historical than is philosophy? Would it in the long run help poetry, or poetics, if we rewrote Aristotle in some such twentieth-century sense? Has the imagination retreated from its encounter with time as a sacral or religious reality only to engage in mortal combat against the terrors of history's profane time? If so, does not the vitality of our poetry stand most to suffer? Do we not run the risk, which Alexander Pope describes in the third book of the *Dunciad,* of generalizing and absolutizing Dullness in terms of History?

> But where each Science lifts its modern type,
> History her Pot, Divinity her Pipe,
> While proud Philosophy repines to show
> Dishonest sight! his breeches rent below.[65]

[64] Archibald MacLeish, *J.B.* (Boston: Houghton Mifflin, 1956), Scene 9, p. 120. See Bildad's speech on page preceding. "God is far within in History / Why should God have time for you?"

[65] *Dunciad III,* ll. 195–9.

Bernard J. Muller-Thym has reminded us that "there are histories as many and as diverse as there are human knowledges"; even for poetry, there would seem to be much wisdom in recognizing that the skyline of history is often no more than a mirage. Absolutely as knowledge, as human science, "there is no such thing as history," but only a "manifold of singulars," "a process made possible, conditioned, and regulated by the knowledge which is divine providence." [66] Muller-Thym, who is no Hegelian, calls this knowledge the "calculus" of history. "If the Greeks did not have history as Christians do," he notices, "they did possess something which stood in its place. That was tragedy."

With these two notions of Muller-Thym on providence and on tragedy, we come back by a "commodious vicus of recirculation" to the thought of the philosopher-theologian, whose positive Christian orientation toward time and history has been the most congenial of Christian influences on our modern men of letters, oddly enough not our contemporary but, for all the differences of the worlds they moved in, the contemporary of Alexander Pope: the eighteenth-century Neapolitan Giambattista Vico. A. Robert Caponigri, in his magisterial study *Time and Idea: The Theory of History in Giambattista Vico*, has admirably summarized the radical contradiction perceived by Vico in his defiinition of man ("a finite principle of possibility, of knowing and of willing which tends to the infinite": *posse, nosse, velle finitum quod tendit ad infinitum*):

> Of this contradiction providence is the ultimate rectifying force. It is here, therefore, that the principle of progress is to be found. For providence, while guaranteeing the overall movement of history toward ideality, does not cancel the deviations, the contradictions, the retrogressive and paralogical movements of the human spirit in history. . . . Progress is part of that wider conception of providence in which the radical trauma of human history is healed. And the sense of progress is balanced, indeed at times very nearly outweighed, by the sense of the immanent tragic element or potentiality of history.[67]

[66] Bernard J. Muller-Thyn, "Of History as a Calculus Whose Term Is Science," *Modern Schoolman*, 19 (March, 1942; May, 1942), 42, col. 2; 76, col. 1. In *The Theologian*, 11 (Spring, 1956), 11–22, H. R. Burns, S.J., develops suggestively, from a theologian's point of view, these philosophical points of Muller-Thym. See "The Paradox of History": ". . . we are equivalently saying that history finally depends on principles which are a-historical" (18).

[67] A. Robert Caponigri, *Time and Idea: The Theory of History in Giambattista Vico* (Chicago: Regnery, 1953), p. 123.

Vico's approach to the problem of time, establishing as it does a tension between the retrogressive forces of man and the rectifying force of the ideal, has nothing in common with discredited Deistic theories about the linear movement of history, nor with other purely humanistic constructs of history, positive or negative, of exclusively secularistic-minded man. Far from renouncing the past, Vico argues for its constant recall, not as an object of scientific knowledge but as a felt ground of present insight and choice which poetry is best suited to illuminate, to reveal. Neither is the primacy of the poetic moment established, as in Eliot's *Four Quartets* or in Proust's *Recherche*, by affective reactions of the sensibility: as, for example, Eliot's "hint half guessed," "gift half understood," or the multiple sense impressions of Proust's Marcel when he hears again a part of Venteuil's sonata, or tastes again of the *madelein*.[68] Vico's "recall" is to be understood as an awareness (*Coscienza*) of the reflective consciousness which recognizes its own responsibilities at the level of creative freedom to interpret the past with intelligence, and to give footroom, in its symbolic reflections about the transhistorical future, for the choices and decisions which contingent events, unique and equivocal, will call for, and which human history will never fail to provide.[69] In this respect, so substantial and central, Vico's *corsoricorso* movement of history is not even on the same plane with the repetitive cyclic "returns" of the archaic cultures, fatalistic gestures of the spirit which sought to eliminate profane existence, or, at least, to annul the seeming meaninglessness of "becoming," which is inseparable from our common sense experience of time. Mircea Eliade in our own day has wonderfully drawn our attention to the spiritual positions manifested by the men of archaic societies in their intolerance of history, the need they felt to abolish or at least regenerate themselves from time. It is not to Eliade's purpose in his germinal study *The Myth of the Eternal Return* to consider Vico's *New Science*, nor to point out the radical differences between Vico's historical principle of *ricorso* and the primitive versions of cyclic recurrence.[70] It is not here to our purpose to detail these dif-

[68] See for example, for Proust, *Remembrance of Things Past*, I, "Swann's Way," p. 160; or, again, *Remembrance*, II, "The Past Recaptured," p. 992.
[69] *The New Science of Giambattista Vico*, tr. Thomas Goddard Bergin and Max Harold Fisch (Ithaca: Cornell University Press, 1948), p. 91.
[70] Mircea Eliade, *The Myth of the Eternal Return*, tr. Willard R. Trask. Bollingen Series 46 (New York: Pantheon, 1954).

ferences, either, beyond recalling that Vico wrote his *New Science* precisely to demonstrate that even for the Gentiles, who lacked the special dispensation of the Chosen People, there was yet a special providence which in spite of the catastrophes of history led men to a now widening, now narrowing awareness of the presence of God, and which forbade the human spirit to assume a posture of alienation from time. Eliade, as a matter of fact, without mentioning Vico, very well describes Vico's position on the last page of *The Myth of the Eternal Return:* "Since the 'invention' of faith, in the Judaeo-Christian sense of the word . . . the man who has left the horizons of archetypes and repetition can no longer defend himself against that terror [of history] except through the idea of God." [71]

With the possible exception of Proust's *À La Recherche du Temps Perdu* ("Remembrance of Things Past" and "The Past Recaptured"), the most extraordinary and concentrated symbolic effort of our century to discover some principle of unity, some single synoptic view, at least imaginatively, in the fluctuating flow of time, and to express it in language, in James Joyce's *Finnegans Wake.* The quasi-circular, or cyclical, concept of time which pervades this remarkable, many-leveled work, written in the perspectives of Vico's *corso-ricorso* theory of history, a kind of ascending spiral, is well known and has often been pointed out. What is less well known and, consequently, less noted is the distinctively Christian slant of Joyce's fictional glass through which, in spite of himself, it would seem, he views the "wrunes" which time past—its theologies, its mythologies, and its poetry— has left for the poet to decipher, to interpret. Here the Catholic bias or basis of Joyce's work is inescapable; it is this which more than anything else gives to the *Wake* a tone of comic serenity almost totally absent from the deterministic and pessimistic generalizations about history of such works as Spengler's *Decline of the West* and Toynbee's more recent monumental, cinemascopic

[71] *Ibid.,* pp. 161–2. See *The New Science,* p. 99: "Divine providence has so conducted human affairs that, starting from the poetic theology which regulated them by certain sensible signs believed to be divine counsels sent to men by the gods, and by means of the natural theology which demonstrates providence by eternal reasons which do not fall under the senses, the nations were disposed to receive revealed theology in virtue of a supernatural faith, superior not only to the senses but to human reason itself" (Nicolini par. 366).

Study of History. One senses in the *Wake* a gravitational pull toward a Catholic theological center which is humorlessly absent in Toynbee's syncretic and ludicrous litany: "*Sancta Dei Genetrix, intercede pro nobis*. Mother Mary, Mother Isis, Mother Cybele, Mother Ishtar, Mother Kwanyin, have compassion on us . . .," or "*Sancte Petre, intercede pro nobis*. Tender-hearted Muhammad. . . ." [72]

Finnegans Wake is remarkable for a number of reasons. It is not now to our point to note the complex theory of language which the work undertakes to develop and illustrate.[73] It is to the point, however, to note well at the outset that this work is in no explicit sense a defense of a Christian theory of time or of history; on the contrary, it asks us to accept its "monomyth" of history, undatable in its symbolically articulated atemporality, as a purely secular construct, part of the effort of the "post-Christian," or even "post-modern" age so-called (though one might be forgiven here for wondering what content such current terms are supposed to have) to find a lay substitute for Vico's ideal-eternal Christian structure of time. What is remarkable, first of all, is that a sense of hope survives at all with Joyce in spite of the catastrophes of history, global and personal, which he experienced so sharply right up to the end (though he attempted to stop his clock in 1904), and which his work sets out as comprehensively as possible to record. Secondly, in spite of the bitterness ("Agenbite of Inwit") of Joyce's personal apostasy and the absence in his work of any personal avowal of faith, the *Wake* is remarkable for the plus value which it gives to time, a kind of involuntary witness to the Christian dogma that a moment in time is God's creation as well as is a moment of "timelessness." Without the "innocence" or "luck" of Dante, but with great good humor, it dramatizes a theological sense of the past as being that alone which can give meaning to the future, a center to history, and a tolerance to time.

In the "millwheeling vicociclometer" of Everyman's (Earwicker's) dream, Adam's story ("Der Fall Adams") is subsumed by the story of Finnegan, the supernatural giant who lived before

[72] Arnold J. Toynbee, *A Study of History*, Part XIII, Vol. 10 (London: Oxford University Press, 1954), 143.
[73] I have attempted to account for the *Wake's* theory of language in my *Joyce and Aquinas*, ch. 8, "The Root Language of Shem," 144–60, Yale Studies in English 133 (New Haven: Yale University Press, 1957).

the dawn of recorded human history: "Bygmester Finnegan . . . lived in the broadest way immarginable . . . before joshuan judges had given us numbers or Helviticus committed deuteronomy." Finnegan is the "agent," who on a "thundersday" brought about "this municipal sin business." [74] But even at his own wake, the Bygmester wants to rise. His natural descendants are content enough to mourn his passing, but some Irish spirits (*Usqueadbaugham:* "water of life," in Gaelic) splash on him, and with this *baptism*, the supernatural man in Finn again asserts himself, and much to the distress and confusion of those who mourn, or pretend to, his death: "Now be aisy, good Mr Finnimore, sir. And take your laysure like a god on pension and don't be walking abroad. Sure you'd only lose yourself in Healiopolis now the way the roads in. . . ." [75] The rest of the story is to be dominated by the fleeting presence of the resurrected giant, who *seems* to be sleeping by Howth's Head. But is he? "We'll wake and see." [76]

For the God of the creation, there is no past or future. Everything occurs for Him in an ever present Now. The story of all men, of all Finn's descendants, is resumed by Joyce, the artist of creation, without regard to differences of time or space, in the character of Everyman, whom sometimes he calls Humphrey Chimpden Earwicker, sometimes *Here Comes Everybody,* or *Haveth Childers Everywhere,* sometimes just H. C. E., or even H_2CE_3 (a "telesmell" stink, "big brewer's belch"). [77] Between (Everyman) Earwicker's sense of shame and sorrow, and the primeval fall of (Adam) Finnegan from his ladder, there exists a mysterious, all-important link, the time-shrouded connection between archaic and historical man. Rumor goes about that Earwicker, who has a guilty stutter, committed a crime of exhibitionistic sexuality in the precincts of Dublin's Phoenix Park (an "Edenborough" of "sombrer opacities" and "sphoenix spark"), [78] but the crime remains nameless; though Earwicker owns up to it, the impression grows that, guilty as he is of other crimes and criminalities, the (original) sin in the Park is one in which he took no personal, voluntary part. This impression

[74] *Finnegans Wake,* pp. 614, 70, 4, 5.
[75] *Ibid.,* p. 24.
[76] *Ibid.,* p. 375.
[77] *Ibid.,* p. 95.
[78] *Ibid.,* pp. 29, 473.

of an imputability which is both atemporal and impersonal survives the Cad's accusing allegations, who after the sin tries to
disconcert Earwicker by asking him for the time ("By the watch,
what is the time, pace?").[79] "The point of eschatology" is stated
forthrightly by Matty Armagh, only after St. Patrick's arrival in
Ireland: "He is cured by faith who is sick of fate." [80]

Besides creating man, God created nature, and God taught
Adam how to give to the things of nature their proper sounding
names. Anna Livia Plurabelle is one of Joyce's names for nature:
"as happy as the day is wet, babbling, bubbling, chattering to
herself . . . giddygaddy, grannyma, gossipaceous Anna Livia." [81]
Just as the river Liffey flows cleansingly through Dublin, so does
Anna Livia flow with cleansing waters through the guilt-laden
change and permanence (between the elmtree and the stone) of
Earwicker's ever dissolving, ever renewed dream of dreams.
"O'Cronione lags acrumbling in his sands but his sunsunsuns
still tumble on.[82]

At another level, Anna Livia Plurabelle (the Universal
Woman) is a name for Maggie, Earwicker's wife, grown old and
undesirable. When the "heroticisms, catastrophes and eccentric-
ities transmitted by the ancient legacy of the past" have passed
by in the dream, and the dream is dissolving, H. C. E. turns
back, quite simply, to Anna.[80] And Anna accepts him though
she knows that their old love is dead. "Forbeer, forbear! For
nought that is has bane. In mourenslaund. Themes have thimes
and habit reburns." [84]

At a third level, Anna Livia is Everyman's soul, or *anima*. It
is through her that *Here Comes Everbody* learns the hard, hard
lesson of submission, and it is in her act of faith, made in the
throes of doubt as she lies dying, that Everyman goes back to the
Father, as the dream dissolves with Finn coming back ("Finn,
again!") : "If I seen him bearing down on me now under white-
spread wings like he'd come from Arkangels, I sink I'd die down
over his feet, humbly dumbly, only to washup." [85]

[79] *Ibid.*, p. 154.
[80] *Ibid.*, p. 482.
[81] *Ibid.*, p. 195.
[82] *Ibid.*, p. 415.
[83] *Ibid.*, p. 614–15.
[84] *Ibid.*
[85] *Ibid.*, p. 628.

In between Finn's death and resurrection, the dream of Earwicker re-enacts symbolically all the antagonisms of history. As a result of Finnegan's fall, Everyman Earwicker leads a divided life. He cannot bring unity into the world of his dreaming; he cannot even unify himself. He identifies himself now with one son, Kevin, now with the other, Jerry, in their ceaseless brother battle ("What a zeit for the goths!").[86] Kevin and Jerry have names and faces that shift and merge, but the brother battle knows no arresting, just as the division in Earwicker's character remains a constant right up to the end: Shem the Penman (Shem Macadamson), or Shaun the Postman? Shun the Punman (the literary artist), or "dear dogmestic Shaun"? [87]

At the end, as Everyman's sin-soiled soul goes on to lose itself in the ocean of the Father, its ultimate "at-one-ment" is "humbly dumbly" symbolized in an act of washing up (worship). For Earwicker, the dreamer, the *corso-ricorso* has come full circle. In his case, the movement of the human spirit between time and idea has been acted out. But Earwicker stands for Everyman ("Here Comes Everybody"), and in the case of Everyman, the drama of history still goes on. The unfinished sentence on the last page finds its completion on the first page at the beginning of the book. Thus it is that "the Vico road" of *Finnegans Wake* "goes round and round to meet where terms begin." [88]

As the tone of some of the quoted phrases incorporated into the above greatly simplified synopsis of the *Wake* suggests, many clusters of non-Christian mythic attitudes orbit around its Christian core in such a way as greatly to distort Vico's creative Christian structure of time. In spite of the *Wake's* insistent refrain, "O foenix culprit," the redemptive role of Christ at the center of history is by-passed almost altogether, and where it is incidentally enacted at all, it is mostly by way of ironic allegory or parody. Neither Our Lord nor Our Lady is present in the traditionally positive and active senses for which the central dogmas of the Incarnation and the Redemption provide the clues for a Christian historical stance. This Joycean substitution of myth for theology, this confusion of poetry with revelation is by no means a unique phenomenon. It is, perhaps, the most per-

---

[86] *Ibid.*, pp. 415, 551.
[87] *Ibid.*, p. 411.
[88] *Ibid.*, p. 452.

vasive heresy of modern literature. "Time surely would scatter all," Stephen Dedalus reflects in *Ulysses:* "History is a nightmare from which I am trying to awake." [89] *Finnegans Wake,* as the title hints, is in a sense an awakening, but the fatalistic trauma of Joyce's nightmare has not been healed. Hope to be hope must have a rational foundation. The rational grounds for hope must seem dim to us as we view with Joyce the shambles in the city of man, the city of Tim Healy's Dublin. Until there is a recovery or a discovery of theological faith, there seem to be slight rational grounds for hoping that in our modern poetry another sun-city of the Phoenix, "Heliotropolis, the castellated, the enchanting," will rise out of the ashes of these "wrunes" of time.[90]

[89] *Ulysses,* p. 35.
[90] *Finnegans Wake,* pp. 594, 19–20.

D. S. BLAND

ENDANGERING THE READER'S NECK
BACKGROUND DESCRIPTION IN THE NOVEL

> We want, I think, very much a Discourse on De-
> scription, carried through all the Species of Writing.
> To show us from what Objects, and how, to draw
> the finest Circumstances
> —Thomas Purney, Preface to *Pastorals* (1717)

In spite of the establishment of the novel in a dominant position by the middle of the nineteenth century, it is only in the last fifty years that there has been any really profitable discussion of its nature and processes. Even so, one aspect of the novelist's art, the role and technique of background description, has been somewhat neglected. Book after book can be read, broadcast after broadcast can be listened to, without the subjects ever coming up. The moral purpose of the novelist, the nature of the hero, the

Reprinted from Criticism, *III (1961) by permission of The Wayne State University Press, Copyright, 1961, Wayne State University Press.*

novel as epic or symbol or what you will, these topics are discussed with unfailing regularity. But the critic who does more than make a conventional nod in the direction of Egdon Heath or the environs of Wuthering Heights is hardly ever to be encountered.

One reason for this neglect is that description—of a sort—is so easy to do, and so frequently done for its own sake, without relevance to the totality of the novel, that the critic avoids so obvious a field for adverse comment. Relevance, in fact, is the key, as Elizabeth Bowen has pointed out in her "Notes on Writing a Novel": "Scene is only justified in the novel where it can be shown, or at least felt, to act upon action or character. In fact, where it has dramatic use." [1] It is this use of relevant, dramatic description that I propose to examine, though within the limits of this article I can do no more than sketch out the sort of approach I consider desirable. [2] It is easy and tempting to regard descriptive passages in a novel as having little or no relation to problems of plot and character, particularly if these passages strike us as being no more than examples of "fine" writing. But we are learning to pay the same attention to "the words on the page" in a novel as in poetry and drama, and I believe that this attention, directed towards passages of background description, will show that not all of them are as irrelevant as we are sometimes led to believe.

At the same time, we have to recognize that, in its early days at least, the novel owed a great deal to the practice of the landscape painters in the matter of natural description. This relationship between the two arts has introduced a complication into our response to description in the novel which may lie behind the quite sharp division between those who enjoy description and those who find it irrelevant. The history of landscape painting shows that it succeeds in establishing itself as a fully independent genre, unrelated, in the hands of a Constable or a Cézanne, to story-telling or moral issues. When we encounter its equivalent in a novel, then, we tend, according to our temperament, either to welcome it for its own sake, finding in it those

[1] Elizabeth Bowen, *Collected Impressions* (London, 1950), p. 254.
[2] These limits compel me to confine my attention to English examples. Any extended survey would have to take account, for example, of the carpentry of Balzac's theatre-workshop, the panoramic range of Tolstoy, the *genius loci* of Henry James, and the subjective intensity of Proust.

emotional satisfactions we find in painting, or to dismiss it because (such is our experience of landscape painting) it seems to have little or nothing to do with the things that the novel ought to be doing.

Because of this complication, therefore, I shall confine my examination entirely to landscape description. But before turning to the influence of landscaping painting on the novel I must draw attention to one recent book, Mr. Robert Liddell's *Treatise on the Novel*, which does indeed broach the subject of description, but only to dismiss it as a side issue.

> The aesthetics of descriptive writing have not yet received sufficient attention—it is commonly held in too great esteem, particularly when it occurs in works of fiction. Painting or music that has a strong literary element is now severely criticised. It is time for an attack to be made upon the pictorial element in literature. Mr. Richards, in *Practical Criticism*, has done much to teach us not to look for "pictures" in Poetry—nevertheless, the Novel is still in need of a purge.[3]

Mr. Liddell makes a relevant point when he says that descriptive writing is generally too much esteemed by the reader. It is this esteem which once exalted Mary Webb and which can still miss the true nature of Conrad's achievement. Nevertheless, background description is there in the novel, and has been from the very beginning of its development, and must be taken into account in any comprehensive account of its nature and achievements. I do not wish to suggest that there is anything to be gained by rhapsodising over the "beauties" of a description, particularly when the passage can be detached from the novel without doing much damage to its fabric. But equally, I think, Mr. Liddell is wrong to go so far to the other extreme and ask for nothing more than the sign-posting we get in Elizabethan stage-directions: "a street in London," "another part of the forest"— a map-reference sufficient to enable us to orientate ourselves, but no more. He argues as follows: "Too many stage-directions are boring and confusing if we read a play; if we see them carried out on the stage, the result is a fussy and undignified ritualism. They are worst of all in a novel."[4]

This view can be countered immediately. In his recent study, *The Rise of the Novel*, Professor Ian Watt has shown that one

---

[3] Robert Liddell, *A Treatise on the Novel* (London, 1947), p. 110.
[4] Liddell, p. 112.

of the distinguishing characteristics of the novel is that it gives its personages "a local habitation and a name." Robinson Crusoe, Pamela Andrews, Tom Jones, these normal forms are distinct from the single names of older heroes and heroines, Macbeth, Portia, and from the type-names of allegory, such as Mr. Badman. The novelist's characters are contemporary figures, moving in a solid world of everyday life. In the more timeless worlds of tragic or comic drama it does not matter that the characters are not so localised. Very often, in fact, they cannot be. In *A Midsummer-Night's Dream* we are told that the wood is near Athens, but it turns out to be peopled with very English artisans and fairies. But even if there were not this point to be made about the localisation of characters in a novel, Mr. Liddell could still be criticised for equating too rigidly the stage-direction and the novel's descriptive passages. Properly used, the latter are rather to be equated with the dramatically presented descriptions that we get from the *characters* in a drama. While many of these arise from the nature of the Elizabethan stage and are merely utilitarian, others of them have a deeper significance. Thus, when Duncan and Banquo describe Macbeth's castle, they are certainly letting us know where we are supposed to be; but phrases like "a pleasant seat" and "the air is delicate" have a dramatic irony that lifts the description beyond utility.

As I have indicated, the approach I propose to make towards an examination of the place of description in the novel involves some consideration of landscape painting as an independent genre. The situation is similar to that obtaining in the realm of descriptive poetry. That is, the work of the painter comes first and educates the eyes of the writer.[5]

Professor Watt's point about the localisation of the setting in the pioneer English novels is perfectly valid; but description is put to other uses than this, and it is with the development of these uses that I am concerned. Localisation is a practical matter of placing the characters in an environment within which they can act out their stories. It is equivalent of both the dramatically presented description and the stage scenery of the drama. Thus the interest attaching to Crusoe's island is that of seeing what he

[5] See, for example, Jean H. Hagstrum, *The Sister Arts: The Tradition of Literary Pictorialism and English Poetry from Dryden to Gray* (Princeton, 1958).

can make of it. It is far from being a romantic Treasure Island or Blue Lagoon. In Pamela's case we must be made aware that Mr. B's house has closets to which she can retire to write her letters or avoid a rape. And in *Joseph Andrews* and *Tom Jones* a distinction must be made between a good inn and a bad one, between Allworthy's orderly house and Squire Western's free-and-easy one. The nearest we come in Fielding's work to a piece of natural description for its own sake is a short passage in *Joseph Andrews*.

> Adams continued his subject till they came to one of the beautifullest spots of ground in the universe. It was a kind of natural amphitheatre, formed by the winding of a small rivulet, which was planted with thick woods, and the trees rose gradually above each other by the natural ascent of the ground they stood on; which ascent as they hid with their boughs, they seemed to have been disposed by the design of the most skilful planter. The soil was spread with a verdure which no paint could imitate; and the whole place might have raised romantic ideas in elder minds than those of Joseph and Fanny, without the assistance of love (Bk. III, Chap. V).

But even this, as we shall see, is not "pure" description, though it will appear to be alongside the picture we are given in *Tom Jones* of Allworthy's house and estate, which is much more in line with eighteenth-century taste in landscape description:

> It stood on the south-east side of a hill, but nearer the bottom than the top of it, so as to be sheltered from the north-east by a grove of old oaks which rose above it in a gradual ascent of near half a mile, and yet high enough to enjoy a most charming prospect of the vale beneath.
>
> In the midst of the grove was a fine lawn, sloping down towards the house, near the summit of which rose a plentiful spring, gushing out of a rock covered with firs, and forming a constant cascade of about thirty feet, not carried down a regular flight of steps, but tumbling in a natural fall over the broken and mossy stones until it came to the bottom of the rock, then running off in a pebbly channel, that with many lesser falls winded along, till it fell into a lake at the foot of the hill, about a quarter of a mile below the house on the south side, and which was seen from every room in the front. Out of this lake, which filled the center of a beautiful plain, embellished with groups of beeches and elms, and fed with sheep, issued a river, that for several miles was seen to meander through an amazing variety of meadows and woods till it emptied itself into the sea, with a large arm of which, and an island beyond it, the prospect was closed.

On the right of this valley opened another of less extent, adorned with several villages, and terminated by one of the towers of an old ruined abby, grown over with ivy, and part of the front, which remained still entire.

The left-hand side presented the view of a very fine park, composed of very unequal ground, and agreeably varied with all the diversity that hills, lawns, wood, and water, laid out with admirable taste, but owing less to art than to nature, could give. Beyond this, the country gradually rose into a ridge of wild mountains, the tops of which were above the clouds (Bk. I, Chap. IV).

The significance of the chapter-heading here should not be overlooked: "The reader's neck brought into danger by a description." Here Fielding is apparently warning us to expect something unusual, but what in fact he offers us is something to which no good Augustan would take exception. Allworthy's estate displays the expected taste of an eighteenth-century landowner who has accepted the changes in landscape gardening brought about by the influence of painters such as Poussin and Claude. What Fielding gives us is not a piece of natural description for its own sake (this *would* have brought the reader's neck into danger in the middle of the century) but the panorama of a situation in which nature is so manipulated as to form a setting for man.[6] We are here at a transitional stage between the complete formality of the continental garden of the seventeenth century, and the appreciation of *natural* nature that is to be a characteristic of the Romantic movement. It is on the principles of this transitional stage that Pope laid out his five-acre plot at Twickenham, and the river that meanders through Allworthy's estate is at one with Hogarth's "line of beauty," the serpentine line that has given its name to the ornamental water in Hyde Park. How transitional the situation was can be seen by comparing the close of the passage from *Tom Jones* with the paragraph from *Joseph Andrews*. In the latter the trees are approved of because "they seemed to have been disposed by the design of the

[6] Mr. Christopher Hussey has suggested that "the man-made humanised landscape" of the eighteenth century is "England's greatest contribution to the visual arts of the world." See his introduction to Margaret Jourdain, *The Work of William Kent* (London, 1948), p. 15. His introduction to the companion volume, Dorothy Stroud, *Capability Brown* (London, 1950, rev. 1957), should also be consulted. The two together form an excellent analysis of the aesthetics of landscape gardening.

most skilful planter," whereas in *Tom Jones* the left-hand scene pleases because it owes *less* to art than to nature.

Fielding's object in going into such detail should now be obvious. By this means he both places Allworthy on the social map and displays his character, that of a quiet-living man of taste, in contrast to Squire Western, of whose estate we get no such picture. In *Joseph Andrews* the description is used for another purpose. The charm of the natural amphitheatre chimes in with and underlines the romantic mood of the lovers, and this, the use of "mood" landscape, is the next stage in the development of description in the novel. In each case, however, the reader is being invited to participate by being reminded of visual experiences with which Fielding supposes him to be familiar, experiences derived from his acquaintance with neo-classical landscape painting and the garden-design based on it.

Both Poussin and Claude had painted "mood" landscapes; in Claude's case, a mood of calm contemplation of an idealised Nature. In the hands of Salvator Rosa the mood becomes wildly picturesque, inducing feelings of awe and terror. From looking at pictures of this sort it is only a step to seeking for passages in literature in which the thrill can be experienced. This demand was met by the writers of the novel of terror, and the extent to which they relied on what had been done by the landscape painters is indicated by the following passage from *The Mysteries of Udolpho* in which Mrs. Radcliffe gives the game away completely:

> The scene of barrenness was here and there interrupted by the spreading branches of the larch and cedar, which threw their gloom over the cliff, or athwart the torrent that rolled in the vale. No living creature appeared—except the lizard scrambling among the rocks, and often hanging upon points so dangerous that fancy shrunk from the view of them. This was such a scene as Salvator would have chosen, had he then existed, for his canvass. St. Aubert, impressed by the romantic character of the place, almost expected to see banditti start from behind some projecting rock, and he kept his hand upon the arms with which he always travelled (Chap. III).

There is no question that Salvator Rosa would have painted such a scene. He *had* painted it, not once but many times, and without his example Mrs. Radcliffe might have written very differently. Here we have something that is characteristic of the very essence of *Udolpho*. Even Mr. Liddell would hardly claim that the novel would still be what it is if such passages were reduced to mere stage-directions.

Another characteristic passage is to be found in the prototype of the novel of terror, *The Castle of Otranto:*

> Theodore at length determined to repair to the forest that Matilda had pointed out to him. Arriving there, he sought the gloomiest shades, as best suited to the pleasing melancholy that reigned in his mind. In this mood he roved insensibly to the caves which had formerly served as a retreat to hermits, and were now reported round the country to be haunted by evil spirits.

In *Joseph Andrews* "one of the beautifullest spots of ground in the universe" happens to accord with the mood of Fanny and Joseph. But Horace Walpole's Theodore actually seeks a setting for his melancholy, and this deliberate association of mood and situation with setting remains a staple feature of fictional description thereafter. This is particularly the case in the nineteenth century. In Disraeli's *Henrietta Temple* (close of Book III) and in Wilkie Collins' *The Woman in White* (first narrative, section XV), for example, the settings are in perfect accord with the emotional crises of the story. In better novels this manipulation rises to the level of symbol, as in the use made of the chestnut tree in *Jane Eyre*. Under it, on a balmy evening, Jane and Rochester become engaged. During the night that follows, it is blasted in a storm. At an earlier period in our literature this would have been an omen merely. Here it is both omen and symbol. The hitherto solid growth is split into two halves. Nor did this use of the device die out with the passing of the Victorian novel. It has been used quite recently by L. P. Hartley in the symbolic deadly nightshade plant in *The Go-Between*.

In Walpole and Mrs. Radcliffe the situation is, of course, deliberately rigged, and it was therefore easy for Jane Austen to poke fun at the practice in *Northanger Abbey*, particularly as her own tendency in landscape description (as in other aspects of her work) is to look back to a central eighteenth-century position. Now Jane Austen is a writer whom Mr. Liddell especially admires for her restraint in landscape description, so it is worth while pausing to examine her practice in some detail.

We may take as typical of her normal practice the following passage from *Emma:*

> Their road to this detached cottage was down Vicarage Lane, a lane leading at right angles from the broad though irregular main street of the place; and, as may be inferred, containing the blessed abode of Mr. Elton. A few inferior dwellings were first to be passed, and then, about a quarter of a mile down the lane, rose the vicarage; an old and not very good house, almost as close to the road as it could be (Vol. I, Chap. X).[7]

Here every word is utilitarian, with the exception of the ironically used "blessed," and the passage adequately meets Mr. Liddell's call for description that is no more than a map-reference.

But Jane Austen does not always work at this level of utility. Some of her descriptions can be very subtle indeed, and careful reading is required to pierce the surface of restraint. Of this subtlety the following passage will serve as an example:

> It was hot; and after walking some time over the gardens in a scattered, dispersed way, scarcely any three together, they insensibly followed one another to the delicious shade of a broad short avenue of limes, which stretching beyond the garden at an equal distance from the river, seemed the finish of the pleasure grounds. It led to nothing; nothing but a view at the end over a low stone wall with high pillars, which seemed intended, in their erection, to give the appearance of an approach to the house, which had never been there. Disputable, however, as might be the taste of such a termination, it was in itself a charming walk, and the view which closed it extremely pretty. The considerable slope, at nearly the foot of which the Abbey stood, gradually acquired a steeper form beyond its grounds; and at half a mile distant was a bank of considerable abruptness and grandeur, well clothed with wood; and at the bottom of this bank, favourably placed and sheltered, rose the Abbey-Mill Farm, with meadows in front, and the river making a close and handsome curve around it.
>
> It was a sweet view—sweet to the eye and the mind. English verdure, English culture, English comfort, seen under a sun bright, without being oppressive (*Emma*, Vol. III, Chap. VI).

The close of this passage certainly puts the manipulation of Walpole and Mrs. Radcliffe in its place. But though the whole

---

[7] My quotations are taken from the standard Oxford edition, edited by R. W. Chapman.

scene has much in common with Fielding (Mr. Allworthy would have felt quite at home here), there is something more to it.[8] The description is divided equally between the Abbey grounds and the Abbey-Mill Farm. Now the latter, of course, is where Robert Martin lives, the farmer whose interest in Harriet Smith has been thwarted by Emma. This description, said Mr. Wilson, helps to "point up" Emma's mistaken and snobbish view of him. In her eyes he is only a common farmer, unfit to be the husband of a Woodhouse protégée. But through the eyes of Jane Austen herself we are able, in this description, to see Martin at his proper level, the respectable level of the successful yeoman farmer, a rank which Jane Austen herself by no means despised. It is the view of the farm which is sweet and English, and the air of restraint in the closing sentence, though owing something to an eighteenth-century dislike of "enthusiasm," is also appropriate for placing Martin in the social order. Were he a degree lower, he would be indifferent to appearances. A degree higher, and he too would have gone in for "improvements," and would then have run the risk of producing the effect of pretentiousness which *is* criticised in the description of the Abbey estate of Mr. Knightley. This use of the description is of greater importance than the impression which a first or superficial reading of the last sentence will arouse—the impression of a prim withdrawal from the temptations of natural description.

This is not to deny that Jane Austen *is* chary of description. Her attitude in this matter is bound up with her criticism of the "improvements" of the Abbey estate, a criticism which has parallels elsewhere in her work. Thus, the panorama of Bath is humorously dismissed in *Northanger Abbey* for its failure to conform to the picturesque standards of landscape beauty; an element of Marianne's "sensibility" is a belief in those standards; and in *Mansfield Park* considerable areas of the dialogue are given over to discussing improvements. There is no doubt where Jane Austen stands in this matter. It is on the side of restraint; understandably so, when a lack of restraint which had its origin in the same fashionable taste for the picturesque could lead to the over-emphasis of Mrs. Radcliffe's descriptive passages.

[8] In what follows here I am indebted to some points made by Mr. Edmund Wilson in a talk on the B.B.C. a few years ago.

It is sometimes claimed that Jane Austen let herself go beyond her normal limits in her treatment of Fanny Price's Portsmouth environment in *Mansfield Park*. Here, indeed, she goes into far more detail than she usually permits herself. But it is not detail in isolation. Cramped living rooms, deficiency of manners, lack of privacy and paucity of books, all the details are intermingled in a picture which is meant to provide a counterbalance to Mansfield Park. Only once in this part of the novel does Jane Austen seem to depart from this strict obedience to the needs of relevance:

> The day was uncommonly lovely. It was really March, but it was April in its mild air, brisk soft wind, and bright sun, occasionally clouded for a minute; and everything looked so beautiful under the influence of such a sky, the effect of the shadows pursuing each other, on the ships at Spithead and the island beyond, with the ever-varying hues of the sea now at high water, dancing in its glee and dashing against the ramparts with so fine a sound, produced altogether such a combination of charms for Fanny, as made her gradually almost careless of the circumstances under which she felt them (Vol. III, Chap. XI).

At first it seems that Jane Austen has for once looked at a scene with a painter's eye rather than a novelist's. Even here, however, we are carefully brought back to situation. When our first surprise is over, the passage begins to look something like the Radcliffian concordance of place and mood. What more can Fanny want than a fine day, her family in their Sunday best, and her arm in Henry Crawford's? But the circumstances of which she is almost careless are not of a piece with this idyllic situation:

> Nay, had she been without his arm, she would have soon known that she needed it, for she wanted strength for a two hour's saunter of this kind, coming as it generally did upon a week's previous inactivty. Fanny was beginning to feel the effect of being debarred from her usual, regular exercise; she had lost ground as to health since her being in Portsmouth, and but for Mr. Crawford and the beauty of the weather, would soon have been knocked up now.

Above all, Crawford is not Edmund, even though he is improving upon acquaintance. And so it finally appears that description here is not being used to enhance situation, as in Mrs. Radcliffe, but to act as a foil to it, and to that end some expansiveness of detail is necessary.

What Jane Austen withdraws from, then, is the artificiality of the *Udolpho* use of description. She does not withdraw from description which is organic, description which reveals character, mood and situation. Sir Walter Scott had no such scruples. Like Mrs. Radcliffe (from whom he probably learned) he will use a dramatic setting if it suits his purpose, and he is as aware as she is of the influence on vision of the work of the picturesque painters:

> If India be the land of magic . . . this is the country of romance. The scenery is such as nature brings together in her sublimest moods; sounding cataracts—hills which rear their scathed heads to the sky— lakes that, winding up the shadowy valleys, lead at every turn to yet more romantic recesses—rocks which catch the clouds of heaven. All the wildness of Salvator here, and there the fairy scenes of Claude (*Guy Mannering*, Chap. XVII).

But in his best work he goes further than Mrs. Radcliffe in that he does not invent such settings, or take them at second-hand from painitngs. He uses what is actually present. This comes out clearly in the description of Jeanie Deans' moonlight meeting with the mysterious Wilson, in *The Heart of Midlothian* (Chap. XV):

> It was situated in the depth of the valley behind Salisbury Crags, which has for a background the north-western shoulder of the mountain called Arthur's Seat, on whose descent still remain the ruins of what was once a chapel or hermitage, dedicated to Saint Anthony the Eremite. A better site for such a building could hardly have been selected; for the chapel, situated among the rude and pathless cliffs, lies in a desert, even in the immediate vicinity of a rich, populous, and tumultuous capital: and the hum of the city might mingle with the orisons of the recluses, conveying as little of worldly interest as if it had been the roar of the distant ocean. Beneath the steep ascent on which these ruins are still visible, was, and perhaps is still pointed out, the place where the wretch Nicol Muschat, who has been already mentioned in these pages, had closed a long scene of cruelty towards his unfortunate wife, by murdering her, with circumstances of uncommon barbarity. The execration in which the man's crime was held extended itself to the place where it was perpetrated, which was marked by a small cairn, or heap of stones, composed of those which each chance passenger had thrown there in testi-

mony of abhorrence, and on the principle, it would seem, of the ancient British malediction, "May you have a cairn for your burial-place!"

As our heroine approached this ominous and unhallowed spot, she paused and looked to the moon, now rising broad on the north-west, and shedding a more distinct light than it had afforded during her walk thither. Eyeing the planet for a moment, she then slowly and fearfully turned her head towards the cairn, from which it was at first averted. She was at first disappointed. Nothing was visible beside the little pile of stones, which shone grey in the moonlight. A multitude of confused suggestions rushed on her mind. Had her correspondent deceived her, and broken his appointment?—was he too tardy at the appointment he had made?—or had some strange turn of fate prevented him from appearing as he proposed?—or, if he were an unearthly being, as her secret apprehensions suggested, was it his object merely to delude her with false hopes, and put her to unnecessary toil and terror, according to the nature, as she had heard, of those wandering demons?—or did he propose to blast her with the sudden horrors of his presence when she had come close to the place of rendezvous? These anxious reflections did not prevent her approaching to the cairn with a pace that, though slow, was determined.

The language is that of Mrs. Radcliffe—"ominous and unhallowed," "sudden horrors"—but the details of the setting are not fictional, and the occasion of the meeting at such a place and hour is not merely designed to make the reader's flesh creep (though such a motive is of course involved) but is a logical outcome of the situation in which Wilson is placed. Some manipulation of mood and circumstance there certainly is, but there is no law which says that a creative artist shall not manipulate his material. The most we can do is to condemn him if he fails to bring it off, and Scott can successfully plead "not guilty" on this occasion, as on many others.

A subsequent writer who does not always get away with it is Dickens. Much of his description is utilitarian scene-setting, as it is in the work of his eighteenth-century masters, and here his selection of what is relevant and characteristic is usually under control. But he is also one of the first English novelists (if not the first) to raise description to a symbolic level, and when he does so he runs much greater risks. The opening of *Bleak House* is justly famous for its transition from the actual level of a London "pea-souper" to the symbolic fog at the heart of the High Court of Chancery. By contrast, the attempt to make the rain and floods in this novel symbolise the desolation of Lady Dedlock must be adjudged a failure. As a piece of pure description the passage is well enough done:

> The waters are out in Lincolnshire. An arch of the bridge in the park has been sapped and sopped away. The adjacent low-lying ground, for half a mile in breadth, is a stagnant river, with melancholy trees for islands in it, and a surface punctured all over, all day long, with falling rain. . . . The weather, for many a day and night, has been so wet that the trees seem wet through, and the soft loppings and prunings of the workman's axe can make no crash or crackle as they fall. The deer, looking soaked, leave quagmires, where they pass. The shot of a rifle loses its sharpness in the moist air, and its smoke moves in a tardy little cloud towards the green rise, coppice-topped, that makes a background for the falling rain.

I agree with Mr. Liddell's view of this passage. What spoils its adequacy as symbol is not the quality of the description itself, but the situation, the melodramatic situation, which it is intended to emphasize.

No particular principle lay behind my original choice of examples to illustrate this article beyond that of relevance, but it so happens that a pattern of ebb and flow in the effectiveness of these passages does emerge. We began with the utilitarian description required by the novel to localise its characters and their actions to a degree not met with in the older narrative or dramatic forms. The next stage was to place the character in his social setting, as well as within a geographical one, and then followed the manipulation of landscape in the novel of terror to suit the emotions and situations of the characters. This may not seem very effective to us, and the fashion for the novel of terror among the educated classes did not last very long. One would hesitate to attribute its decline to *Northanger Abbey* alone; but Jane Austen does come out strongly against it, and returns to description used as a means of social placing. Scott, however, continues to use atmospheric description (though he does so more naturally than Mrs. Radcliffe) because the nature of his work requires it. Finally, description rises to the level of symbolism in Dickens.

In my next example, the current changes once more. No one could be more utilitarian than Trollope, no one less likely to be suspected of rigging the description to suit a mood or to fashion a symbol. His general level of achievement can be illustrated by the account of Hiram's Hospital in the first chapter of *The Warden:*

> Hiram's Hospital, as the retreat is called, is a picturesque building enough, and shows the correct taste with which the ecclesiastical architects of those days were imbued. It stands on the banks of the little river, which flows nearly round the cathedral close, being on the side furthest from the town. The London road crosses the river by a pretty one-arched bridge, and, looking from this bridge, the stranger will see the windows of the old men's rooms, each pair of windows separated by a small buttress. A broad gravel walk runs between the building and the river, which is always trim and cared for; and at the end of the walk, under the parapet of the approach to the bridge, is a large and well-worn seat, on which, in mild weather, three or four of Hiram's bedesmen are sure to be seen seated. Beyond this row of buttresses, and further from the bridge, and also further from the water which here suddenly bends, are the pretty oriel windows of Mr. Harding's house, and his well-mown lawn. The entrance to the hospital is from the London road, and is made through a ponderous gateway under a heavy stone arch, unnecessary, one would suppose, at any time, for the protection of twelve old men, but greatly conducive to the good appearance of Hiram's charity. On passing through this portal, never closed to anyone from six a. m. till ten p. m., and never open afterwards, except on application to a huge, intricately hung, medieval bell, the handle of which no unitiated intruder can possibly find, the six doors of the old men's abodes are seen, and beyond them is a slight iron screen, through which the more happy portion of the Barchester elite pass into the Elysium of Mr. Harding's dwelling.

Everything in this passage, with one exception, is devoted to the business of localisation, a rough test of which is whether one can draw a map or make a picture from the data. Here the facts are more than adequate for this purpose. The exception is the word "Elysium." Like the adjective "blessed" in the description of Mr. Elton's house, it is a means of connecting utilitarian description with the immediate situation of the characters. It points the contrast between the situation of the bedesmen, kept strictly to the letter of Hiram's will, and the happier lot of the Warden. The two areas are separated by a screen; a slight screen, it is true, but one of iron nevertheless, a barrier which shuts these poor Adams out of Paradise. And further, there is an irony on "Elysium," because the peace for which it stands is about to be rudely invaded by the forces of reform.

If this example is a regression, the next is so subtle and complicated that it can almost stand as a summary of the various uses to which description can be put:

> On a grey but dry November morning Dorothea drove to Lowick in company with her uncle and Celia. Mr. Casaubon's home was the manor-house. Close by, visible from some parts of the garden, was the little church, with the old parsonage opposite. In the beginning of his career, Mr. Casaubon had only held the living, but the death of his brother had put him in possession of the manor also. It had a small park, with a fine old oak here and there, and an avenue of limes towards the south-west front, with a sunk fence between park and pleasure-ground, so that from the drawing-room windows the glance swept uninterruptedly along a slope of greensward till the limes ended in a level of corn and pastures, which often seemed to melt into a lake under the setting sun. This was the happy side of the house, for the south and east looked rather melancholy even under the brightest morning. The grounds here were more confined, the flower-beds showed no careful tendance, and large clumps of trees, chiefly of sombre yews, had risen high, not ten yards from the windows. The building of greenish stone, was in the old English style, not ugly, but small windowed and melancholy-looking; the sort of house that must have children, many flowers, open windows, and little vistas of bright things, to make it seem a joyous home. In this latter end of autumn, with a sparse remnant of yellow leaves falling slowly athwart the dark evergreens in a stillness without a sunshine, the house too had an air of autumnal decline, and Mr. Casaubon, when he presented himself, had no bloom that could be thrown into relief by that background (*Middlemarch*, Book I, Chap. IX).

Here, obviously, is localisation. We know where we are and could paint the scene. Here too are the remains of the man-made, man-centred landscape of the eighteenth century in the mention of the avenue of limes and the sunk fence, and the (probably unconscious) glance back to the paintings of Claude: "a level of corn and pastures, which often seemed to melt into a lake under the setting sun." Added to this is a selection of detail and colour which helps to present character and situation. Casaubon is at one with the autumnal decline; like the November morning, he too is grey and dry. The choice of season is deliberate, and provides an emphasis which is parallel to the concordance of mood and scene which we have noted in the novel of terror, but raised here by George Eliot to the level of symbol. The happy side of the house stands for the sort of life that Dorothea will renounce in her marriage; there will be no children, no vistas of bright things on her side of the house of marriage.

All this, however, is still in the future, and we need to be reminded of the situation again when Dorothea and Casaubon are actually married. George Eliot does this in describing their arrival at Lowick after the honeymoon, and the bright contrasts in the final sentence leave us in no doubt that Dorothea has reached the winter of her discontent:

> Mr. and Mrs. Casaubon, returning from their wedding journey, arrived at Lowick Manor in the middle of January. A light snow was falling as they descended at the door, and in the morning, when Dorothea passed from her dressing-room into the blue-green boudoir that we know of, she saw the long avenue of limes lifting their trunks from a white earth, and spreading white branches against the dun and motionless sky. The distant flat shrank in uniform whiteness and low-hanging uniformity of cloud. The very furniture in the room seemed to have shrunk since she saw it before; the stag in the tapestry looked more like a ghost in his ghostly blue-green world; the volumes of polite literature in the bookcase looked more like immovable imitations of books. The bright fire of dry oak-boughs burning on the dogs seemed an incongruous renewal of life and glow—like the figure of Dorothea herself as she entered carrying the red-leather cases containing the cameos for Celia (Book III, Chap. XVIII).

The same contrast of light and shade can be seen in the next example, from *The Mayor of Casterbridge*. But where the passages from *Middlemarch* look back to the restrained landscapes of Claude, Hardy's description continues many features of the Salvator Rosa landscape, and the cult of the picturesque which it inspired:

> These precincts embodied the mournful phases of Casterbridge life, as the south avenues embodied its cheerful moods. The whole way along here was sunless, even in summer time; in spring, white frosts lingered here when other places were steaming with warmth; while in winter it was the seed-field of all the aches, rheumatisms, and torturing cramps of the year. The Casterbridge doctors must have pined away for want of sufficient nourishment, but for the configuration of the landscape on the north-eastern side.
> The river—slow, noiseless, and dark,—the Schwarzwasser of Casterbridge—ran beneath a low cliff, the two together forming a defence which had rendered walls and artificial earthworks on this side unnecessary. Here were ruins of a Franciscan priory, and a mill attached to

the same, the water of which roared down a back-hatch like the voice of desolation. Above the cliff, and behind the river, rose a pile of buildings, and in the front of the pile a square mass cut into the sky. It was like a pedestal lacking its statue. This missing feature, without which the design remained incomplete, was, in truth, the corpse of a man; for the square mass formed the base of the gallows, the extensive buildings at the back being the county gaol. In the meadow where Henchard now walked the mob were wont to gather whenever an execution took place, and there to the tune of the roaring weir they stood and watched the spectacle.

The exaggeration which darkness imparted to the glooms of this region impressed Henchard more than he had expected. The lugubrious harmony of the spot with his domestic situation was too perfect for him, impatient of effects, scenes and adumbrations. It reduced his heartburning to melancholy, and he exclaimed, "Why the deuce did I come here!" He went on past the cottage in which the old local hangman had lived and died, in times before that calling was monopolized all over England by a single gentleman; and climbed up by a steep back lane into the town (Chap. XIX).

Good as it is, this passage is a retrogressive step. Like Mrs. Radcliffe, Hardy gives the game away and admits to manipulation when he tells us how much the scene harmonised with Henchard's mood. All the same, the thing is better done than it is by Disraeli or Wilkie Collins, partly because, as with Scott, the locality is actual and not imagined.

But the time has come to sum up. The nature of the novel, in its beginnings, was such that a greater degree of localisation of the characters was required than in the older literary forms, because these characters were less universal, more closely related to their own day and age. This localisation was achieved by setting them in a solidly constructed environment. But it is not long before description is being used more widely, to reveal, first, general characteristics, and then particular moods. There is not much point in telling the reader that So-and-so felt melancholy and leaving it at that. In drama participation in the moods of the characters is achieved through the direct contact between actor and audience, and is embodied in action, in pauses and tones of voice, and so forth. But participation in the novel is much less direct (we read it all in our own internal tone of voice, for example) and one way to make the connection is through the evocative power of descriptive passages. Here, as we have seen, the novelist was able to learn something from the development of landscape painting at this time.[9]

Next description can rise to the level of symbol, and so stand for more than the writer expresses directly, or else express in succinct form what otherwise might have been more laborious. And there is also that aspect of the question which has only been implicit in my discussion, an aspect put at its plainest by L. P. Hartley in *A Perfect Woman*, a novel published in 1955: "There was surely no sympathetic fallacy in the idea that the earth reflected one's own moods and that one could project oneself into it; not to have felt akin to it would have argued insensitiveness, lack of imagination" (Chap. XVIII). But everywhere the primary requirement is that of relevance, and next to relevance, refusal to rig the description. When these essentials have been observed, the descriptive passages take their place in the texture of the novel, and cannot be detached and enjoyed for their own sake, nor wished away from the novel without damaging its fabric.

---

[9] It is worth noting that painting is still having an influence on the descriptive powers of the novelist in our own day. The following passage is taken from Virginia Woolf's *Between The Acts:* "The roof was weathered red-orange; and inside it was a hollow hall, sunshafted, brown, smelling of corn, dark when the doors were shut, but splendidly illuminated when the doors at the end stood open, as they did, to let the wagons in— the long, low wagons, like ships of the sea, breasting the corn, not the sea, returning in the evening, shagged with hay." If we compare this with Jane Austen's passage describing Mr. Elton's house we can see a decisive change from utility to evocation; and evocation, I would suggest, is a dominant characteristic of contemporary fictional description, and can be found at its best in the work of women novelists like Elizabeth Bowen, Rosamund Lehmann and Iris Murdoch. It is not too much to say that, in Virginia Woolf's case, she would not have written quite as she did without the example of the Impressionists before her, and without the modification of visual awareness which their work brought about. We remember in this connection that her sister, Vanessa Bell, is a sensitive painter, that her brother-in-law is the critic Clive Bell, and that she was the close friend and biographer of Roger Fry.

8

SYMBOL

A good many of the aspects of fictional theory are, however intricate, at least comfortably parochial. Only fiction, for example, alternates summary, narrative, analysis, and scene; and only in narrative art is point of view a relevant category. Symbol, on the other hand, is a frustratingly broad subject. As William York Tindall points out, taking the word symbol in one sense, virtually all human activity is symbolic. Certainly all of literature, in a sense, is symbolic—and so is all of language. The critic of fiction is obliged to keep in mind these general, philosophical senses by which any novel, even the most literal and single-leveled, can properly be described as a system of symbols. When the critic of fiction uses the word symbol, however, he is likely to mean something a good deal more limited. It is the purpose of Tindall's discourse to sift through the various senses of that difficult word so as to find the precise sense which is useful in describing that specialized use of language which results in the fog in Bleak House, the darkness in Heart of Darkness, and the bowl in The Golden Bowl.

Once one has decided on a working definition, the job of practical criticism still remains. At the beginning of Gide's Pastoral Symphony the snow is falling. Is that snow a symbol, or is it snowing because Gide simply wished his novella to begin in winter and falling snow is a reasonable way to make concrete that time of year? If one comes to Gide's novella after having read Joyce's "The Dead," at the end of which the snow indisputably has a large and quite explicit symbolic value, one is predisposed to find a symbolic value in Gide's snow. But what, on the other hand, if one comes to Gide after having read one of countless Russian novels in which the snow is falling because it often snows in Russia? To a reader who is inclined to see Gide's snow as background description, a symbolic interpretation of it will seem over-ingenious. And to a reader who is inclined to see it as symbol, a literal reading of it will seem hopelessly obtuse. It is hardly surprising that deep and often passionate differences occur over the questions of symbol since one critic will seem to another to be reading literature as a branch of cryptography while his opposite will seem to him to be wilfully ignoring the dimension of literature which gives to it depth of texture, resonance, breadth, and richness of significance—a dimension, moreover, which writers such as Joyce make clear is intentionally there. Something of the nature of these differences can be seen in items in the bibliography under Philip Rahv, Robert Wooster Stallman, Harry Levin, and Saul Bellow, as well as in such classic works on symbol as Susanne Langer's Philosophy in a New Key.

In any given case, of course, the relevance of a symbolic reading must be established by a sensitive insight into the tone and mode of a work. But some general guidelines can be established, and it is the intent of Ursula Brumm's essay to suggest some of the limits of symbolic interpretation, to redefine the nature of the fictional symbol, and to form some classifications by way of clarifying the way in which symbols operate. One of the incidental pleasures of Professor Brumm's essay, appearing as it does beside the beginning chapter of William York Tindall's The Literary Symbol, is that it provides not only a perspective different from Tindall's but a pointed dissent from his position. The theory of the novel, like the theory of anything else, becomes more precise in a direct relation to the capacity of critics to say no to each other. It is one of the misfortunes of fictional theory that the affirmations so heavily outweigh the dissents.

WILLIAM YORK TINDALL

EXCELLENT DUMB DISCOURSE

That symbols present thought and feeling while celebrating or constructing suitable worlds, though plain to Moses and other authors before the time of Blake, has been plainer since then. Melville, Baudelaire, and Ibsen come readily to mind, but the twentieth century brought with it an even thicker crowd of romantic symbolists, including the greatest writers of our period. Not only Yeats and Joyce, Valéry and Proust, Wallace Stevens and Faulkner, Mann, Kafka, and Conrad—all writers of the first order—but even more popular, though no less important, writers such as F. Scott Fitzgerald and T. S. Eliot, making symbolic worlds of symbolic elements, have shaped our vision of reality.

Consider Dr. T. J. Eckleburg's eyes in *The Great Gatsby:*

About half way between West Egg and New York the motor road hastily joins the railroad and runs beside it for a quarter of a mile, so as to shrink away from a certain desolate area of land. This is a valley of ashes—a fantastic farm where ashes grow like wheat into ridges and hills and grotesque gardens, where ashes take the forms of houses. . . . But above the gray land and the spasms of bleak dust which drift endlessly over it, you perceive, after a moment, the eyes of Doctor T. J. Eckleburg. The eyes of Doctor T. J. Eckleburg are blue and gigantic—their retinas are one yard high. They look out of no face, but, instead, from a pair of enormous yellow spectacles which pass over a nonexistent nose. Evidently some wild wag of an oculist set them there to fatten his practice in the borough of Queens, and then sank down

From The Literary Symbol *(New York, 1955), where the essay appears as Chapter One. Reprinted by permission of Columbia University Press.*

himself into eternal blindness, or forgot them and moved away. But his eyes, dimmed a little by many paintless days, under sun and rain, brood on over the solemn dumping ground.

Fitzgerald's desolating image, which recurs throughout the novel, is what most would call a symbol. If this vision of eyes is a functioning part of a larger structure, as the single eye on a signboard near the end of Faulkner's *The Sound and the Fury* or the eyes of Beatrice in Eliot's "The Hollow Men" are obscurely portentous but essential constituents of that novel and this poem, it becomes apparent that symbols may serve as elements of a work. That the work itself may be as symbolic as its elements is not unlikely.

The Cocktail Party seems a symbol composed of symbols, not there to be explained but to play their part in a conspiracy. Peripheral suggestions of gin and water, of making dishes out of nothing, and of single eyes may limit or deepen the total effect and excite the critic, but the audience, taking them as they come, enjoys the experience to which they contribute. As if referring to members of this audience, Eliot's Thomas Becket says: "They know and do not know."

The masters of those who know tell us that symbol-making is our natural activity and our condition. Catching up with artists or trying to account for them, recent philosophers provide an assurance that the value we place on symbols is not misplaced. Whitehead regards symbolism, if I understand him correctly, as a mode of perception and a cause of error, but, although he talks about literature at times, he is too general and indifferent to help us with the literary symbol. Cassirer, who seems more to the point, says man is a symbolic animal whose languages, myths, religions, sciences, and arts are symbolic forms by which he projects his reality and comes to know it: "What reality is apart from these forms is irrelevant."

As these philosophers assure us, all perception, all our fanatical pursuits, and all our arts may be symbolic in some fundamental sense at all times, but at certain times symbolism has become conscious and deliberate. It is with one of these periods that I am concerned and with one of the arts. Before approaching the literary symbol as it is used in our time, I must accost symbol and tell the difference between symbol and sign or at least fix their usage. Webster says that a symbol is "that which stands for or suggests something else by reason of relationship, association, convention or accidental but not intentional resemblance; especially, a visible sign of something invisible, as an idea, a quality or a totality such as a state or a church." Something that stands for or suggests something else is an attractive account of the word as we use it in the market place but too general and maybe too clear for the closet. I prefer "a visible sign of something invisible," although this would seem to exclude unwritten music or music as we hear it. Webster's echo of the catechism or the prayer book might be intensified and the definition made more inclusive by saying that a symbol seems the outward sign of an inward state, if by inward state we refer to feeling or thought or a combination of the two. However, this gets us, as it got Webster, into trouble with the word sign.

The words symbol and sign are commonly interchangeable, yet at times some of us mean one thing by sign and another by symbol. That is a cause of trouble and this is another: sign, taken to mean an exact reference, may include symbol, and symbol, taken to mean a suggestive device, may include sign. Since Dr. T. J. Eckleburg's eyes occupy a signboard, they are plainly a sign, yet we agree or, I think, should agree that they are as plainly a symbol, which, in this case, must consist of a sign. If we define a sign as an exact reference, it must include symbol because a symbol is an exact reference too. The difference seems to be that a sign is an exact reference to something definite and a symbol an exact reference to something indefinite. Less of a paradox than they appear, exact and indefinite will get along more comfortably together if we consider the senses of exact, one of which is suitable. Dr. Eckleburg's eyes are a sign referring to Dr. Eckleburg and his business. As a symbol they suggest, to use Webster's word, more thoughts and feelings than we could state; for if we stated as many as we could—the wasteland, the suburb, the modern world, futility, or moral censure—some would be left over and some would remain unstatable.

As I shall use it, the word sign means a one-to-one correspondence. Example: the American flag is a sign of the United States, used to identify post offices, income tax bureaus, and ships. The flag may also suggest Iwo Jima, General Grant's cigar, and graduation day—as the sign TIMES SQUARE on that corner suggests as much as it indicates. The sign may have symbolic values; but ignoring connotations, overtones, and suggestions, I shall regard the sign as a pointer. Indifferent to the sign as symbol or as the container of a symbol, I prefer to look at the symbol as a container of a sign—upon the flag, for example, as a symbol which happens by proximity and custom to indicate a post office. Those eyes as suggesters of many things, some of them nameless, seem more entertaining than as references to an oculist.

If we receive sign as pointer and my variation upon Webster's second try as a provisional account of symbol, we may proceed to art as symbol and symbol in the arts. According to Cassirer's *Essay on Man,* as we have seen, art is a symbolic form, parallel in respect of this to religion or science. Each of these forms builds up a universe that enables man to interpret and organize his experience; and each is a discovery, because a creation, of reality. Although similar in function, the forms differ in the kind of reality built. Whereas science builds it of facts, art builds it of feelings, intuitions of quality, and the other distractions of our inner life—and in their degrees so do myth and religion. What art, myth, and religion are, Cassirer confesses, cannot be expressed by a logical definition.

Nevertheless, let us see what Clive Bell says about art. He calls it "significant form," but what that is he is unable to say. Having no quarrel with art as form, we may, however, question its significance. By significant he cannot mean important in the sense of having import, nor can he mean having the function of a sign; for to him art, lacking reference to nature, is insignificant. Since, however, he tells us that a work of art "expresses" the emotion of its creator and "provokes" an emotion in its contemplator, he seems to imply that his significant means expressive and provocative. The emotion expressed and provoked is an "aesthetic emotion," contemplative, detached from all concerns of utility and from all reference.

Attempting to explain Bell's significant form, Roger Fry, equally devoted to Whistler and art for art's sake, says that Flaubert's "expression of the idea" is as near as he can get to it, but neither Flaubert nor Fry tells what is meant by idea. To "evoke" it, however, the artist creates an "expressive design" or "symbolic form," by which the spirit "communicates its most secret and indefinable impulses."

Susanne Langer, who occupies a place somewhere between Fry and Cassirer, though nearer the latter, once said in a seminar that a work of art is an "unassigned syntactical symbol." Since this definition does not appear in her latest book, she may have rejected it, but it seems far more precise than Fry's attempt. By unassigned she probably intends insignificant in the sense of lacking sign value or fixed reference; syntactical implies a form composed of parts in relationship to one another; and a symbol, according to *Feeling and Form*, is "any device whereby we are enabled to make an abstraction." Too austere for my taste, this account of symbol seems to need elaboration, which, to be sure, her book provides. For the present, however, taking symbol to mean an outward device for presenting an inward state, and taking unassigned and syntactical as I think she uses them, let us tentatively admire her definition of the work of art.

Parallel symbolic forms, says Mrs. Langer, the arts differ from one another in materials and in what is symbolized. As music uses sounds, painting colors, and sculpture stuff, so literature uses words to create an image of time, space, or dynamic patterns of feeling. Music attends to virtual time, painting to the semblance of space, and literature to vital patterns. However referential or discursive the materials and elements or constituent parts of painting or literature, these arts are as irrelevant and nondiscursive as music.

Words, which she finds trivial in themselves, seem more than materials of literature. Its elements may be character, action, and image; but words, more than the matter from which these elements that compose the form are made, also serve as elements in their own right as her metaphor of syntax should imply. The potency of the real thing, Cassirer says in *Language and Myth*, is contained in the word that creates it. If language, as he says elsewhere, is a symbolic form, literature uses elements of one symbolic form as those of another. Words are symbols, but like most symbols they are not without significance or sign value, as the grammarian's connotation and denotation imply. If words are elements as well as materials of literature, a poem, differing in this respect from a sonata or a plastic abstraction, is a symbolic whole composed in part of references. At once assigned and unassigned, literature troubles aesthetic philosophers and moralists alike.

My interest in literature is not that of the philosopher, still less that of the moralist. Cassirer talks about art in general as symbolic form, and Mrs. Langer about poems as symbols, whereas I have in mind not only that but the symbolic elements that compose the poem. My examination of the literary symbol will proceed from constituent images to whole works. Since the image seems an approximate epitome of the whole, we may acquire understanding of the literary symbol from a return to Dr. Eckleburg's eyes.

Taking that signboard as the image, we recognize it as a definite object, or at least as the semblance of an object, which, though nothing much in itself, has received import from experience and memory. We know that eyes, even virtual eyes, are for looking, watching, rebuking; and with them we associate many other activities and attitudes, which we can feel more easily than explain. If the signboard were alone in a kind of nothing, we might not know which of these implications to pick from memory or feeling and which to reject. Situated as it is, however, near a commuters' railroad between Wall Street and a suburb, near a highway for homing brokers, and in the middle of a waste of ashes and shacks, which is presented by charged, desolating words, that signboard or rather its meaning is at once enriched and limited by context. I agree that this would be no less true if the signboard found itself in a kind of nothing, for nothing as context becomes something. No constituent image is without context, and every image owes context part of what it bears. Since context owes as much to image, the roads and ashes and all the implied commuters acquire import from those eyes. By reciprocal limitation and expansion, image and context, two interacting components of what they create, carry feelings and thoughts at once definite and indefinite. This composite of image and context constitutes that symbol.

This image in context is an element of *The Great Gatsby*, but if it is an epitome of the symbolic whole in which it functions, it is no more than approximate; for although work and image alike are made up of elements which, working together, present a feeling and maybe an idea, the constituent image has immediate literary context and the work has not. Of course we may take the state of society, the literary tradition, what we know of the hand that wrote the book and what we feel of the hand that holds it, time, place, and the weather as a kind of context with which the work may interact; but such circumstance, of the sort that surrounds all our affairs, is too general and remote to serve as more than a parallel to the surroundings of Dr. Eckleburg's signboard. The work as symbol, therefore, differs from the image as symbol in lacking the limitation and enlargement provided by immediate context. Work and image may have similar syntactical structure and function, but without immediate context, the work, less narrowly directed, is harder to apprehend. This lack is more or less supplied by the greater richness and complexity of the internal relationships that, providing control and enhancement, compose the whole.

The literary symbol, whether a work or one of its parts, is clearly an embodiment. As the spirit or vital principal occupies our bodies and shines out, so thought and feeling occupy the form, shape, or body that we call symbol. With the symbol or something like it in mind, Shakespeare's Theseus in *A Midsummer-Night's Dream*, considering madmen and poets, speaks of "shaping fantasies, that apprehend more than cool reason ever comprehends."

> And, as imagination bodies forth
> The forms of things unknown, the poet's pen
> Turns them to shapes, and gives to airy nothing
> A local habitation and a name.

If we may take these verses as references to the literary symbol, it is a thing made by the shaping imagination to body forth an unknown airy nothing. Although made by the poet's pen and composed of words, these words, no longer in the service of cool or discursive reason, serve nondiscursive purposes; neither practical nor logical, the poet's speech is the builder of symbolic forms. Shakespeare again has the words for this kind of speech, no longer speech but shape, in *The Tempest*, where, speaking of shapes, gesture, and sound, one of his people calls nondiscursive though expressive form "a kind of excellent dumb discourse."

Unlike the sign, which interests us less for what it is than what it points to, this dumb discourse is interesting in itself. Unlike the sign, it cannot be separated from what it stands for; for it is what it stands for or else part of it by a kind of synecdoche. Not entirely translatable and without substitute, it resists what Wilbur Marshall Urban in *Language and Reality* calls "expansion." That transcendental philosopher, who believes that a symbol is a "condensation of meaning, of unexpressed reference," holds that it may be "expanded into expressed reference" or discourse. If that were so, there would be no need to employ symbols; for as the dancer said, "If I could say what it means, I should not have to dance it." Justly rebuked for those notions, Urban has retired to the arms of New Critics. But the symbol remains, calling for explanation and resisting it. Though definite in itself and generally containing a sign that may be identified, the symbol carries something indeterminate and, however we try, there is a residual mystery that escapes our intellects. As Carlyle said, and what he said is true to our impression, the symbol at once reveals and conceals.

The symbol conceals what it carries and resists total explanation because it is founded upon analogy, which, philosophers say, is primitive, childish, and irrational. Cassirer has told how primitive man confused analogy with fact, and Whitehead, seeking things as they are, has found in analogy a cause of modern error; but men of letters, recovering an ancient illusion, have made of it a device for presenting apprehensions, counteracting the world of fact, and creating something more suitable. If symbol is analogy, it is related to metaphor, but the account of that relationship can wait awhile. For the present it is enough to say that the symbol seems a metaphor one half of which remains unstated and indefinite. As in metaphor, the halves of the equation may be related by partial similarity, which is qualitative at times and structural or functional at others but hardly ever imitative or representative. Dr. Eckleburg's eyes and their environment are an analogy for an unexpressed feeling and thought about our condition, not an imitation of it.

The creator of such a symbol is not unlike Henry James's antique dealer, who, taking the golden bowl from its box, "left the important object—for as 'important' it did somehow present itself—to produce its certain effect." Certain from one point of view, this effect is uncertain from another, and the producer of the effect or the symbol itself is definite enough to call for definition—to call in vain maybe; for, if we may judge by the definitions I have reviewed and by my own approaches and withdrawals, the enterprise is difficult. Here, nevertheless, is my attempt to establish the important object:

The literary symbol, an analogy for something unstated, consists of an articulation of verbal elements that, going beyond reference and the limits of discourse, embodies and offers a complex of feeling and thought. Not necessarily an image, this analogical embodiment may also be a rhythm, a juxtaposition, an action, a proposition, a structure, or a poem. One half of this peculiar analogy embodies the other, and the symbol is what it symbolizes.

I am afraid that this approach to a working definition, hopelessly general, might fit all literature at all times, but there are differences in degree between *Tom Jones,* let us say, and *Moby Dick.* What I have in mind is less literature in general than symbolist literature, my term for writing deliberately symbolic and for writing in symbolist periods which, though not necessarily deliberate, takes its method from current practice. Most of the writers I shall consider are conscious symbolists—not that it matters whether they are or not; for what matters is the kind of thing they made. I think we can recognize the difference in degree that separates their work, if symbolist, from *Tom Jones,* which, like all literature, is symbolic. The mark of distinction is embodied or immanent analogy.

Returning to the conscious or unconscious use of analogy, let us consider the statements of four symbolists. In a letter to Mrs. Hawthorne about *Moby Dick,* Melville said:

> Your allusion for example to the "Spirit Spout" first showed to me that there was a subtle significance in that thing—but I did not, in that case, *mean* it. I had some vague idea while writing it, that the whole book was susceptible of an allegoric construction, & also that *parts* of it were—but the specialty of many of the particular subordinate allegories, were first revealed to me, after reading Mr. Hawthorne's letter, which, without citing any particular examples, yet intimated the part-&-parcel allegoricalness of the whole.

By allegory he meant, I think, what we mean by symbol. Happy to discover what he had made and tolerantly aware that what his creation carries is an affair between the reader and a book, no longer the creator's but an object for creating feelings and ideas in others, Melville appears to have been no more than partly conscious of what he was creating. In his Preface to *Paludes,* an early work, André Gide says:

> Before explaining my book to others, I wait for them to explain it to me. To explain it first is to limit its sense; for if we know what we wished to say, we do not know if we have said only that.—One always says more than that.—And my interest is what I have put into the work without knowing it,—the unconscious part that I like to call God's.— A book is always a collaboration, and the greater its value, the smaller the part of the scribe. As we expect all things in nature to reveal themselves, so let us expect our books to be revealed by readers.

Speaking in a letter of the symbolic character of all art and of unconscious and conscious symbolism, D. H. Lawrence said that while much of his own symbolism was intentional, some of it escaped his notice until later. In an interview William Faulkner, speaking of how critics take his images, said: "I'm just a writer. Not a literary man. . . . Maybe all sorts of symbols and images get in. I don't know. When a good carpenter builds something, he puts the nails where they belong. Maybe they make a fancy pattern when he's through, but that's not why he put them in that way." Although Faulkner's statements to his public not uncommonly reveal tongue in cheek, maybe those nails are an analogy for analogies.

Whether consciously, unconsciously, or with a profession of this or that, authors make symbols and readers receive them. We must discover, if we can, the function of symbols and for whom they are designed. As for the second of these, a symbol in a novel may serve a character, the author, the reader, or the critic.

Some symbols, plainly for a character in the book, are there to carry something to him and by his reaction to enlighten us about him. If like the green-eyed man in Joyce's "An Encounter," the character responds to hair and whips, we understand his nature a little better. To find how the symbol serves the author we must consult psychology and history (which I do not propose to do here); for time and fixation may determine usage. Beyond these he may use symbols to embody what he cannot think, to discover what he feels or to express it, or, if he is an artist like Faulkner, to function as elements in a design. Convinced of the inadequacy of discourse for all that lies outside the rational and the prosaic or persuaded that things as they are are not entirely explicable, he may resort to analogical embodiment, which is useful too for supplementing a discursive meaning with overtones, qualities, and implications beyond logical handling. "Where there is an obscurity too deep for our Reason," says Sir Thomas Browne, " 'tis good to sit down with [an] . . . adumbration." Dissatisfied with what is, the author may use the symbol to create something better. For the philosopher, the psychologist, or the historian it is all right to inquire into the relation of author to symbol, but not for the critic, lest he commit the "intentional fallacy."

To a point the reader may share the author's concerns and find in the symbol a reminder of his own; but for him the principal function of symbol is organizing his experience and enlarging it. This supposes apprehension of the symbol, but even if careless of it, the reader may respond beneath the level of awareness and find himself surprised by an enrichment he cannot account for. Perhaps this is the commonest and best way to take symbolist writing. For critics, however, unawareness is a fault. Their response to symbolism, far keener than that of most authors and readers, is of two kinds: exercising ingenuity as over a puzzle, they may explain meaning and reduce embodiment to discourse; or, if aesthetic, they may try to fix the function of parts in the whole.

For author and reader the symbol is unitive. By its roots, as the dictionary tells us, the word symbol implies throwing or putting together. Taken from one realm of experience, vegetable nature for example, to serve in another, let us say the moral, the symbol joins those realms. By uniting the separate it can organize experience into a kind of order and, revealing the complex relationships among seemingly divided things, confer peace. Men of God praise the symbol's mediatory power. Whether verbal or iconographic, the religious symbol, and the political too, can unite man with man and man with something greater than he, society or God. Jung, speaking of the symbol as reconciler, finds it uniting the unconscious with the conscious, and Whitehead finds it connecting modes of experience. In a world as scattered as our own this ability is not without value. More important or at least more immediate for us is the power of the symbol to put parts of a literary work together in the service of the whole.

The symbol may put things together, but we must find if it puts author and reader together by establishing communication between them. The trouble with the symbol as communicator is that, although definite in being the semblance of an articulated object, it is indefinite in what it presents. In the first place the symbol is an analogy for something undefined and in the second our apprehension of the analogy is commonly incomplete. Moreover, the terms of the analogy are confused. Since one is embodied in the other, our search for a meaning apart from the embodiment must return to it and we are left with a form, at once definite and indefinite, and significant perhaps only by seeming so.

For communication there must be reference to actuality or to something accepted. The symbol may communicate by incorporating a sign or a traditional association. In so far as it has significance in the sense of containing a sign, it may unite author, reader, and fact, but significance is the symbol's lesser part. The greater part, remaining mysterious, carries no guarantee of communicating. As we have seen, the author's community with his symbol is often incomplete; therefore what passes between him and the reader through intermediary embodiment must be less nearly complete. When we pass beyond significance, communication is uncertain or partial at best. What the reader gets from a symbol depends not only upon what the author has put into it but upon the reader's sensitivity and his consequent apprehension of what is there. The feeling of profundity that accompanies it comes from a gradual but never final penetration of the form. T. S. Eliot's remarks about the poem seem relevant here: an independent object, the poem (or symbol) stands between author and reader, related in some fashion to each, but the relationship between author and object is not necessarily similar to that between object and reader. It may express the author and suggest to the reader, but expression and suggestion need not coincide. I. A. Richards, Eliot's opposite, who finds poetry the highest form of communication, finds it so by reducing symbol to sign. If the symbol, apart from incorporated sign, has little value as communicator between author and reader, its value may lie in communication between itself and the reader. What it submits to him and what he receives, however, may be different things. Nevertheless the value of the symbol to readers must be sought in this imperfect relationship.

Maybe the symbol has value as a way of knowing; but the meaning of knowing depends upon one's school. If one belongs to the scientific school, knowledge means acquaintance with fact, the sign becomes the instrument of knowing, and, as Ernest Nagel has pointed out, the symbol of science, a fiction ancillary to sign, is only a means of arriving at it. In the sense of direct reference to fact, the literary symbol, like that of science but worse, is so far from cognitive that even the sign it incorporates seems useless or vague. If we take knowledge to mean acquaintance with truth, the literary symbol, equally uncertain, may seem a more suitable instrument. However, Yeats, an old man at the time, said: "Man can embody truth but he cannot know it." By "know" in this place he seems, like a rationalist, to mean apprehend by discursive reason, though we should expect a romantic poet to find the symbol a way to another kind of knowledge—intuitive (immediate apprehension without logical interference) or else emotional. For him, the symbol, embodying intuitive truth and feeling, might present something which, although imperfectly received, feels like knowledge. As a character puts it in a novel by Charles Williams: "I sometimes think the nearest we can get to meaning is to feel as if there was meaning." Virtual knowledge, addressed to our feelings, might be what the symbol carries. But "virtual" implies that true knowledge is scientific and so does the quotation from Yeats.

Before we accept that meaning of knowledge we should consult Cassirer, an enemy of "naive realism," to whom scientific knowledge is one of many kinds, each a symbolic form for showing what reality is like. The literary symbol, which presents knowledge of its own reality, may not communicate this knowledge, but by its form, which corresponds in quality to a nature of things, creates it. In so far as we apprehend the form we too are informed. The value of the symbol, if we accept this account of it, lies therefore in creating a vision of reality and submitting it to our apprehension. Not only creative but heuristic, it serves to discover the reality it shapes. Perhaps in view of the narrow sense of "knowledge" it would be better to speak of the literary symbol not as a way of knowing but of embodying awareness or of conceiving in the sense of becoming filled with or pregnant.

If feeling is part of conceiving, we must consider feeling, which may be of several kinds. Aside from that experienced and embodied by the author, feeling may be our reaction to the stimulus afforded by the embodiment, a sign for us, if we are sensitive and experienced, that something of value is there. But those who find fallacies congenial tell us that this is subjective and, except for indication of possible value, unreliable. In the second place, the feeling may be that embodied in the symbol and offered to us. This, as T. S. Eliot says in "Tradition and the Individual Talent," is objective, impersonal, and "significant." In the third place, the feeling may be what the embodiment creates. Equivalent to an apprehension of the feeling in the symbol, this is not so much a feeling of our own as an awareness, at once distant and sympathetic, of immanence—by a kind of empathy. If that is the case, contemplation of feeling rather than feeling itself marks our happiest encounter with these fictions.

As the feeling in the symbol is more important than our emotional response, so the symbol is more important than what it suggests. Lacking embodiment and the semblance of actuality, what it suggests turns back to its source to recapture a body and enlarge it. The symbol is not there like a sign to point to something else, to take the place of something else, or even to stand for it, but to display itself with all it has created and welcomed home. The trouble with Whitehead in this connection is that he thinks a symbol may be exchanged with what it symbolizes, as if the halves of the peculiar equation were of equal importance. This may be true of certain signs or of symbols that only convenience recommends, but it is far from true of literary symbols. Our concern, less with disembodied souls than with embodied ones, keeps our metaphysics warm—or, to call upon a more classical poem, the symbol haunts us with its body on.

Since his region is on the other side of logic, the critic of such embodiments has no rational way of proceeding from analysis of part and function to a judgment of the whole. If he feels that symbols offer something that analysis fails to guarantee, he must call upon intuition and feeling for help, not only the sudden intuition and feeling that accompany discovery of the object but the feeling that accompanies the apprehension of feeling in it. Analysis, justified by these feelings, may help to account for them: "I no sooner felt," says Coleridge in *Biographia Literaria*, "than I sought to understand." However impersonal the critic or the work itself, the criticism of literature is a transaction between an impersonal object and a person. However cold-blooded and objective the "exegetical inquirer" may pretend to be, he is a feeler; for we feel more than we think. If he is sensitive, feeling must attend and direct his analysis and assist his apprehension of feeling in the object. Maybe such feeling is another word for taste or for what Eliot calls sensibility. If, ignoring his commendation, we fear the subjective with all its horrors of irrelevance and eccentricity, we must try to endure our condition; and if, in this doubtful region, fearing the danger of obscurantism, we long for Euclid, we must recall that the symbol, occupying another region, does what discourse cannot do. The best equipment for a critic of symbolist literature may be what Keats called Negative Capability: "being in uncertainties, mysteries, doubts, without any irritable reaching after fact and reason," and "remaining content with half-knowledge."

The principal justification of the analyses which constitute the greater part of this essay is displaying the text and calling those parts to notice that might be missed by a more casual approach. Partly intended, moreover, to illustrate the kinds of symbol, my analyses are exemplary in that sense alone. Far from exhausting the texts or preventing further interpretation, they invite the reader's rivalry, and if his response is better than mine, pleased by having helped, I applaud. If, however, the reader protests that since texts embody the indefinite, his interpretations may be infinite, I reply that indefinite does not mean infinite and hasten to add that all interpretation, his or mine, is limited by what is there before us—by the symbol in its context, both immediate and more generally circumstantial. For the attempt, however vain, to find exactly what the text presents, analysis, which keeps it before us, seems as good a way as any, though not so all-sufficient as the austere prefer.

For vain attempts, whether austere or warmly moral, upon a haunting body, let us turn to critics of Moby Dick, that great yet exemplary symbol. In *The Enchafed Flood,* an investigation of "romantic iconography," W. H. Auden says: "A symbol is

felt to be such before any possible meaning is consciously recognized; i.e., an object or event which is felt to be more important than reason can immediately explain." This seems
almost unobjectionable, but, he continues: "A symbolic correspondence is never one to one but always multiple, and different
persons perceive different meanings." He illustrates this point by
stating what Moby Dick means to Starbuck, Ishmael, Ahab, and
the captains of other ships. Since each interpretation differs
from the others and each is thoroughly explicit, we must conclude that the meaning of the whale is both multiple and
definite. This seems Auden's own position; for although he
allows multiplicity of meaning, he inclines to allegory and sign,
and we are left with a series of clear equations. Not multiplicity
of definite meanings, however, but indefiniteness is the mark
of the symbol, a conclusion too obscurantist perhaps for Auden's
brilliant mind, a reasoning engine which, making signs of symbols, provides a fitting introduction to commentators who, like
Auden's mariners, are devoted to significance.

During the course of *Studies in Classic American Literature*
D. H. Lawrence comes to Moby Dick: "Of course he is a symbol.
Of what? I doubt if even Melville knew exactly. That's the best
of it." Later on, however, reproving Melville for a transcenden-
talism unlike his own, and refusing to accept the story as "a
voyage of the soul," Lawrence prefers to take it literally as a
"sea yarn." That is a good beginning: the whale is a whale—but
he also seems more than whale, and Lawrence, unable to resist,
leaves the literal story he has been enjoying for a definite interpretation in the light of his philosophy: "What then is Moby
Dick?—he is the deepest blood-being of the white race. . . .
And he is hunted . . . by the maniacal fanaticism of our white
mental consciousness." If we contemplate the image of the
whale, we must admit that it embodies sexual suggestions. That
it presents the phallic being endangered by the mind is possible,
but it seems illiberal to exclude possibilities which are as plainly
embodied. Each of us, carrying his own baggage to the symbol,
admires what he has brought without care for what the pile
obscures. The symbol seems to invite this undertaking; and our
excuse must be that we find it hard to endure the indefinite.

The mediaeval bestiary includes the whale. In the first part
of the verses devoted to that "fish," he is described, and in the

second his significance is defined. This emblematic habit of mind, persisting to our day, limits or disembodies Moby Dick, who, becoming a mirror for critics, "represents" or "signifies" their anthropological, political, sociological, or psychological concerns. Almost as if he had such critics in mind, Melville includes the following quotation in his prefatory extracts: " 'My God! Mr. Chace, what is the matter?' I answered, 'We have been stove by a whale.' "

Although William Ellery Sedgwick calls the whale an "emblem" of the mystery of creation, he refuses to make definite equations of symbols: "No statement as to their meaning can convey how vital, how meaningful these symbols are. Separately and in relation to each other [the whale, Ahab, and the sea] will not be held to any final definition or any fixed subject-object relationship." Interrelated yet unlimited, he continues, they baffle the intellect. Charles Feidelson, who agrees that the symbol is supralogical, finds *Moby Dick* a philosophical quest. Seeking vision through images of whale and sea, the voyaging mind approaches Emersonian knowledge of reality. Although Newton Arvin confuses Melville with himself at times and parodies Dante at others, the literal, Freudian, moral, and mythical meanings of his whale fail, as he says, to exhaust it. For other men other whales.

Not entirely aware, perhaps, of what he was composing, Melville was conscious enough to include passages which serve not only as elements of his book but apparently as clues to how we are to take it and how not. At the Spouter Inn, for example, Ishmael confronts a painting "so thoroughly besmoked, and every way defaced, that in the unequal cross-lights by which you viewed it, it was only by diligent study and a series of systematic visits to it, and careful inquiry of the neighbors, that you could any way arrive at an understanding" of "such unaccountable masses of shades and shadows." Contemplating this obscure and marvelous object, he is puzzled yet compelled by its "indefinite sublimity" to try to find what it is. "Ever and anon a bright, but, alas, deceptive idea would dart you through.—It's the Black Sea in a midnight gale.—It's a blasted heath.—It's a Hyperborean winter scene.—It's the breaking-up of the ice-bound stream of time. But at last all these fancies yielded to that one portentous something in the picture's midst." His "theory," tentative and based in part upon the opinions of many aged persons, is that the portentous something in the middle is a whale. This painting is plainly an analogy for the book. Ishmael's compulsive attempt at explanation corresponds to the predicament and endeavor of reader, critic, and maybe the author. It is worth noting that Ishmael, content at last with discovering the image, stops short of its significance—though his preliminary speculations about it are better than those of most critics.

A little later Father Mapple finds a definite lesson in the story of Jonah and the whale. That this, however, is not how to take the story of Ahab and the whale is suggested by the Ecuadorian doubloon, nailed by Ahab to the mast as an incentive to the discovery of Moby Dick. This golden coin from the center of the earth, richly stamped with a design of three mountains, a tower, a flame, a cock, and half the zodiac, revered by the mariners as the White Whale's talisman, invites interpretation. In "some monomaniac way" Ahab finds these strange figures significant; for as they say in Emersonian Concord, "some certain significance lurks in all things, else all things are little worth, and the round world itself but an empty cipher, except to sell by the cartload, as they do hills about Boston, to fill up some morass in the Milky Way." Not only monomaniac but egocentric, Ahab sees the coin as an image of himself and the world, which "to each and every man in turn but mirrors back his own mysterious self." Healthier but allegorical, Starbuck sees the sun as God, the valleys as our life, and the three mountains, "in some faint earthly symbol," as the Trinity. Stubb, fixing upon the zodiac, thinks of Bowditch and the cycle of life. Flask sees the coin as money for cigars: "There's another rendering now; but still one text." Only feeble-minded Pip, a critic of critics, makes an admirable comment: "I look, you look, he looks; we look, ye look, they look." We are left with the object and lookers at it; but whether monomaniac, eccentric, or practical, these lookers are mistaken. Far from being a clue to the interpretation of the book, as some critics have taken it, this episode of the doubloon shows how not to interpret *Moby Dick* or any other symbolic form.

The chapter on the whiteness of the whale seems more exemplary. "What the White Whale was to Ahab, has been hinted," says Ishmael. "What, at times, he was to me, as yet

remains unsaid." Taking a quality for the whole, he finds whiteness ambivalent, full of warring contraries, and universal. A
"vague, nameless horror" on the one hand, it serves on the other
to "symbolize whatever grand or gracious thing." Few are "entirely conscious" of the effect of whiteness in either of its aspects.
Even Ishmael, who is conscious enough, finds the meaning of
whiteness so "well nigh ineffable" that he almost despairs of
putting it into "a comprehensible form"; and "to analyse it
would seem impossible." By analogy and example, calling upon
white towers, white mountains, and white seas, he suggests "the
nameless things of which the mystic sign gives forth such hints."
Is it "a dumb blankness, full of meaning?" he asks. "Is it that
by its indefiniteness it shadows forth the heartless voids and
immensities of the universe?" After such questions, analogies,
examples, and contradictions which build up the feeling and
idea of indefiniteness, he concludes: "And of all these things
the Albino Whale was the symbol."

Let us see how that symbol is composed. By description Melville presents the whale's indifference, its ferocity, and its "uncommon bulk." By the action and the nature of the sea, the ship,
and the quest he improves the whale's solidity and complicates
his import. "The overwhelming idea of the great whale himself" is further qualified by the thoughts of those in quest of
him: Ahab's idea of him as the "incarnation" of all evil and
Ishmael's idea of him as a thing of the "wonder-world," a
"grand hooded phantom" which, midmost in the "endless pro-
cessions of the whale" that floated through his soul, seemed "a
snow hill in the air." From discursive chapters on the whale's
anatomy, the history of whaling, the process of trying whales
out, and the like, the image acquires greater body and depth—
as Somerset Maugham, omitting these elements from his edition, failed to see. "Taken with context," however, as Father
Mapple observes, "this is full of meaning." His observation,
which refers to an incident of Jonah's life, may be taken as a
reference to Melville's whale; for the monster, like Dr. Eckleburg's eyes, is made by an interaction of image and context.

Melville's success in shaping them to embody his vision of
reality is proved by the variety of critical interpretation. Working within the limits of his fixation or his gift, each critic takes
an aspect or two of Melville's vision as the whole, and each is
more or less justified by parts of image or context. Those who

are fitted to find sociological or political significance are encouraged by the emblematic ending of the book. Those who are devoted to Freud find evidence in Ahab's missing leg. Those who prefer the metaphysical find ample corroboration everywhere. But that whale in context is more than a thing to a man. All things in heaven and earth, unassigned and indefinite, he embodies our feeling and thought when face to face with ourselves and with what surrounds us.

To every dog his patch; but what of the undogmatic critic? If, preferring the whale to the part, he finds the image a general vision of reality, inexpressible save by itself, he incurs the danger of monotony; for the same thing might be said of *Ulysses, The Trial,* or "Bateau ivre." But, however general, each symbol is particular in feeling and quality, and the critic, without trying to define the indefinable, may suggest its singularity. By analysis of image and context he may reveal the shape of the image, the relation of part to part and to the whole, and the function of each part. For aid he may consult the author's intention, if he can, and the circumstances of time and place. Anything goes as long as, decently skeptical of all else, we remember that the text is the thing and that the symbol, an apparent object, is the object. Contemplating that appearance, we may find it becoming what Wallace Stevens calls a "transparence," but if, like Ahab and his critics, we find it becoming a mirror, we must look again.

URSULA BRUMM

SYMBOLISM AND THE NOVEL

We live in the age of symbolism in literature. But we accept the fact calmly, if with no particular enthusiasm. For symbolism makes no burdensome demands on us; it exacts neither tragic

From Partisan Review, *XXV (1958). Reprinted by permission of* Partisan Review *and the author,* © *1958 by* Partisan Review.

participation nor the effort of precise reflection, above all it entails no decision for or against anything. Indeed we are scarcely conscious of its ascendency. Symbolism has pervaded poetry long enough for us to be perfectly accustomed to it. Its conquest of the novel and the drama has been gradual and unobtrusive. And in both these fields its ascendency has for the most part been discreetly camouflaged under a deliberate show of realism. The triumph of symbolism as a habit of thought is most strikingly evidenced by the considerable number of critics who, in their enthusiasm for symbols, more and more unqualifiedly equate literature with symbolism. The symbol has come to be the major criterion of literary value. "Since symbolism is the necessary condition of literature, all novels are symbolic," says William York Tindall in his *The Literary Symbol* (1955). So far as I am aware, this flat statement and others similarly dogmatic have not so far aroused objections except from Philip Rahv in his essay "Fiction and the Criticism of Fiction" (*Kenyon Review*, Spring 1956). To support his thesis Tindall adduces a number of modern novels (by Henry Green, Virginia Woolf, and James Joyce), the symbolic elements in which he merely assembles and presents without critical evaluation. To go symbol hunting in the novel is a highly popular sport these days. If a novel contains symbols that you can pick out like raisins from a bun, it can claim to be literature.

The purpose of this essay is to examine the nature and function of symbols in the novel. Lyric poetry, which is governed by wholly different laws, lies outside the scope of the discussion. Our aim is to define, as exactly as possible, the role played by symbols in prose literature. This is no simple task, for both symbol and novel are essentially collective concepts, which respectively lump together the most diverse varieties of symbolism and narrative fiction. Precision, perhaps even extreme simplification in statement, can alone shed light on the very complex relations between novel and symbol, and I am well aware of the dangers inherent in this approach. I am also aware that finding even one critical flaw in the armor of symbolism is a sure way of making oneself unpopular these days.

Although the historical approach to any critical problem is now considered hopelessly outmoded, we do need the perspective of history, if only as a check against our private prejudices and currently accepted views. And in fact the historical test shows that the prevailing opinion cannot be right: Symbolism, in the specific sense developed by modern writers, is not the necessary condition of literature, nor are all novels symbolic. (For neither we nor the proponents of the dogma take it to mean every work of art is vaguely symbolic for the simple reason that it represents life.) The great nineteenth-century novel is not the product of an imagination working in symbolic forms. It is a representation of life, but not a symbolic representation. Stendhal, Balzac, Tolstoy, to mention only the greatest, did without symbols in the specific sense; for many good reasons, there is no room for the symbol in their works. This most significant tradition of the novel is non-symbolic, or at least neutral in regard to the symbol.

In its origins the European novel, in contrast to the early American novel, is a child of the Age of Enlightenment and of historicism. The so-called realistic novel of the late eighteenth and early nineteenth centuries is empirical in both its attitudes and its technical procedures. It is realistic, not because it set out to produce an absolutely faithful re-creation of reality, but because it holds that only what actually is can furnish trustworthy data concerning our destiny as human beings. In this sense it is agnostic, sceptical, empirical, and secular. In his *The Rise of the Novel* (1957) Ian Watt has shown that the novels of Defoe, Fielding, and Richardson were born of the same *Zeitgeist* as the philosophies of Locke and Descartes. They are critical and unprejudiced studies of life as represented by memorable personages whose destiny is determined by their individual character, by their particular place in society, and by the times they lived in and the ideas prevalent in those times. (That our contemporary critics choose to regard these characters simply as the product of their social status is another prejudice that will not stand the historical test.) The same is true of the novels of Stendhal, Balzac, and Tolstoy. The particular classical form of the novel which they created and which has received the rather dubious designation of "realistic" (for simplicity's sake we shall use the term too) is in a certain sense anti-symbolic, for it is opposed to the entire class of elements to which the symbol belongs. The realistic novel owes its origin to rejecting the paradigms that had for centuries determined literary forms:

fable, legend, myth, and the traditional, typical stories and characters from the storehouse of world literature that were constantly being reworked (i.e., the "archetypes" that have become so popular again today). The realistic novel is against types, against the changeless decked out in varying guises, against the authority of the eternal and the accepted. It is concerned with the individual and idiosyncratic, that is, the particular in its particular circumstances, with reality as experienced by the individual as constituting the only genuine version of reality. The realistic novel is the purest embodiment in literature of the modern scientific sceptical approach (but how quickly the "modern" becomes old and passé!) for which only an observed and measured reality was valid as the raw material for cognition and creation. Only this kind of reality seemed reliable enough to serve the novelist as the basis for a portrayal of life. This attitude has little use for symbols, since a symbol always represents something that remains to be demonstrated, unless it has already been accepted on faith.

In its empiricism the classical novel was at one with historiography, which, just at this time, and setting out from similar intellectual principles, was tremendously enlarging its field of operations and its horizon. Like historiography, the novel proposed to investigate and depict the concrete and specific form of reality at a particular time in a particular place. Hence the historical element, and especially the element of contemporary history, has an important and indeed indispensable place in these novels. There is scarcely one of them that does not establish the historical period of the events within the first few pages. *"Le 15 mai 1796, le général Bonaparte fit son entrée dans Milan"*—so Stendahl begins *La Chartreuse de Parme*, and this event is the fulcrum in the life and destiny of Fabrizio del Dongo. But it is never the mythopoeic aspect of history which these writers seek out and emphasize; history is always referred to the individual. Even situations that invite mythopoeic treatment are passed over, and indeed, whatever illusion naturally attaches to such situations is consciously destroyed. Stendahl "disenchants" Napoleon's battles; Tolstoy "demythifies" the great fire of Moscow. He states emphatically that it was not set by the inhabitants to demonstrate their and Russia's spirit of resistance. It was no patriotic beacon and no symbol; the city was built of wood, and therefore was bound to go up in flames when the citizens left and enemy soldiers moved in. The exact empirical truth means more to Tolstoy than even the most apt symbolic interpretation. A symbolist would say that here the artist in Tolstoy was defeated by the historian. But the truth is that we here have a manifestation of the principle of the historical novel, which derives the meaning of events solely from experienced and duly established reality.

What are the principles of artistic creation in this kind of novel? The most important principle has to do with subject matter. Almost all of these novels were written for the sake of the great discovery of the age, the personality of the individual; it is this that shapes the novel. Julien Sorel, Fabrizio del Dongo, Balzac's many heroes, Pierre Bezukhov, Prince Andrey, and Anna Karenina are personalities of fascinating interest, and as such they justify the work of art. They are characteristic, but they are not typical. On the contrary, they are unique and incomparable, but they are so constructed that in them the problems of the human situation stand out with particular force. If it is the task of the novel to show how character, milieu, historical period, and the individual's relations to others shape his destiny, there can be no further question as to what principle governs the selection of subject matter. It must be the principle of a causality, not precisely demonstrable but accepted because factually present, between the external world and human actions, the same causality that in a wider context is also the concern of the historian. Certain elements in the specific circumstances shape the actions and destiny of the hero. Hence certain details of the circumstances are important; and so the novelist depicts them for the reader. Stendhal begins his *Le rouge et le noir* with a quite full description of the small and not especially interesting village of Verrières. Verrières is significant only with respect to Julien Sorel. It constitutes the particular reality into which he was born and which he tries to leave behind; in addition it is characteristic for petit-bourgeois life in provincial France at that particular time. Or take Ippolito Nievo's great novel of 1867, *Confessions of an Octogenarian*,[1] recently rediscovered in Italy, with its description of the picturesque but shabby castle of

[1] The original title of the posthumously published book was *Confessions of an Italian*.

Fratta, north of Venice, where the hero, a penniless relative of
the castellan, spent his youth toward the end of the eighteenth
century. Nievo depicts the dilapidated towers, the archaic cavern
of a kitchen, the incompetent administrative hierarchy, the inhabitants of the castle and their diversions.

Are these symbols? In the specific sense, they are not. They are
genuine components of empirical reality, taken into the novel as
such components and not because they have the capacity to be
images. But they are components in which the forces that shape
this empirical reality concentrate and become visible. From
this point of view they are seen to concretize the meaning sought
in reality. The castle of Fratta, though not the village of Verrières, comes close to being a symbol. It is in a certain sense "a
visible sign of something invisible," insofar as it is taken to express forces that remain partially invisible because they can only
be conceived in the abstract. The old castle, still managed in
accordance with feudal custom, is among other things also a
symbol of the superannuated and chaotic conditions prevailing
in Italy at the time. Or better, it is the concrete and particular
expression of the ideas and forces that shape the reality, and as
such it can assume the functions of a symbol. The outstanding
difference between such "realistic" symbols and the symbols
of modern literature is that, unlike the latter, the former are not
compact images that make a single strong sensual impression,
but are often extensive and not easily delimitable segments of
reality. In addition they are always genuine components of
reality, actually to be found in it (the true realist does not
manipulate reality to produce them); they are not indications
added by the author simply to make his meaning clear. This
difference already shows the difference between the realistic and
the symbolic novel. The former seeks meaning in actual experience and is content to be taught by it; the latter imposes a particular meaning on reality. Correspondingly, the symbol in the
realistic novel is always causally related to its meaning—the
symbol represents the hidden cause; whereas in the symbolic
novel it is a transcendent embodiment of the intended meaning:
for example, a lamb can stand for an innocent victim or a bird
with a broken wing for a frustrated longing.

Because the structure of the Italian states had degenerated in
the eighteenth century, life in Fratta had precisely these charac-

teristics, and hence the castle can also be seen as a symbol of conditions in Italy. In this case the symbolic function is a secondary, subordinate quality of the phenomena, their primary role remaining in their import as reality. This of course does not mean that the realistic novel excludes phenomena and images which the characters in the novel interpret metaphorically in relation to their own lives, as for example, when the defeated hero sees the gallows by the roadside as a symbol of his unsuccessful life. These and similar symbols are always subjective interpretations by the characters in the novel, not by the author. The realistic author wants to see the phenomena of this world in their objectivity, and he sees them in all their characteristic configuration and multiplicity, for their particular configuration is precisely what holds at least a partial meaning for him. In contrast, the symbolist boldly undertakes to reduce the multiplicity of phenomena to the level of signs. He dematerializes the world, and in so doing deindividualizes it, deprives it of specific characteristics. It is not an accident that modern symbolic novels grow shorter and shorter.

Since the realistic symbol is a direct reflection of the intended meaning, it has "expressionistic" potentialities, which, boldly conceived, lead directly to the Expressionist technique of the twentieth century. The symbolic novel, on the other hand, descends not from the realistic but from the romantic novel. To voice whatever meaning is intended, Expressionism renounces the empirical probability of events. Symbolism achieves the same end by renouncing the causal connection between meaning and image; it gives the image a transcendent meaning. The difference between the realistic and the transcendent symbol can be illustrated by a comparison. In *The Literary Symbol,* W. Y. Tindall cites only one example from the realm of the realistic novel. Referring to Tolstoy's *Anna Karenina,* he writes: "When Vronsky . . . rides his mare to death at the races, breaking her back by his awkwardness or zeal, his action, unnecessary to the plot and far from realistic, embodies his relationship with Anna." Here we have a situation, of rare occurrence in Tolstoy, where the author manipulates events in the interest of a symbolic foreshadowing. Yet the symbol remains realistic, for horse-racing, as every reader of the novel knows, is a natural element in the life of the Russian aristocracy. The animal that Vronsky kills clearly belongs in his world. Its death is brought about by his impetuosity and thoughtlessness. And in so far as these contribute to Anna's ruin, the episode can assume the functions of a symbol for the relationship between Anna and Vronsky. If we compare this to Henry James's golden bowl with its mysterious crack, which similarly serves as symbol for the relationship between two lovers, the difference is at once apparent. The bowl exists in the novel solely for the sake of its symbolic character, and by possessing this character it controls the structure of the plot. Tolstoy's symbol is a possible interpretation of a subordinate event which the reader can also take at its face value. But a reader who misses the meaning of James's golden bowl will miss the entire novel. Only in *The Golden Bowl* do we have symbolism in the full sense of the term—the symbol is image, expressing the meaning it is meant to convey in image and not in a causal nexus. For the strange way in which the bowl is found and bought at the no less strange art dealer's establishment after all bears merely a semblance of causal relation to the plot, a semblance that will not stand up under the slightest scrutiny. And between symbol and meaning, between the bowl and the relationship of the two lovers, there is no causal nexus at all but only a mysterious parallel. In addition, the bowl was not cracked by any of the characters in the novel. It is a motif outside the realm of reality, with magic powers. Its breaking releases magic effects which bring the two lovers together again.

I have called this kind of symbol "transcendent" because here an image embodies a meaning with which it has no direct connection. The golden bowl with its crack stands for little Maggie Verver's imperiled relationship to her princely husband. This kind of transcendent symbol is a belated manifestation of faith, a last faint reflection of religious convictions, a surviving vestige of magic amid the secularization of our world. For the transfer of meaning to the image does not arise, as in the case of the less pretentious metaphor, from a daring comparison. It stems from the world of faith, myth, legend, fairy tale, magic. It is a parallel, with magic as connecting link. In *The Golden Bowl* the fairy tale elements are clearly visible through the modern disguise. The beautiful daughter of the (dollar-King) father who is looking for a son-in-law; the motif of the wedding gift with the secret flaw or curse, which is rendered harmless by cleverness and persistence—these are age-old fairy tale situations, familiar in a thousand variations. There is even an interesting variation of the wicked stepmother motif. It is this world of fairy tale and myth to which the symbol traces its origin, and it has maintained the closest relationship with it down to this day. It is no coincidence that mythological and legendary motifs, which the early realistic novel would have rejected, appear today in the novel together with the symbol. How strong is the connection between modern symbolism and its mythological origins is apparent from Eliot's "Notes on The Waste Land." "Not only the title," Eliot writes, "but the plan and a good deal of the incidental symbolism of the poem were suggested by Miss Jessie L. Weston's book on the Grail legend, *From Ritual to Romance.*" As a further source Eliot mentions Frazier's *Golden Bough.* After all, meaning and image are not comparable in rational terms; the connection between them is metasensory.

Even when the symbolic novel does not make use of more or less disguised mythological material, it tends to draw its images from the realms of religion and myth. And this is not so simply because the most striking images are to be found in religion and myth but rather because it is only these realms that provide an authoritative interpretation of the symbol through the belief, or at least a memory of the belief, that genuinely links meaning and image. Symbols without such a mythological past are private inventions, and as such they cannot be counted on to affect our imagination. Virginia Woolf's lighthouse and Eliot's cocktails are feeble results of private symbol-making, as are the railway terminals and gas stations which have recently been so popular as symbols of man's homelessness. On the other hand, when Henry James uses not any random precious object with a crack in it his symbol, but a golden bowl, he establishes a connection with our memories of the sacred symbol of the Grail, which—and James alludes to this—traditionally expresses the sublime and supernatural meaning of human relations.

Symbolism, which has been considered "one of the most sophisticated movements in literary history," [2] still actually draws its basic sustenance from the faith of a magic-mythical past. The presuppositions for a symbolic literature in our time are two, an imagination hungry for images, and a vague idea that our lives

[2] Charles Feidelson, *Symbolism and American Literature,* 1953, p. 4.

are somehow determined by indefinable principles which operate outside the domain of cause and effect but which have a hidden meaning that manifests itself in external phenomena. This is more or less the credo at which modern man has arrived, and to it the symbolic novel addresses itself. Here lies the secret of its origin and its success. In our souls we are still, or once again, romantics, whether we like it or not. The basic tendency of symbolic literature is its orientation toward the intuited, intangible, indeterminate. To be a Christian is as out of fashion as to be an atheist; one is simply a symbolist, for that leaves all roads open and involves no commitment. "Indirection," "suggestion," and "allusion" are key words of symbolistic criticism and are used as positive criteria in literary appraisal. W. Y. Tindall defines the symbolic novel thus: "As tight and reflexive as poems, symbolist novels *insinuate* their meanings by a concert of elements. Images, *allusions, hints,* changes of rhythm, and tone—in short *all the devices of suggestion*—support and sometimes carry the principal burden" (italics minc). Here vagueness of content has become a criterion of value. It demands the counterbalancing effect of concise form, which hence has assumed such great importance today.

We have tried to reduce the innumerable variations of the symbol in the novel to its two major types: the cause-linked "realistic" symbol, and the transcendent or magic symbol of the poetic novel. Both are creatures of man's imagination in its quest for meaning, and in some of their variants they approach each other quite closely. Thus, for example, we find the realistic symbol for the sake of which reality has to be decidedly tampered with, and the transcendent symbol which is convincingly anchored in reality. Nevertheless, these two types of symbol are of different origin, and it would be false to assume that one has evolved from the other. That they have not is proved by the basically different mentalities expressed in their opposing attitudes toward reality.

How did the magic symbol enter the novel, the literary form which by its very nature is tied to reality? It is tempting to find the answer in the great influence and great prestige of symbolist poetry, especially that of the French symbolists. And in fact this is essentially true so far as the modern novel is concerned. But it is interesting to note that the lyrical symbolists in their turn found an influential model in the novel. I refer to Novalis's fragmentary poetic novels, especially his *Heinrich von Ofterdingen,* which centers around the "blue flower," the most famous symbol of German Romanticism. In the author's conception, *Heinrich von Ofterdingen* is a "poetic" and "romantic" novel, that is, a radically unrealistic novel which loftily and deliberately disregards all the conditions of real life. The medieval poet Heinrich von Ofterdingen roams the world searching for the meaning of nature and its laws, the meaning of love and poetry. The revelation of their meaning occurs, in typically romantic fashion, in the form of legend and fairy tale. Here we have a world completely dominated by the miraculous and the symbolic, with the "blue flower" functioning as a sort of symbol of symbols, representing the most secret meaning of the poet's art. This novel shuns the realities of human life to a degree that has scarcely been attempted since. Henry James's *Golden Bowl,* in which the symbol also has a dominant role, at least maintains the appearances of nineteenth-century reality, even if on closer scrutiny the timeless fairy tale elements show through.

The important role of the symbol in the American novel cannot, however, be adequately explained by models in European romanticism or by the influence of the French symbolists. Symbolism is a native American growth, which flourished in this country earlier and more vigorously than elsewhere. It draws its sustenance from the soil of Calvinism, a fact that again corroborates, in a different way, our observation concerning the ancestry of the symbol in the world of faith. American symbolism is a form of secularized and aestheticized Calvinism. Hawthorne's allegories, Emerson's principle that "every natural fact is a symbol of a spiritual fact," and Melville's scarcely maintained faith in the meaningfulness of the world—"some certain significance lurks in all things, else all things are of little worth and the round world itself but an empty cipher"—are steps in the progressive secularization of the Calvinist interpretation of the world, which in its turn is indebted to medieval typology and exegesis of the Scriptures. The Calvinist is a realist who accepts the facts of his world and does not try to alter them. He considers it his task to interpret them in the light of Biblical precedents, and to this end he contrives a structure of parallels between Biblical and secular events. Thus he distinguishes himself from other realists by his technique of interpretation, which is not secular and causal but transcendental, which is based on faith, and which establishes supra-sensory points of reference for all things earthly. From this it is only a step to the transcendent symbol, which also operates according to the system of an inner parallelism between meaning and phenomenon, but which has freed itself both from rigid dependence on reality and from the dogmatic bonds of the Calvinist faith. This emancipation was accomplished by the American Transcendentalists, abetted by the European romanticists and romantic philosophers with their faith in fairy tale and myth.

The religious basis of American symbolism was already noted by F. O. Matthiessen in his *American Renaissance,* and observed even more clearly by Yvor Winters. Winters recognized that the Calvinist tradition gave its particular stamp to American literature far into the nineteenth century. Winters's well known essay is an attack on romanticism, and this includes symbolism, though he does not specifically condemn it. Charles Feidelson, in his *Symbolism and American Literature,* has an interesting essay in which he too demonstrates the Calvinist ancestry of this American symbolism. He discusses the same authors as Winters, but his sympathies are decidedly symbolist. His claims for the services rendered by symbolism are of the broadest. "In the central work of Hawthorne, Whitman, Melville and Poe, symbolism is at once technique and theme. It is a governing principle; not a stylistic device, but a point of view." This is no longer literary criticism; as the tone of the passage shows, it is a literary manifesto. The particular *hybris* of the symbolist faith is apparent in the assumption that the symbol is to determine the perspective of the work of art, the "point of view," as Feidelson puts it. Yet Feidelson does see some of the problems inherent in symbolism: arbitrariness of interpretation, anti-rationalism, and, as the final consequence of the speculative nature of the image-symbol, "the possibility of the meaninglessness of meaning." He tries to meet these problems by improvising a philosophy of symbolism. Starting out from Cassirer, for whom poetry is still a world of illusion and fantasy, distinct from that of logical truth, Feidelson argues: "It is quite possible to take poetry as the norm and to regard logical statements as the fantasy; this indeed seems the more natural outcome of a philosophy which begins in a contrast between logical sign and creative symbol. . . . The symbolist . . . redefines the whole process of knowing and the status of reality in the light of poetic method. He tries to take both poles of perception into account at once, to view the subjective and objective worlds as functions of the forms of speeches in which they are rendered." Such a definition is no more than philosophical sleight-of-hand. It is a dialectically dressed up version of a faith whose principal dogma is obviously redemption by "poetic method," by "forms of speech," by style. The dyed-in-the-wool symbolists accepted this faith early; they are even now sacrificing at its altar.

For Melville's Moby Dick, which has both a real existence and a symbolic function, the Biblical-typological interpretation is still partly determinative. For Henry James and his generation the images of the Calvinistic typology have grown pale, and a purely aesthetic motivation replaces the religious one. In Stephen Crane's colorful imagery we see a last reflection of religious symbolism— "the red sun was pasted in the sky like a wafer"—but here, as Philip Rahv has pointed out, it assumes a purely decorative function. Here we have the beginning of the aesthetic playing with symbols as images and embodiments of meaning, a typical trap for overzealous critics who try to ascribe a profoundly symbolic value to every image used. It is interesting to note that in other literatures, too, symbolism begins to flourish just at the moment when the religious symbols that had earlier dominated imagination lose their dogmatic hold. James Joyce's *A Portrait of the Artist as a Young Man* derives its dense symbolic structure from the aesthetic use of religious symbols, a technique which in this case is justified and even necessitated by the subject matter, for the hero's road leads from the Church to art. His constant practice of reinterpreting the religious symbols of his childhood in secular terms gives the reader convincing insight into his state of mind.

Symbolism becomes questionable when themes concerning modern man and his dilemma in a world full of facts and problems are represented in novels composed in the technique of all-dominating symbolism. The result is a discrepancy between theme and technique, for the symbolist has neither sympathy nor patience with the nature of facts and their consequences for man. Writers like Truman Capote, Frederick Buechner, or Jean

Stafford escape the dangers of this discrepancy by sublimating contemporary history into a personal essence, depriving it of almost any import. At best they can show contemporary problems as reflected in a mentality which takes refuge in symbols. The case is different with symbolists like Paul Bowles and Malcolm Lowry. In such novels as *The Sheltering Sky* or *Under the Volcano* these writers attempt to use the technique of symbolism in portraying the destiny of politically conscious characters thoroughly aware of contemporary events. Their theme is the failure and final disintegration of the highly civilized mentality of Europeans or Americans; but they do not attempt to evolve their symbols from the reality that is inseparable from the theme; instead, they prefer to take them from some colorful exotic setting. Or rather, they make the entire exotic setting a symbol for the mental state of their heroes. In consequence, they have to transport their heroes to the exotic setting where image-symbols adequate to their problems flourish, to North Africa or to Mexico. But this procedure results not only in negating the causal connection between symbol and meaning, it actually inverts their relationship. Since the image-symbols of disintegration are to be found only in exotic countries, these unfortunate occidentals have to go where they can perish both in reality and symbolically, but under circumstances that bring about their downfall only in the transcendent meaning of the symbol and exclude the realm of causality. The true causes remain unrepresented, just as the world that formed these characters is pushed aside with the symbolist's typical disregard for the factual and characteristic.

Contrary to the widely held opinion, this marks not the high point but the dead end of symbolic fiction. For the sober medium of prose remains bound to the solidity of the world of realities. Its most significant subject matter is man as a spiritual being conditioned by material reality. Dismissing this objective in favor of pure subjectivity is something that only lyric poetry can risk with impunity. Conrad's colonials who perish in the tropics follow their profession—making money—and their greed, and suffer the fate they themselves have thereby challenged. But Bowles's and Lowry's heroes drift without will or desire, like lost children, in exotic places that have every appearance of being under the spell of a wicked witch, so deceitful, malicious, and inexplicable is everything that happens there. These novels are fairy tales of evil. Here excessive speculation over meanings has not only robbed the world of reality, but emptied it of meaning.

Much more to the point, even if less spectacular than the oppressive symbolism of these novels, is for example Saul Bellow's comparable story, "Seize the Day." Its literary technique holds to the theme and evolves its images from the theme.

It may be suggested that many young writers today are influenced more than is good for either them or their work by critics who have swallowed symbolism whole and who nourish their enthusiasm by providing symbolic interpretations of all past and present literature without any sense of differences in style. This results in a vicious circle of criticism and creative literature. The natural relationship between the two is reversed and writers are made to go to school to critics. In this way criticism acquires a concealed power to lay down laws and determine the future. No such power rightfully belongs to it. Let us maintain the separation of powers in literature too. Let the critics be content with their judicial functions and let them keep their hands off legislation.

(*Translated from the German by Willard R. Trask*)

9

LIFE AND ART

A departure from the preceding sections in its inclusions, the last section, which follows, is intended first to simplify, second to complicate. The first selection, by Robert Scholes and Robert Kellogg, takes certain aesthetic theories out of the position in which they seem to be irreconciliably opposed to each other, placing them instead in a continuum of possible theories. A fair amount of unnecessary argument can be saved simply by following Scholes and Kellogg to their conclusion that different aesthetic formulas are appropriate to different kinds of fiction. The selections from the novelists, however, a group of classic statements on the relation between experience at large and art, have the opposite effect. That is, they present that relation as being so intensely personal a problem for each individual novelist that the question of life and art seems, as it should, the largest and most elusive question of all.

Lying behind Scholes' and Kellogg's argument are two basic and opposed ways of approaching the problem of life and art. The first position takes art, including the art of fiction, to be a made thing, subject to its own laws, answerable only to the imagination of the artist, autotelic or having no purpose beyond its own existence, a self-contained, self-sufficient formal complex. It is the position implied in MacLeish's famous line, "A poem should not mean but be." It is also the position one is likely to come to when approaching fiction from general aesthetics. One does not ask, after all, except in the most indirect of ways, what the relation between a Greek amphora or a painting by Mondrian and experience at large might be. The opposite position takes art to be, in Arnold's phrase, a criticism of life, a position which implies that art is answerable to experience and, far from being its own purpose, an active force in the life of its culture. From this point of view, a novel concerned, say, with the Spanish Civil War is responsible not only to the artistic conscience of the author, not only to human nature, but to history and to politics. As long as both positions are held by their proponents in an exclusive way, an impasse is, of course, inevitable. What Scholes and Kellogg do is to replace the either/or with a both/and, insisting that different kinds of fiction stand in different relations to experience, that some kinds of fiction come remarkably close to pure pattern, some remarkably close to history, that some fiction refers only to aspects abstracted from experience while other fiction seeks a more-or-less direct imitation.

What is likely to be most striking in the responses of the novelists to the problem of life and art is first the large variety of tones which the novelists take, from fervent to earnestly analytical to casual to flippant. Second, one is likely to be forcibly reminded of the number of dimensions which the problem of life and art really has. As the selections indicate, the problem embraces the biographical events and the temperament of the novelist's life in their relation to his art, the subjective nature of perceived experience, the conventions of art and the expectations of the audience, the obligations of the author to empirical reality and his freedom to invent, the way in which his vision of experience is likely to differ from that of the philosopher, the historian, or the common reader. In this particular collection, Joyce has the last word. But it is a subject toward which no novelist's response is identical with any other's and one in which there are no last words.

ROBERT SCHOLES AND ROBERT KELLOGG

THE PROBLEM OF REALITY
ILLUSTRATION AND REPRESENTATION

Meaning, in a work of narrative art, is a function of the relationship between two worlds: the fictional world created by the author and the "real" world, the apprehendable universe. When we say we "understand" a narrative we mean that we have found a satisfactory relationship or set of relationships between these two worlds. In some narratives the author tries to control the reader's response more fully than in others. The most extreme attempts at this sort of control we recognize as allegory and satire, and because of the special problems raised by them, we have devoted the second part of this chapter to a discussion of the nature and history of attempts to control meaning. But for the moment we are concerned with more fundamental problems, the first of which must be the relationship between the actual worlds of the author and the reader.

In an oral culture this problem does not exist. Singer and listeners share the same world and see it in the same way. Those elements in a traditional tale which in the course of time might become irrelevant or confusing to the singers and their audiences are, in the course of time, eliminated or accommodated to the new ways; and, conversely, the oral tales themselves act as a conservative element in a culture, tending to curb new ways of living or of perceiving the cosmos. In a culture of written letters, however, such as our Western civilization has become, a fixed text will tend to survive its native milieu and be forced to make its way in alien surroundings. Not only will its language become archaic and obsolete, but the assumptions about man and nature and about the proper way to tell a story, upon which the tale is built, will also recede farther and farther from the assumptions of living men.

To understand a literary work, then, we must first attempt to bring our own view of reality into as close an alignment as possible with the prevailing view in the time of the work's composition. Even a contemporary work, if it springs from a milieu or a mind quite alien to the reader's, must be approached by him with a special effort if he wants to understand its meaning rather than merely to see what he can make it mean. Thus, the approach of a modern reader to a work from an alien milieu, ancient or modern, must depend to some extent upon historical scholarship or what used to be called "learning." This learning should be used for the sake of the literary work—not the other way round —and it should be used imaginatively, in order to bring the world of the reader and the author into as close an alignment as possible before confronting that ultimate mediator between them —the literary work itself.

This problem of the alignment of "real" worlds can be solved by the imaginative use of learning. A much more complicated problem, however, and one less easily resolved, is the nature of the relationship between the author's fictional world and his real world. This is a creative problem for the author, and it is a critical problem for the reader. It is the very problem upon which much criticism of narrative literature founders. We can best approach it by schematizing the possible kinds of relationship between these two worlds in what may seem at first to be an overneat and oversimple way. To begin with, not all narrative works are seriously concerned with meaning at all. There are different, and significant, ways in which this unconcern with meaning can manifest itself, but they are best understood after an attempt to confront those works which definitely do aspire not merely to "be" but to "mean" as well. Works which aspire to meaning do not all seek to create or convey their meanings in the same way. They adopt a variety of ways which are intimately connected to the varieties of narrative form themselves, and can be seen as presenting a similar spectrum of possibilities shading into one another. The connection between the fictional world and the real can be either *representational* or *illustrative*. The images in a narrative may strike us at once as an attempt to create a replica of actuality just as the images in certain paintings or works of sculpture may, or they may strike us as an attempt merely to remind us of an aspect of reality rather than convey a total and convincing impression of the real world to us, as certain kinds of visual art also do. That kind of art, literary or plastic, which seeks to duplicate reality we will designate by the word "represent" in its various forms. For that kind of art which seeks only to suggest an aspect of reality we will use the word "illustrate." In art the illustrative is stylized and stipulative, highly dependent on artistic tradition and convention, like much oriental painting and sculpture, while the representational seeks continually to reshape and revitalize ways of apprehending the actual, subjecting convention to an empirical review of its validity as a means of reproducing reality. The illustrative is symbolic; the representational is mimetic. In the visual arts illustration ranges between almost pure meaning—the ideogram or hieroglyph—and almost pure pleasure—the non-representational design. It is tied to ends, not means. But the representational is tied to the means of reproduction and varies as new ways of seeing or new artistic techniques of reproducing are discovered.

We can approach a painting in terms of its design and try to see it in a purely esthetic way. When we do this we are deliberately removing it from the area of meaning, even though we may recognize in the shapes on the canvas suggestions of actual shapes and things. Literature can never become quite so "pure," but the highly patterned and virtually meaningless configurations of the romance of adventure are a near equivalent. We can also approach a painting in terms of its symbolic meaning, interpreting the forms according to a system of stipulated meanings from traditional or other sources. This is an iconographical way of "understanding," whether the iconography be Augustinian or Freudian. Interpretation of purely illustrative literary works must be analogous to the iconographical approach to works in the plastic arts. We can also approach a painting in terms of its mimetic meaning, attempting to read the character of persons depicted and to comprehend the milieu in which we find them—an approach we are most likely to employ with portraits or other historically oriented artworks. Here, we are on the verge of considering the painter as psychologist or sociologist, an approach considered at best unfashionable as a mode of art criticism today, but quite the way in which the young James Joyce approached the canvases of Munkácsy or the mature Tolstoy represented the visual artist in the Italian chapters of *Anna Karenina*.

Western painting and Western literature have both distinguished themselves from much of the world's art by the extent to which they have emphasized the mimetic or representational potential of their forms; and the high tide of realism in both arts seems to have been reached in the later nineteenth century and then begun to recede, the plastic arts since carrying the nonrepresentational to an extent which literature will hardly be likely to match. Realism has proved so powerful an agent in narrative art that its influence may never wholly disappear; literary artists may never recapture totally the innocence of pre-novelistic romance. It has even been possible for one of the most formidable and influential attempts to see Western narrative whole—Auerbach's *Mimesis*—to consider the subject purely in terms of the development of realism. Still, in our consideration of meaning in narrative literature, we must be prepared to come to grips with the illustrative way of meaning as well as the representational, and especially, we must be prepared to note the way in which these different kinds of meaning combine and interact with esthetic design in the greatest of our narrative works.

Representational narrative can carry specific meaning, referring to actual individuals and events. History, biography, and autobiography do just this. Illustrative reference can also be specific, as it is in the historical allegory of Book V of *The Faerie Queene* or Part I of *Gulliver's Travels*. But both history proper and historical allegory seek continually for higher and more generalized meanings. The diarist or chronicler may simply record specific data, but the autobiographer or historian seeks a pattern which drives him in the direction of generalization. His story will become generalized to the extent that he discovers a pattern in it, and he may by direct commentary on the action he narrates or through a device like Plutarch's parallel Lives make his individual characters into types. The historical allegorizer has already generalized his subject in the establishment of an illustrative connection betwen fiction and reality, the link betwen fact and fiction being an aspect of general resemblance. Swift's Flimnap resembles the actual Walpoe mainly through a generalized concept of political dexterity symbolized by the fictional character's capers on the tightrope. The specific reference of figures in historical allegory is invariably accompanied by a generalized reference as well.

In representational narrative the notion of specific connection between the "real" world and the world of the story seems to precede the notion of a more generalized mimetic connection. From diarist and historian the narrative artists learn to present a world of apparent specificity, the world of mimetic fiction. Robinson Crusoe is not a real individual but he is an attempt to present an individual whose most important attribute is that he may pass for real. This kind of specific though not factual mimetic presentation shades into a more generalized kind of mimesis dominated by the notion of the typical rather than the notion of the apparently factual. Robinson Crusoe is a type of the middle class man and may be seen as such, but he is not so typical a character as Fielding's Squire Western, for example, in whom potential individuality has been suppressed for the sake of the typical. Fielding, in fact, locates his justification of this new kind of historical or biographical fiction precisely in its function as a way of presenting generalized human types, thus asserting its superiority to so-called history and biography, which present specific lies rather than general truth. Fielding's preference for the general (which he shares with Aristotle) makes him an intellectualizer, a didactic writer. The didactic assumes importance in narrative art whenever that art seeks a generalized connection with the real world.

We have been considering the connection between real and fictional worlds as a spectrum dominated by three hues—the recording of specific fact, the representation of what resembles specific fact, and the representation of generalized types of actuality. With the fourth hue of this spectrum these shaded differences in degree become so marked as to require a difference in terminology. The differences in degree have become a difference in kind. The ways of linking the two worlds which we have just enumerated are all "empirical": they are three different ways of "representing" reality. Confronted with a character in one of these fictional worlds we are justified in asking questions about his motivation based on our knowledge of the ways in which real people are motivated. Though Squire Western is not "realistic" in the same sense that Robinson Crusoe is, or Clarissa Harlowe is, he derives his justification and his meaning from his "realness," his representative quality. When Dr. Johnson defended Shakespearian characterization against the accusation of impropriety, he observed that "there is always an appeal open from art to life." In this, as in other formulations, Johnson is of great use to us because his observation marks an important watershed in critical assumptions about the relationship between the real and fictional worlds. It is of the essence of that century in which the novel came into its own that art should be seen as a representation rather than an illustration of life, that it should be seen empirically and judged so, that criticism should abandon the tottering edifice of rules and decorum and rush into marshy ground after the *ignis fatuus* we have learned to call "realism." In the twentieth century we should be able to avoid critical impetuosity and see the representational and the illustrative as simply two solutions to the essentially unsolvable problem of putting life into art, of reconciling truth and beauty.

Illustration differs from representation in narrative art in that it does not seek to reproduce actuality but to present selected aspects of the actual, essences referable for their meaning not to historical, psychological, or sociological truth but to ethical and metaphysical truth. Illustrative characters are concepts in anthropoid shape or fragments of the human psyche masquerading as whole human beings. Thus we are not called upon to understand their motivation as if they were whole human beings but to understand the principles they illustrate through their actions in a narrative framework. An example or two may help to reinforce the distinction: a Theophrastian characterization of a miserly man would be a highly generalized mimetic type; Moliére's Miser a somewhat more specifically rendered human being; Balzac's Old Grandet a highly individualized personality. All three are "representational," intended as literary reproductions of a type of man which can (or could) be apprehended empirically in life and presented in literature according to psychological or sociological principles. But Spenser's Mammon in Book II of *The Faerie Queene* is the essence of acquisitiveness itself, given a temporary shape as a character in a narrative framework. He is illustrative. Milton's Mammon, on the other hand, though he shares many of the traditional illustrative qualities of Spenser's allegorical figure, especially as he is presented in Book I of *Paradise Lost,* emerges after his speech in the Great Consult of Book II as more representational than illustrative. His characteristics are derived, principally, from Milton's personal feeling about the nature of a mind dominated by things, rather than from literary or theological tradition, even though this Mammon is not placed in the sort of representational milieu which would enable us to recognize him immediately as a "realistic" figure. To understand properly what Milton is doing with a characterization such as Mammon we must be aware of the difference between illustrative and representational characterization, and to give Spenser his proper due as a narrative artist we must realize that he has something in mind very different from Milton's quite representational kind of characterization.

There are of course some narrative works which gain many of their effects precisely by straddling this precipitous border between the illustrative and the representational. The tales and romances of Hawthorne are a case in point. To some critics it seems evident that these stories should be read symbolically or allegorically; to others it seems equally clear that the meaning of Hawthorne's fiction lies in an understanding of the psychology which motivates his characters. Obviously, both critical approaches depend on an assumption about the nature of the work, an assumption which ought itself to be examined closely in the context of each narrative. It is highly likely that Hawthorne himself never settled consistently into a posture of either representation or illustration, and that the power and intellectual complexity of his fiction is derived from an intricate process of oscillation between these two ways of creating a simulacrum of the real world. A proper understanding of Hawthorne, then, must be based on a grasp of the way in which this oscillation operated in his performance of the creative task.

Much of the more interesting literary characterization can be seen as deriving from the instinct or desire of narrative artists to work on both sides of the gap we have postulated, to make their characters at once representative and illustrative. But this instinct or desire takes a different form in different writers, depending partly on the extent to which the writer is conscious of his technique. One suspects that Hawthorne may have operated more instinctively than deliberately, and one feels even more strongly that his method, instinctive or not, is to blur rather than to bridge, to fuse rather than to juxtapose, to present not a work that can be read on several levels but a work that must be read between two levels. A critic considering this aspect of Hawthorne might build a favorable value judgment into his criticism by referring this phenomenon to Hawthorne's "unified sensibility," or he might equally allow his terminology to masquerade as judgment by calling this a "fuzziness" of focus. We must avoid invidious distinctions arrived at through question-begging terminology, but it may help to clarify the way in which Hawthorne deals with the gap between the illustrative and the representational if we consider some other great narrative artists who have clearly confronted the problem of this gap in ways quite different from Hawthorne.

James Joyce grew up as a narrative artist in a tradition dominated by realistic and naturalistic theory and practice, in which the representation of slices of "real life" could be seen as the true end of narrative literature. His earliest narrative efforts, *Dubliners* and *Stephen Hero*, are clearly efforts in this tradition. Gradually he grew more and more impatient with the limitations of realism and shaped his art accordingly. We can even catch him in revisions of *Dubliners* actually "putting in symbols" so as to lift the stories from their flat naturalistic level, and we can see that the later stories in that collection become more and more concerned with symbolic richness. The very titles of his works, from *Dubliners* and *A Portrait* to *Ulysses* and *Finnegans Wake*, reveal a shift from the representational to the illustrative as the dominant mode of Joyce's thought. From the beginning Joyce was aware of the division between the realistic and the symbolic —it had been one of the great literary battlegrounds of the *fin de siècle*—and his determination as a narrative artist became more and more clearly to bridge the gap between these two modes of narrative with as wide a bridge as possible, hanging on to the naturalistic and representational with stark intensity but insisting on a scheme of correspondences that made the petty objects and creatures of his literary foreground illustrative of heroic and universal types and principles. We can take Molly Bloom as an example—a representational portrait, psychologically sound enough to astonish Jung with its validity and profoundness, but also clearly and deliberately connected to the nymph Calypso and the wife Penelope of literary tradition, and to the *gea tellus* of primitive myth and the general principles of earthiness and undiscriminating fecundity which Molly illustrates through her highly "realistic" stream of thoughts and sensations. The deliberate nature of Joyce's bridge between the illustrative and the representational, and the width of the gap he has chosen to span, is in sharp contrast with Hawthorne's instinctive blurring of this gap. Proceeding in this manner we could formulate quite explicitly the reasons why Joyce and Mann, for example, can be properly treated as members of one narrative school, while Hawthorne and Melville belong to another.

* * *

The interaction between illustration and representation in the fictional world is but one aspect of the complexity of meaning in narrative literature. We can see in the representational a further division between the psychological and the sociological. Most representational meaning in narrative lies in that area contested by the individual and society. Some novelists are more concerned with social portraiture, others with psychological, but representational values must be seen both psychologically and sociologically. They are the product of the novelist's concern for the identity of the individual and the welfare of society. Similarly, we can see the illustrative as varying radically depending on whether its symbols are orthodox and traditional or heterodox and personal. In Western narrative not only has the representational tended to displace or dominate the illustrative; the heterodox or personal symbol system has also tended to replace the orthodox. Even when traditional symbols are employed by a modern narrative artist, they are frequently employed in non-traditional and unorthodox ways. For a writer like James Joyce, symbolic reference to Freud, Frazer, de Sade, and Masoch is placed on a par with reference to Catholic liturgy or theology—the "Holy Office" is both a priestly function and a puberty rite. And for a writer like D. H. Lawrence it is quite natural to create a symbol system drawn primarily from a combination of Freud and the Book of Revelation, the relative dominance of the two being reflected in the titles of his two main symbolic essays—*The Fantasia of the Unconscious* and *The Apocalypse.*

Another significant aspect of meaning in narrative, which we have barely considered thus far, depends upon a connection between the fictional and real worlds so tenuous as to be almost a denial of connection. In some fictions the apparent humanity of the characters and the apparent reference of some of the events to possible human events are not meaningful in any sense, they merely exist so as to engage the interest of the reader in fictional happenings. In pure romance the characters do not represent real individuals or types, nor do they illustrate essences or concepts. They merely borrow human shapes or human characteristics because these have become in most Western fiction a necessary minimum of narrative equipment. This kind of fiction is as close as literature can come to the non-representational in art. Such "meaningless" narratives employ "esthetic" types which short-circuit meaning by keeping its referential potential within the context of the narrative. Villains, heroes, heroines: these are esthetic types which operate strongly on the reader's emotions but with virtually no meaningful impact. In *Tom Jones* Mr. Blifil (the villain) and Sophia Western (the heroine) are virtually pure esthetic types.

The intellectual vacuity of pure romance makes it a ready vehicle for illustrative or allegorical narrative, but when esthetic types are merged with illustrative types, and purely emotional situations or events are combined with allegorical situations or events, the tension between ethical and esthetic impulses can become complex, working modifications in both story and meaning. In a narrative by Hawthorne it is quite conceivable that some elements take the shape they do because of their illustrative content and some because of their representational quality (as we have already suggested), and that some are shaped by the purely esthetic exigencies which require the tale to adopt a form capable of satisfying the reader's purely emotional expectations.

We can observe with some clarity the ways in which these different kinds of connection between the real and fictional worlds manifest themselves in narrative works, if we consider for a moment some of the varieties of characterization employed by Fielding in *Tom Jones*. In this novel the tutors, Thwackum and Square, are primarily illustrative or allegorical characters. They do not mainly represent sociological or psychological types, but illustrate philosophical and theological positions which are always in perfect opposition. And in the same novel Squire Western is a representative or mimetic character, representing a psychological type or humour—the choleric man, perhaps—and a sociological type for which his name provides the label—a Tory squire from the West of England. Because Western is both a permanent type of human nature—choleric—and a specifically localized sociological type—eighteenth-century country squire—Fielding was able to assert that the basis for this kind of characterization was truth to general human nature, regardless of time and space; while Sir Walter Scott was able to praise this particular characterization, Fielding's own view notwithstanding, for its unmistakable specialness, remarking the accuracy of the portrayal and observing that no other time and place had produced anything exactly like the eighteenth-century Tory squire of England. For us, it seems easy to reconcile these views by noting that the effectiveness of the characterization stems from the fact that it indeed does just what both Fielding and Scott say about it. It is representative of both general and specific human qualities.

In this sort of discussion a certain amount of oversimplification is inevitable, but we may be able to guard against an excess of it by looking a bit harder at the ways in which illustrative, representational, and esthetic elements are combined in Fielding's characterization. Thwackum and Square, on the one hand, and Western, on the other, though different in the ways we have just been considering, are also united by a number of characteristics. Though Western is essentially a mimetic type, he is too typical to be quintessentially mimetic. Fielding's contemporary, Richardson, presents much more highly individualized characters, whose inner lives are far more complex. In a very real sense the psychological is more mimetic than the sociological. Characterization by sociological situation involves an inevitable generalizing process; it opens the way to illustrative characterization and allegory; whereas, characterization by presentation of thought process does not inevitably include reference to systems of psychological classification. The psychological impulse tends toward the presentation of highly individualized figures who resist abstraction and generalization, and whose motivation is not susceptible to rigid ethical interpretation. When Tom Jones acts, the question of whether he is "right" or "wrong" is always important to the story and to its meaning. The question or rightness or wrongness cannot be put so easily to the actions of Leopold Bloom, or even to the actions of Clarissa Harlowe. The inner lives of Richardson's characters are much more thoroughly realized and much more complex than those of Fielding's. In fact, Fielding's inability to understand Richardson is mainly the result of his inability to understand Richardsonian complexity of characterization. For Fielding, Pamela was a scheming hypocrite and Clarissa an angel— and he was equally wrong in both judgments because he could not "see," simply could not perceive the Richardsonian tangle of motivation. This difference between the two men was what Dr. Johnson had in mind when he distinguished Richardson from Fielding as one who could see into the mechanism of a clock while the other merely knew how to tell the time. Johnson's metaphor is unfair to Fielding but it perfectly describes the difference between the two kinds of characterization. The strong influence of Fielding on English fiction for the past two hundred years accounts in part for the tendency of the English novel to resist realism and maintain a persistent hospitality toward the typical and the allegorical.

In responding to Richardsonian characterization, the reader does not make a connection between the fictional character and an actual type or concept; he makes a connection between the character's psyche and his own. Richardson's characterizations are much more personal—drawn more deeply from the author's own being—than Fielding's, and the reader's response is also much more personal. The Richardsonian kind of characterization tends to take the character out of the area of "meaning." We can see Clarissa as a type of the bourgeoise and Lovelace as a type of the aristocrat, and we can read the rape of Clarissa as a symbol of the class struggle; but we do considerable violence to the individuality of the characters by considering them too seriously in this way. Still, by raising the possibility we can see that we do less violence to Lovelace than to his victim by seeing him as a type. His characterization is less personal than Clarissa's, and much of his character is composed of standard elements of Restoration Rake. But Lovelace is not the character we hold up as being typically Richardsonian. Pamela and Clarissa are creatures of true Richardsonian complexity, and this is illustrated perfectly by the injustice Richardson does his own creation when he insists on an exemplary interpretation of Pamela as a figure illustrative of Virtue Rewarded. Richardson's intellectual grasp of his own achievement is a slender one. He was a genius of the psyche but in all other things a rather ordinary individual, with an intellect far inferior to Fielding's.

In addition to being something of a social type—Restoration Rake—Lovelace is something of an esthetic type—the Villain— also, without whom Richardson's finely wrought timepiece would lack a mainspring. But Lovelace is too deeply and complexly motivated himself to be a pure esthetic type. He has too rich a personality. Normally we do not empathize at all with the esthetic villain, nor do we criticize the esthetic heroine. We are not interested in connections between the psyches of Mr. Blifil or Sophia Western and our own, nor do they suggest interesting correspondences to the types and concepts through which we apprehend the real world. They are of the story, serving mainly to polarize the reader's emotions and to assist in generating that raw desire for the consummation of the plot which hurries us so precipitously through the last part of Fielding's novel. Such esthetic types have great emotional value within the fictional world but no intellectual connection with reality; therefore, we can say that they have little to do with "meaning" as we have been using that term. In a quite different way the most mimetic characterizations seem also to exist largely outside the area of meaning. The highly individualized character draws the reader into a very intimate connection with the fictional world and makes that world assume something like the solidity of reality. By awakening complex correspondences between the psyches of character and reader, such characterization provides a rich and intense "experience" for the reader— an experience which may not only move him but also exercise his perception and sensibility, ultimately assisting him to perceive and comprehend the world of reality more sharply and more sensitively than he otherwise might. This is obviously a worthy function and it is on this basis that "realism" in fiction has quite properly sought its justification. But a narrative work, if such could exist, which presented only this kind of relationship between its fictional world and the real world would not be "meaningful" as we are using the term here. This is not to say that such a work could not be of great power and beauty, or even of great ethical value. We are deliberately narrowing the scope of that word "meaning" at this point, so as to include only those narrative works which project some generalized and therefore intellectual connection between the specific characters, action, and background of their fictional worlds and the general types and concepts which order our perception and comprehension of actuality.

MIGUEL DE CERVANTES

SANCHO TELLS A TALE

Don Quixote then bade him tell a tale for his entertainment, as he had promised; and Sancho replied that he would, if his dread of the noise would allow him. 'But, for all that,' he said, 'I will endeavour to tell you a story and, if I manage to tell it without interruption, it'll be the best story in the world. Pay good attention, your worship, for I'm going to begin.—Once upon a time; may good befall us all and evil strike the man who seeks it. Notice, your worship, that the ancients didn't begin their stories just as they pleased, but with a sentence by Cato, the Roman censor, who says—"Evil strike the man who seeks it"; and that fits in here like a ring on a finger, meaning that your worship must stay quiet and not go anywhere seeking harm, but that we must turn up some other road, since nobody is making us follow this one, where there are so many terrors to frighten us.'

'Go on with your story, Sancho,' said Don Quixote, 'and leave the road we are follow to me.'

'I tell you, then,' Sancho resumed, 'that in a village in Estremadura there was once a shepherd—a goatherd I should say, for he kept goats—and this shepherd or goatherd, as my story tells, was called Lope Ruiz. Now this Lope Ruiz fell in love with a shepherdess called Torralba, which shepherdess

From Don Quixote, *translated by J. M. Cohen, 1950. Reprinted by permission of Penguin Books Ltd.*

called Torralba was the daughter of a rich herdsman; and this rich herdsman . . .'

'If you tell your story that way, Sancho,' said Don Quixote, 'and repeat everything you have to say twice over, you will not be done in two days. Tell it consequentially, like an intelligent man, or else be quiet.'

'The way I'm telling it,' replied Sancho, 'is the way all stories are told in my country, and I don't know any other way of telling it. It isn't fair for your worship to ask me to get new habits.'

'Tell it as you like,' replied Don Quixote, 'and since it is the will of Fate that I cannot help listening, go on.'

'And so, my dear master,' Sancho went on, 'as I said, this shepherd fell in love with the shepherdess Torralba, who was a plump, high-spirited girl, and rather mannish, for she had a slight moustache—I can almost see her now.'

'Really, did you know her, then?' asked Don Quixote.

'I didn't know her,' replied Sancho, 'but the man who told me this story said that it was so true and authentic that when I told it to anyone else I could swear on my oath that I had seen it all. So, as the days came and the days went, the Devil, who never sleeps and tangles everything up, brought it about that the love which the shepherd had for the shepherdess turned to hatred and ill-will; and the reason was, as evil tongues told, that she caused him a number of little jealousies, such as exceeded the bounds and trespassed on the forbidden; and thenceforth the shepherd loathed her so much that, to avoid her, he decided to leave that country and go where his eyes should never see her again. But when Torralba found that Lope scorned her, she immediately fell to loving him more than she had ever loved him before.'

'That is natural in women,' said Don Quixote, 'to scorn those who love them, and love those who loathe them. Go on, Sancho.'

'It came about that the shepherd put his resolution into effect,' said Sancho, 'and set out driving his goats across the plains of Estremadura to cross into the kingdom of Portugal. Torralba heard of his plan, and followed him at a distance, on foot and bare-legged, with a pilgrim's staff in her hand and a satchel round her neck, which contained, the story goes, a bit of mirror and a broken comb, and some little bottle or other of washes for her face. But whatever it was she carried, I don't mean to set about inquiring now. I'll only say that the story tells how the shepherd came with his flock to cross the Guadiana river, which at that season was swollen and almost overflowing; and at the place he struck it there wasn't a boat of any kind, nor anyone to ferry him or his flock to the other side. This put him very much out, because he saw Torralba coming near, and she was sure to bother him a great deal with her entreaties and tears. He went on looking about him, however, until he saw a fisherman close beside a boat, which was so small that it could only hold one man and one goat. But, all the same, he hailed him and arranged for him to take himself and his three hundred goats across. The fisherman got into the boat and took one goat over, came back and fetched another, and came back once more and took another. Keep an account of the goats which the fisherman is taking over, your worship, for if you lose count of one the story will end, and it won't be possible for me to tell you another word of it. I'll continue now and mention that the landing-place on the other side was very muddy and slippery, which delayed the fisherman a good deal in his journeys backwards and forwards. But, all the same, he came back for another goat, and another, and another.'

'Take it that they are all across,' said Don Quixote, 'and do not go on coming and going like that, or you will never get them all over in a year.'

'How many have got over so far?' asked Sancho.

'How the devil should I know?' replied Don Quixote.

'There now, didn't I tell you to keep a good count? Well, there's an end of the story. God knows there's no going on with it now.'

'How can that be?' replied Don Quixote. 'Is it so essential to the tale to know exactly how many goats have crossed that if you are one out in the number you cannot go on?'

'No, sir, not at all,' answered Sancho. 'But, when I asked your worship to tell me how many goats had got across and you replied that you didn't know, at that very moment everything I had left to say went clean out of my head, though there were some good and amusing things coming, I promise you.'

'So,' said Don Quixote, 'the story is finished, then?'

'As sure as my mother is,' said Sancho.

'Really,' replied Don Quixote, 'you have told me one of the strangest tales—true or false—that anyone could imagine in the whole world; and never in a lifetime was there such a way of telling it or stopping it, although I expected no less from your excellent intelligence. But I am not surprised, for this ceaseless thumping must have disturbed your brains.'

'That may well be,' replied Sancho, 'but I know that so far as my story goes there is nothing more to say, for it just ends where the error begins in counting the goats that cross over.'

'All right, let it end where it will,' said Don Quixote. 'And now let us see if Rocinante can move.' He dug in his spurs once more, and the horse gave a few more leaps. Then he stood stock still, so fast was he tied.

HENRY FIELDING

NOT AN INDIVIDUAL BUT A SPECIES

I question not but several of my readers will know the lawyer in the stage-coach the moment they hear his voice. It is likewise odds but the wit and the prude meet with some of their acquaintance, as well as all the rest of my characters. To prevent, therefore, any such malicious applications, I declare here, once for all, I describe not men, but manners; not an individual, but a species. Perhaps it will be answered, Are not the characters then taken from life? To which I answer in the affirmative; nay, I believe I might aver that I have writ little more than I have seen. The lawyer is not only alive, but hath been so these four thousand years; and I hope G—— will indulge his life as many yet to come. He hath not indeed confined himself to one profession, one religion, or one country; but when the first mean selfish creature appeared upon the human stage, who made self the centre of the whole creation, would give himself no

From Joseph Andrews, *1742, Chapter I, Book III, "Matter prefatory in praise of biography."*

pain, incur no danger, advance no money, to assist or preserve his fellow-creatures; then was our lawyer born; and, whilst such a person as I have described exists on earth, so long shall he remain upon it.

LAURENCE STERNE

TRISTRAM WRESTLES WITH THE RECORDS

Upon looking into my mother's marriage settlement, in order to satisfy myself and reader in a point necessary to be clear'd up, before we could proceed any further in this history;——I had the good fortune to pop upon the very thing I wanted before I had read a day and a half straight forwards,——it might have taken me up a month;——which shews plainly, that when a man sits down to write a history,——tho' it be but the history of *Jack Hickathrift* or *Tom Thumb*, he knows no more than his heels what lets and confounded hinderances he is to meet with in his way,——or what a dance he may be led, by one excursion or another, before all is over. Could a historiographer drive on his history, as a muleteer drives on his mule,——straight forward;——for instance, from *Rome* all the way to *Loretto*, without ever once turning his head aside either to the right hand or to the left,——he might venture to foretell you to an hour when he should get to his journey's end;—— but the thing is, morally speaking, impossible: For, if he is a man of the least spirit, he will have fifty deviations from a straight line to make with this or that party as he goes along, which he can no ways avoid. He will have views and prospects to himself perpetually solliciting his eye, which he can no more help standing still to look at than he can fly; he will moreover have various

Accounts to reconcile:

Anecdotes to pick up:

Inscriptions to make out:

From Tristram Shandy, *Volume I, 1759, Chapter XIV.*

Stories to weave in:
Traditions to sift:
Personages to call upon:
Panegyrics to paste up at this door:
Pasquinades at that:——All which both the man and his mule
are quite exempt from.

STENDHAL

THE NOVEL AS A MIRROR

A novel is a mirror carried along a high road. At one moment
it reflects the blue skies, at another the mud of the puddles at
your feet. The man who carries this mirror in his pack you will
accuse of being immoral! Blame instead that high road upon
which the puddle lies, or even more the inspector of roads who
allows the water to gather and the puddle to form.

From The Red and the Black, *1830, Volume II, Chapter 49.*

W. M. THACKERAY

BOX AND PUPPETS

Ah! *Vanitas Vanitatum!* Which of us is happy in this world?
Which of us has his desire? Or, having it, is satisfied?—Come,
children, let us shut up the box and the puppets, for our play
is played out.

The last paragraph of Vanity Fair, *1847–1848.*

GUSTAVE FLAUBERT

ART AND PERSONALITY

Yes, it is a strange thing, the relation between one's writing and one's personality. Is there anyone more in love with antiquity than I, anyone more haunted by it, anyone who has made a greater effort to understand it? And yet in my books I am as far from antiquity as possible. From my appearance one would think me a writer of epic, drama, brutally factual narrative; whereas actually I feel at home only in analysis—in anatomy, if I may call it such. By natural disposition I love what is vague and misty; and it is only patience and study that have rid me of all the white fat that clogged my muscles. The books I most long to write are precisely those for which I am least endowed. *Bovary,* in this sense, is an unprecedented tour de force (a fact of which I alone shall ever be aware): its subject, characters, effects, etc.—all are alien to me. It should make it possible for me to take a great step forward later. Writing this book I am like a man playing the piano with leaden balls attached to his fingers. But once I have mastered my technique, and find a piece that's to my taste and that I can play at sight, the result will perhaps be good. In any case, I think I am doing the right thing. What one does is not for one's self, but for others. Art is not interested in the personality of the artist. So much the worse for him if he doesn't like red or green or yellow: all colors are beautiful, and his task is to use them. . . .

Letter to Louise Colet, 1852. From The Selected Letters of Gustave Flaubert, *translated by Francis Steegmuller; reprinted by permission of Farrar, Straus and Giroux, Inc. Copyright 1953 by Francis Steegmuller.*

EVERYTHING ONE INVENTS IS TRUE

The day before yesterday, in the woods of Touques, in a charming spot beside a spring, I found old cigar butts and

Letter to Louise Colet, 1853.

scraps of pate. People had been picnicking. I described such a scene in *Novembre,* eleven years ago; it was entirely imagined, and the other day it came true. Everything one invents is true, you may be sure. Poetry is as precise as geometry. Induction is as accurate as deduction; and besides, after reaching a certain point one no longer makes any mistake about the things of the soul. My poor Bovary, without a doubt, is suffering and weeping at this very instant in twenty villages of France.

GEORGE ELIOT

A FAITHFUL ACCOUNT OF MEN AND THINGS AS THEY HAVE MIRRORED THEMSELVES IN MY MIND

"This Rector of Broxton is little better than a pagan!" I hear one of my readers exclaim. "How much more edifying it would have been if you had made him give Arthur some truly spiritual advice. You might have put into his mouth the most beautiful things—quite as good as reading a sermon."

Certainly I could, if I held it the highest vocation of the novelist to represent things as they never have been and never will be. Then, of course, I might refashion life and character entirely after my own liking; I might select the most unexceptionable type of clergyman, and put my own admirable opinions into his mouth on all occasions. But it happens, on the contrary, that my strongest effort is to avoid any such arbitrary picture, and to give a faithful account of man and things as they have mirrored themselves in my mind. The mirror is doubtless defective; the outlines will sometimes be disturbed, the reflection faint or confused; but I feel as much bound to tell you as precisely as I can what that reflection is, as if I were in the witness-box narrating my experience on oath.

Sixty years ago—it is a long time, so no wonder things have

From Adam Bede, *1858, Chapter XVII, "In Which The Story Pauses a Little."*

392 LIFE AND ART

changed—all clergymen were not zealous; indeed there is reason to believe that the number of zealous clergymen was small, and it is probable that if one among the small minority had owned the livings of Broxton and Hayslope in the year 1799, you would have liked him no better than you like Mr. Irwine. Ten to one, you would have thought him a tasteless, indiscreet, methodistical man. It is so very rarely that facts hit that nice medium required by our own enlightened opinions and refined taste! Perhaps you will say, "Do improve the facts a little, then; make them more accordant with those correct views which it is our privilege to possess. The world is not just what we like; do touch it up with a tasteful pencil, and make believe it is not quite such a mixed, entangled affair. Let all people who hold unexceptionable opinions act unexceptionably. Let your most faulty characters always be on the wrong side, and your virtuous ones on the right. Then we shall see at a glance whom we are to condemn, and whom we are to approve. Then we shall be able to admire, without the slightest disturbance of our prepossessions: we shall hate and despise with that true ruminant relish which belongs to undoubting confidence."

But, my good friend, what will you do then with your fellow-parishioner who opposes your husband in the vestry?—with your newly-appointed vicar, whose style of preaching you find painfully below that of his regretted predecessor?—with the honest servant who worries your soul with her one failing?—with your neighbour, Mrs. Green, who was really kind to you in your last illness, but has said several ill-natured things about you since your convalescence?—nay, with your excellent husband himself, who has other irritating habits besides that of not wiping his shoes? These fellow-mortals, every one, must be accepted as they are: you can neither straighten their noses, nor brighten their wit, nor rectify their dispositions; and it is these people—amongst whom your life is passed—that it is needful you should tolerate, pity, and love: it is these more or less ugly, stupid, inconsistent people, whose movements of goodness you should be able to admire—for whom you should cherish all possible hopes, all possible patience. And I would not, even if I had the choice, be the clever novelist who could create a world so much better than this, in which we get up in the morning to do our daily work, that you would be likely to turn a harder, colder eye on the dusty streets and the common green fields—on the real breathing men and women, who can be cheered and helped onward by your fellow-feeling, your forbearance, your outspoken, brave justice.

So I am content to tell my simple story, without trying to make things seem better than they were; dreading nothing, indeed, but falsity, which, in spite of one's best efforts, there is reason to dread.

ANTHONY TROLLOPE

GETTING THE FACTS RIGHT

The poor fictionist very frequently finds himself to have been wrong in his description of things in general, and is told so roughly by the critics, and tenderly by the friends of his bosom. He is moved to tell of things of which he omits to learn the nature before he tells of them,—as should be done by a strictly honest fictionist. He catches salmon in October; or shoots his partridges in March. His dahlias bloom in June, and his birds sing in the autumn. He opens the opera-houses before Easter, and makes Parliament sit on a Wednesday evening. And then those terrible meshes of the law! How is a fictionist, in these excited days, to create the needed biting interest without legal difficulties; and how, again, is he to steer his little bark clear of so many rocks,—when the rocks and the shoals have been purposely arranged to make the taking of a pilot on board a necessity? As to those law meshes, a benevolent pilot will, indeed, now and again give a poor fictionist a helping hand,— not used, however, generally with much discretion. But from whom is any assistance to come in the august matter of a Cabinet assembly?

From Phineas Finn, *1869, Volume II, Chapter IV, "A Cabinet Meeting."*

GEORGE MEREDITH

NO DUST OF THE STRUGGLING OUTER WORLD

Comedy is a game played to throw reflections upon social life, and it deals with human nature in the drawing-room of civilized men and women, where we have no dust of the struggling outer world, no mire, no violent crashes, to make the correctness of the representation convincing. Credulity is not wooed through the impressionable senses; nor have we recourse to the small circular glow of the watchmaker's eye to raise in bright relief minutest grains of evidence for the routing of incredulity. The Comic Spirit conceives a definite situation for a number of characters, and rejects all accessories in the exclusive pursuit of them and their speech. For, being a spirit, he hunts the spirit in men; vision and ardour constitute his merit: he has not a thought of persuading you to believe in him. Follow and you will see.

From The Egoist, *1879, "Prelude: A Chapter of Which the Last Page Only Is of Any Importance." (It is the first paragraph of the chapter that is quoted here.)*

EMILE ZOLA

EXPERIENCE AND THE NATURALISTIC NOVEL

The greatest praise that could be formerly given to a novelist was to say that "he had imagination." To-day this praise would be looked upon almost as a criticism. This only goes to show

From The Experimental Novel, *1880, translated by Belle M. Sherman, 1893.*

that all the conditions of the novel have changed. Imagination is no longer the predominating quality of the novelist.

Alexander Dumas and Eugène Sue were gifted with imagination. In "Notre Dame de Paris" Victor Hugo imagined characters and a story of the most intense interest; in "Mauprat" George Sand knew how to impassion a whole generation by the imaginary loves of her heroes. But nobody has ever thought of granting imagination to Balzac and Stendhal. Their wonderful faculties of observation and analysis have been spoken of; they are great because they have depicted their epoch, and not because they invented stories. These are the men who lead this evolution; it is dating from their works that imagination no longer counts in the novel. Look at our great contemporaneous writers, Gustave Flaubert, Edmond and Jules de Goncourt, Alphonse Daudet: their talent does not come from what they have imagined, but from the manner in which they show forth nature in its intensity.

I insist upon this fall of the imagination, because in it I see the characteristic of the modern novel. While the novel was a recreation for the mind, an amusement, from which was asked only animation and vivacity, it is easily understood that the important thing was to show an abundance of invention before anything else. Even when the historical novel and the novel with a purpose appeared, even then it was still imagination which reigned omnipresent, either in calling up vanished times or in the form of arguments, which characters, formed according to the need of the author, expounded. With the naturalistic novel and the novel of observation and analysis, the conditions change at once. The novelist invents, indeed, still: he invents a plan, a drama; only it is a scrap of a drama, the first story he comes across and which daily life furnishes him with always. Then in the arrangement of the work this invention is only of very slight importance. The facts are there only as the logical results of the characters. The great thing is to set up living creatures, playing before the readers the human comedy in the most natural manner possible. All the efforts of the writer tend to hide the imaginary under the real.

One could write an interesting paper on the subject of how our great novelists of to-day work. They base nearly all their works on profuse notes. When they have studied with scrupulous care the ground over which they are to walk, when they have gotten information from all the possible sources, and when they hold in their hands the manifold data of which they have need, then only do they decide to sit down and write. The plan of the work is brought to them by the data themselves, because the facts always classify themselves logically, this one before that one. Inevitably the work takes shape; the story builds itself up from all the observations gathered together, from all the notes taken, one leading to the other, through the linking of the lives of the characters, and the climax is nothing more than a natural and inevitable consequence. You can easily see, in this work, how little part imagination has in it all. We are very far removed, for example, from George Sand, who, they say, put herself before a mass of white paper, and, starting out with the first idea, went on and on without stopping, composing in a steady stream, relying solely on her imagination, which brought her as many pages as she needed to complete a volume.

HENRY JAMES

ON WRITING FROM EXPERIENCE

I remember an English novelist, a woman of genius, telling me that she was much commended for the impression she had managed to give in one of her tales of the nature and way of life of the French Protestant youth. She had been asked where she had learned so much about this recondite being, she had been congratulated on her peculiar opportunities. These opportunities consisted in her having once, in Paris, as she ascended a staircase, passed an open door where, in the household of a *pasteur*, some of the young Protestants were seated at table round a finished meal. The glimpse made a picture; it lasted only a moment, but that moment was experience. She had got her direct personal impression, and she turned out her type. She knew what youth was, and what Protestantism; she also had the ad-

From "The Art of Fiction," 1884.

vantage of having seen what it was to be French, so that she converted these ideas into a concrete image and produced a reality. Above all, however, she was blessed with the faculty which when you give it an inch takes an ell, and which for the artist is a much greater source of strength than any accident of residence or of place in the social scale. The power to guess the unseen from the seen, to trace the implication of things, to judge the whole piece by the pattern, the condition of feeling life in general so completely that you are well on your way to knowing any particular corner of it—this cluster of gifts may almost be said to constitute experience, and they occur in country and in town, and in the most differing stages of education. If experience consists of impressions, it may be said that impressions *are* experience, just as (have we not seen it?) they are the very air we breathe. Therefore, if I should certainly say to a novice, "Write from experience and experience only," I should feel that this was rather a tantalizing monition if I were not careful immediately to add, "Try to be one of the people on whom nothing is lost!"

GUY DE MAUPASSANT

A PRESENTMENT MORE STRIKING THAN REALITY ITSELF

The realist, if he is an artist, will endeavour not to show us a commonplace photograph of life, but to give us a presentment of it which shall be more complete, more striking, more cogent than reality itself. To tell everything is out of the question; it would require at least a volume for each day to enumerate the endless, insignificant incidents which crowd our existence. A choice must be made—and this is the first blow to the theory of "the whole truth."

Life, moreover, is composed of the most dissimilar things, the

From the Preface to Pierre et Jean, *1888, trans. Clara Bell, 1902.*

most unforeseen, the most contradictory, the most incongruous; it is merciless, without sequence or connection, full of inexplicable, illogical, and contradictory catastrophes, such as can only be classed as miscellaneous facts. This is why the artist, having chosen his subject, can only select such characteristic details as are of use to it, from this life overladen with chances and trifles, and reject everything else, everything by the way.

To give an instance from among a thousand. The number of persons who, every day, meet with an accidental death, all over the world, is very considerable. But how can we bring a tile on to the head of an important character, or fling him under the wheels of a vehicle in the middle of a story, under the pretext that accident must have its due?

Again, in life there is no difference of foreground and distance, and events are sometimes hurried on, sometimes left to linger indefinitely. Art, on the contrary, consists in the employment of foresight, and elaboration in arranging skilful and ingenious transitions, in setting essential events in a strong light, simply by the craft of composition, and giving all else the degree of relief, in proportion to their importance, requisite to produce a convincing sense of the special truth to be conveyed.

"Truth" in such work consists in producing a complete illusion by following the common logic of facts and not by transcribing them pell-mell, as they succeed each other.

Whence I conclude that the higher order of Realists should rather call themselves Illusionists.

How childish it is, indeed, to believe in this reality, since to each of us the truth is in his own mind, his own organs! Our own eyes and ears, taste and smell, create as many different truths as there are human beings on earth. And our brains, duly and differently informed by those organs, apprehend, analyze, and decide as differently as if each of us were a being of an alien race. Each of us, then, has simply his own illusion of the world —poetical, sentimental, cheerful, melancholy, foul, or gloomy, according to his nature. And the writer has no other mission than faithfully to reproduce this illusion, with all the elaborations of art which he may have learned and have at his command. The illusion of beauty—which is merely a conventional term invented by man! The illusion of ugliness—which is a matter of varying opinion! The illusion of truth—never immutable! The illusion of depravity—which fascinates so many minds! All the great artists are those who can make other men see their own particular illusion.

JOSEPH CONRAD

THE HIGHEST KIND OF JUSTICE TO THE VISIBLE UNIVERSE

A work that aspires, however humbly, to the condition of art should carry its justification in every line. And art itself may be defined as a single-minded attempt to render the highest kind of justice to the visible universe, by bringing to light the truth, manifold and one, underlying its every aspect. It is an attempt to find in its forms, in its colours, in its light, in its shadows, in the aspects of matter, and in the facts of life what of each is fundamental, what is enduring and essential—their one illuminating and convincing quality—the very truth of their existence. The artist, then, like the thinker or the scientist, seeks the truth and makes his appeal. Impressed by the aspect of the world the thinker plunges into ideas, the scientist into facts—whence, presently, emerging they make their appeal to those qualities of our being that fit us best for the hazardous enterprise of living. They speak authoritatively to our common sense, to our intelligence, to our desire of peace, or to our desire of unrest; not seldom to our prejudices, sometimes to our fears, often to our egoism—but always to our credulity. And their words are heard with reverence, for their concern is with weighty matters: with the cultivation of our minds and the proper care of our bodies, with the attainment of our ambitions, with the perfection of the means and the glorification of our precious aims.

It is otherwise with the artist.

Confronted by the same enigmatical spectacle the artist de-

Preface to The Nigger of The 'Narcissus,' *1897.*

400 LIFE AND ART

scends within himself, and in that lonely region of stress and strife, if he be deserving and fortunate, he finds the terms of his appeal. His appeal is made to our less obvious capacities: to that part of our nature which, because of the warlike conditions of existence, is necessarily kept out of sight within the more resisting and hard qualities—like the vulnerable body within a steel armour. His appeal is less loud, more profound, less distinct, more stirring—and sooner forgotten. Yet its effect endures for ever. The changing wisdom of successive generations discards ideas, questions facts, demolishes theories. But the artist appeals to that part of our being which is not dependent on wisdom; to that in us which is a gift and not an acquisition—and, therefore, more permanently enduring. He speaks to our capacity for delight and wonder, to the sense of mystery surrounding our lives; to our sense of pity, and beauty, and pain; to the latent feeling of fellowship with all creation—and to the subtle but invincible conviction of solidarity that knits together the loneliness of innumerable hearts, to the solidarity in dreams, in joy, in sorrow, in aspirations, in illusions, in hope, in fear, which binds men to each other, which binds together all humanity—the dead to the living and the living to the unborn.

It is only some such train of thought, or rather of feeling, that can in a measure explain the aim of the attempt, made in the tale which follows, to present an unrestful episode in the obscure lives of a few individuals out of all the disregarded multitude of the bewildered, the simple, and the voiceless. For, if any part of truth dwells in the belief confessed above, it becomes evident that there is not a place of splendour or a dark corner of the earth that does not deserve, if only a passing glance of wonder and pity. The motive, then, may be held to justify the matter of the work; but this preface, which is simply an avowal of endeavour, cannot end here—for the avowal is not yet complete.

Fiction—if it at all aspires to be art—appeals to temperament. And in truth it must be, like painting, like music, like all art, the appeal of one temperament to all the other innumerable temperaments whose subtle and resistless power endows passing events with their true meaning, and creates the moral, the emotional atmosphere of the place and time. Such an appeal to be effective must be an impression conveyed through the senses; and in fact, it cannot be made in any other way, because temperament, whether individual or collective, is not amenable to persuasion.

All art, therefore, appeals primarily to the senses, and the artistic aim when expressing itself in written words must also make its appeal through the senses, if its high desire is to reach the secret spring of responsive emotions. It must strenuously aspire to the plasticity of sculpture, to the colour of painting, and to the magic suggestiveness of music—which is the art of arts. And it is only through complete, unswerving devotion to the perfect blending of form and substance; it is only through an unremitting never-discouraged care for the shape and ring of sentences that an approach can be made to plasticity, to colour, and that the light of magic suggestiveness may be brought to play for an evanescent instant over the commonplace surface of words: of the old, old words, worn thin, defaced by ages of careless usage.

The sincere endeavour to accomplish that creative task, to go as far on that road as his strength will carry him, to go undeterred by faltering, weariness, or reproach, is the only valid justification for the worker in prose. And if his conscience is clear, his answer to those who, in the fullness of a wisdom which looks for immediate profit, demand specifically to be edified, consoled, amused; who demand to be promptly improved, or encouraged, or frightened, or shocked, or charmed, must run thus: My task which I am trying to achieve is, by the power of the written word to make you hear, to make you feel—it is, before all, to make you *see*. That—and no more, and it is everything. If I succeed, you shall find there according to your deserts; encouragement, consolation, fear, charm—all you demand— and, perhaps, also that glimpse of truth for which you have forgotten to ask.

To snatch in a moment of courage, from the remorseless rush of time, a passing phase of life, is only the beginning of the task. The task approached in tenderness and faith is to hold up unquestioningly, without choice and without fear, the rescued fragment before all eyes in the light of a sincere mood. It is to show its vibration, its colour, its form; and through its movement, its form, and its colour, reveal the substance of its truth— disclose its inspiring secret: the stress and passion within the core of each convincing moment. In a single-minded attempt of that kind, if one be deserving and fortunate, one may perchance attain to such clearness of sincerity that at last the presented vision of regret or pity, of terror or mirth, shall awaken in the hearts of the beholders that feeling of unavoidable solidarity; of the solidarity in mysterious origin, in toil, in joy, in hope, in uncertain fate, which binds men to each other and all mankind to the visible world.

It is evident that he who, rightly or wrongly, holds by the convictions expressed above cannot be faithful to any one of the temporary formulas of his craft. The enduring part of them—the truth which each only imperfectly veils—should abide with him as the most precious of his possessions, but they all: Realism, Romanticism, Naturalism, even the unofficial sentimentalism (which, like the poor, is exceedingly difficult to get rid of), all these gods must, after a short period of fellowship, abandon him —even on the very threshold of the temple—to the stammerings of his conscience and to the outspoken consciousness of the difficulties of his work. In that uneasy solitude the supreme cry of Art for Art, itself, loses the exciting ring of its apparent immorality. It sounds far off. It has ceased to be a cry, and is heard only as a whisper, often incomprehensible, but at times and faintly encouraging.

Sometimes, stretched at ease in the shade of a roadside tree, we watch the motions of a labourer in a distant field, and after a time, begin to wonder languidly as to what the fellow may be at. We watch the movements of his body, the waving of his arms, we see him bend down, stand up, hesitate, begin again. It may add to the charm of an idle hour to be told the purpose of his exertions. If we know he is trying to lift a stone, to dig a ditch, to uproot a stump, we look with a more real interest at his efforts; we are disposed to condone the jar of his agitation upon the restfulness of the landscape; and even, if in a brotherly frame of mind, we may bring ourselves to forgive his failure. We understood his object, and, after all, the fellow has tried, and perhaps he had not the strength—and perhaps he had not the knowledge. We forgive, go on our way—and forget.

And so it is with the workman of art. Art is long and life is short, and success is very far off. And thus, doubtful of strength to travel so far, we talk a little about the aim—the aim of art, which, like life itself, is inspiring, difficult—obscured by mists. It is not in the clear logic of a triumphant conclusion; it is not in the unveiling of one of those heartless secrets which are called the Laws of Nature. It is not less great, but only more difficult.

To arrest, for the space of a breath, the hands busy about the work of the earth and compel men entranced by the sight of distant goals to glance for a moment at the surrounding vision of form and colour, of sunshine and shadows; to make them pause for a look, for a sigh, for a smile—such is the aim, difficult and evanescent, and reserved only for a very few to achieve. But sometimes, by the deserving and the fortunate, even that task is accomplished. And when it is accomplished—behold!—all the truth of life is there: a moment of vision, a sigh, a smile—and the return to an eternal rest.

ANDRE GIDE

EDOUARD ON THE TYRANNY OF RESEMBLANCE

"Is it because the novel, of all literary *genres*, is the freest, the most *lawless*," held forth Edouard, ". . . is it for that very reason, for fear of that very liberty (the artists who are always sighing after liberty are often the most bewildered when they get it), that the novel has always clung to reality with such timidity? And I am not speaking only of the French novel. It is the same with the English novel; and the Russian novel, for all its throwing off of constraints, is a slave to resemblance. The only progress it looks to is to get still nearer to nature. The novel has never known that 'formidable erosion of contours,' as Nietzsche calls it; that deliberate avoidance of life, which gave style to the works of the Greek dramatists, for instance, or to the tragedies of the French XVIIth century. Is there anything more perfectly and deeply human than these works? But that's just it—they are human only in their depths; they don't pride themselves on appearing so—or, at any rate, on appearing real. They remain works of art."

Edouard had got up, and, for fear of seeming to give a lecture, began to pour out the tea as he spoke; then he moved up and down, then squeezed a lemon into his cup, but, nevertheless, continued speaking:

From The Counterfeiters with Journal of "The Counterfeiters," *1925, translated by Dorothy Bussy and Justin O'Brien.* © *Copyright 1955 by Alfred A. Knopf, Inc. Reprinted by permission.*

"Because Balzac was a genius, and because every genius seems to bring to his art a final and conclusive solution, it has been decreed that the proper function of the novel is to rival the *état-civil*.[1] Balzac constructed his work; he never claimed to codify the novel; his article on Stendhal proves it. Rival the *état-civil!* As if there weren't enough fools and boors in the world as it is! What have I to do with the *état-civil? L'état c'est moi!* I, the artist; civil or not, my work doesn't pretend to rival anything."

Edouard, who was getting excited—a little factitiously, perhaps—sat down. He affected not to look at Bernard; but it was for him that he was speaking. If he had been alone with him, he would not have been able to say a word; he was grateful to the two women for setting him on.

"Sometimes it seems to me there is nothing in all literature I admire so much as, for instance, the discussion between Mithridate and his two sons in Racine; it's a scene in which the characters speak in a way we know perfectly well no father and no sons could ever have spoken in, and yet (I ought to say for that very reason) it's a scene in which all fathers and all sons can see themselves. By localizing and specifying one restricts. It is true that there is no psychological truth unless it be particular; but on the other hand there is no art unless it be general. The whole problem lies just in that—how to express the general by the particular—how to make the particular express the general. May I light my pipe?"

"Do, do," said Sophroniska.

"Well, I should like a novel which should be at the same time as true and as far from reality, as particular and at the same time as general, as human and as fictitious as *Athalie,* or *Tartuffe* or *Cinna.*"

"And . . . the subject of this novel?"

"It hasn't got one," answered Edouard brusquely, "and perhaps that's the most astonishing thing about it. My novel hasn't got a subject. Yes, I know, it sounds stupid. Let's say, if you prefer it, it hasn't got *one* subject . . . 'a slice of life,' the naturalist school said. The great defect of that school is that it always cuts its slice in the same directions; in time, lengthwise. Why not in breadth? Or in depth? As for me I should like not

[1] The state records of each individual citizen, in which are noted the legal facts of his existence—*Translator's Note.*

to cut at all. Please understand; I should like to put everything into my novel. I don't want any cut of the scissors to limit its substance at one point rather than at another. For more than a year now that I have been working at it, nothing happens to me that I don't put into it—everything I see, everything I know, everything that other people's lives and my own teach me. . . ."

"And the whole thing stylized into art?" said Sophroniska, feigning the most lively attention, but no doubt a little ironically. Laura could not suppress a smile. Edouard shrugged his shoulders slightly and went on:

"And even that isn't what I want to do. What I want is to represent reality on the one hand, and on the other that effort to stylize it into art of which I have just been speaking."

"My poor dear friend, you will make your readers die of boredom," said Laura; as she could no longer hide her smile, she had made up her mind to laugh outright.

D. H. LAWRENCE

THE ONE BRIGHT BOOK OF LIFE

Now I absolutely flatly deny that I am a soul, or a body, or a mind, or an intelligence, or a brain, or a nervous system, or a bunch of glands, or any of the rest of these bits of me. The whole is greater than the part. And therefore, I, who am man alive, am greater than my soul, or spirit, or body, or mind, or consciousness, or anything else that is merely a part of me. I am a man, and alive. I am man alive, and as long as I can, I intend to go on being man alive.

For this reason I am a novelist. And being a novelist, I consider myself superior to the saint, the scientist, the philosopher, and the poet, who are all great masters of different bits of man alive, but never get the whole hog.

The novel is the one bright book of life. Books are not life. They are only tremulations on the ether. But the novel as a tremulation can make the whole man alive tremble. Which is more than poetry, philosophy, science, or any other book-tremulation can do.

JAMES JOYCE

A DIVIDUAL CHAOS, PERILOUS, POTENT, COMMON TO ALLFLESH

Then, pious Eneas, conformant to the fulminant firman which enjoins on the tremylose terrian that, when the call comes, he shall produce nichthemerically from his unheavenly body a no uncertain quantity of obscene matter not protected by copriright in the United Stars of Ourania or bedeed and bedood and bedang and bedung to him, with this double dye, brought to blood heat, gallic acid on iron ore, through the bowels of his misery, flashly, faithly, nastily, appropriately, this Esuan Menschavik and the first till last alshemist wrote over every square inch of the only foolscap available, his own body, till by its corrosive sublimation one continuous present tense integument slowly unfolded all marryvoising moodmoulded cyclewheeling history (thereby, he said, reflecting from his own individual person life unlivable, transaccidentated through the slow fires of consciousness into a dividual chaos, perilous, potent, common to allflesh, human only, mortal) but with each word that would not pass away the squidself which he had squirtscreened from the crystalline world waned chagreenold and doriangrayer in its dudhud.

SELECTED BIBLIOGRAPHY

The bibliography that follows is limited to works in English, and, with a few exceptions, to works published after 1900. For the most part it excludes works on particular novelists or special periods in the history of the novel where the main intent of such works is practical and the theoretical insights are subordinate.

Adams, Ken. "Notes on Concretization," *British Journal of Aesthetics*, IV (1964), 115–125.
Adams, Robert M. *Strains of Discord: Studies in Literary Openness*. Ithaca, N.Y., 1958.
> Only partly concerned with fiction, but an articulation of the uses of formal "openness" indispensable in judging a good many novels.
Aldridge, John W., ed. *Critiques and Essays on Modern Fiction: 1920–1951*. New York, 1952.
> A large, exceptionally rich collection of essays on modern novelists with an extensive bibliography.
———. *In Search of Heresy*. New York, 1956.
———. *Time to Murder and Create: The Contemporary Novel in Crisis*. New York, 1966.
Allen, Walter. *The English Novel: A Short Critical History*. London, 1954; New York, 1955.
> An excellent brief history.
———. *The Modern Novel in Britain and the United States*. New York, 1964.
———. *Reading a Novel*. London, 1949; Denver, 1949.
———. *Writers on Writing*. London, 1948.
> An anthology of brief passages, half by novelists, on their art.
Allott, Miriam. *Novelists on the Novel*. New York and London, 1959.
> A diverse collection of remarks by novelists, English, French, and Russian, on aspects of their craft; the best of several such books.
———. "The Temporal Mode: Four Kinds of Fiction," *Essays in Criticism*, VIII (1958), 214–216.
Alter, Robert. *Rogue's Progress*. Cambridge, Mass., 1964.
> On the picaresque novel.
Ames, Van Meter. *Aesthetics of the Novel*. Chicago, 1928.
———. "Butor and the Book," *Journal of Aesthetics and Art Criticism*, XXIII (1964), 159–165.
> On the "new" French novel.

———. "The New in the Novel," *Journal of Aesthetics and Art Criticism,* XXI (1963), 243–250.

———. "The Novel: Between Art and Science," *Kenyon Review,* V (1943), 34–48.

Auerbach, Erich. *Mimesis: The Representation of Reality in Western Literature.* Princeton, 1953.

> One of the indisputably great works of criticism; of special interest for the theory of the novel are chapters on Petronius, Cervantes, the Abbé Prevost, Schiller, the brothers Goncourt, and Virginia Woolf.

Arnold, Aerol. "Why Structure in Fiction: A Note to Social Scientists," *American Quarterly,* X (1958), 325–337.

Baker, Ernest A. *A History of the English Novel.* 10 vols. London, 1924–39.

> Useful for its amplitude but uneven in its judgments.

Baker, Joseph E. "Aesthetic Surface in the Novel," *The Trollopian,* II (1947), 91–106.

Barnes, Hazel E. "Modes of Aesthetic Consciousness in Fiction," *Bucknell Review,* XII (1964), 82–93.

Bateson, F. W. and B. Shahevitch. "Katherine Mansfield's 'The Fly': A Critical Exercise," *Essays in Criticism,* XII (1962), 39–53.

Bayley, John. *The Characters of Love: A Study in the Literature of Personality.* New York, 1960.

> Accomplishes an important revival of the study of character in literature.

Beach, Joseph Warren. *The Twentieth Century Novel: Studies in Technique.* New York, 1932.

Beardsley, Monroe C. *Aesthetics: Problems in the Philosophy of Criticism.* New York, 1958.

> Most general works on aesthetics form their concepts and choose their examples from the visual arts, often omitting a treatment of fiction altogether. Beardsley's book is not only readable and highly intelligent but also sensitive to the values and problems of literature.

Beck, Warren. "Conception and Technique," *College English,* XI (1950), 308–317.

Becker, George J. *Documents of Modern Literary Realism.* Princeton, 1963.

> A large, useful anthology.

———. "Realism: An Essay in Definition," *Modern Language Quarterly,* X (1949), 184–197.

Belgion, Montgomery. "The Testimony of Fiction," *Southern Review,* IV (1938), 143–155.

Bellow, Saul. "Facts That Put Fancy to Flight," in *Opinions and Perspectives from The New York Times Book Review,* ed. Francis Brown, Boston, 1964.

———. "Deep Readers of the World, Beware," in *Opinions and Perspectives from The New York Times Book Review,* ed. Francis Brown, Boston, 1964.

Bennett, Arnold. *Books and Persons.* New York, 1917.

Bentley, Phyllis. *Some Observations on the Art of Narrative.* New York, 1948.

Besant, Walter. *The Art of Fiction.* London, 1902.

Blackmur, R. P. "Between the Numen and the Moha: Notes Towards a Theory of the Novel," *Sewanee Review,* LXII (1954), 1–23.

———. *Eleven Essays in the European Novel.* New York, 1964.

———. "Notes on Four Categories," *Sewanee Review,* LIV (1946), 576–590.

    "Superficial techniques," "linguistic technique," "the ulterior use of the imagination," "the symbolic imagination."

———. "Notes on the Novel: 1936," in *The Expense of Greatness,* New York, 1940.

Bland, D. S. "Endangering the Reader's Neck: Background Description in the Novel," *Criticism,* III (1961), 121–139.

Bluestone, George. "Time in Film and Fiction," *Journal of Aesthetics and Art Criticism,* XIX (1961), 311–315.

Booth, Bradford A. "Form and Technique in the Novel," in *The Reinterpretation of Victorian Literature,* ed. Joseph E. Baker, Princeton, 1950.

———. "The Novel," in *Contemporary Literary Scholarship,* ed. Lewis Leary, New York, 1958.

Booth, Wayne C. "Distance and Point-of-View: An Essay in Classification," *Essays in Criticism,* XI (1961), 60–79.

———. *The Rhetoric of Fiction.* Chicago, 1961.

    A strongly reasoned, brilliantly supported reassessment of the question of point of view. One of the few books in the field that one must know.

Boulton, Marjorie. *The Anatomy of Prose.* London, 1954.

Bowen, Elizabeth. "Notes on Writing a Novel," in *Collected Impressions,* London, 1950; reprinted in *Myth and Method: Modern Theories of Fiction,* ed. James E. Miller, Lincoln, Nebraska, 1960.

    Wise, aphoristic statements on plot, characters, scene, dialogue, etc.

———. "Rx for a Story Worth Telling," in *Opinions and Perspectives from The New York Times Book Review,* ed. Francis Brown, Boston, 1964.

———. "The Search for a Story to Tell," in *Highlights of Modern Literature: A Permanent Collection of Memorable Essays from The New York Times Book Review,* ed. Francis Brown, New York, 1954.

———. "The Writer's Peculiar World," in *Highlights of Modern Literature: A Permanent Collection of Memorable Essays from The New York Times Book Review,* ed. Francis Brown, New York, 1954.

Bowling, L. E. "What is the Stream of Consciousness Technique?," *PMLA,* LXV (1950), 333–345.

Brace, Gerald Warner. "The Essential Novel," *Texas Quarterly,* VIII (1965), 28–38.

Brace, Marjorie. "Thematic Problems of the American Novelist," *Accent,* VI (1945), 44–54.

Breit, Harvey. *The Writer Observed*. Cleveland, 1956.
>   Interviews with a wide range of writers.
Brooks, Cleanth and Robert Penn Warren. *Understanding Fiction*. New York, 1943.
Brooks, Peter. "In the Laboratory of the Novel," *Daedalus*, XCII (1963), 265–280.
>   On Robbe-Grillet, Nathalie Sarraute, and the "new" novel.
Brown, E. K. *Rhythm in the Novel*. Toronto, 1950.
>   On repetition, symbolic interrelation, etc.
————. "Two Formulas for Fiction: Henry James and H. G. Wells," *College English*, VIII (1946), 7–17.
Brown, Huntington. *Prose Styles: Five Primary Types*. Minneapolis, 1966.
Brown, Rollo Walter, ed. *The Writer's Art*. Cambridge, Mass., 1921.
Brumm, Ursula. "Symbolism and the Novel," *Partisan Review*, XXV (1958), 329–342.
Bruner, Jerome S. *On Knowing: Essays for the Left Hand*. Cambridge, Mass., 1962.
>   See especially "Identity and the Modern Novel."
Buchan, John. *The Novel and the Fairy Tale*. Oxford, 1931.
Buckler, William E. *Novels in the Making*. Boston, 1961.
>   Classic statements of novelists on the origins of their work.
Bullough, Edward. "Psychical Distance as a Factor in Art and an Aesthetic Principle," *British Journal of Psychology*, V (1912–13), 87–118; largely reprinted in Melvin Rader, ed. *A Modern Book of Esthetics*, 3rd ed. New York, 1960.
>   An important, original study which any treatment of distance must take into account.
Burgum, Edwin Berry. *The Novel and the World's Dilemma*. New York, 1963.
Burns, Wayne. "The Novelist as Revolutionary," *Arizona Quarterly*, VII (1951), 13–27.
————. "The Panzaic Principle," *Paunch*, 22 (January, 1965), 2–31.
>   "In life the rightness of the guts (as against the mind) will depend on one's point of view. In Lawrence's as in all other novels, however, the guts are always right; it is an axiom or principle of the novel that they are always right, that the senses of even a fool can give the lie to even the most profound abstractions of the noblest thinker."
Burton, Richard. *Forces in Fiction and Other Essays*. Indianapolis, 1902.
Butor, Michael. "Intervention at Royaumont," *Odyssey Review*, I (1961), 176–179.
————. "Thoughts on the Novel," *Encounter*, XX (June, 1963), 17–24.
Cannavo, Salvator and Lawrence W. Hyman. "Literary Uniqueness and Critical Communication," *British Journal of Aesthetics*, V (1965), 144–158.
Cary, Joyce. *Art and Reality: Ways of the Creative Process*. New York, 1958.

————. "On the Function of the Novelist," in *Highlights of Modern Literature: A Permanent Collection of Memorable Essays from The New York Times Book Review,* ed. Francis Brown, New York, 1954.

————. "The Way a Novel Gets Written," *Harper's,* CC (February, 1950), 87–93.

Cather, Willa. *On Writing: Critical Studies on Writing as an Art.* New York, 1949.

"The Characteristic Form," in *The American Imagination: A Critical Survey of the Arts from The Times Literary Supplement,* London, 1960.

Chase, Richard. *The American Novel and Its Tradition.* New York, 1957.
    A highly original study of the American novel in relation to its culture; theoretically perceptive on the difference between novel and romance.

————. *Quest for Myth.* Baton Rouge, 1949.

Chekhov, Anton. *The Personal Papers of Anton Chekhov.* New York, 1948.

Church, Margaret. *Time and Reality: Studies in Contemporary Fiction.* Chapel Hill, N.C., 1963.
    A theoretical chapter on Bergson and Proust; fine essays on time sense in Joyce, Virginia Woolf, Mann, Faulkner.

Cockshut, A. O. J. "Sentimentality in Fiction," *Twentieth Century,* CLXI (April, 1957), 354–364.

Collins, Norman. *The Facts of Fiction.* London, 1932.

Colum, Mary. *From These Roots: The Ideas that Have Made Modern Literature.* New York, 1938.

Comfort, Alex. *The Novel and Our Time.* London, 1948.
    A somewhat sketchy attempt to describe "the social role of the novel" at the present time.

Cook, Albert. *The Meaning of Fiction.* Detroit, 1960.
    A dense, original book.

Cooper, William. "Reflections on Some Aspects of the Experimental Novel," *International Literary Annual,* II (1959), 29–36.
    A spirited attack on the position of Robbe-Grillet. *See* Robbe-Grillet.

Cowie, Alexander. *The Rise of the American Novel.* New York, 1948.
    A standard work.

Cowley, Malcolm. *The Literary Situation.* New York, 1954.

————, ed. *Writers at Work: The Paris Review Interviews.* New York, 1958.

Crane, R. S. "The Concept of Plot and the Plot of Tom Jones," in *Critics and Criticism, Ancient and Modern,* ed. R. S. Crane, Chicago, 1952.

Cruttwell, Patrick. "Makers and Persons," *Hudson Review,* XII (1959–60), 487–507.
    An impressive treatment of the relation between the writer and his literary projection of himself.

Dahlberg, Edward and Herbert Read. *Truth is More Sacred*. New York, n.d.

An exchange of letters on Joyce, Lawrence, James, *et al.*

Daiches, David. "The Criticism of Fiction: Some Second Thoughts," in *Literary Essays*, London, 1956.

———. *Literature and Society*. London, 1938.

———. "The Nature of Fiction," in *A Study of Literature: For Readers and Critics*, Ithaca, 1948.

———. *The Novel and the Modern World*, rev. ed. Chicago, 1960.

———. "Time and Sensibility," *Modern Language Quarterly*, XXV (1964), 486–492.

Davis, Robert Gorham. "Fiction and Thinking," *Epoch*, I (1948), 87–96.

———. "The Sense of the Real in English Fiction," *Comparative Literature*, III (1951), 200–217.

DeVoto, Bernard. *The World of Fiction*. Boston, 1950.

Dickie, George. "Bullough and the Concept of Psychical Distance," *Philosophy and Phenomenological Research*, XXII (1961), 233–238.

Dodsworth, Martin. "'The Truth of Fiction,'" *Essays in Criticism*, IX (1959), 443–446.

Cf. the article by A. E. Rodway.

Douglas, Wallace W. "The Meanings of 'Myth' in Modern Criticism," *Modern Philology*, L (1953), 232–242.

Drew, Elizabeth A. *The Modern Novel*. New York, 1926.

Dubois, Arthur E. "The Art of Fiction," *South Atlantic Quarterly*, XL (1941), 112–122.

Duncan, Hugh Dalziel. *Language and Literature in Society*. Chicago, 1953.

The best book on the sociology of literature; an extensive bibliography.

Eastman, Richard M. "The Open Parable: Demonstration and Definition," *College English*, XXII (1960), 15–18.

Edel, Leon and Gordon Ray. *Henry James and H. G. Wells: A Record of their Friendship, their Debate on the Art of Fiction, and their Quarrel*. Urbana, 1958.

———. *The Modern Psychological Novel*. New York, 1955.

Both theoretical and practical; an indispensable work in its field.

Edgar, Pelham. *The Art of the Novel: from 1700 to the Present Time*. New York, 1933.

Ehrenpreis, Irwin. *The "Types" Approach to Literature*. New York, 1945.

Elliott, George P. "A Defense of Fiction," *Hudson Review*, XVI (1963), 9–48.

An excellent essay, insisting, among other things, on the need for flexibility in responding to the varieties of fiction.

———. "The Novelist as Meddler," *Virginia Quarterly Review*, XL (1964), 96–113.

On the moral relations between author, fictive world, and reader.

Embler, Weller B. "The Novel as Metaphor," *Etc.*, X (1953), 3–11.

Erlich, Victor. "Some Uses of Monologue in Prose Fiction: Narrative Manner and World-View," in *Stil- Und Formprobleme in Der Literatur,* ed. R. W. Zandvoort, Heidelberg, 1959.

Farber, Marjorie. "Subjectivity in Modern Fiction," *Kenyon Review,* VII (1945), 645–652.

Farrell, James T. "Some Observations on Naturalism, So Called, in Fiction," *Antioch Review,* X (1950), 247–264.

Fasel, Ida. "Spatial Form and Spatial Time," *Western Humanities Review,* XVI (1962), 223–234.

Fergusson, Francis. "Myth and the Literary Scruple," *Sewanee Review,* LXIV (1956), 171–185.

> The illustrations come more from Dante than from prose fiction, but this is a stimulating essay in definition.

Fernandez, Ramon. *Messages,* trans. Montgomery Belgion. New York, 1927.

Feuchtwanger, Lion. *The House of Desdemona, or The Laurels and Limitations of Historical Fiction,* trans. Harold A. Basilius. Detroit, 1963.

Fleming, William. "The Newer Concepts of Time and Their Relation to the Temporal Arts," *Journal of Aesthetics and Art Criticism,* IV (1945), 101–106.

Flint, F. Cudworth. "Remarks on the Novel," *Symposium,* I (1930), 84–96.

Follett, Wilson. *The Modern Novel: A Study of the Purpose and Meaning of Fiction.* New York, 1918.

Ford, Ford Madox. *The English Novel: From the Earliest Days to the Death of Joseph Conrad.* London, 1930.

> Opinionated.

————. *Joseph Conrad: A Personal Remembrance.* London, 1924.

> Contains a brilliant discussion of technique in the account of the collaboration between Ford and Conrad.

Forster, E. M. *Aspects of the Novel.* New York, 1927.

> Too witty and personal a book to deserve the epithet "standard"; but one of the few essential books on the novel.

Fox, Ralph. *The Novel and the People.* New York, 1945.

> Doctrinaire Marxist.

Frank, Joseph. "Spatial Form in Modern Literature," *Sewanee Review,* LIII (1945), 221–240; 433–456; 643–653.

> Widely reprinted in abridged versions. *See* Sutton.

Frey, John R. "Past or Present Tense? A Note on the Technique of Narration," *JEGP,* XLVI (1947), 205–208.

> Based on Rumer Godden's *Take Three Tenses: a Fugue in Time.*

Friedman, Alan. "The Stream of Conscience as a Form in Fiction," *Hudson Review,* XVII (1965), 537–546.

Friedman, Melvin. *Stream of Consciousness: a Study in Literary Method.* New Haven, 1955.

> On the subject, *see also* Humphrey, which complements rather than duplicates Friedman's study.

Friedman, Norman. "Criticism and the Novel," *Antioch Review*, XVIII (1958), 343–370.
> A tightly reasoned defense of the understanding of plot as a prerequisite for understanding cause in fiction.

———. "Forms of the Plot," *Journal of General Education*, VIII (1955), 241–253.

———. "Point of View in Fiction: The Development of a Critical Concept," *PMLA*, LXX (1955), 1160–1184.

———. "What Makes a Short Story Short?" *Modern Fiction Studies*, IV (1958), 103–117.
> A closely reasoned essay which incidentally implies an answer to the question, "What makes a novel long?"

Frye, Northrop. *Anatomy of Criticism*. Princeton, 1957.
> Much more of this highly influential book is relevant to the theory of the novel than the section reprinted in this volume.

Garnett, David. "Some Tendencies of the Novel," *Symposium*, I (1930), 96–105.

Garvin, Paul L., ed. and trans. *A Prague School Reader on Esthetics, Literary Structure, and Style*. Washington, D.C., 1958.
> See especially Havránek, "The Functional Differentiation of the Standard Language."

George, W. L. *A Novelist on Novels*. London, 1918.

Gerould, Gordon Hall. *How to Read Fiction*. Princeton, 1937.

Ghiselin, Brewster. "Automatism, Intention, and Autonomy in the Novelist's Production," *Daedalus*, XCII (1963), 297–312.

Gibbon, F. P. "The Truth of Fiction," *Essays in Criticism*, X (1960), 480–483.

Gibson, Walker. "Authors, Speakers, Readers, and Mock Readers," *College English*, XI (1950), 265–269.

Gide, André. *Pretexts: Reflections on Literature and Morality*, ed. Justin O'Brien. New York, 1959.

Gillie, Christopher. *Character in English Literature*. New York, 1965.
> A group of related studies extending from *Everyman* to D. H. Lawrence. A stimulating book.

Glasgow, Ellen. *A Certain Measure*. New York, 1943.
> Critical prefaces to her own novels.

Glicksberg, Charles I. "Fiction and Philosophy," *Arizona Quarterly*, XIII (1957), 5–17.

———. "The Numinous in Fiction," *Arizona Quarterly*, XV (1959), 305–313.
> On the possibilities of mystery, a sense of metaphysical infinity, in the novel.

———. *The Self in Modern Literature*. University Park, Penna., 1963.

Gold, Herbert. "The Lesson of Balzac's Stupidity," *Hudson Review*, VII (1954), 7–18.

———. "The Mystery of Personality in the Novel," *Partisan Review*, XXIV (1957), 453–462.

———. "Truth and Falsity in the Novel," *Hudson Review*, VIII (1955), 410–422.

Goldberg, M. A. "Chronology, Character, and the Human Condition: A Reappraisal of the Modern Novel," *Criticism*, V (1963), 1–12.

Goodman, Paul. *The Structure of Literature*. Chicago, 1954.

Goodman, Theodore. *The Techniques of Fiction*. New York, 1955.

Gordon, Caroline and Allen Tate. *The House of Fiction*. New York, 1950.

Gordon, Caroline. *How to Read a Novel*. New York, 1958.

———. "Some Readings and Misreadings," *Sewanee Review*, LXI (1953), 384–407.

Grabo, C. H. *The Technique of the Novel*. New York, 1928.

Graham, Kenneth. *English Criticism of the Novel, 1865–1900*. Oxford, 1965.

Gransden, K. W. "Thoughts on Contemporary Fiction," *Review of English Literature*, I (April, 1960), 7–17.

Grant, Douglas. "The Novel and Its Critical Terms," *Essays in Criticism*, I (1951), 421–429.

Gray, James. *On Second Thought*. Minneapolis, 1948.

Green, F. C. "Some Observations on Technique and Form in the French Seventeenth and Eighteenth Century Novel," in *Stil- Und Formprobleme in Der Literatur*, ed. R. W. Zandvoort, Heidelberg, 1959.

Greenberg, Alvin. "The Novel of Disintegration: Paradoxical Impossibility in Contemporary Fiction," *Wisconsin Studies in Contemporary Literature*, VII (1966), 103–124.

Greene, Theodore M. *The Arts and the Art of Criticism*. Princeton, 1940. A large, impressive treatment of dozens of aesthetic problems relevant to the theory of fiction.

Gregor, Ian and Brian Nichols. *The Moral and the Story*. London, 1962.

Grundy, Joan and G. Ingli James. "The Mode of the Novel," *Essays in Criticism*, IX (1959), 201–209.

Haines, Helen E. *What's in a Novel*. New York, 1942.

Hale, Nancy. *The Realities of Fiction*. Boston, 1962.

Hamilton, Clayton. *Materials and Methods of Fiction*. New York, 1908.

Handy, William. "Toward a Formalist Criticism of Fiction," *Texas Studies in Language and Literature*, III (1961), 81–88.

Hansen, Agnes. *Twentieth Century Forces in European Fiction*. Chicago, 1934.

Harding, R. M. *An Anatomy of Inspiration*. Cambridge, Mass., 1940.

Hardison, O. B., Jr. "Criticism and the Search for Pattern," *Thought*, XXXVI (1961), 215–230.

Hardy, Barbara. *The Appropriate Form: An Essay on the Novel*. London, 1964.

"My subject is the variety of narrative form, illustrated by a sample of a few novels and novelists sufficiently representative and distinctive."

———. "Formal Analysis and Common Sense," *Essays in Criticism*, XI (1961), 112–115.

Harrah, David. "Explication of 'Depth,' 'Level,' and 'Unity,' " *Journal of Philosophy*, LV (1958), 781–785.

Harris, Robert T. "Plausibility in Fiction," *Journal of Philosophy*, XLIX (1952), 5–10.

Harris, Wendell V. "Style and the Twentieth-Century Novel," *Western Humanities Review,* XVIII (1964), 127–140.

Hartley, L. P. "The Novelist's Responsibility," *Essays and Studies,* XV n.s. (1962), 88–100.

Hartt, Julian N. *The Lost Image of Man.* Baton Rouge, La. 1963.

Hatcher, Anna Granville. "*Voir* as a Modern Novelistic Device," *Philological Quarterly,* XXIII (1944), 354–374.

Hauser, Arnold. "The Conceptions of Time in Modern Art and Science," *Partisan Review,* XXIII (1956), 320–333.

Harvey, W. J. *Character and the Novel.* Ithaca, N.Y., 1965.
  A brilliant, essential book.

Hicks, Granville, ed. *The Living Novel.* New York, 1957.
  Diverse essays by living American novelists on their art.

Hirsch, David. "Reality, Manners, and Mr. Trilling," *Sewanee Review,* LXXII (1964), 420–432.
  Sees Trilling's view of the novel as too limiting.

Hoffman, Frederick J. *Freudianism and the Literary Mind.* Baton Rouge, La., 1945.
  A standard work in its field and a model for studies of intellectual influence.

———. *The Modern Novel in America, 1900–1950.* Chicago, 1951.

———. "The Self in Time," *Chicago Review,* XV (1961), 59–75.

Holloway, John. *The Victorian Sage.* London, 1953.
  The "sages" include novelists as well as writers of discursive prose; excellent rhetorical analysis.

Honig, Edwin. *Dark Conceit: The Making of Allegory.* Evanston, Ill., 1959.
  Definition and historical criticism of allegory, application to such novelists as Melville and Kafka.

———. "In Defense of Allegory," *Kenyon Review,* XX (1958), 1–19.

Horne, Charles F. *The Technique of the Novel.* New York, 1908.

Hough, Graham. "Morality and the Novel," in *The Dream and the Task,* London, 1963.

Howe, Irving. "Mass Society and Post-Modern Fiction," in *A World More Attractive,* New York, 1963.

———. *Politics and the Novel.* New York, 1957.

Hughes, Helen Sard. "The Middle-Class Reader and the English Novel," *JEGP,* XXV (1926), 362–378.

Humphrey, Robert. *Stream of Consciousness in the Modern Novel.* Berkeley, 1954.

———. "'Stream of Consciousness': Technique or Genre?" *Philological Quarterly,* XXX (1951), 434–437.

James, Henry. *The Art of the Novel,* with intro. by R. P. Blackmur. New York, 1934.
  James's critical prefaces, many of which are excerpted in this volume, together with a fine introduction.

———. *The Future of the Novel: Essays on the Art of Fiction,* ed. with intro. by Leon Edel. New York, 1956. The same collection appears as *The House of Fiction.* London, 1957.

————. *Literary Reviews and Essays,* ed. Albert Mordell. New York, 1957.

Jameson, Storm. "The Craft of the Novelist," *English Review,* LVIII (1934), 28–43.

Janeway, Elizabeth. "Fiction's Place in a World Awry," in *Opinions and Perspectives from The New York Times Book Review,* ed. Francis Brown, Boston, 1964.

————. "What's American and What's British in the Modern Novel," in *Highlights of Modern Literature: A Permanent Collection of Memorable Essays from The New York Times Book Review,* ed. Francis Brown, New York, 1954.

Jelly, Oliver. "Fiction and Illness," *Review of English Literature,* III (January, 1962), 80–89.

Jessup, Bertram E. "Aesthetic Size," *Journal of Aesthetics and Art Criticism,* IX (1950), 31–38.

————. "On Fictional Expressions of Cognitive Meaning," *Journal of Aesthetics and Art Criticism,* XXIII (1965), 481–486.

Johnson, Pamela Hansford. "The Genealogy of the Novel," *The New Hungarian Quarterly,* V (1964), 97–107.

Johnson, R. Brimley, ed. *Novelists on Novels.* London, 1928.

Jolly, R. A., R. H. Copland, E. B. Greenwood. "Katherine Mansfield's 'The Fly,' " *Essays in Criticism,* XII (1962), 335–347.

Jordan, Robert M. "The Limits of Illusion: Faulkner, Fielding, and Chaucer," *Criticism,* II (1960), 278–305.
    A critique of "organicism." "Much of the excellence and peculiar excitement of the fiction of Fielding and Chaucer result from the very insistence upon distinguishing content from form."

Kahler, Erich. "The Forms of Form," *Centennial Review,* VII (1963), 131–143.

————. "Transformation of Modern Fiction," *Comparative Literature,* VII (1955), 121–128.

Kayser, Wolfgang. *The Grotesque in Art and Literature,* trans. Ulrich Weisstein. Bloomington, Ind., 1963.
    Contains discussions of such novelists as Gogol, Dickens, Kafka.

Kazin, Alfred. *On Native Grounds.* New York, 1942.

Kennedy, Margaret. *The Outlaws on Parnassus.* London, 1958.

Kettle, Arnold. *An Introduction to the English Novel,* 2 vols. London, 1951; New York, 1960.
    Analyses of classic novels within an historical framework; morally serious, formally acute, socially perceptive, Marxist but not thesis-ridden.

Kiely, Robert. "The Craft of Despondency—The Traditional Novelists," *Daedalus,* XCII (1963), 220–237.

Killham, John. "The Use of 'Concreteness' as an Evaluative Term in F. R. Leavis's 'The Great Tradition,' " *British Journal of Aesthetics,* V (1965), 14–24.

Kohler, Dayton. "Time in the Modern Novel," *College English,* X (October, 1948), 15–24.

Kolnai, Aurel. "On the Concept of the Interesting," *British Journal of Aesthetics,* IV (1964), 22–39.

Krey, Laura. "Time and the English Novel," in *Twentieth Century English*, ed. W. S. Knickerbocker, New York, 1946.

Krieger, Murray. *The Tragic Vision: Variations on a Theme in Literary Interpretation*. New York, 1960.

Kris, Ernst. *Psychoanalytic Explorations in Art*. New York, 1952.
> See especially "Daydream and Fiction," "The Aesthetic Illusion," the section on the comic.

Kronenberger, Louis, ed. *Novelists on Novelists: An Anthology*. New York, 1962.

Krutch, Joseph Wood. *Five Masters: A Study in the Mutations of the Novel*. New York, 1930.
> Admittedly old-fashioned criticism, a mixture of biography and literary description; warmly affectionate essays on Boccaccio, Cervantes, Richardson, Stendhal, and Proust.

Langer, Susanne K. *Feeling and Form*. New York, 1953.
> A general aesthetic with important implications for the theory of the novel.

——. *Philosophy in a New Key*. Cambridge, Mass., 1942.

Lathrop, Henry Burrowes. *The Art of the Novelist*. London, 1919.

Lawrence, D. H. "Morality and the Novel," in *Selected Literary Criticism*, ed. Anthony Beal, New York, 1956.
> "The novel is the highest example of subtle interrelatedness that man has discovered. Everything is true in its own time, place, circumstance, and untrue outside of its own place, time, circumstance."

——. "Why the Novel Matters," in *Selected Literary Criticism*, ed. Anthony Beal, New York, 1956.

Leavis, F. R. "The Novel as Dramatic Poem (I): 'Hard Times,'" *Scrutiny*, XIV (1947), 185–203.
> Substantially the same essay appears in *The Great Tradition*. But in *Scrutiny* the essay inaugurated a series of essays on novels as "dramatic poems," the phrase and the theoretical point of view becoming very influential.

——. *The Great Tradition*. London, 1948.
> Stimulating readings of individual novels within a dogmatic, very limiting framework.

Leavis, Q. D. *Fiction and the Reading Public*. London, 1932.

Lee, Vernon [Violet Paget]. *The Handling of Words, and Other Studies in Literary Psychology*. New York, 1923.

Lees, F. N. "Identification and Emotion in the Novel: A Feature of Narrative Method," *British Journal of Aesthetics*, IV (1964), 109–113.

Leggett, H. W. *The Idea in Fiction*. London, 1934.
> An interesting treatment of the novelist's values in relation to technique.

Lemon, Lee T. "The Illusion of Life: A Modern Version of an Old Heresy," *Western Humanities Review*, XVII (1963), 65–74.

Lemon, Lee T. and Marion J. Reis, trans. and ed. *Russian Formalist Criticism: Four Essays*. Lincoln, Nebr., 1965.

Two essays by Victor Shklovsky, one each by Boris Tomashevsky and Boris Eichenbaum, the first three of considerable significance to the theory of fiction.

Lerner, Laurence. *The Truest Poetry: An Essay on the Question What is Literature?* London, 1960.

Lesser, Simon O. "The Attitude of Fiction," *Modern Fiction Studies,* II (1956), 47–55.

>Response to fiction differs from response to experience both in the concentration and the ambivalence of the former.

———. *Fiction and the Unconscious.* Boston, 1957.

>Most of this deals less with fiction than with response to fiction, but the chapter on "The Language of Fiction" makes a good many useful distinctions between language put to imaginative and discursive purposes.

———. "The Functions of Form in Narrative Art," *Psychiatry,* XVIII (1955), 51–63.

Levi, Albert William. *Literature, Philosophy and the Imagination.* Bloomington, Ind., 1962.

>*See* Chapter II: "Forms of Literary Imagination: Poetry and the Novel."

Levin, Harry. *Contexts of Criticism.* Cambridge, Mass., 1957.

>*See especially* "What is Realism?", "Observations on the Style of Ernest Hemingway" as a masterful piece of applied stylistic criticism, "Society as its Own Historian," and "Symbolism and Fiction."

———. "The Novel," in *Dictionary of World Literature,* ed. Joseph Shipley, revised edition, New York, 1953.

———. "Toward a Sociology of the Novel," *Journal of the History of Ideas,* XXVI (1965), 148–154.

Lewis, R. W. B. *The Picaresque Saint: Representative Figures in Contemporary Fiction.* New York, 1959.

Lewis, Wyndham. *Men Without Art.* London, 1934.

>*See especially* "Appendix: The Taxi-Cab Driver Test for 'Fiction.' "

———. *Time and Western Man.* New York, 1928.

Liddell, Robert. *Some Principles of Fiction.* London, 1953.

>A provocative collection of remarks (Liddell's and others') on aspects of fictional craftsmanship, capricious in organization, often dogmatic.

———. *A Treatise on the Novel.* London, 1947.

>Somewhat more systematic than the above, but the tendency to announce rather than to demonstrate is common to both.

Littlejohn, David. "The Anti-realists," *Daedalus,* XCII (1963), 250–264.

Lodge, David. *Language of Fiction: Essays in Criticism and Verbal Analysis of the English Novel.* London, New York, 1966.

>A brilliant synthesis of theories of style in fiction (though Lodge avoids the word "style") and some fine essays in practical stylistic criticism. The best single book on fictional style.

Lord, Catharine. "Aesthetic Unity," *Journal of Philosophy*, LVIII (1961), 321–327.

Lowenthal, Leo. *Literature and the Image of Man: Sociological Studies of the European Drama and Novel, 1600–1900*. Boston, 1957.

Lukács, George. "Essay on the Novel," *International Literature*, 5 (1936), pp. 68–74.

———. *The Historical Novel*, trans. H. and S. Mitchell. London, 1962. Thoroughly Marxist in its orientation; still the best study of the historical novel.

———. "The Intellectual Physiognomy of Literary Characters," *International Literature*, 8 (1936), pp. 55–83.

———. *Studies in European Realism: A Sociological Survey of the Writings of Balzac, Stendhal, Zola, Tolstoy, Gorki, and Others*, trans. Edith Bone. London, 1950.

Lutwack, Leonard. "Mixed and Uniform Prose Styles in the Novel," *Journal of Aesthetics and Art Criticism*, XVIII (1960), 350–357.

Lytle, Andrew Nelson. "The Image as Guide to Meaning in the Historical Novel," *Sewanee Review*, LXI (1953), 408–426.

———. "Impressionism, the Ego, and the First Person," *Daedalus*, XCII (1963), 281–296.

———. "The Working Novelist and the Mythmaking Process," *Daedalus*, LXXXVIII (1959), 326–338.

Macauley, Robie and George Lanning. *Technique in Fiction*. New York, 1964.
One book on how to write fiction that is theoretically sophisticated and sensitive in its values.

Mann, Thomas. "The Art of the Novel," in *The Creative Vision: Modern European Writers on Their Art*, ed. Haskell M. Block and Herman Salinger, New York, 1960.

———. *The Genesis of a Novel*, trans. Richard and Clara Winston. London, 1961.

Mansfield, Katherine. *Novels and Novelists*, ed. J. Middleton Murry. London, 1930.

Marcus, Steven. "The Novel Again," *Partisan Review*, XXIX (1962), 171–195.

Maurois, André *The Art of Writing*, trans. Gerard Hopkins. New York, 1960.

Martin, Harold C., ed. *Style in Prose Fiction: English Institute Essays, 1958*. New York, 1959.
The first essay is reprinted here. The essays that follow contain some models for applied stylistic analysis and the volume contains a useful bibliography of stylistic studies.

Maugham, W. Somerset. *The Summing Up*. New York, 1938.

de Maupassant, Guy. "Essay on the Novel," in *The Portable Maupassant*, New York, 1947.
Originally the preface to *Pierre et Jean*.

Mauriac, Claude. "The 'New Novel' in France," in *Opinions and Perspectives from The New York Times Book Review*, ed. Francis Brown, Boston, 1964.

May, Derwent. "The Novelist as Moralist and the Moralist as Critic," *Essays in Criticism*, X (1960), 320–328.

Mayhead, Robin. *Understanding Literature*. Cambridge, 1965.

McCarthy, Mary. "Characters in Fiction," in *On the Contrary*, New York, n.d.

> On what makes characters substantial and memorable and how the ability to make characters has given way to a kind of narrative ventriloquist act.

———. "The Fact in Fiction," *Partisan Review*, XXVII (1960), 438–458; reprinted in *On the Contrary*, New York, n.d.

> A definition of the novel in terms of factuality, veracity, etc., a qualified despair over the possibility of such traditional fiction in the present time.

McCormick, John. *Catastrophe and Imagination: An Interpretation of the Recent English and American Novel*. London, 1957.

McHugh, Vincent. *Primer of the Novel*. New York, 1950.

McKillop, Alan Dugald. *The Early Masters of English Fiction*. Lawrence, Kansas, 1956.

MacShane, Frank, ed. *Critical Writings of Ford Madox Ford*. Lincoln, Nebr., 1964.

Melchiori, Giorgio. *The Tightrope Walkers: Studies in Mannerism in Modern English Literature*. London, 1956.

Mendilow, A. A. *Time and the Novel*. London, 1952.

> A remarkably thorough treatment of technique. For further reading on the subject, one might well complement Mendilow by consulting some of the criticism that takes a more philosophical view of the subject, one of the volumes of Poulet, e.g., or the work by Meyerhoff which follows.

Meyerhoff, Hans. *Time in Literature*. Berkeley, 1955.

Mizener, Arthur. *The Sense of Life in the Modern Novel*. Boston, 1964.

> Defense, and practical criticism, of the novel of manners.

Monroe, N. Elizabeth. *The Novel and Society*. Chapel Hill, N.C., 1941

> The record of a fruitless search for a great visionary novelist.

Montague, C. E. *A Writer's Notes on His Trade*. London, 1930.

Moore, Patrick. *Science and Fiction*. London, 1957.

> The bibliography on science fiction is a large one, very little of which is included here. This is a good British study.

Morris-Jones, H. U. W. "The Language of Feelings," *British Journal of Aesthetics*, II (1962), 17–25.

Moss, Howard. "Notes on Fiction," *Wisconsin Studies in Contemporary Literature*, VII (1966), 1–11.

Mothersill, Mary. " 'Unique' as an Aesthetic Predicate," *Journal of Philosophy*, LVIII (1961), 421–437.

Mudrick, Marvin. "Character and Event in Fiction," *Yale Review*, L (1960), 202–218.

> "In the beginning of poetry is the word; in the beginning of fiction is the event."

Mueller, William R. *The Prophetic Voice in Modern Fiction*. New York, 1959.

Muir, Edwin. *The Structure of the Novel.* New York, 1929.
    To some extent an argument with Forster's *Aspects of the Novel;* an account of the operation of different kinds of fictional structures in time and space.
Muller, H. J. "Impressionism in Fiction," *American Scholar,* VII (1938), 355–367.
————. *Modern Fiction: A Study of Values.* New York, 1937.
Murry, John Middleton. *The Problem of Style.* Oxford, 1922.
Myers, Walter L. *The Later Realism: A Study of Characterization in the British Novel.* Chicago, 1927.
Noon, William T. "Modern Literature and the Sense of Time," *Thought,* XXXIII (1958), 571–603.
Norris, Frank. *The Responsibilities of the Novelist.* New York, 1903.
Nicholson, Norman. *Man and Literature.* London, 1943.
O'Connor, Frank. *The Mirror in the Roadway: A Study of the Modern Novel.* New York, 1956.
    Its theses, general constructs, and methods are less interesting than its insights into particular novels, which are intuitive and highly original.
O'Connor, William Van, ed. *Forms of Modern Fiction.* Minneapolis, 1948.
    An impressive collection of essays, various in their methods, most directed toward particular modern novelists.
————. *The Grotesque: An American Genre and Other Essays.* Carbondale, Ill., 1962.
————. "The Novel as a Social Document," *American Quarterly,* IV (1952), 169–175.
————. "The Novel of Experience," *Critique,* I (1956), 37–44.
O'Faolain, Sean. *The Short Story.* London, 1948.
    A genial, personal, penetrating commentary on craftsmanship, directed toward the short story but often applicable to larger forms.
————. *The Vanishing Hero: Studies in the Novelists of the Twenties.* London, 1956.
O'Grady, Walter. "On Plot in Modern Fiction: Hardy, James, and Conrad," *Modern Fiction Studies,* XI (1965), 107–115.
O'Hare, Charles B. "Myth or Plot? A Study in Ways of Ordering Narrative," *Arizona Quarterly,* XIII (1957), 238–250.
Opel, Harold. "The Double Symbol," *American Literature,* XXIII (1951), 1–6.
    On Hawthorne, but a useful point for wider application.
Ortega y Gasset, José. *The Dehumanization of Art and Other Writings on Art and Culture.* New York, n.d.
    Contains "Notes on the Novel," "On Point of View in the Arts," "The Self and the Other."
Orvis, Mary Burchard. *The Art of Writing Fiction.* New York, 1948.
Overton, Grant. *The Philosophy of Fiction.* New York, 1928.
Pascal, Roy. "The Autobiographical Novel and the Autobiography," *Essays in Criticism,* IX (1959), 134–150.

———. "Tense and Novel," *Modern Language Review*, LVII (1962), 1–11.

An interesting discussion of a German critic who proposes a difference in grammatical tense between history and fiction.

Paul, David. "The Novel Art," *Twentieth Century*, CLIII (June, 1953), 436–442.

———. "The Novel Art: II," *Twentieth Century*, CLIV (October, 1953), 294–301.

———. "Time and the Novelist," *Partisan Review*, XXI (1954), 636–649.

Penzoldt, Peter. *The Supernatural in Fiction*. London, 1952.

Perry, Bliss. *A Study of Prose Fiction*. Boston, 1902.

Peter, John. "Joyce and the Novel," *Kenyon Review*, XVIII (1956), 619–632.

Peyre, Henri. *Literature and Sincerity*. New Haven, 1963.

See especially Chapter 6, "The Personal Novel," Chapter 10, "The Perils and Benefits of Literary Sincerity."

Piper, Warrene. "Sources and Processes in the Writing of Fiction," *American Journal of Psychology*, XLIII (1931), 188–201.

Plimpton, George, ed. *Writers at Work: The Paris Review Interviews, Second Series*. New York, 1963.

Poulet, Georges. *The Interior Distance*. Baltimore, 1959.

An extension of *Studies in Human Time*, treating Balzac, Hugo, Musset, and others.

———. *Studies in Human Time*. Baltimore, 1956.

Concerned with the sense of time in major French writers, an appendix on American writers; a dense, rewarding book.

Priestley, J. B. "Some Reflections of a Popular Novelist," *Essays and Studies*, XVIII (1932), 149–159.

Pritchett, V. S. "The Future of English Fiction," *Partisan Review*, XV (1948), 1063–1070.

———. *The Living Novel*. London, 1946.

Witty, penetrating esays on some classic novels, and some minor ones.

Proust, Marcel. *Marcel Proust on Art and Literature, 1896–1919*, trans. Sylvia Townsend Warner. New York, 1958.

Rahv, Philip. "Fiction and the Criticism of Fiction," *Kenyon Review*, XVIII (1956), 276–299.

Mainly a protest against over-ingenious symbolic readings.

———. *Image and Idea*. New York, 1957.

Ransom, John Crowe, "Characters and Character," *American Review*, VI (January, 1936), 271–288.

———. "The Content of the Novel," *American Review*, VII (1936), 301–318.

———. "The Understanding of Fiction," *Kenyon Review*, XII (1950), 189–218.

A speculative and inconclusive essay on the possibility of applying methods of criticizing poetry to the criticism of fiction.

Rathburn, Robert C. and Martin Steinmann, Jr., eds. *From Jane Austen to Joseph Conrad*. Minneapolis, 1958.

Reiss, H. S. "Style and Structure in Modern Experimental Fiction," in *Stil- Und Formprobleme in Der Literatur*, ed. R. W. Zandvoort, Heidelberg, 1959.

Rickword, C. H. "A Note on Fiction," in *Forms of Modern Fiction*, ed. William Van O'Connor, Minneapolis, 1948.
    A rather acrimonious attack on the location of the interest and value of fiction in character, a promotion of the importance of narrative method and organic structure.

Robbe-Grillet, Alain. "From Realism to Reality," *Evergreen Review*, X (1966), 50–53, 83.

———. "Reflections on Some Aspects of the Traditional Novel," *International Literary Annual*, I (1958), 114–121.
    An attack on the values associated with the categories "character," "story," and "content."

Rodway, A. E. "The Truth of Fiction: A Critical Dialogue," *Essays in Criticism*, VIII (1958), 405–417.

Rogers, W. H. "Form in the Art-Novel," *Helicon*, II (1939), 1–17.

Romberg, Bertil. *Studies in the Narrative Technique of the First-Person Novel*. Stockholm, 1962.

Rosenheim, E. W., Jr. *What Happens in Literature: A Student's Guide to Poetry, Drama and Fiction*. Chicago, 1960.

Rovit, Earl H. "The Ambiguous Modern Novel," *Yale Review*, XLIX (1960), 413–424.

Saintsbury, George. "Technique," *Dial*, LXXX (April, 1926), 273–278.

Sale, Roger, ed. *Discussions of the Novel*. Boston, 1960.

Sarraute, Nathalie. *The Age of Suspicion: Essays on the Novel*, trans. Maria Jolas. New York, 1963.
    A manifesto for the spare, objective novel.

Sartre, Jean-Paul. *What is Literature?*, trans. Bernard Frechtman. New York, 1949.

Savage, D. S. *The Withered Branch*. New York, 1950.
    Essays on the modern novel.

Schlauch, Margaret. *Antecedents of the English Novel, 1400–1600*. Warsaw and London, 1963.
    A far more usable account of the same material covered in the early volumes of E. A. Baker.

Scholes, Robert. *Approaches to the Novel*. San Francisco, 1961.

Scholes, Robert and Robert Kellogg. *The Nature of Narrative*. New York, 1966.
    A broad, impressive treatment of all major narrative forms, viewing the novel not as an evolutionary culmination but as one of several narrative possibilities.

Schorer, Mark. "Fiction and the 'Matrix of Analogy,'" *Kenyon Review*, XI (1949), 539–560.

———. *Society and Self in the Novel: English Institute Essays, 1955*. New York, 1956.

———. "Technique as Discovery," *Hudson Review*, I (1948), 67–87.

Scott, Nathan A., Jr. *Forms of Extremity in the Modern Novel*. Richmond, Va., 1965.

Theologically oriented essays on Kafka, Hemingway, Camus, Graham Greene.

Scrutton, Mary. "Addiction to Fiction," *Twentieth Century*, CLIX (April, 1956), 363–373.

Sherman, Caroline B. "A Brief for Fiction," *South Atlantic Quarterly*, XXXVI (1937), 335–347.

Sherwood, Irma Z. "The Novelists as Commentators," in *The Age of Johnson: Essays Presented to Chauncey Brewster Tinker*, ed. F. W. Hilles, New Haven, 1949.

Shumaker, Wayne. *Literature and the Irrational*. Englewood Cliffs, N.J., 1960.

> *See especially* Chapter 5: "Fictive Plot: Its Genesis and Some Recurrent Motifs."

Shroder, Maurice Z. "The Novel as a Genre," *Massachusetts Review*, IV (1963), 291–308.

Singer, Godfrey Frank. *The Epistolary Novel*. Philadelphia, 1938.

Smart, Charles A. "On the Road to Page One," *Yale Review*, XXXVII (1947), 242–256.

Smith, Janet Adam, ed. *Henry James and Robert Louis Stevenson: A Record of Friendship and Criticism*. London, 1948.

Snow, C. P. "Science, Politics, and the Novelist," *Kenyon Review*, XXIII (1961), 1–17.

Sontag, Susan. "On Style," *Partisan Review*, XXXII (1965), 543–560.

Sorenson, Virginia. "Is it True?—The Novelist and his Materials," *Western Humanities Review*, VII (1953), 283–292.

Spencer, John. "A Note on the "Steady Monologuy of the Interiors,' " *Review of English Literature*, VI (April, 1965), 32–41.

Stafford, Jean. "The Psychological Novel," *Kenyon Review*, X (1948), 214–227.

Stallman, Robert Wooster, ed. *The Critic's Notebook*. Minneapolis, 1950.

> A collection of brief excerpts from many critics, few of them directed specifically toward the novel but most of them relevant to the novel. An extensive bibliography.

——. "Fiction and Its Critics: A Reply to Mr. Rahv," *Kenyon Review*, XIX (1957), 290–299.

> A defense of symbolic exegesis; cf. Rahv above.

Stang, Richard. *The Theory of the Novel in England, 1850–1870*. New York, 1959.

Stegner, Wallace. "A Problem in Fiction," *Pacific Spectator*, III (1949), 368–375.

> A personal account of the genesis of a story.

Stein, Gertrude. *Narration*, intro. Thornton Wilder. Chicago, 1935.

Stern, Madeline B. "Counterclockwise: Flux of Time in Literature," *Sewanee Review*, XLIV (1936), 338–365.

Stevenson, David L. "The Activists," *Daedalus*, XCII (1963), 238–249.

Stevenson, Lionel. *The English Novel: A Panorama*. Boston, 1960.

> A first-rate one-volume history.

Stevenson, Robert Louis. "A Gossip on Romance," in *Works*, Vol. XIII, New York, 1895.

————. "A Humble Remonstrance," in *Works*, Vol. XIII, New York, 1895.

Stevick, Philip. "Fictional Chapters and Open Ends," *JGE: The Journal of General Education*, XVII (1966), 261–272.

————. "The Theory of Fictional Chapters," *Western Humanities Review*, XX (1966), 231–241.

Struve, Gleb. *"Monologue Interieur:* The Origins of the Formula and the First Statement of its Possibilities," *PMLA*, LXIX (1954), 1101–1111.

Sutton, Walter. "The Literary Image and the Reader: A Consideration of the Theory of Spatial Form," *Journal of Aesthetics and Art Criticism*, XVI (1957), 112–123.
> Cf. Joseph Frank's "Spatial Form in Modern Literature."

Svoboda, Karel. "Content, Subject and Material of a Work of Literature," *Journal of Aesthetics and Art Criticism*, IX (1950), 39–45.

Swinnerton, Frank. "Variations of Form in the Novel," *Essays and Studies*, XXIII (1937), 79–92.

Symons, Julian. "Politics and the Novel," *Twentieth Century*, CLXX (Winter, 1962), 147–154.

Sypher, Wylie. *Loss of the Self in Modern Literature and Art*. New York, 1962.

Tate, Allen. "Techniques of Fiction," *Sewanee Review*, LII (1944), 210–225.
> On "completeness of presentation in the art of fiction," the model being Flaubert. Widely reprinted.

Taylor, H. W. "Modern Fiction and the Doctrine of Uniformity," *Philological Quarterly*, XIX (1940), 226–236.

————. " 'Particular Character': an Early Phase of a Literary Evolution," *PMLA*, LX (1945), 161–174.

Thompson, Denys. *Reading and Discrimination*. London, 1949.

Tilford, John E. "Point of View in the Novel," *Emory University Quarterly*, XX (1964), 121–130.

————. "Some Changes in the Technique of the Novel," *Emory University Quarterly*, IX (1953), 167–174.

Tillotson, Kathleen. *The Tale and the Teller*. London, 1959.

Tillyard, E. M. W. *The Epic Strain in the English Novel*. London, 1958.
> Since almost no novels, in Tillyard's view, attain epic stature, this is an oddly negative approach.

————. "The Novel as Literary Kind," *Essays and Studies*, IX (1956), 78–86.

Tindall, William York. *Forces in Modern British Literature, 1885–1946*. New York, 1947.

————. *The Literary Symbol*. New York, 1955.

Toynbee, Philip. "Experiment and the Future of the Novel," in *The Craft of Letters in England*, ed. John Lehmann, London, 1956.

Trilling, Lionel. *The Liberal Imagination*. New York, 1950.
> *See especially* "Manners, Morals, and the Novel," "Art and Fortune," "The Meaning of a Literary Idea."

————. *The Opposing Self*. New York, 1955.

Turnell, Martin. *The Novel in France.* New York, 1951.
   See especially the first chapter, "The Language of Fiction."
Ullman, Stephen. "Style and Personality," *Review of English Literature,* VI (April, 1965), 21–31.
"The Uses of Comic Vision," in *The British Imagination: A Critical Survey from The Times Literary Supplement.* New York, 1961.
Uzzell, Thomas H. *The Technique of the Novel.* New York, 1959.
   Rather cynically formulaic.
Van Ghent, Dorothy. *The English Novel, Form and Function.* New York, 1953.
   Ingenious, stimulating essays on classic novels employing a variety of methods.
Vivas, Eliseo. *The Artistic Transaction and Essays on Theory of Literature.* Columbus, Ohio, 1963.
———. "The Self and its Masks," *Southern Review,* I (1965), 317–336.
Wagenknecht, Edward. *Cavalcade of the English Novel.* New York, 1943.
Wagner, Geoffrey. "Sociology and Fiction," *Twentieth Century,* CLXVII (February, 1960), 108–114.
Walcutt, Charles Child. "From Scientific Theory to Aesthetic Fact: The 'Naturalistic' Novel," *Quarterly Review of Literature,* III (1946), 167–179.
———. "Interpreting the Symbol," *College English,* XIV (1953), 446–454.
Warburg, Jeremy. "Idiosyncratic Style," *Review of English Literature,* VI (April, 1965), 56–65.
Watt, Ian. *The Rise of the Novel.* London and Berkeley, 1957.
   By far the best treatment of the sociological, formal, and philosophical problems surrounding the beginnings of the novel. Varies as practical criticism, from brilliant on Defoe and Richardson to somewhat procrustean on Fielding.
Wellek, René and Austin Warren. *Theory of Literature.* New York, 1949.
   See especially Chapter XVI: "The Nature and Modes of Narrative Fiction."
Welty, Eudore. "Words into Fiction," *Southern Review,* I (1965), 543–553.
Wescott, Glenway. *Images of Truth: Remembrances and Criticism.* New York, 1962.
West, Paul. *The Modern Novel.* London, 1963.
   International in scope; a broad, highly intelligent survey.
———. "The Nature of Fiction," *Essays in Criticism,* XIII (1963), 95–100.
West, Ray B., Jr. and R. W. Stallman. *The Art of Modern Fiction.* New York, 1949.
West, Rebecca. *The Strange Necessity,* New York, 1928.
Weston, Harold. *Form in Literature.* London, 1934.
Wharton, Edith. *The Writing of Fiction.* New York, 1925.
Wheelwright, Philip. *The Burning Fountain.* Bloomington, Ind., 1954.
   An important book on symbolism.
Williams, Raymond. *Culture and Society, 1780–1950.* London, 1958.

An exemplary study of the relations between certain literary works, among them a good many novels, and the growth of industrial culture.

————. *Reading and Criticism*. London, 1950.

————. "Realism and the Contemporary Novel," *Partisan Review*, XXVI (1959), 200–213.

Wilson, Angus. "The Novelist and the Narrator," in *English Studies Today: Second Series; Lectures and Papers Read at the Fourth Conference of the International Association of University Professors of English Held at Lausanne and Berne, August, 1959*. Berne, 1961.

Wilson, Edmund. *Axel's Castle: A Study of Imaginative Literature of 1870–1930*. New York, 1931.

Wolfe, Thomas. "The Story of a Novel," in *The Thomas Wolfe Reader*, ed. C. Hugh Holman, New York, 1962.

Woodman, Ross. "Literature and Life," *Queens Quarterly*, LXVIII (1962), 621–631.

Woolf, Virginia. *The Common Reader*. London, 1925.

————. *Granite and Rainbow*. London, 1958.

————. *The Second Common Reader*. London, 1932.

"The Workaday World that the Novelist Never Enters," in *The British Imagination: A Critical Survey from The Times Literary Supplement*. New York, 1961.

Wright, Andrew. "Irony and Fiction," *Journal of Aesthetics and Art Criticism*, XII (1953), 111–118.

Wright, Walter Francis, ed. *Joseph Conrad on Fiction*. Lincoln, Nebr., 1964.

Wyndham, Francis. "Twenty-five Years of the Novel," in *The Craft of Letters in England*, ed. John Lehmann. London, 1956.

Zabel, Morton Dauwen. *Craft and Character: Texts, Method, and Vocation in Modern Fiction*. New York, 1957.

Excellent eclectic criticism; especially good on Conrad and Dickens.

Zola, Emile. *The Experimental Novel and Other Essays*, trans. Belle M. Sherman. New York, 1893.

INDEX

An Act of Faith (Irwin Shaw), 164
Adam Bede (George Eliot), 236, 391–93
Adams, Henry, 294, 301
Addison, Joseph, 95
Albright, Evelyn May, 114*n*
Alice in Wonderland (Carroll), 14, 39, 50
All the King's Men (R. P. Warren), 154, 164
The Ambassadors (James), 13, 62, 90, 91, 144*n*, 208, 212, 232–33
Amelia (Fielding), 181
Ames, Van Meter, 116*n*
Amis, Kingsley, 238
Amory, Thomas, 41
"Anatomy," 40–43
The Anatomy of Melancholy (Burton), 31, 40
Anderson, Sherwood, 81
Anna Christie (O'Neill), 16
Anna Karenina (Tolstoy), 54, 374
Antigone (Sophocles), 159
The Apocalypse (D. H. Lawrence), 379
Apologia pro Vita Sua (Newman), 35
Appearance and reality, 7, 14
Apuleius, 37, 38, 41
Aristotle, 1, 13, 20, 89, 110, 132*n*, 293, 305, 375
Arms and the Man (G. B. Shaw), 165
Arnold, Matthew, 27, 110*n*, 206, 370
Arvin, Newton, 351
As I Lay Dying (Faulkner), 102–3
The Aspern Papers (James), 184
Athenaeus, 39
Auden, W. H., 301, 349–50
Auerbach, Erich, 163, 374
Augustine, Saint, 35, 290, 293
Austen, Jane, 2, 5, 15, 18, 20, 27, 32, 34, 36–38, 48, 52, 87–88, 93, 99, 100, 106, 140, 165, 176, 183, 186, 223, 228–31, 239, 254, 320–23, 324, 326
"The author's second self," 92–93

Autumn (Strindberg), 165
The Awkward Age (James), 95, 105, 130
Ayer, A. J., 202*n*

Background characters, 236
Bader, A. L., 117*n*
Baker, Harry T., 115*n*
Balzac, Honoré de, 15, 22, 23, 30, 261, 269, 314*n*, 356, 358, 376, 395
Barbauld, Mrs. A. L., 260*n*, 273
Barchester Towers (Trollope), 52, 96, 276
Barth, Karl, 299, 303
Barzun, Jacques, 139
Battenhouse, Roy W., 293
Baudelaire, Charles, 23, 26, 335
Beach, Joseph Warren, 108, 112–13, 116, 131, 275, 276
Beach, Stewart, 116*n*
The Bear (Faulkner), 161
Beardsley, M. C., 148*n*
Beckett, Samuel, 2, 254, 283, 284*n*, 289
Behn, Aphra, 2
Bell, Clive, 338
Bellow, Saul, 96, 101, 334, 368
Bement, Douglas, 116*n*
Bennett, Arnold, 48, 49, 241, 254
Benson, Stella, 263
Bentley, Phyllis, 46–57, 116
Berger extravagant (Sorel), 17
Bergson, Henri, 27, 287–88, 289
Berrigan, Daniel, 284
Besant, Walter, 108, 114*n*
Beware of the Dog (Roald Dahl), 164
Blake, William, 335
Bland, D. S., 255, 312–330
Bleak House (Dickens), 8, 325–26, 334
Bloomfield, Leonard, 190*n*, 203
Boccaccio, Giovanni, 38, 106
Boethius, 41
Boileau, Nicolas, 264
Booth, Bradford, 108, 131
Booth, Wayne C., 87–107, 134*n*, 254

Borrow, George, 31, 32, 41
Bouvard et Pecuchet (Flaubert), 40
Bowen, Elizabeth, 83, 118*n*, 142*n*, 314, 331*n*
Bowles, Paul, 367
Bowling, Lawrence, 129*n*
Bradley, A. C., 221
Brave New World (Huxley), 37, 91, 263, 295
Brée, Germaine, 248–49
The Bride of Lammermoor (Scott), 225
Brighton Rock (Graham Greene), 98
Brontë, Charlotte, 34, 48, 52, 55, 231
Brontë, Emily, 5, 6, 32, 34, 48, 52, 55, 67, 69–71, 79, 140, 185, 254, 276, 320
Brook Kerith (George Moore), 255
Brooks, Cleanth, 117*n*, 118*n*
The Brothers Karamazov (Dostoevsky), 6, 141
Brower, Reuben A., 205*n*
Browne, Sir Thomas, 35, 345
Browning, Robert, 104
Brumm, Ursula, 334, 354–68
Brunetière, Ferdinand, 29
Buechner, Frederick, 366
Buffon, Georges Louis Leclerc, comte de, 82
Bullough, Edward, 111*n*
Bultmann, Rudolf Karl, 299
Bunyan, John, 6, 13, 34, 35, 119, 316
Burke, Edmund, 8
Burke, Kenneth, 175, 205, 232
Burns, Robert, 34
Burton, Robert, 40
Butler, Samuel, 37, 119, 125–26, 150*n*, 183–84
Butterfield, Herbert, 281
By Love Possessed (Cozzens), 219
Byron, George Gordon, Lord, 19, 27, 160

Cabell, J. B., 263
The Caine Mutiny (Wouk), 154
Caldwell, Erskine, 81
Callahan, John F., 293

Campbell, Joseph, 15
Camus, Albert, 86, 96, 101
Candide (Voltaire), 16, 37, 295
Caponigri, Robert, 306
Capote, Truman, 366
The Captive and the Free (J. Cary), 90
The "Card," 238–42
The Card (Bennett), 241
Carlyle, Thomas, 31, 34, 41, 215, 342
Carroll, Lewis, 14, 39, 50
Cary, Joyce, 86, 90
"A Cask of Amontillado" (Poe), 91
Cassirer, Ernst, 336, 338–40, 342, 347, 365
Castiglione, Giovanni, 39
The Castle of Otranto (Walpole), 320
The Catcher in the Rye (Salinger), 96
La Celestina (Rojas), 277*n*
The central consciousness, 61–62, 94, 112
Cervantes, Miguel de, 2, 14–28, 384–87
Cézanne, Paul, 314
The Changeling (Middleton), 160
La Chartreuse de Parme (Stendhal), 18, 22, 24
Chase, Richard, 9, 28
Chaucer, Geoffrey, 4, 40, 94
Chekhov, Anton, 28, 33, 156, 158, 163, 224
Chesterton, G. K., 239
Cicero, 189
Clarissa (Richardson), 4, 86, 98, 178–79, 211, 255, 262, 273, 277, 375
Clark, Glenn, 115*n*
Claude Lorrain, 318, 319, 328, 329
Clayhanger (Bennett), 49
The Cocktail Party (Eliot), 336
Coleman, Elliott, 297
Coleridge, Samuel Taylor, 1, 110*n*, 349
Collins, Wilkie, 158, 320, 330
Comfort, Alex, 118*n*
The Compleat Angler (Walton), 41

Confessions of a Justified Sinner (Hogg), 41
Confessions of an Octogenarian (Nievo), 358–60
Confessions of Zeno (Svevo), 87
Congreve, William, 2
Connolly, Francis, 118n
The Conquest of Granada (Dryden), 161
Conrad, Joseph, 5, 12, 29–30, 34, 71, 73, 80, 83, 86, 125, 133, 140, 152, 157, 161, 236, 270, 315, 334, 367, 399–403
The Consolation of Philosophy (Bocthius), 41
Constable, John, 314
Cook, Albert S., 7
Cooper, James Fenimore, 214, 236
Cornford, Francis, 19, 25
The Counterfeiters (Gide), 24, 403–405
A Country Love Story (Jean Stafford), 165
Cozzens, J. G., 219
Crabbe, George, 6
Crane, R. S., 140, 141–45, 149n, 151–54, 157
Crane, Stephen, 158, 366
Cross, Ethan Allen, 115n
Cullman, Oscar, 299, 300–301
Cymbeline (Shakespeare), 160

Dahl, Roald, 164
Daisy Miller (James), 165
Daniélou, Jean, 303
Darkness at Noon (Koestler), 149
Daudet, Alphonse, 395
David Copperfield (Dickens), 48, 215, 234
Davis, H. L., 161
Dawson, Christopher, 281
"The Dead" (Joyce), 94, 334
Death of a Salesman (A. Miller), 158
The Death of Ivan Ilyich (Tolstoy), 164
Death in Venice (Mann), 250–51
La Débâcle (Zola), 22
Decameron (Boccaccio), 36
Decline and Fall (Waugh), 100

Defoe, Daniel, 2, 3, 4, 32, 36, 48, 51, 57, 67–69, 84, 86, 114n, 134n, 177–78, 223, 228, 253, 255, 259, 260–61, 316, 356, 375
Deipnosophists (Athenaeus), 39
Deloney, Thomas, 4, 32
"Demythification," 17, 357
DeQuincey, Thomas, 41
Descartes, René, 6–7, 356
DeVoto, Bernard, 117
D. H. Lawrence: A Personal Record (E. T.), 75
Dialogue, 53, 95, 276–79
Diana of the Crossways (Meredith), 161
Dickens, Charles, 3, 8, 12, 15, 22, 35, 46, 48, 51, 52, 60, 73, 80, 88, 93, 98, 99, 127, 131, 134, 149, 152–53, 155–56, 161, 215, 216, 221, 222, 227, 234, 237, 239, 240, 241, 242, 250, 256, 325–26, 334
The disappearance of the author, 24–25, 108, 130–31
Disraeli, Benjamin, 320, 330
Distance, 70, 96–100
The Doctor (Southey), 41
Doctor Faustus (Mann), 30, 93, 96, 159
Don Juan (Byron), 19
Don Quixote (Cervantes), 2, 13–28, 34, 41, 90, 134n, 141, 172, 221, 384–87
Dos Passos, John, 81, 217
Dostoevsky, Feodor, 6, 28, 231, 235, 237, 295
Douglas, Norman, 226–27
Doyle, Sir Arthur Conan, 158
Drew, Elizabeth, 115n
Dr. Thorne (Trollope), 49
Dryden, John, 89, 90, 110n, 161
Dubois, Arthur E., 117n
Dubliners (Joyce), 36, 378
The Duchess of Malfi (Webster), 159
Dumas, Alexandre, 29, 395

The Education of Henry Adams (H. Adams), 294

L'Education Sentimentale (Flaubert), 17
The Egoist (Meredith), 13, 32, 48, 52, 90, 94, 394
Either/Or (Kierkegaard), 41
Eliade, Mircea, 307, 308
Eliot, George, 8, 41, 48, 51, 60, 61, 90, 182, 183, 233, 248, 328–29, 391–93
Eliot, T. S., 67, 110, 111n, 133, 263, 281, 283, 288, 297, 298–99, 300–301, 307, 335, 336, 346, 348, 349, 362
Ellsperman, Dom Gerard, 302–303
Emerson, R. W., 364
Emile (Rousseau), 37
Emma (Austen), 2, 18, 20, 100, 176, 223, 320–22
The Emperor Jones (O'Neill), 163
Erasmus, 37, 39, 40
Erewhon (Butler), 37
Esenwein, J. Berg, 115n
"An Essay of Dramatic Poesy" (Dryden), 89
E. T., 75, 135
Evan Harrington (Meredith), 226

A Fable (Faulkner), 296
The Faerie Queene (Spenser), 374, 376
The Fall (Camus), 101
The Fantasia of the Unconscious (Lawrence), 379
A Farewell to Arms (Hemingway), 146, 212–13, 217
Farrell, James T., 78, 79, 83, 84, 217
Faulkner, William, 3, 81, 86, 90, 97, 101, 102–103, 161, 254–55, 265–66, 278, 296, 335, 336, 344, 345
Feidelson, Charles, 351, 365–66
Fernandez, Ramon, 128n
Ficelle, 63, 237, 242–47
Fielding, Henry, 2, 4, 11, 17, 27, 32, 35, 47, 52, 87, 93, 97, 102, 103, 105, 114n, 121, 133, 140, 172, 179–82, 208–210, 214, 215, 231, 274, 317–19, 320, 322, 356, 375, 380–83, 387–88

Finnegans Wake (Joyce), 13, 42–43, 81, 172, 284, 308, 309–13, 378, 406
Fitzgerald, F. Scott, 125, 146, 163, 335–36, 337, 340, 341
Flaubert, Gustave, 1, 8, 13, 17, 18, 21, 25, 26, 27, 34, 40, 43, 45, 80, 93, 140, 144n, 231, 269, 305, 338, 390–91, 395
Földes, Jolán, 266
Ford, Ford Madox, 71, 85, 116n, 268n, 270
Forster, E. M., 9, 13, 28, 87, 142n, 165–66, 222, 223–31, 243, 244–46
For Whom the Bell Tolls (Hemingway), 162
Foster-Harris, William, 117n
Four Quartets (Eliot), 307
Franklin, Benjamin, 119
Frazer, Sir James G., 27, 362
Frederick, John T., 116n
Freud, Sigmund, 8, 27, 354
Friedman, Norman, 108–137, 140, 145–66
From Here to Eternity (Jones), 157, 158
Fry, Roger, 338, 339
Frye, Northrop, 5, 12–13, 15, 19, 31–43

Gallishaw, John, 116n
Galsworthy, John, 49, 172, 263
Gargantua (Rabelais), 4
de Gaultier, Jules, 18
Gerard, Alexander, 110n
Germinal (Zola), 8, 237
Gerould, Gordon Hall, 116n
Gide, André, 24, 27, 80, 334, 344, 403–405
Giraud, Raymond, 15
Glasgow, Ellen, 117
The Go-Between (L. P. Hartley), 320
Go Down, Moses (Faulkner), 265–66
Goethe, Johann W., 160
Gogol, Nikolai, 28
The Golden Bowl (James), 296, 334, 361–64

Golden Wedding (Ruth Suckow), 165
Goncharov, Ivan, 28
de Goncourt, Edmond and Jules, 395
Goodbye to Berlin (Isherwood), 130
de Gourmont, Rémy, 17
Gordon, Caroline, 118*n*, 137
Gorki, Maxim, 164
Grabo, Carl H., 115*n*, 116*n*
Grace Abounding (Bunyan), 35
The Grapes of Wrath (Steinbeck), 217, 230
Graves, Robert, 255, 257
Great Expectations (Dickens), 98, 99, 127, 134, 149, 153, 155–56, 161
The Great Gatsby (Fitzgerald), 95, 100, 125, 146, 165, 335–36, 337, 340, 341
Green, Henry, 355
Greene, Graham, 98, 102
Gulliver's Travels (Swift), 16, 31, 37, 91, 295, 374

Hagstrum, Jean H., 316
Haircut (Lardner), 96
The Hairy Ape (O'Neill), 165
Hamilton, Clayton, 115*n*
Hamlet (Shakespeare), 92, 159
Hardy, Thomas, 24, 26, 27, 121–24, 146, 158, 230, 254, 257, 295, 329–30
Harkness, Bruce, 147*n*
Hartley, L. P., 320, 331
Harvey, Gabriel, 274*n*
Harvey, W. J., 222, 231–51
Hasley, Louis, 129*n*
Hawthorne, Nathaniel, 28, 34, 154, 162, 254, 364, 365, 377–78, 379, 380
Hayakawa, S. I., 199
Hazlitt, William, 110*n*
Heart of Darkness (Conrad), 5, 80, 334
The Heart of Midlothian (Scott), 257, 324
Hedda Gabler (Ibsen), 160
Hellman, Lillian, 160

Hemingway, Ernest, 81–82, 92, 120, 130, 134, 146, 162, 186, 211–13, 217, 219
Henderson the Rain King (Bellow), 101
Henrietta Temple (Disraeli), 320
Henry Esmond (Thackeray), 91, 256, 263
Henry, Paul, 303
Hills Like White Elephants (Hemingway), 134
Hoffman, Arthur Sullivant, 116*n*
Hogarth, William, 4, 318
Hogg, James, 41
Holloway, John, 206*n*
Homer, 111, 179, 180, 185
Horne, Charles F., 115*n*
The Horse's Mouth (Joyce Cary), 101
Hoskins, John, 110*n*
The House of the Seven Gables (Hawthorne), 28, 34
"How Beautiful with Shoes" (Steele), 164
Howells, William Dean, 114*n*
Huckleberry Finn (Twain), 3, 95, 96, 97, 101, 104, 215
Hugo, Victor, 22, 395
Hume, David, 8
Humphrey, Robert, 129*n*
Hussey, Christopher, 318*n*
Huxley, Aldous, 37, 39, 49, 50, 80, 91, 98, 108, 123, 133, 160, 263, 295

Ibsen, Henrik, 6, 156–57, 160, 162, 335
I Claudius (Graves), 255
The Iliad (Homer), 111
Imaginary Conversations (Landor), 39
Immediacy in narration, 53, 130, 264–67, 275–79, 384–87
"The implied author," 99
Intruder in the Dust (Faulkner), 101
Irony, 6, 20–26, 97, 147
Isherwood, Christopher, 130
Ittelson, W. H., 194*n*
Ivanov (Chekhov), 163

Jacob's Room (Woolf), 52–53
James, Henry, 1, 13, 21, 22, 27, 29, 32, 36, 39, 46, 58–65, 71, 87, 88, 90, 91, 94, 95, 101, 105, 107, 108, 112–14, 114*n*, 129, 130, 131, 140, 142, 144*n*, 149, 161, 165, 168–70, 171, 172, 174, 183, 184, 208, 211–14, 217, 218, 232–34, 237, 247, 248, 258, 263, 271, 274, 278, 296, 314*n*, 334, 342, 361–62, 363, 364, 366, 396–97
Jameson, Storm, 48
Jane Eyre (C. Brontë), 48, 52, 55, 320
Jankélévitch, Vladimir, 20
J.B. (MacLeish), 305
Jespersen, Otto, 197*n*
Johann, Robert, 304
John Buncle (Amory), 41
Johnson, Samuel, 1, 4, 186, 376, 382
Jonathan Wild (Fielding), 97
Jones, James, 157, 158
Jonson, Ben, 160
Joseph Andrews (Fielding), 4, 103, 179–80, 210, 317, 320, 387–88
Joseph and his Brethren (Mann), 255
Joseph, Michael, 115*n*
Joyce, James, 1, 13–17, 25, 27, 28, 36, 42–43, 67, 71, 76–78, 80–81, 83, 86, 88, 90, 94, 104, 110, 111, 128–29, 134, 136–37, 140, 161, 165, 172, 197, 208, 234, 243, 258, 263, 271, 278, 284, 288, 308, 309–313, 334, 335, 344, 354, 355, 366, 373, 378–79, 406
Julius Caesar (Shakespeare), 154, 159
Jung, C. G., 345
Jurgen (Cabell), 263

Kafka, Franz, 98, 335, 354
Kahn, Gustave, 16, 22, 23
Kames, Henry Home, Lord, 110*n*
Kant, Immanuel, 288
Keats, John, 65, 110*n*, 291, 349

Kellogg, Robert, 369–84
Kempton, Kenneth P., 118*n*
Kierkegaard, S., 41
"The Killers" (Hemingway), 92, 95
Kilpatrick, F. P., 194*n*
King Lear (Shakespeare), 159
Kingsley, Charles, 39
Knights, L. C., 221
Knot of Vipers (Mauriac), 98
Koestler, Arthur, 149
Köhler, Wolfgang, 172
Komroff, Manuel, 118*n*
Korzybski, Alfred, 199

de La Fayette, Mme., 1, 20, 27
Lamb, Charles, 267
Lancelot (Anon.), 13
Landor, W. S., 39
Langer, Susanne, 173, 176, 204–205, 207, 334, 339–40
Lanier, Sidney, 114*n*
Lardner, Ring, 96, 97
Larkin, Philip, 284
Lathrop, Henry Burrowes, 115*n*
Lavengro (Borrow), 31
Lavrin, Janko, 130*n*
Lawrence, D. H., 67, 73–76, 83, 135, 146, 176, 226, 258, 344, 350, 379, 405–406
Lazarillo de Tormes (Anon.), 172
Leavis, F. R., 222
Lee, Vernon, 111*n*
Lehmann, Rosamund, 331
Lettres provinciales (Pascal), 25
Levin, Harry, 15, 20, 22, 334
Lewis, C. S., 19, 281, 293
Liddell, Robert, 315, 316, 320, 321
The Life and Death of Mr. Badman (Bunyan), 316
Light in August (Faulkner), 90
Linn, James Weber, 116*n*
de Lisle, Leconte, 26
"A Little Cloud" (Joyce), 165
Little Dorrit (Dickens), 35
The Little Foxes (Hellman), 160
Lloyd, Donald, 197*n*
Location in the novel
  specificity of, 120, 315–17
  in relation to landscape painting, 314–15

as symbol, 325–26
relevance of, 321–30
Locke, John, 6–7, 356
Lord Jim (Conrad), 34, 133, 152, 161
Loughran, Charles P., 280*n*
Love and Freindship (Austen), 20
The Loved One (Waugh), 238
The Lovely Ship (Storm Jameson), 48
Löwith, Karl, 302
Lowry, Malcolm, 367
Lubbock, Percy, 49, 54, 86, 87, 95, 113, 117, 173–74
Lucian, 4, 37
Lucky Jim (Amis), 238
Lutwack, Leonard, 186, 208–218
Lynch, William, 284–85

MacKenzie, Henry, 114*n*
Mackintosh (Maugham), 165
MacLeish, Archibald, 305, 370
Macrobius, 39
Madame Bovary (Flaubert), 8, 13, 18, 34, 43, 140, 144*n*
Maggie: A Girl of the Streets (Crane), 158
Malone Dies (Beckett), 2
The Man of Property (Galsworthy), 49
Mann, Thomas, 27, 30, 86, 93, 96, 159, 250–51, 255, 258, 335, 379
Mansfield, Katherine, 33
Mansfield Park (Austen), 20, 228, 322–23
Maritain, Jacques, 281
Marius the Epicurean (Pater), 164
Marx, Karl, 4, 8
Mason, Ellsworth, 129*n*
The Master of Ballantrae (Stevenson), 100
Masters, Edgar Lee, 133
Mattheissen, F. O., 365
Matthews, Brander, 114*n*
Maturin, C. R., 41
Maugham, W. S., 165, 353
de Maupassant, Guy, 114*n*, 397–99
Mauprat (George Sand), 395
Mauriac, François, 27, 98

The Mayor of Casterbridge (Hardy), 329–30
McCarthy, Mary, 238–39, 240, 241
McCleary, Dorothy, 118*n*
McHugh, Vincent, 118*n*
McLaughlin, Charles A., 110*n*, 147*n*, 160*n*
Mehl, Roger, 280*n*
Melmoth the Wanderer (Maturin), 41
Melville, Herman, 2, 32, 41, 42, 91, 98, 102, 134*n*, 211, 216, 218, 236, 246, 295, 335, 343–44, 349–54, 364, 365, 366
Memoirs of Barry Lyndon (Thackeray), 101
Mendilow, A. A., 118*n*, 254, 255–80
Menippean satire, 37–40
Menippus, 37, 39
Meredith, George, 13, 26, 32, 48, 52, 90, 93, 94, 110*n*, 161, 185, 226, 277, 278, 394
Merton, Thomas, 137
The Metamorphosis (Kafka), 98
Meyerhoff, Hans, 289–90, 292–93, 296
Middlemarch (G. Eliot), 8, 48, 51, 90, 182, 183, 248, 328–29
Middleton, Thomas, 160
Mill, J. S., 36, 192
Miller, Arthur, 158
Miller, Henry, 86
Millet, Fred B., 118*n*
Milton, John, 159, 286, 288, 376–7
Mirrilees, Edith, 116*n*
Mirsky, D. S., Prince, 130*n*
Moby Dick (Melville), 2, 32, 41, 42, 91, 102, 134*n*, 211, 216, 218, 236, 246, 343–44, 349–54, 366
Molière, 26, 94, 160, 376
Moll Flanders (Defoe), 4, 36, 48, 51, 67–69, 86, 95, 134*n*, 177–78, 223, 255, 260–61
Moloney, Michael, 297
Montaigne, 36
Moore, George, 255
More, St. Thomas, 294
Morley, Christopher, 263
Morozov, Mihail M., 110*n*

Morris, Charles W., 195
Morris, William, 33, 34, 263
Mister Roberts (Thomas Heggen), 161
Muller-Thym, Bernard J., 306
Mumford, Lewis, 253
Munsterberg, Hugo, 111*n*
Murder in the Cathedral (Eliot), 298
Murdoch, Iris, 331
Murry, J. M., 200
Mutability, 285–87
My Oedipus Complex (O'Connor), 165
The Mysteries of Udolpho (Radcliffe), 319, 320

Nagel, Ernest, 347
Nashe, Thomas, 2, 4
Natural Child (Willingham), 101
Naturalism, 81
"The Necklace" (Maupassant), 98
Newman, John Henry Cardinal, 35, 206, 285
News from Nowhere (W. Morris), 263
Nievo, Ippolito, 358–60
The Nigger of the 'Narcissus' (Conrad), 236, 399–403
Night and Day (Woolf), 48
Nine Stories (Salinger), 88
1984 (Orwell), 146, 149, 295
Noctes Ambrosianae (Various), 41
Noon, William T., 254, 280–311
Norris, Frank, 114*n*
Northanger Abbey (Austen), 20, 34, 320, 322, 326
The Notebooks of Henry James (James), 144*n*
Notre Dame de Paris (Hugo), 395
Novalis, 364
The novel
difficulties of definition, 11–12, 13–14, 31–32
its essential theme, 14–15
as a gestalt, 172–75
and autobiography, 35
and essay, 210–11
and history, 35, 255–58, 357–58, 374

and the philosophical tale, 16, 20–21
and romance, 6, 15, 16–21, 32–35, 374
and "prophetic fiction," 28
and empirical reality, 6–7, 356–58, 388–99
The novelistic hero, 15–28
"Nuns at Luncheon" (Huxley), 98

O'Brien, Edward J., 116*n*
O'Connor, Frank, 165
O'Connor, William Van, 10
Oedipus at Colonnus (Sophocles), 126*n*
Oedipus Rex (Sophocles), 126*n*, 141, 142, 159
Of Time and the River (Wolfe), 79
Ohmann, Richard, 186, 190–208
The Old Wives' Tale (Bennett), 48
Olson, Elder, 150*n*
One Autumn Night (Gorki), 164
O'Neill, Eugene, 116, 163, 165, 278
"Open Winter" (H. L. Davis), 161
The Ordeal of Richard Feverel (Meredith), 26
Orphée (Ballanche), 13
Orlando (Woolf), 263
Ortega y Gasset, José, 17, 111*n*
Orvis, Mary Burchard, 116*n*, 118*n*
Orwell, George, 146, 149, 295
Othello (Shakespeare), 156, 159
The Other Two (Wharton), 165
Overton, Grant, 116*n*

Pamela (Richardson), 4, 5, 41, 134*n*, 208, 273, 316
Paradise Lost (Milton), 376–77
Pascal, Blaise, 25
A Passage to India (Forster), 244–6
"Paste" (James), 165
Pastoral Symphony (Gide), 334
Pater, Walter, 142, 164, 257
Peacock, Thomas Love, 27, 32, 37, 38, 39
A Perfect Woman (Hartley), 331
Perry, Bliss, 114*n*
Persuasion (Austen), 140, 230
Petronius, 37, 38, 39
Phineas Finn (Trollope), 393

Pieper, Josef, 280–81, 303
The Pilgrim Hawk (Wescott), 81–2
The Pilgrim's Progress (Bunyan),
    13, 34, 119
Pillars of the Community (Ibsen),
    156–57, 162
Pitkin, Walter B., 115n
Plato, 39, 110, 111, 205, 276–77,
    293, 294
Plotinus, 293
Plutarch, 374
Poe, E. A., 33, 91, 365
Poetics (Aristotle), 89
Point Counterpoint (Huxley), 37,
    50, 123
Point of view, 27, 85–137
    control of, as a means to artistic
        success, 59–62, 68–70, 73–
        76
    consistency of, 113–16, 134
    consistency of, as a spurious
        principle, 89
Pope, Alexander, 305, 306, 318
Porter, Katherine Anne, 82, 102
The Portrait of a Lady (James),
    59–62, 142, 161, 247, 248
A Portrait of the Artist as a Young
    Man (Joyce), 36, 67, 76–78,
    104, 128–29, 134, 136–37,
    161, 294, 288, 366, 378
The Possessed (Dostoevsky), 237
Poulet, Georges, 287, 291
Pound, Ezra, 301
Poussin, Nicolas, 318, 319
The Power and the Glory
    (Greene), 102
The Prairie (Cooper), 236
The Prelude (Wordsworth),
    244
Pride and Prejudice (Austen), 48,
    52, 100, 165
Priestley, J. B., 296
The Princess Casamassima
    (James), 247
La Princesse de Clèves (La
    Fayette), 1, 20
Prometheus Unbound (Shelley),
    295
Proust, Marcel, 15, 27, 28, 41, 93,
    96, 211, 225, 231, 235, 242,
    243, 248–49, 254, 260, 284,
    290–91, 292, 297, 307, 308,
    314n, 335
Puech, Henri-Charles, 297–98
Purney, Thomas, 313

Quentin Durward (Scott), 263
The Quiet American (Greene), 98
Quintilian, 22, 39, 110n

Rabelais, François, 4, 37, 38, 40, 41
Radcliffe, Mrs. Ann, 319–25, 330
Rader, Melvin, 111n
Rahv, Philip, 334, 355, 366
The Red and the Black (Stend-
    hal), 89
Redburn (Melville), 98
The Regent (Bennett), 241
Reliable and unreliable narrators,
    100–102
Religio Medici (Browne), 35
Remembrance of Things Past
    (Proust), 93, 96, 260, 307
Representative and illustrative fic-
    tion, 372–84
Response to characters, 221–22,
    225–31, 233–51
    in relation to plot, 151–52, 156,
        158–66
    in relation to point of view, 69–
        70, 75–77, 100, 103–104,
        136–37
    as representatives of "real life,"
        223, 385
The Return of the Native (Hardy),
    24
Rhoda Fleming (Meredith), 278
Richard III (Shakespeare), 160
Richards, I. A., 192–93, 195, 201–
    202, 346
Richardson, Dorothy, 271, 278
Richardson, Samuel, 2–5, 41, 86,
    114n, 134n, 178–79, 208, 211,
    228, 254, 255, 259, 261–62,
    273–74, 277, 316, 356, 375,
    381–83
Robbe-Grillet, Alain, 88
Roberts, Paul, 197n
Roderick Hudson (James), 168–
    70, 171

Robinson Crusoe (Defoe), 4, 253, 259, 316, 375
Rogers, W. H., 117*n*
de Rojas, Fernando, 277*n*
Rosa, Salvator, 319, 329
Rousseau, J. J., 35–37
Roxana (Defoe), 260
Runyan, Damon, 260

Salinger, J. D., 88, 96
Saltykov, Mikhail, 28
Sand, George, 22, 395–96
Sandburg, Carl, 133
Santayana, George, 239
Saroyan, William, 82, 84
Sartor Resartus (Carlyle), 31, 41
Sartre, Jean Paul, 95
Saturnalia (Macrobius), 39
Savage, D. S., 74
The Scarlet Letter (Hawthorne), 154, 162
Scarron, Paul, 20
Scene, 52–54, 64–65, 95, 103, 120
Scholes, Robert, 369–84
Schorer, Mark, 46, 65–84, 109, 117, 118*n*, 135
Schweitzer, Albert, 299
Scott, Sir Walter, 12, 22, 34, 35, 50, 60, 114*n*, 131, 214, 221, 225, 257, 263, 277, 324, 325, 330, 381
The Seagull (Chekhov), 156, 163
The Secret Sharer (Conrad), 157, 161
Sedgwick, William Ellery, 351
Seize the Day (Bellow), 368
Senior, Nassau William, 114*n*
The Sense of the Past (James), 263
A Sentimental Journey (Sterne), 277
Shakespeare, William, 14–15, 60, 92, 98, 154, 156, 159, 160, 221, 224, 242–43, 256, 286, 293, 298, 316, 341, 376
Shapiro, Karl, 282, 304
Shaw, G. B., 73, 165
Shaw, Irwin, 164
Shelley, P. B., 295
The Sheltering Sky (Bowles), 367
Shroder, Maurice Z., 11, 12–28
Sidney, Sir Philip, 32, 110*n*

Sinclair, Jo, 150*n*
The Skin of Our Teeth (Wilder), 283
Smollett, Tobias, 11
Snow, C. P., 27
Socrates, 22
Sons and Lovers (Lawrence), 67, 73–76, 135, 146, 176
Sophocles, 126*n*, 141, 142, 159
Sorel, Charles, 17, 20, 257*n*, 264
The Sound and the Fury (Faulkner), 97, 101, 336
Southey, Robert, 41
Southwell, Robert, 280
The Spectator (Addison and Steele), 95
Spengler, Oswald, 290, 308
Spenser, Edmund, 286, 303, 374, 376
The Spinner of Years (Bentley), 51
Spitzer, Leo, 208
The Spoils of Poynton (James), 101
Stafford, Jean, 82, 165, 366–67
Stallman, Robert W., 334
Stebbing, Susan, 201*n*
Stein, Gertrude, 197
Steinbeck, John, 81, 217, 230, 236
Stendhal, 18, 21, 22, 24, 89, 278–79, 356–58, 389, 395
Stephen Hero (Joyce), 77, 378
Sterne, Laurence, 12, 31, 40, 42, 90, 91, 93, 95, 96, 97–98, 99, 172, 182–83, 211, 216, 221, 234, 258, 277, 388–89
Stevens, Wallace, 335, 354
Stevenson, R. L., 60, 86, 100, 114*n*, 187–89, 251
Stevick, Philip, 171–184
The Story of a Novel (Wolfe), 136*n*
The Storyteller (O'Conner), 165
The Stranger (Camus), 96
The Street of the Fishing Cat (Földes), 266
A Streetcar Named Desire (T. Williams), 154, 158
Strindberg, August, 165
Struve, Gleb, 129*n*
Studs Lonigan (Farrell), 217
Sturt, M., 267

Style, 185–219
and syntax, 197–203
and feeling, 204–208
and colloquial speech, 216–18
as evaluation, 76–78, 79–82
Suckow, Ruth, 165
Sue, Eugène, 395
Summary, 47–52, 95, 120
Summers, Richard, 118n
The Sun Also Rises (Hemingway),
81
Svevo, Italo, 87
Swift, Jonathan, 16, 31, 37, 38,
91, 295, 374
Symbol, 333–68
and sign, 337–38
defined, 343
as a vehicle of meaning, 343–54
and the realistic novel, 356–61
and the American novel, 364–66

Tale of Two Cities (Dickens), 256
Tarski, Alfred, 202n
Tartuffe (Molière), 160
Tate, Allen, 116, 118n, 144n, 292
Taylor, Houghton Wells, 116n
"Telling and showing," 88, 90,
113–14, 116, 127–28, 128n
Ten (Nuhn), 161
Tender is the Night (Fitzgerald), 163
Tess of the d'Urbervilles (Hardy),
24, 121–24, 146, 158, 257
Thackeray, William M., 5–6, 15,
17, 24, 49, 55–57, 91, 101,
114n, 172, 226, 231, 254,
256, 263, 268, 277, 389
Thompson, Daniel Greenleaf, 114n
Thompson, J. A. K., 25
Thoreau, Henry David, 215
The Three Sisters (Chekhov), 158
Thunder on the Left (Morley), 263
Tillich, Paul, 299
Tillotson, Kathleen, 88
Time and the Conways (Priestley),
296
Tindall, William Y., 333, 334,
335–54, 355, 360, 363
Tintern Abbey (Wordsworth), 244
Tobit Transplanted (Benson), 263
Tolstoy, Leo, 25, 28, 39, 54, 121,

133, 164, 231, 295, 314n, 356,
357, 358, 360–61, 374
Tom Jones (Fielding), 4, 17, 24,
35, 47, 52, 90, 91, 94, 95, 96,
102, 105, 121, 133, 142, 151,
180–81, 208–211, 262, 274,
316, 317–19, 342, 375, 380–83
Tono Bungay (Wells), 67, 71–73,
227
To the Lighthouse (Woolf), 127–
28, 134, 164, 296–97
Toynbee, Arnold, 281, 308–309
Traven, B., 160
The Treasure of Sierra Madre
(Traven), 160
The Trial (Kafka), 354
Trilling, Diana, 135
Trilling, Lionel, 4, 12, 14
Tristan and Iseult (Anon.), 253
Tristram Shandy (Sterne), 31, 40,
42, 90, 91, 93, 95, 96, 97–98,
99, 182–83, 211, 216, 234,
258, 267, 388–89
Troilus and Criseyde (Chaucer), 94
Trollope, Anthony, 3, 33, 35, 46,
49, 52, 96, 103, 189, 257n,
258, 268, 276, 326–27, 393
Tropic of Cancer (H. Miller), 86
True History (Lucian), 4
Tucker's People (Wolfert), 81
Turgenev, Ivan, 27, 28, 62
Twain, Mark, 3, 27, 95, 96, 97,
101, 104, 185, 186, 215, 216

Ulysses (Joyce), 17, 28, 42–43,
77–80, 90, 208, 218, 263, 288,
354, 378
Uncle Vanya (Chekhov), 163
Under the Volcano (Lowry), 367
The Unfortunate Traveller
(Nashe), 2
Urban, Wilbur Marshall, 342
Utopian fiction, 39, 264, 294–95
Uzzell, Thomas H., 116n

Valéry, Paul, 335
Van Ghent, Dorothy, 7
Vanity Fair (Thackeray), 5–6, 15,
24, 49, 55–57, 91, 172, 226,
256, 268, 389

Varro, 37, 39
Verga, Giovanni, 24
Verne, Jules, 73
Vico, Giambattista, 294, 306–309
The Victim (Bellow), 96
Victory (Conrad), 83
Virgil, 179, 285
Volpone (Jonson), 160
Voltaire, 16, 21, 37, 38, 39, 40, 295

Waiting for Godot (Beckett), 283
Walpole, Horace, 320, 321
Walton, Izaac, 39, 41
Wanning, Andrews, 190n, 191n, 203n
War and Peace (Tolstoy), 121, 133, 164, 231
The Warden (Trollope), 326–27
Warren, Austin, 1, 118n
Warren, Robert P., 117n, 118n, 154, 164
Washington Square (James), 149
Wasteland (Jo Sinclair), 150n
The Water-Babies (Kingsley), 39
Watt, Ian, 6–7, 23, 253–54, 315
Waugh, Evelyn, 12, 100, 238
Waverly (Scott), 35, 50
The Way of All Flesh (Butler), 37, 119, 125–26, 150n, 161, 183
Webb, Mary, 315
Webster, John, 159
Weisman, Herman M., 130n
Wellek, René, 1, 118n
Wells, H. G., 67, 71–73, 84, 227
Welty, Eudora, 82
Wertheimer, Max, 175
Wescott, Glenway, 81–82
West, Nathanael, 81
Weston, Jessie L., 362
Wharton, Edith, 112, 115n, 165
Whitcomb, Selden L., 114
Whitehead, A. N., 336, 342, 345, 348

Whitman, Walt, 133, 365
Whorf, Benjamin Lee, 198
Wilbur, Richard, 292
Wilder, Thornton, 283
Williams, Blanche C., 115n
Williams, Charles, 347
Williams, Raymond, 9
Williams, Tennessee, 154, 158
Williams, William Carlos, 81
Willingham, Calder, 101
Wilson, Edmund, 86, 322
Wimsatt, W. K., 148n, 200
The Wings of the Dove (James), 71, 172, 247
Winters, Yvor, 365
Winterset (Anderson), 164
The Winter's Tale (Shakespeare), 298
Wittgenstein, Ludwig, 191, 201
Wolfe, Thomas, 78, 79, 83, 84, 134n, 136n, 271
Wolfert, Ira, 81
The Woman in White (Collins), 320
Woolf, Virginia, 12, 27, 48, 52–53, 54, 57, 79, 86, 127–28, 131, 134, 164, 263, 278, 296–97, 331n, 355, 362
Worcester, David, 20
Wordsworth, William, 34, 243, 244, 258n
Worringer, Wilhelm, 111n
Wouk, Herman, 154
Wright, Andrew, 181n
Wuthering Heights (E. Brontë), 6, 32, 67, 69–71, 276

The Years (Woolf), 54
Yeats, William Butler, 26, 104, 286–287, 289, 291, 335, 347

Zola, Emile, 8, 22, 23, 25, 27, 237, 263, 269, 394–96